D1380774

Edmund Fawcett was born in London in 1946. After taking a degree at Oxford, he served for three years as European correspondent for the *Economist* and then, since 1976, as its Washington bureau chief.

Tony Thomas was born in Zimbabwe in 1940. After working on newspapers there and in Britain, he joined *The Times* as United States economics correspondent. For the *Economist*, he was American business correspondent before his return to London as business editor.

Edmund Fawcett

and Tony Thomas

AMERICA AND THE AMERICANS

Fontana/Collins

First published as *The American Condition*
in the USA by Harper & Row 1982
Published in Great Britain as *America, Americans*
by William Collins 1983
First issued in Fontana Paperbacks 1983

Made and printed in Great Britain by
William Collins Sons & Co. Ltd, Glasgow

To my parents
EF

For Sarah
TT

CONTENTS

INTRODUCTION

A Maturing Nation

Americans are quick to believe that everything familiar about their lives is subject to constant change. Restless movement is their guiding image. America belongs to the New World, which, after all, is always being completed but never finished. This is a young country, it is sometimes still said, with its face to the future and its back to the past. Americans have always been ready to move on and start again. On the frontier, Tocqueville wrote, the American would build a house for his old age and move away before the roof was on. "We want to live in the present," said Henry Ford, "and the only history that is worth a tinker's damn is the history that we make today." Such self-confidence is meant to run in the American blood. However daunting the obstacle, Americans would roll up their sleeves to shove it out of the way. Where else, the historian Eric Goldman has asked, would people joke: "The difficult we do immediately. The impossible takes a little longer"?

In its third century, is America so young, so supple, and so thoroughly forward-looking? After talking with several hundred Americans about their country and getting to know all its regions—we have traveled, between us, to all but a handful of the fifty states—we think it is time to look through a new face of the prism. How modern is modern America? The many people we met, who were so generous with their thoughts and their time, live in a mature country, a mature economy, a mature society, with all the strengths and weaknesses the word "maturity" implies. Heirs, it seemed to us, more than pioneers, few of them appeared to think that anything of importance in their vast and complicated nation could be made over easily anymore. The economic dynamo no longer roars, and as its reassuring din dies away, sharp ears can pick up in places a clashing of gears in a prodigiously rich but still far from equal society.

We talked to farmers in the Texas panhandle, businessmen in Saint Louis, and politicians in Cleveland; we spoke with priests in Chicago, rabbis in Brooklyn, and ministers in Los Angeles; we heard from teachers in Oregon, from psychiatrists in Manhattan, and from professors everywhere, not to mention top bankers and lawyers on Wall Street as well as diplomats and legislators and officials in Washington. Almost everyone showed that personal energy and openness which foreigners, with envy and wonder, have so often noted in Americans and which make working as a journalist in the United States so straightforward and rewarding. Yet the figure of the country that emerged—and that we offer in this book—was far more mixed.

An unmodern America does not fit the usual preconceptions of the country. It did not, entirely, fit ours. For each of us—and we suspect for plenty of others who grew up outside America after the Second World War—modern life meant American life. America had not only dazzled would-be consumers by originating private cars, drive-in banks, restaurants, movies, and churches, supermarkets, long-distance telephones that worked, high-speed elevators, and color television. It was in the United States that the gap between the most extravagant technical ambitions and their execution—the tallest building, the longest bridge, or the first moon shot—seemed smallest. It was America that seemed best able to put science to use and gave the world the two inventions that bracket the modern age, the computer and the atomic bomb.

Quite apart from any of this, America struck foreigners as a society that canceled tradition, where sex and psychiatry flourished, where men and women got divorced many times, and where children stood up to and often walked all over their parents. Next to almost any other Western country, the United States looked democratic and free of class-consciousness. Americans, or so it seemed, just did not let themselves get stuffed into narrow social pigeonholes the way people did in other countries. The American would chuck his work in midcareer and go off to Alaska or Arizona in a trailer. Lawyers could become carpenters and vice versa. In a country that preached hard work and worshiped the dollar, many Americans seemed strangely capable of separating a sense of their own worth from the type of work they did or the size of their income.

If all this was modern, then America no longer has its modernity to itself. America has shared its consumption culture with the world; its science and engineering, if second to none, does not stand alone; modern capitalist success long ago began weakening tradition and overturning social chessboards in West Europe and in Japan as well. Much of the cultural carping from the Old World at the expense of the New and its supposedly vulgar, commercial civilization—a line of work much favored in Britain and France, with which many Americans are still gullible—depends for its success on ignoring these rather obvious truths. Using the traditions of Europe as a stick to beat modern America might have been plausible a half century ago. Today it sounds simply quaint.

After writing for foreigners about America for more than eight years, each of us, we are struck more and more not by what is new in the United States but by what is old. American political institutions are venerable. The roots of a formidably elaborate legal system reach back to medieval England. The Constitution combines practical arrangements designed originally for colonial legislatures with the political ideas of the Enlightenment. The older American banks, companies, and universities long ago acquired not only pasts but hallowed traditions.

The American economy is a senior citizen compared with those of Western Europe or Japan, rejuvenated as they were with American capital. Set against the more rapidly industrializing countries of the third world, many American industries look positively ancient. There are of course regions of the country—the Oil South and the West—where rapid money can still be made, but overall, the country is no longer bursting with its old possibilities of natural-seeming, unthought-out economic growth.

A fluid society long ago began to solidify. Almost all Americans now enjoy a material standard of living their grandparents could only have dreamed about. This is an undeniable achievement. Yet the income gaps between the rich, the poor, and the great middle-in-between would be almost exactly the same as they were at the end of the 1940s if not for social welfare payments, once again under attack. Americans, too, have always been justly proud of their job mobility. Yet most sons or daughters of blue-collar parents are still likely to have to skip college and go into low-paying or low-status jobs themselves. To the universal astonishment of visitors who remember the United States in the early 1960s, the Americans have dismantled almost without trace the legal apparatus of racial discrimination. Yet too many black Americans must still watch at the very bottom of the economic heap as immigrants from Asia and Latin America leapfrog past them.

More and more Americans are looking not only for jobs but also for job security. Trade unions are for the most part as interested in protecting the gains of the members they have as in continued expansion. In the winter of 1982, when about ten million Americans were looking for work, many big unions, following the auto workers, had agreed to make heavy contract concessions in order to keep their jobs. The concern for job security by the four working Americans in five who do not belong to unions is hardly less keen. In the professions, growing specialization has brought specialists ever better rewards but has greatly reduced the ability to maneuver from job to job.

The largest American companies are as bureaucratic as any government department. Today's Horatio Alger heroes would begin at Harvard or Stanford business school, join a corporation, and soldier their way up the hierarchy. To counter discrimination against women and racial minorities, government offices and many businesses must now take on a corrective ration of women and black workers. Welcomed or contested—as from certain quarters this is, with increasing shrillness—such affirmative action has added further rigidity to a supposedly fluid market in jobs.

America is maturing in a quite different and more literal way as well. Taken as a whole, the population is itself aging. America will be graying, not greening, for the next couple of decades. Until the end of the 1950s, large families were the rule. The American population grew by an average of 2.9 million people, or by some 1.9 percent, a year. Small families are now far commoner than large ones. In the 1970s, the population was growing about 2 million a year, or by just more than 1 percent.

Sheer pressure of numbers lent weight to the exuberant spirits of the 1960s. Many found it bliss to be students in those years; for some, to be at Berkeley was very heaven. To all, university was better than being sent to Vietnam. Not every elder agreed, although some later adopted their children's looser cultural style. Later still, the same parents discovered how marriage-and-mortgage-minded their children could become on reaching their thirties. Just as America was unusually young in the 1960s, so it is becoming disproportionately middle-aged in the 1980s.

Some of the more predictable results are already apparent. Young men and women have become, in the language of real estate agents, "nesters," if less prolific than their parents were. There is a large pent-up demand for housing. Classrooms have begun to empty. Schools are laying off teachers. Universities send out recruiters looking for students. Rock music sales are on the slide, and the Gerber company is trying to diversify away from baby food and other infant products.

This settling of ways has coincided—although it is not otherwise obviously connected—with a conservative narrowing of aim elsewhere in American life. Economic hard times, uncertainty about the future, class resentments against liberal elites—all have been thrown out as explanations for the gathering political reaction of the late 1970s, which culminated in the election of Ronald Reagan and the loss of the Democratic majority in the Senate. Yet there was more to it than this. Crime, poor schools, pornography, and that useful but amorphous catchall "permissiveness" bothered plenty of ordinary Americans beyond the committed letter senders of the New Right.

Every new society quickly finds itself in need of a graveyard and a prison, wrote Hawthorne, and since the first Puritan settlements, Americans have tended to oscillate in treating wrongdoers as perfectible and as incorrigibly bad. Today's Americans seem to be swinging back to the gloomier reading, as reform ideas about crime and prisons fade. In schooling, too, experimentation is being discounted. The down-to-earth view commonly heard is that a school's most ambitious aim ought to be to turn out seventeen-year-olds who can read and write.

It did sometimes seem, ten years ago or so, as if the nation had linked hands in a collective group therapy session. No taboo, not even incest, was barred from frank and presumably ratings-boosting discussion on television. Americans burdened by stuffy or hypocritical standards were, it must be hoped, glad to be rid of them. Discovering one is not bad, however, does not reliably make one feel good. Permissiveness and self-searching brought problems of their own. Fundamentalist preachers came forward to say "We told you so." Praising the Lord and passing the collection plate, these Bible-thumpers bought time on radio and television—or founded their own networks—to rail at the new morality with a success that took liberal-minded politicians and opinion makers by surprise.

Political historians can take a long view and hunt for parallels. Journalists, who look for news, have to be professionally startled by events. After the 1980 election, there was much debate as to whether the conservative victory was, in reverse, another 1932, which inaugurated close to half a century of Democratic rule, or something closer to 1952, which proved to be only a modest deflection from the course of welfare capitalism. Either way, the election did suggest that the resilience of a hard and uncompromising brand of conservatism had been badly underestimated.

In *The American Mind*, the historian Henry Steele Commager described the national outlook as he saw it, two years before that 1952 election. He wrote that for all their uncertainties—Americans were about to go abroad again to war and the anticommunism of the cold war was reaching a height—Americans still believed three basic things about themselves: (1) that they lived in the most favored of all countries; (2) that theirs was the happiest and most virtuous of all societies; and (3) that the best was still to come. The Americans Commager was describing had, for all their disquiet, just won a global war that left the country astride the world. Depression and war had been great levelers and a huge mass of Americans shared in a new prosperity.

It is a safe bet that most Americans would still embrace the first belief. Many would also still defend the second, especially if the claim were taken in a comparative and not an absolute sense, although the black experience and the Vietnam War exposed widespread disillusionment on this score as well. As for the third—that the best is still to come—it can only be said that despite the thumbs down given Jimmy Carter's rather wet jeremiads and the thumbs up given Ronald Reagan's nice-guy optimism, there are large and possibly uncharacteristic doubts.

The new generation that has pretty well taken over now in politics and business is not in for an especially easy time. It comes in with old party coalitions weak or broken up. The electorate it faces is better educated, more independent, and more questioning, but also, to judge from the numbers of nonvoters, more turned off, than at any recent time. In the past decade, the country rounded an important economic corner. For the first time in nearly a century, America became a net importer—that is, got less in return for the goods it sold abroad than it paid for the foreign goods it bought. This was most obvious with oil and cars, but Americans also began buying from overseas other goods they had up till then managed to provide for themselves: bottled water, blue jeans, radio and television sets, and spectator sports. Far from feeling that they bestrode the world, Americans felt buffeted by it as seldom before—by competitive friends, superpower rivals, and nationalist governments in the third world.

This generation's task is helped neither by a national trust in superlatives nor by the common expectation of constant improvement. It is not easily accepted in America that the United States could be very favored without being most favored; happy without being happiest; or that its future might be good without being better, let alone best. Yet success, in America, is almost invariably measured in relative ways. Doing well means doing better—either than others or than one's own past best. Winning is an American passion. Grades, rankings, and statistical comparisons are made in every conceivable sphere of life. Games are seldom allowed to end in ties. Imported games—like soccer —have had invented for them sudden-death endings.

It is common in America to speak as if "winning" and "succeeding" meant the same, as if rivalry, not cooperation, were the surer spur to achievement. That success could mean something other than a race against oneself or against others strikes many Americans as foreign and weak-spirited. Advertisers rarely call products "good." They are "new and improved." The very logic of economic success has encouraged Americans to believe that they can always do better and that to do less is to fail. Challenging this cuts against the American grain.

On getting encouragement to pursue an ambitious and, in many respects, impertinent book, we were told that Americans like reading about themselves. They may be optimists—or feel they should be—but they are not complacent. Indeed, an all-or-nothing quality grips them when they turn to self-examination, which suggests that the task, if it is to be done at all, may well be best left to foreigners. Americans do sometimes seem determined to boast about what does not much matter while forgetting everything they should be proud of in their country.

In a country with large inequalities of wealth and income, most Americans will still make an assumption of equality about each other. They are democrats in their bones and can show a lack of deference to authority that would make a libertarian anarchist's blood race. The Americans in the last decade removed an openly criminal President and checked blatant excesses in the national security system. There are few other countries boasting such a vigorous tradition for the protection of individual rights. Americans like to complain about their bureaucrats —who doesn't?—but where else is government as accountable, as open, and as constitutionally bad at keeping secrets as in the United States?

While we were gathering material for this book, it was also said to us that embarking on America Today was rather like setting off to write about The World Today. There were several layers of truth to this remark, which was not meant to be encouraging. For a start, the subject matter of America was practically as forbidding and unmanageable as that of the world. Then again, American capital, technology, and popular culture have so stamped other nations that it was easy to lose track of where America stopped and the rest of the world began.

Straying into America's Place in the World was a temptation we think we have successfully resisted. Japanese and European imitators have left America both less distinctive and less preeminent than it was. In two ways, America remains the exception. As a superpower, with a military arsenal second to none, it cannot be treated as just another country. Alone among the capitalist economies of the West, America has given the socialist tradition least quarter. With that twin qualification, the world system to which America, West Europe, and Japan all belong is no longer uniquely and unarguably American.

Most tellingly, the remark about America being like the world, which was meant as polite discouragement, hinted at a conjecture that nobody who has traveled widely inside America with any curiosity or enjoyment can before long have possibly avoided making. This is the hunch that if the traveler goes far and looks long enough in America, he will stumble across every possible variety of human enterprise, as in a gigantic, living Museum of Man.

Many books have been and will be written about the strange, the bizarre, the eccentric, and the unexpected that can be found in America. For every claim about "Americans," there are hundreds, perhaps millions, of counterexamples. Yet our aim was not to write a Ripley's Believe It or Not. *America and the Americans* is not a book version, with sharp edges, of *That's Incredible!* or *Real People*. It is never possible to generalize convincingly about people, but it is necessary to generalize about a society.

Our book is about one country in America: the United States. Apologies are due in advance to Canadians and Latin Americans. Throughout we have adopted the common, if strictly incorrect, usage by which "America" and "the Americans" mean the United States and its people. To us, America is not many countries, many peoples and many nations. We find the forces shaping people's everyday lives more rather than less alike from region to region. This view is taken in full knowledge that there are four continental time zones, leaving out Alaska's and Hawaii's, and four census regions: the West, the South, the Northeast, and the North Central—that is, the Midwest. We recognize that foreign observers are warned not to concentrate on the East Coast and the Coast—meaning California—while ignoring the real America in between. We know that America has recently been carved into a Frostbelt, where industry is depressed, elites are shaken, and people are worried, on the one hand, and a Sunbelt, where business booms, the new rich are confident, and the people are optimistic, on the other. Treating America as one is done in the knowledge, as well, that the great cliché pencil has drawn a competing line down our Rand-McNally wall maps at the 100th meridian, separating an angry, dry, and freedom-loving West from a congested, complacent, and bureaucratized East.

In treating Americans as a single people, we do not overlook the renewed preoccupation with ethnic differences or the mountain of social science devoted recently to showing that the melting pot "did not happen." There is still Black America and White America, as well as Spanish-Speaking America and English-Speaking America, but racial divisions are less deep than they were, as the lives of the black and Hispanic middle class suggest.

Treating America as one nation is done in the knowledge that it is a federal system of fifty states and that a half century's concentration of power in Washington has come, at least temporarily, to an end, but also in the belief that what happens politically in Washington, for all the rude things said about the place, still matters more decisively for every American, and indeed the rest of the world, than anything that happens in the capital of even the biggest of the states.

Our book offers a portrait, done between late 1979 and early 1982, of a maturing, not to say middle-aged, America. In it we think we have caught the main social forces that are shaping ordinary Americans' daily lives, at work, at home, at school, in court, in church, and at the polls. Much more should have been said about the arts and popular culture, but our book, which is not an encyclopedia, was already long.

For the Hollywood film and for jazz, the two indisputably American art forms, this is a particular matter of regret. Yet in the movies, seen the world over, is recreated a Mythic America that could well have served as a commentary on the Real America we describe were it not for the fact that this would have doubled our length and for the fact that the image of America in Hollywood film should stand as a book on its own. America in jazz, and in the blues, would also be its own story.

In describing America, certain themes keep coming back. What is the balance between diversity and conformity, between "pluralism" and "Americanism," between local interests and national pressures? What on earth, the question recurs, holds the American system together when national institutions—political parties, unions, churches, newspapers—are so weak? "With liberty and justice for all," the phrase from the pledge of allegiance—a patriotic oath which first appeared, as far as it is known, some ninety years ago in a Boston boys' magazine —catches the leading tension in American politics between a conservative tradition which emphasizes freedom and a progressive tradition that stresses equality. Which is likelier to come to the fore in a maturing America where economic success cannot be relied on to cushion political conflicts and where a strong tradition of the left is largely missing? America and the Americans does not set out to provide the answer, but this question is the red thread in what follows.

1

A RICH AND VARIED SAMENESS
Regions and People

As the plane flies, it is farther from New York to San Francisco than from Paris to Baghdad, a longer trip from Chicago to San Antonio than from London to Warsaw. For the unprepared traveler, a first hint of the variety of this continent-sized nation is the discovery that America has no climate. It may be snowing in Chicago, sunny in San Antonio, raining in New York, and foggy in San Francisco. During the especially bad winter of 1977, it snowed in Florida while sunshine baked Alaska. The land varies as much as the weather. Farmers in cold Vermont used to complain that the easiest crop to grow there was rocks. In the damp South, virtually anything grows. The kudzu vine that covers trees and hangs from telephone lines creeps so fast it is said to smother drivers in their pickups. Almost nothing grows in the desert West unless the land is expensively irrigated. Between October and April, on the other hand, in the lumber forests of the Pacific Northwest it never seems to stop raining.

Even in today's citified America, it is still possible to come across a continental range of wildlife. In Minnesota there are timber wolves that must be protected from weekend hunters. Alligators leave their swamps and turn up in the town drains of Florida. Mountain lions and wild sheep roam the national parks of the Southwest. In the suburbs of East Coast cities, garbage can lids are pried loose by raccoons. Newcomers to Houston are warned about snakes that swim onto front porches during summer rainstorms.

Americans live in a continent of extremes. Considering how comfortable they have made themselves, it is easy to forget the many different ways in which theirs is such an inhospitable land. Blizzards have been known to keep Bostonians indoors for days at a time. Tornadoes tear through towns in the Midwest. Hurricanes—called, without bias, Alberto and Chris now, as well as Beryl and Debby—roar up from the Caribbean. Earthquakes have shaken cities as distant from each other as Charleston and San Francisco. Thunderheads toss 747s about on the Gulf Coast. Volcanoes in the West blow out mountainsides. Is it any surprise that after struggling over the Rockies, the Great Desert Basin, and the Sierras, early settlers coming down on California's narrow central valley thought they had found paradise?

Money and ingenuity have helped rub away the bigger differences. It was bad luck for the Puritans to fetch up in Massachusetts, but living through a few New England winters was a great spur to their inventiveness. A lot today is made of the economic success of the Sunbelt, the southeastern corner of which ought more accurately to be called the Steambelt. Without air conditioning, the region would be hard put to attract new migrants. Houston's yearly bill for air conditioning is roughly $700 million. It is difficult to imagine economic takeoff in the old Confederacy, cooled only by ceiling fans. Nor could the southwestern quadrant of the Sunbelt, typified by Phoenix, the country's fastest-growing city, long survive without the billions of gallons of specially pumped water it needs every year. Not ones to brave when they can tame the elements, Americans are able to live at a comfortable 68 degrees, winter and summer, pretty much anywhere in the country, providing they can afford the bills.

Big as the United States is, the second thing the traveler soon realizes is that it is almost empty, at least of people. Americans do not, in fact, live pretty well anywhere. They bunch. Fly coast to coast on a northern route. Beyond the Mississippi, going west, is farmland. The talkative Khrushchev gasped for words when he saw the amount of cropland on his cross-country trip in 1959. The rest is mountain and desert, until the thin Pacific strip. People are concentrated in the Northeast, in the South, around the Great Lakes, along a narrow band on the West Coast, and at a few urban outposts in between, such as Denver and Saint Louis. Even within these broad regions, Americans long ago went to town. Theirs is a rich and varied land, but few know it closely today except on weekends or holidays. Three Americans in four live in what the Census Bureau calls "metropolitan areas"—that is, cities or suburbs. Most of the rest live in small towns that are fast becoming middle-sized as their popularity and population grow.

Empty as the land may look from the air, down below the settled bits are filling up, some faster than others, according to the latest census. The 1980 census was contested for being inaccurate, expensive, and discriminatory, but it is still the freshest statistical picture there is of the American people today. It confirmed that the populations of the South and West were growing rapidly, while those of the Midwest or Northeast were growing slowly or hardly at all. Between 1970 and 1980, the American population as a whole rose 11 percent, to 226 million. The West's grew 24 percent, the South's 21 percent, the Midwest's 4 percent, and the Northeast's 1 percent. If numbers alone are cause for regional pride, the South and West had reason to cheer. Migration from the North, though, played only one part. Pensioners from Ohio or Pennsylvania did retire to Arizona or Florida. Young workers in Detroit or Cleveland did look for work in Texas. As telling a difference, however, lay in the simple fact that the South and West had higher birth rates than the rest of the country. This in turn was largely because their populations, overall, have a bigger share of young people of child-bearing age.

Faster growth in the South and West did mean that the 435 seats in the House of Representatives, fixed at that number some seventy years ago, had to be shared out again among the states. The North and Midwest lost seventeen seats. Beyond that it is hard to gauge what it means that almost exactly half the country now lives in the South and West, half in the Northeast and Midwest. For these regions are, to a large extent, head-counting devices. This makes them rather arbitrary at the edges. The census categories are slightly different, but the South, typically, is taken to include the eleven states of the Old Confederacy as well as West Virginia, Kentucky, and Oklahoma. The Northeast usually means New England, the big Mid-Atlantic states, as well as Maryland, Delaware, and the District of Columbia, although the census puts these last three in the South. The Midwest covers the five Great Lakes states and the Plains states, including Missouri. The West is the rest.

Regions exist in ways that matter only to the extent that people who live in them believe they do. Although both states are in the West, the residents of Oregon have little Western distinctiveness in common with those of New Mexico. Within the South, there is the Oil South, the Deep South, and the New South, as well as Texas, which includes all three, and Florida, as hard to pigeonhole as its shape. The industrial Great Lakes are different in character from the farmbelt. Rural Maine could not be mistaken for Manhattan. Why four regions and not fourteen, or forty? Ask an American where he is from. The answer will be a city or town first, a state second, and a region last, if at all. Ask an Italian, in Paris or Berlin, where he is from and the answer will most probably not be "Italy" but "Rome," "Milan," or "Bologna." Local pride still rivals national pride. Ask an American the same question abroad and he will say: "I'm American." National pride is greater than regional pride.

Yet regional pride persists. The regions are not simply matters of convenience for the Census Bureau. Nor are they simply regional coalitions lobbying together for bigger shares of the federal pie. The bumper stickers on Texan cars that read: "Drive at 90, freeze a Yankee," or the T-shirt covering a large Colorado chest and even larger belly at Stapleton Airport outside Denver that said: "If God had meant Texans to ski he'd have made bullshit white," do not suggest that the spirit of section is entirely dead.

The four main regions have typically been given characters as distinct as the different soils and climates. Regional character had such obvious underpinnings that until quite recently it would have been absurd to question this. The struggle to keep the South in the Union was waged with a methodical ferocity that introduced the world to modern warfare, and for a century afterward the South remained a place apart. A backward South, bypassed by new immigrants, preoccupied with race, and suspicious of outsiders, turned in on itself, although it was not starved of outside capital.

Stand under the broad sky in Iowa, where there is continent in every direction for a thousand miles or more, and then travel across to the great band of industrial cities along the Great Lakes. Run down as many of them may be, it is not difficult to get a feel for the isolationism of the old Midwest and its quarrels with the East. Corn, cattle, steel, and cars made the Midwest a self-sufficient dynamo that needed the rest of America for markets and the rest of the world hardly at all. Its very compactness—as well as its history—pulled together the Northeast just as the conviction that the West represented the future united that region. Are these regional differences what they were?

The South has many distinctions, but it is no longer utterly distinct. It is more violent than the rest of the country. The old South's do-or-die tradition of settling arguments lives on in the homicide rate. Two murders in five are committed in Southern states, a finding that prompted a University of North Carolina professor, John Reed, to suggest that the Mason-Dixon line should be renamed the Smith & Wesson line. Southern courts are likelier to have hanging judges and juries than the North. At the start of 1980, Florida had 138 prisoners on death row, Texas 117, and Alabama 43. The total for the states outside the Old Confederacy was 138.

The South is also more religious. Southerners still tend to be more churchgoing and more Protestant than other Americans. Having more spending money has not weakened their observance. Middle-class suburban Southerners can be as keen churchgoers as the rural converts of tent revivalists. Nor has greater wealth brought much taste for more tolerant creeds. Southern Baptists, thirteen million strong, can still work up a passion arguing over whether every word in the Bible, from creation in seven days to Gog and Magog, is literally true.

The South, particularly, in its upper social reaches, remains more obviously clannish than the rest of America. Southerners of a certain class keep informal social registers and like to place each other as precisely as diamond-sorters. Sizing up of this kind goes on in drawing rooms everywhere, of course, and not just in Boston or Philadelphia, but in Cleveland, Denver, and San Diego. It is an innocent indeed who thinks otherwise. Southerners, nonetheless, seem to do it with greater conviction. In a more closed society that failed to keep up in the American business of making money, caste and rank, not surprisingly, remained unusually important. A sense of family and a sense of place were also easier to hang on to in a region so long insulated from change. The millions of European immigrants who came over around the turn of the century had not come to live in the South, a depressed, agrarian region that itself exported people. In this the South used to be thought of as the opposite pole from California, where people went to make a new start, the past was rewritten, and all were on equal footing. There may have once been something in this, although the South now has quite enough new money as well as newcomers to make it more open than it was.

The South is also more black than the rest of the nation, more conservative, less unionized, less educated, and in most places, poorer, although the differences are much less than they were, and the South has lost the peculiarities that were once strong enough to threaten the stability of an entire nation. To borrow the words well known to so many black Southern preachers, it could be said by whites in the South today: "We ain't what we ought to be. We ain't what we're going to be. But, thank the Lord God Almighty, we ain't what we was." Rural blacks are no longer plagued by beriberi and pellagra. Racist groups like the Invisible Circle, the Pale Faces, the Knights of the White Camellia, and the White League are historical curiosities. The Ku Klux Klan remains an ugly force, as it does outside the South, but it is no longer widely condoned. Race-baiting oratory from campaigning politicians has gone the way of the braces-and-shirtsleeves harangue from the back of a flatbed truck. Formal segregation, backed by the law, is a thing of the past.

Progress is far from complete. Fifteen years after the Voting Rights Act, a black had still to win a statewide election in the South. Blacks make up 18 percent of the Southern population but account for fewer than three in a hundred of all elected officials. Blacks, though, have become mayor of some of the South's largest cities: Andrew Young and Maynard Jackson in Atlanta, Henry Marsh in Richmond, Ernest Morial in New Orleans, and Richard Arrington in Birmingham, where in 1963, Bull Connor, the police commissioner, set his police dogs on civil rights marchers.

Southern politics has changed in step. The region is no longer distinguished by one-party rule. The South stopped being dependably Democratic in presidential elections as long ago as 1948, and this change is now coming about lower down as well. Ten of the old Confederacy's twenty-two senators at the start of the Ninety-seventh Congress in 1981 were Republicans. In 1978, Texas elected a Republican governor. This does not mean the South is becoming a Republican or even a two-party region. Like the rest of the country, it is more and more a "no-party" region, with a conservative tilt in which candidates matter more than parties. Old racist politicians like Strom Thurmond began to appeal for black votes. As it grows in weight, the black vote may mute Southern conservatism in places, assuming blacks continue to vote alike. Easier race relations have lessened Southerners' sense that they are an outnumbered few. This, in turn, has weakened that talent for resistance and delay which stamped the South's political style and drove its politicians to excel at tactics, procedure, and ingenious legalism.

Spreading wealth played a large part in these changes. When the Black South challenged segregation, the White South divided between resistance and compromise. Black politicians, appealing to whites, argued that freeing blacks from segregation would liberate whites as well. Jimmy Carter, then the nationally unknown governor of Georgia, echoed the theme. Southern businessmen, especially in the bigger cities, such as Atlanta, boosted as "too busy to hate," had already heard the message that segregation was commercially profitless, and this argument helped carry the day. Economic progress in the South has brought other changes, lamented by traditionalists. The gothic, the tragic, and the bizarre, so easy to brood on in the South, are draining away. Yet only a bigot could regret the loss of much that made the South so different, as the historian C. Vann Woodward has described it: the one-horse farm, one-crop agriculture, one-party politics, the share-cropper, the poll-tax, the white primary, the Jim Crow car, the lynching bee.

Economic growth in the South has brought a more varied economy than the region used to have. This itself has made the South's economy less distinctive from the rest of the nation's and has also meant that there is less tying the South itself together as an economic area. In trying to attract Yankee capital, Southern businessmen turned some time ago from advertising a labor force that was "ninety percent pure Anglo-Saxon" to touting one that was barely unionized. In North Carolina, for example, fewer than one worker in ten belongs to a union, although one worker in three has an industrial job. Right-to-work laws, inhibiting union organizers, are the rule throughout the South. Cheap labor and low taxes did lure outside investors, but many labor-intensive industries that bought the South's pitch, such as textiles or shoes, face competitors from the third world in such places as South Korea, Mexico, Taiwan, or Hong Kong. The South used to want free trade to sell cotton and later soybeans and rice on world markets in return for cheap machinery. Now it has a strong protectionist constituency. Were matters that simple, a neat switch in traditional roles might be expected as a low-wage, protectionist Sunbelt with declining industries falls back again economically while a high-wage, high-technology Northeast revives. Matters are not that simple. For the South's economy is now too complex and varied to allow such tidy change. North Carolina has more than its share of noncompetitive industries, but it also has knowledge-based firms linked with the Research Triangle near the University of North Carolina. Texas, the one state in the Union that was an independent republic for any length of time, is really a region of its own. It has oil and gas, oil engineering, medical and space technology, aerospace, and agriculture. Florida has got rich, so locals like to say, on farming, tourism, and drug smuggling. Southerners would be hard put to say now what is distinctively Southern about their economy.

The South's remaining claims to distinctiveness—its feel for the language and its sense of place, black country blues and white country music, its novelists and its journalists—the South and the rest of the country can welcome. There are dry counties to this day and states like North Carolina with no bars where liquor can only be served in restaurants, but Northerners have less grounds for suspecting Southern uprightness than they once had. A few years behind the West Coast and the North, the South, in country music and a copious supply of marijuana, got its own counterculture in the university towns. Learning that there was more to politics than race and that race was not the South's problem alone was a liberation for white Southerners. The South is still pocketed with areas of poverty. Despite the boosterism of the Sunbelt, it is still, on average, poorer than the Northeast or Midwest, although the gap is smaller than it was. Southerners, all the same, are better off and on much better racial terms with one another than they were only twenty years ago. By any count, that is a remarkable change. It makes it hard for Southerners to go on thinking of themselves as a people apart. Southerners still have a flag, but in truth, today theirs is really just another region.

So much a part of the national mainstream had the South become when a former Georgia governor from a rural backwater won the 1976 presidential election without carrying a single Western state, political writers began wondering whether the West had not replaced the South as the most alienated part of the country. The election of Ronald

Reagan four years later seemed to confirm for many that the West was indeed different, even if those who thought it alienated had a difficult time squaring that with those who thought it the leading edge of a new political majority.

Though born and raised in the Midwest, Reagan has identified himself much more closely in the public mind with the West—at least the West of the imagination—than native Californian politicians such as Jerry Brown and Richard Nixon. Reagan's cowboy hats, barbecue clothes, and "Aw, shucks" manner went down well in the West, where he piled up heavier majorities against Carter in 1980 than the Midwest-erner Gerald Ford had done in 1976.

Governor Richard Lamm of Colorado, a Democrat, went so far as to say that "A new Mason-Dixon line is being drawn at the 100th meridian." This is a geographers' line running north-south, to the west of which, outside the mountains, rain falls on average under—and often far under—twenty inches a year.

The estrangement found among Westerners can be both diffuse and highly specific. On the booming Colorado Front Range, with the Rockies, an hour's drive away, for scenic backdrop, it is easy to feel detached from the problems of the dense industrial crescent of the Midwest and Northeast. Crowded as most Westerners themselves are into urban oases with too many cars and too much smog, the sheer emptiness all around gives a sense of elbow room Easterners do not have. Western landowners, ranchers, and mineral developers have more particular reasons for feeling estranged from the East, at least they had until James Watt, their paid representative, became secretary of the interior. The target of their anger was federal officialdom that administered the West's vast public lands—86.6 percent of Nevada, 66.1 percent of Utah, 47.8 percent of Wyoming, 42.8 percent of Arizona, and 36.1 percent of Colorado. So long as federal regulators interfered with their development schemes, they lobbied for handing over more control of public lands to tame state legislatures and to local officials who could be counted on to make more pliant overseers.

Plenty of Westerners, old and new, wealthy or not, share these resentments against overzealous federal bureaucrats, believe that they are misunderstood in Washington, and like to think of themselves as independent, self-sufficient types living close to the land. In phrases borrowed from the third world, Westerners have also taken to complaining about the neocolonial status of their region. By this they mean the using of the West as a raw-material exporter or the region's dependence on big oil companies, multinational corporations, the New York and Eurocurrency capital markets, and venture capitalists in Los Angeles, Texas, or elsewhere. The man in the T-shirt at Stapleton Airport was merely bearing on his chest what many local Colorado businessmen feel in their hearts.

It takes more than shared resentments, though, to create a shared identity. The West has a jumble of conflicting aims and ambitions. This is true even when one narrows down the West to include only the Rocky Mountain states of Montana, Wyoming, Colorado, Utah, Nevada, Arizona, and New Mexico, leaving out the West Coast states of Washington, Oregon, and California—a state big and rich enough to be an independent country and virtually impossible to typify—as well as Idaho, which, in the north at least, belongs with the Pacific Northwest.

Even when narrowed down, quite as much divides as unites the Mountain West. Patriarchal Mormons in Utah have little in common with the get-rich-quick hucksters who flew in to Denver to cash in on the energy boom. The interests in Albuquerque that made a once-beautiful city as ugly with highway billboards as Elizabeth, New Jersey, share few ideals with the "Don't Californicate Colorado" lobbyists, who helped wreck the state's plans to act as host for the 1976 Winter Olympics. The old from the Midwest who gather to retire in "sunshine homes" like Sunset City outside Phoenix have different needs and different outlooks from the students at Boulder with their dope, their Buddhist temple, and their sensory deprivation baths. Independent ranchers futilely struggle to compete against rich operators with many business interests who in bad years treat their cattle losses as a tax break. In Montana, ranchers and Indians have made unlikely common cause against mineral developers.

Thoughtful Westerners reply that the same may be said of any region. There are usually as many likenesses or differences as need to be found to make a case for or against a region's identity. They insist, all the same, that the West does face political dilemmas that are different from those of the rest of the country. Western life is dominated by resources. How should its water, land, and minerals be used? Perhaps in the apparent simplicity of this question lies a lot of the appeal of today's West. How can the West be preserved while the urban oases are allowed to grow? Maintaining the lonely grandeur of the West—for all man has done, there is still plenty left—is not a trivial matter for Westerners. A National Park Service ranger, a bespectacled man who looked a bit like a youthful Harry Truman, put the matter clearly when he said that he sometimes wished that all the modern settlers in the Southwest would fold up their oil derricks, abandon their ranch houses, and drive away in their cars. The land could then once again, said the ranger, revert to those who knew it best—the animals, the Utes, the Shoshones, the Crows, and the Navajos.

This particular ranger was touched by the thoroughgoingness of a true believer. When a mountain lion had stalked him once for nearly a mile, he said, he had time to reflect on what he should do if attacked. After pushing the matter back and forth in his head, he decided that he would try to fight the lion off with the butt of his rifle. In no circumstances would he shoot at it or do it serious harm, even if this cost him his life. His justification was unusual but clear. The world could spare him, he said, since it had plenty of people, perhaps too many, already. Mountain lions were rarer and so more precious.

The ranger's dilemma was not unlike the question many Westerners ask themselves. In the words of Governor Bruce Babbitt of Arizona, this is: "How do you have growth without destroying the values that brought people here in the first place?" Easterners or West Coast Americans visiting the Mountain states easily become impatient with this question. Rocky Mountain Westerners are doing very nicely, thank you, or so state boosters would have outsiders believe, and so why should they grumble if their scenery gets a bit battered in the process? The West, besides, is not all breathtaking vista. Fly across the Rockies in a small plane to Colorado's Western Slope. Below, in full daylight, almost no features can be seen on the dark tundra. It is as if one were orbiting the moon. The only sign of human presence is an occasional experimental oil shale plant. Eastern impatience increases when Westerners ask for money to help small towns cope with actual or hoped-for mining booms. Parachute, Colorado, a collection of houses, a closed gasoline station, and a broken-down whitewashed wooden church beside the Colorado River on the Western Slope, was one such town. During the most recent brief flirtation with oil shale in the Piceance Basin nearby, Parachute for a while became a boom town. Westerners say boom towns need help. Easterners say let them look after themselves. What values, they ask, were wrapped up in Parachute?

The West's value is broader than these squabbles suggest. It affects how Americans think of their country, and matters to Easterners who have never set foot there and do not even want to. This is partly an imaginative matter. An America with no West would be a room with no view, a house with no cellar or attic. It would be as difficult to grasp as Northern Europe without the Mediterranean. It is partly because the West is—or was, since it is quickly filling up—an inner frontier in that peculiarly American sense not of a line separating two jurisdictions but of the temporary boundary to an old life that is asking to be crossed. Most tangibly, it is because today's West faces Americans with a question of how they see their country: as a plentiful land full of room and riches, or as an increasingly crowded one without inexhaustible resources.

The Mountain West is deceptive. For all its space and despite the fact that it has ten million people living on 780,000 square miles, it is running out of water. The Mountain West cannot simultaneously cope with more people, irrigate its farmland, and provide water needed to exploit its huge mineral and coal deposits. Washington will not come to the rescue. Most of the efficient water projects in the West are already built. New ones proposed are pork-barrel projects, at least so Eastern politicians tend to believe. Easterners will not spend money to help Westerners avoid hard choices, not at least so long as Western conservatives vote against programs to help Eastern cities.

The Mountain West, some would argue, is facing, in economists' jargon, physical limits to growth. It must now choose between different uses for its limited supplies of water. In the process, it should be added, the states of the West quarrel quite as fiercely among themselves about water allocations as the West as a whole does on other matters with the rest of the nation. There is a counterview, represented by James Watt, the Colorado lobbyist whom Reagan put in charge of the Interior Department. Like many boosterish Westerners, Watt sees little contradiction in mining the West for its resources and preserving its environment. To Watt, there are few obstacles to growth in the West that human ingenuity and less government interference cannot get around. Watt represents a traditional view of the West and of America. The country started with so few settlers and such abundance of resources that the unthinking answer when more oil, more minerals, more timber, or more water were needed was to sink another well, dig another mine, cut another forest, or vote funds for a new dam and damn the expense.

Many Americans think such profligacy is no longer possible. At an early staff meeting in the Interior Department, Watt told his officials his philosophy of the environment. A fundamentalist Christian, Watt said that he was following the work of Christ, who was steward of God's resources on this earth. "If that's so," came the loud voice of a Democratic holdover from the back of the room, "how come he made his only son a carpenter?"

Even if the scale of the limits to growth in the West is exaggerated or their character misunderstood, it is difficult to see how Colorado, for example, can continue to add 700,000 people, or 31 percent, to its population each decade, as it did between 1970 and 1980, at least if they are to be squeezed, as most are today, on a narrow strip on either side of Route 25 running through Denver along the eastern slope of the Rockies. And even if Americans cannot agree on an answer to the rather abstract question of whether the limits to the old attitude of "take as much as you want" are matters of physical supply or price, they are showing a practical awareness that the time of simultaneously cheap and plentiful resources is over. Westerners experiment with solar energy and wind power. Elsewhere, habits are changing, too. Rooms are not invariably kept cooler in summer than Americans find comfortable in winter. New Englanders pay fancy prices for wood stoves of the kind their grandparents threw out. Detroit, at last, is making Japanese-sized cars. To take advantage of the ground's near-constant temperature of 55 degrees, and so cut fuel bills, Minnesotans are experimenting with half-burying their houses underground.

The South was, but no longer is, a country apart. The West, at least the Mountain West, superficially so different, is coming up against choices and limits not unlike those the rest of America is having to face. The Midwest, by contrast, has long been thought of as typically American. In *Inside USA*, John Gunther gave as its hallmarks "middleness" and "typicalness." When the "heartland" is spoken of, it is usually the Midwest that is meant. In *The Real Majority*, a political report on Middle America by Richard Scammon and Ben Wattenberg, based on the 1970 census, just after the upheavals of the preceding years, the "typical American voter" was set down in Dayton, a service and manufacturing town on the Miami River in southwestern Ohio. This voter was a housewife whose husband was a machinist—perhaps with National Cash Register or with Frigidaire—and whose brother-in-law was a policeman. She considered herself a Democrat but often voted Republican. That was a decade ago and the jobs might have to be changed to bring the stereotype up to date. Few would dispute that the Midwest is still average, typical. Columbus, sitting flat in the central Ohio plain, boasts that it is a city where companies like to test-market new products because it offers such a good cross section of the country as a whole.

The "middleness" of the Midwest is not hard to grasp. The Great Lakes states—Wisconsin, Illinois, Indiana, Michigan, and Ohio—are bounded on every side by major waterways that link them with the Northeast and the South, the Mississippi, the Lakes, the Ohio. Chicago, a rail center in the past, today has one of the world's busiest airports. The Plains states—Minnesota, Iowa, Missouri, the Dakotas, Nebraska, and Kansas—are, geographically, the country's middle. Their rich topsoil—good enough to eat without putting through vegetables, Robert Frost called it—provides corn and wheat for the United States and for much of the rest of the world. Physically isolated—at least far from East and West coasts—the farmbelt is no longer isolationist, now that foreign harvests and international politics vitally affect the prosperity of American farmers.

In rural Iowa, patriotism, commercial need, and family feeling were juggled in the arguments over the grain embargo against the Soviet Union imposed by President Carter in January 1980, after the Russian action in Afghanistan. At the grain elevator in Searsboro, a small farm township east of Des Moines, the pros and cons were weighed on the night of the Iowa political caucuses. J. T. Ross, a minister who also operates the grain elevator, argued strongly that the President should be supported in his efforts to mount a boycott of the Moscow Olympic Games. The grain embargo was approved of, so long as other Americans bore some burden along with the farmers. The shrewder farmers knew that the embargo would not much hurt them—as it, in fact, did not. Amid the overheated talk of sending American troops to protect oil supplies in the Persian Gulf, it was generally agreed that nobody wanted his sons or grandsons sent off to foreign parts to fight.

Iowa boosters like to say their state is no longer narrowly agricultural. Narrowly, this is true. Iowa produces machinery besides farm equipment. Des Moines has banks and insurance companies. More Iowans work off the land than on. There are limits, though, to the extent to which the farmbelt can become just another region. Crops may be grown by fewer and fewer farmers, but the wheat and corn cannot readily be grown elsewhere. So perhaps the farmbelt is the exception to the rule that the regions are growing more alike as the old divisions of the country into readily identifiable economic blocs are disappearing. Ames, Iowa, has a famous agricultural research center at the university there. In the main hall, there is a mural by Grant Wood and assistants, done with the support of the WPA. The mural celebrates hard, sober work on the farm and in the machine shop. In the middle is a saying of Daniel Webster's: "When tillage begins, other arts follow." The saying remains true of the farm Midwest.

To find the nation writ small it is necessary to go to Ohio. Divided between the Saint Lawrence and the Mississippi basins, Ohio is as typical of the Midwest as the Midwest is of the country at large. Third or fourth behind California and New York in manufacturing, Ohio also has farms and mines. It reproduces fairly closely the nation's racial groups, its city and rural problems, as well as the American conviction, in the words of Ohio's longtime Republican governor, James Rhodes, that "profit is not a dirty word." Scattered across the state's flat surface are half a dozen cities with half a million people or more, but none with very many more. Like the country, Ohio has no focus. Cincinnati, home of the Tafts, is a solid, middle-class bastion on the Ohio River, with hills and neighborhoods watched over by a wealthy Republican business establishment. Ohio is typical in having been the stopping place for settlers from abroad or from inside the United States, with the exception of the Hispanics. Yankees came from the Northeast. From across the Ohio River came settlers from the border country and the South. Below the old national road that ran roughly from Wheeling through Columbus to Dayton, rural Ohio is more Dixiefied. This used to be Wallace country. Jimmy Carter, campaigning as a Southerner, did well. Confederate flags can be seen on farm porches. In the Civil War, it was Copperhead territory. Barns, as in the South, are painted with signs saying: "Chew Mail Pouch Tobacco—Treat Yourself to the Best." Farther up the Ohio, toward Youngstown and Steubenville, is industrial Ohio, once great but now weak. Cleveland, to the north, on Lake Erie, typifies the troubles of the cities of the industrial Midwest. From Superior Street Bridge it is possible to look down at a jumble of unused plants and old redbrick warehouses that block the city from the lake. When Cleveland grew great, nobody bothered much with town planning. Cleveland's population fell by 165,000 in the past decade. This, say many, is a good thing. It means people are moving out of cities that depend on uncompetitive, high-wage industries, to look for jobs in industries that sell goods at prices people will pay. America makes this sort of adjustment look easier than it is elsewhere. It is possible, especially if one is young, to pack up belongings in a U-Haul trailer and move on to another city. Americans are mobile. But this only works if a few Americans, a few Clevelanders, do it. What about those who remain? Many ex-Clevelanders, after all, simply moved to the suburbs. Despite getting its finances in order, Cleveland continues to have terrible problems of economic adjustment. These are not made easier by the ethnic politics. East of the Cuyahoga, Cleveland has black slums. To the west are run-down, respectable wards with as many distinct European ethnic groups as can be found anywhere in the world. At the covered Western Market, shoppers get pierogi from Ida Kotelewec, meat from Iwaskewych Brothers, or cakes from Konditorei Kühlein, as well as cheeses, paprikas, and sausages from Kaufman, Bartosch, Dohar, or Farkas.

Cleveland's troubles are not the end of Ohio's story. Columbus, a white-collar and university town, has overtaken Cleveland in population. Its unemployment has kept well below the national average, just as the unemployment rate in the old industrial towns of northern Ohio have kept well above average. Columbus, on its face, does not have much to offer. It is flat. Its newspapers are dreadful. It typifies small-city provincialism. Yet its boosters call it a Sunbelt success in the Frostbelt. High-technology companies following in the steps of the Battelle Laboratories have set up business there, and the city offers many things —clean air, reasonably cheap housing, a manageable crime rate, fair public schools—that many average American couples want.

Imagined maps of the boundaries of the Midwest and most other regions of the United States are as various as geographers' stabs at the African interior a couple of centuries ago. Whether the states that were most divided in their loyalties during the Civil War are Southern states or border ones can still get a good row going, as public figures who have described Kentucky, the birthplace of both Jefferson Davis and Abraham Lincoln, as a border state can attest. Where the Midwest begins and ends is not a question that is likely to be solved. Nobody, though, is in any doubt about the boundaries of New England. Six states and six states only—Maine, Vermont, New Hampshire, Massachusetts, Rhode Island, and Connecticut—make up the region. Maine is just about as big as the other five combined; collectively, they are smaller than Idaho or South Dakota, and accommodate fewer people than either Texas or California.

The rest of America has always been of two minds about New Englanders, balancing their supposed Yankee virtues of thrift, artless integrity, hard work, and understatement against their supposed hypocrisy and skepticism and aloofness, as caught in the jest that Yankees believe in the fatherhood of God, the brotherhood of man, and the neighborhood of Boston. The taciturnity of the region's people is commonly thought to be the national obverse of the extrovert spontaneity of Californians, and the claims of New Englanders to a skeptical dry humor are well put in Calvin Coolidge anecdotes. It is remembered, for example, that Cool Cal was presented by the neighbors of his family farm in Vermont with a rake when he left for the White House. In a windy speech, the orator went on at length about the virtues of the hickory wood from which it was made. "Hickory, like the President, is sturdy, strong, resilient, and unbroken," he said. Coolidge picked up the rake, ran his eyes and fingers slowly down it, and said: "Ash." Coolidge, on another occasion, was traveling by train. His companion, made somewhat desperate by the silence, pointed out the window at a field full of sheep. "The sheep have been sheared," he said. Barely glancing up, Coolidge replied: "Looks like it from this side."

This is mostly nostalgia. While New England still has many traces of its Old England yeoman and tradesman heritage, in its rural architecture, its churches, its fish and other dishes, its family and place names, it could, like other regions today, as convincingly celebrate its diversity as its homogeneity. Go to Fenway Park to see the Boston Red Sox and the crowd could be Coca-Cola advertising its worldwide constituency. Or listen to the editor of an eastern Massachusetts newspaper describe his beat, covering a few square miles. "Hamilton-Wenham is Yankee; Newburyport is Irish; Salem is Polish and French-Canadian. In Hamilton they play polo and have a country club; Ipswich doesn't have one, thank God! Each town has its own reason for being there."

As the first part of the country to go in for intensive agriculture of the European sort, and to join the industrial revolution, New England has suffered visibly from its economic age. In southern New Hampshire, old textile mills are as gaunt and eyeless as the industrial archaeology on Old England's Merseyside or Old Scotland's Clydeside. The region's pocket-handkerchief-sized farms were made redundant with the opening of the cornbelt of the Midwest. Today antique and junquetique shops and hobby farms outnumber working farms in rural New England, and at the seaside towns of Cape Cod in the summer it is usual to find fresh fish—mackerel, bluefish, flounder, lobsters, and bass—alongside vegetables that have traveled from half a continent or more away.

In industry, at least, the appearances are misleading. Parts of New England have shown signs of staging an economic recovery on the back of high technology. The turnaround began in earnest about ten years ago, and in 1978 unemployment in New England fell below the average national rate for the first time in forty years, despite the region's dependence on OPEC for four-fifths of its oil needs. This regional defiance of the economic caricature of boom in the Sunbelt and bust in the Frostbelt has, by and large, continued. Route 128 around Boston is as much a hive of high-technology businesses as the Silicon Valley in California. Such New England high-tech multinationals as Wang Laboratories and Digital Equipment have begun to erase internationally the textile-and-shoe industrial image of the place and have made it easier for the area's George Babbitts to entice foreign investment into the region.

The boosters tout, above all, the ready supply of trained, specialist brainpower the region proffers industries in high-growth sectors such as those capitalizing on the technologies of the space race, biological medicine, computers, and the new communications and defense sciences. In the humanities the region has always had a depth and breadth of talent. As the historian Marcus Cunliffe has noted, Boston-Cambridge was in the nineteenth century the only American center that was remotely comparable to England's Oxford or Cambridge; only in Boston could you point to a group of families—Adamses, Holmeses, Lodges, Lowells, Nortons—that it was not absurd to mention with, say, the Huxleys, Stephens, Trevelyans, and Wedgwoods of Victorian England. Since then New England, with its abundance of colleges and universities, which set a standard of excellence that the best educational institutions in the rest of the country and, indeed, abroad strive to emulate, has expanded successfully into the new disciplines of late-twentieth-century capitalism. Harvard vies with Stanford to be acknowledged as the best business school in the country. The Massachusetts Institute of Technology is at the pinnacle in economics and the practical sciences. Such educational excellence can meet, with less strain than many of the Southern states, the demand of the most advanced industries for people with high skills and original minds.

Powerful as they were, regional differences are operating with less and less force. What shapes everyday life for Americans, rich and poor, black and white, is more recognizably alike in the different regions than it was. This is not simply due to the glaring uniformities noticeable from the interstate highway and its margins: the Holiday Inn or Quality Court, the Kentucky Fried Chicken or McDonald's fast-food franchise, and the stereotyped local television news broadcast in the motel bedroom. Americans have been on the move—South to North, East to West, North to South—and by now many regional differences have rubbed off on each other. Extremes of regional wealth and poverty have gone. In 1900, per capita income in the South was less than 50 percent of the national average. In the Northeast it was more than 130 percent and in the Far West more than 160 percent. By 1930, these big discrepancies had narrowed only slightly. Large economic changes since then have narrowed the differences, so that the range of variation in income among all the regions is little more than 20 percent.

The economic identity of the regions has changed in other ways. The work Americans do is no longer a good clue to where they live. Less than 3 percent of the labor force works on the land. As Americans have developed a mature, service economy, they are less and less tied to the industries that stamped whole regions, like mining, steelmaking, or cars. Not every district has farms or industry, but almost every district has a school, a government office, and a hospital, and education, government, and health care now account for one job in three. These are jobs with almost no regional stamp at all.

Someone who can remember America sixty years ago might well find the similarity of the regions today a surprise. What should also flabbergast him is the retreat, almost rout, of the old American assumption that Americanizing newcomers of foreign stock was a high and urgent priority.

Those who think this an exaggeration should look at David Saville Muzzey's An American History, first published in 1911. For more than half a century, this textbook was the main source of information about the country's past for American schoolchildren. Millions of people now middle-aged or older, perhaps the majority of them, were instructed by Muzzey's book, which was amended only slightly over the years. Yet its passages about immigrants, which were uncontroversial, almost unexceptional, only a few years ago, have come to seem like something from a different century. "Can we," he asked, "assimilate or mold into citizenship the millions who are coming to our shores, or will they remain an ever-increasing body of aliens, an undigested and indigestible element in our body politic and a constant menace to our free institutions?" Eugene C. Barker, William E. Dodd, and Henry Steele Commager in another history for schools, Our Nation's Development, first published in the 1930s, were still more outspoken. "Would it be possible," they asked, "to absorb the millions of olive-skinned Italians and swarthy black-haired Slavs and dark-eyed Hebrews into the body of the American people? Would they adjust themselves to their New World environment and understand and contribute to American institutions?"

The implicit assumption in these and other books intended to instruct and inspire children on what their country meant and stood for was that real Americans came out of an Anglo-Saxon, or at least Northern European, culture and it was imperative that the newcomers conform to this American norm as quickly as possible. Blacks, when they were discussed at all, tended to be seen as a problem. Frances FitzGerald, in America Revised, her study of school history books, aimed to show how during the past two decades these have sought to follow changes in popular thought as slavishly as a popular-music radio station follows the hit parade. She notes that the Muzzey text of the

1930s began its first section on the population by saying: "Leaving aside the Negro and Indian population," and then proceeded to do just that.

The world for teachers of history, and the writers and publishers of history books, has since then been turned upside down. American parents who believed the history they learned at school was written in stone look at their children's schoolbooks and marvel to find it was written in sand. The purpose of the texts has become frankly inspirational. The illustrations, too, strive to provide positive role models for children of different colors and foreign backgrounds. Indeed, ethnicity is so celebrated that the child who cannot claim an exotic heritage must sometimes feel deprived. The only Americans still allowed their villains are the WASPs, though it may be only a matter of time before the English-Speaking Union complains that depicting Benedict Arnold as a traitor is an insult to children of British ancestry.

Emphasize the positive is the publishers' golden rule. Pictures of singing blacks slaving in cotton fields or sun-darkened Mexican-Americans stooping to pick lettuce have been cut. No matter that these stereotypes are as historically apt as the pictures of blacks supervising laboratories and of Mexican computer programmers that have replaced them. The publishers of history books have learned to their cost that a plea of historical truth is no defense against the charge of bias and that school systems prefer not to buy "controversial" textbooks. So if they want to turn a profit, they had better present each ethnic group that makes its presence felt in the best possible light and come up with heroic role models for each category of hyphenated American schoolchildren.

In successive amendments made to the books, first, hitherto neglected blacks were inserted: Crispus Attucks in the Boston Massacre; Booker T. Washington, who said his people were the only immigrants to have had their passage to the New World paid for; the diplomat Ralph Bunche, and, eventually, Martin Luther King. When Hispanic-Americans spoke up, the publishers scrambled to order yet further additions and subtractions. Photographs of Anthony Quinn and Senator Joseph Montoya were inserted. There were even photographs of Cesar Chavez in textbooks not expected to sell well in right-to-work states, where union organizers are still commonly regarded as dangerous agitators.

The Indians have been rehabilitated. Barbarous savages always rising up, breaking out, and massacring have become the noble people who, in Tocqueville's words, could not have been destroyed with more respect for the laws of humanity. Children now learn that the Indians were first slaughtered by whites invading their land and then cheated out of what territory they held on to in peace treaties that would be good, so promised the whites, "as long as the waters flow and the grasses grow." If still inhibited about acknowledging black ancestry, white Americans no longer take great pains to conceal Indian forebears. *The Ethnic Almanac* helpfully announces that Johnny Bench is one-eighth Choctaw; Johnny Cash, a quarter Cherokee; Billie Jean King, part Seminole; that Dan Rather's great-grandfather "took an Indian woman," and that Robert Rauschenberg, Burt Reynolds, and Anita Bryant all have some Cherokee ancestry.

Foreigners from countries where class is a more obvious division than national origin are struck by Americans' fascination with these differences as well as by their racial censuses. They are puzzled by the notion of "ethnicity." They know that America is a land of immigrants, a "nation of nations," but how, in practical terms, they want to know, does this really affect Italian-Americans or German-Americans today? Someone, on the other hand, recalling the immigrants from Europe, the nativism, and the urge to Americanize about the turn of the century, would want to know how it is that today's Americans have become so much more relaxed about these differences.

For one thing, he would have to be told, the scale of immigration was quite different then. In 1907, America took 1.3 million immigrants into the population of about 87 million. Today America admits half that number of immigrants each year, with a population almost three times the size. Americans, also, were gripped then by racial stereotypes, which played so large a part in the social science for the "higher races" of the day. Social antagonism between native and immigrants, between Catholic Irish and native Protestant, between Gentile and Jew, threatened—or seemed to—far more then than now.

Tolerance and acceptance from the native majority has come at different speeds for European immigrants, Spanish-speakers, and blacks. Much has been made of the persistence of ethnic pride among descendants of European immigrants. After the civil rights struggles of the 1960s, Italian-Americans, Polish-Americans, Ukrainian-Americans, Lithuanian-Americans, and many others were rediscovered and rediscovered themselves. Membership in Ukrainian fellowship societies increased. Colleges reported a rise in applicants for Scandinavian studies. A lessening of white fears of blacks and an increase in general tolerance no doubt had something to do with this, but so, in reverse, had white ethnic resentments against efforts to help blacks, as George Wallace's successes in the white ethnic strongholds of Michigan and Wisconsin in the mid-sixties showed. Nathan Glazer and Daniel Patrick Moynihan concluded in *Beyond the Melting Pot*, their well-known study of ethnic politics in New York City, that the most striking thing about the melting pot is that it "did not happen."

Shop-floor, office-corridor, barroom, or clubroom conversation, the ethnic joke, and the old city neighborhood should be enough on their own to show any reasonably alert observer that ethnic differences in America still matter. The question is: How much? There is no nationalist movement. America has Basques, in Idaho and Nevada, but no militant separatists campaigning for ETA, "Land of the Basques and Freedom." German-Americans, Slavic-Americans, and Italian-Americans are not refighting old battles for the unification of divided peoples. Nor are any of today's "white ethnics" campaigning as included peoples for separation of some sort—independence, devolution, federation, decentralization—from an unwanted central authority, as do the Scots in Britain, the Basques, Galicians, and Catalonians in Spain, or the Quebecois in Canada. Nor are there bitter sectarian struggles like those in the North of Ireland or in Belgium, where the water cannons and tear gas are periodically brought out to separate warring Dutch-speaking Flemings from French-speaking Walloons. Ethnic pride is tolerated in America today precisely because this is constitutionally toothless and offers no challenge to the political ground rules.

Light can be cast on the question of how much ethnic differences matter—and how they can be made to cease to matter—by looking at the story of the German-Americans. Since the federal government began in 1820 to keep systematic records of immigration, more settlers have come from German-speaking places than from anywhere else; about 7 million of them from Germany and a good share of the over 4 million others from Austria, which included the Austro-Hungarian Empire until 1905, after which Austrian and Hungarian immigrants were recorded separately. They created virtually self-sufficient communities in New York, Philadelphia, and Baltimore, as well as in many of the cities of the Midwest. A Danish visitor to nineteenth-century Milwaukee reported "German houses, German inscriptions over the doors or signs, German physiognomies. Many Germans live here who never learn English, and seldom go beyond German town." By the turn of the century there were nearly eight hundred German-language journals and newspapers published in the United States, and by 1914, German-America, with money rolling in from brewers and with a German-American Alliance claiming two million members, began a resolute campaign to win over the country to strict neutrality to further the cause of the Kaiser and the Fatherland.

The backlash when America entered the Great War against the Kaiser was of an intensity not equaled even in the anti-Communist witch hunts of the McCarthy years. German books were publicly burned, and communities sought to prohibit the playing of music by German composers and even to ban the speaking of German in public. Shops owned by German proprietors were stoned, there were tarrings and featherings, and even, at Collinsville, Illinois, a lynching. German-Americans chose to Anglicize their names, from Schmidt to Smith, Kampf to Camp, Neuhaus to Newhouse. Sauerkraut was renamed "liberty cabbage." Pictures of the old country were hidden away in the attic. At church on Sundays, prayers and hymns were sung in English.

After the virtual halt to immigration from the mid-1920s and with Hitler's rise in the 1930s, most Americans of German origin were no longer hyphenated by the time the country went to war against the Axis powers. Yet President Franklin Roosevelt was still not sure German-Americans could be trusted. According to Attorney General Francis Biddle, the President said: "I don't care so much about the Italians. They are a lot of opera singers, but the Germans are different, they may be dangerous." Not only would nobody today say the Germans were dangerous. Nobody would say they were different. The Germantowns in Philadelphia and New York have all but disappeared. There is no German lobby. Much of the Midwest retains a German air, like Cincinnati with its bratwurst at Riverfront Stadium, its scores of savings and loan offices, and its strictness with jaywalking pedestrians, but this is more a matter of flavor and memory than of real ties to a cultural past. For all the ethnic revival, the German story is repeated—less sharply, more gradually—for other European-Americans.

Like other English-speakers, Americans are not good linguists. Few of those proud to claim Italian, Polish, or Swedish background, for example, speak their parents' or grandparents' mother tongue, and few keep up with life in the home country. Elderly Italians in Chicago not so long ago were still able to get news of Italy from Italian-language radio broadcasts or from *Fra Noi*, a Catholic monthly. Otherwise, Chicago's large Italian population lacked an Italian paper until the small-circulation *L'Italia* was begun in 1977. New York's *Il Progresso* does better. It has a circulation of about seventy thousand, but in a New York–area Italian population of one million, this is still pitifully small. Swedish-Americans make up a large community in Minneapolis, where Swedish Day picnics are held each June in Minnehaha Park, but the men and women gathered at the bandshell decorated with the Swedish flag and a blue banner saying "Välkommen till Svenskarnas Dag" tend to be old. Chicago has a big Swedish-American population, too, but in the whole of the United States there are only five Swedish papers, with a combined circulation of less than fifteen thousand.

America's six million or so Polish-Americans have traditionally kept up the Polish language much better, and Polish-Americans, like Representative Roman Pucinski of Chicago, were leaders of the ethnic revival movement in the early 1970s. Another was the diminutive, articulate Representative Barbara Mikulski of Baltimore, a Polish-American and a liberal Democrat who insists that white ethnics have suffered from discrimination as have blacks and that the two should fight it together. Was this not, in its way, the request that white ethnics be equally treated as Americans?

Ethnic politics still dominates the wards of Milwaukee, Cleveland, Buffalo, and Chicago, but these cities are not returning the dependably huge Democratic majorities they used to. The ward leaders cannot any longer even "deliver a case of milk." Families break up. The young move out to the suburbs. White ethnics are ceasing to vote so predictably or so alike. It may still be true that WASPs own and the Irish run Boston. City politics in Philadelphia means squaring the Italian South Philadelphia of former Mayor Rizzo and *Rocky* with the black wards to the north and with the Irish, but in state and national politics these old formulas are losing currency. As David Glancey, the Philadelphia County Democratic chairman, put it on the eve of the 1980 elections: "Today the precinct captain is the TV set." This is not to say that ethnic politics ends at city hall. Although candidates for national office may no longer feel obliged to take symbolic trips to the "Three I's"—Italy, Ireland, and Israel—Irish-American politicians like Senators Edward Kennedy and Daniel Patrick Moynihan, House Speaker Tip O'-Neill, and Governor Carey of New York speak up loudly when they think the British are doing too little to reach a settlement in the North of Ireland. American Jews speak together as a formidable voice on the foreign policy of the United States as it bears on Israel and the Middle East.

It is as easy to underplay as to exaggerate the heritage of the late-nineteenth-century and early-twentieth-century European immigrants and their American children. Ethnic badges worn with pride in good times can, in bad, quickly become marks of discrimination again. The American majority has shown a Janus face to newcomers, welcoming them and slamming the door, generously granting refuge and sucking in cheaply exploitable labor. Not everyone who came stayed or was admitted. The would-be immigrants in Alfred Stieglitz's famous 1907 photograph, *The Steerage*, were about to return to Europe.

Ethnic stereotyping survives and is even getting spurious support in statistical tables of ethnic earning power and educational achievement. The numbers are hardly necessary. The stereotypes are so well known: the Koreans have taken over the groceries; the Chinese make good engineers and architects; the Jews are running the universities; Italians have big families; undertrained newcomers from India staff the hospitals; Puerto Ricans cannot hold jobs; blacks have fatherless families. To the extent that any of these generalities are supported by fact, nobody is very good at saying what they signify.

Even though this sort of observation becomes grist for prejudice, descendants of turn-of-the-century immigrants are much less its victims than before. With every decade, memories of quotas against Jews at Harvard and Columbia have sunk further away, even if preferential hiring and admissions to help blacks have stirred them up again. So have memories of signs saying "No Irish," of humiliating medical inspections at Ellis Island, of jobs closed to Catholics and neighborhoods restricted to Americans of native stock. A Catholic has been President, a Jewish-American and a Polish-American have been secretaries of state. Of course, not even the impressive array of laws built up against discrimination can guarantee that there will never be a return to explicit prejudice. The position of the grandchildren of turn-of-the-century immigrants and their families looks more secure today, all the same, than ever before. Pressure on them to Americanize, to assimilate in every way, and to forget altogether their background has relaxed from both sides.

Of help there is the fact that today's immigrants are not coming as they used to so overwhelmingly from Europe. In the past decade, about 850,000 came from Europe, while 1.5 million came from Asia and nearly 900,000 from Mexico and Latin America.

Confusingly, those from fartherest away are often the easiest to absorb. The immigrants from Asia, particularly refugees from Southeast Asia whose wealth and status were threatened by war and revolution, came at first from the better-off classes. Unsurprisingly, many of them have quickly found ways to earn good livings in the United States. They encouraged their children to play baseball, to speak accentless English, and to dress in a way that makes them indistinguishable from the others. For them the old melting pot idea is still the ideal and education the passport to advancement, as it was for many Jewish immigrants.

Asian organizations campaign to keep Asian-Americans eligible for minority preference programs, especially for government contracts, even though many Asian-Americans consider this demeaning. Many of them are doing very well by themselves, as is attested by the widely reported finding that they make up a fifth of the undergraduates at Berkeley and outnumber black students by two to one at MIT. After graduating with a straight "A" average at High Point Senior High School in Beltsville, Maryland, and being accepted at Brown University for the fall of 1981, Teresa Chen complained to the *Washington Post:* "The colleges sent me all this minority stuff and I felt insulted. You get the feeling that they weren't interested in me because I'm me but because I'm a minority. . . . They treated me as if I was handicapped. It never occurred to me that I was handicapped because I was Chinese. My parents are very strict by American standards and they really taught us to believe that education is the way to succeed in life. They're proud of the fact that we have been educated and taking tests for thousands of years."

The closest parallel to the turn-of-the-century immigrants from

Europe comes today from the Hispanics, who number anywhere between fourteen and twenty million, depending on the estimate made of "undocumented" immigrants. If it is asked why the same urgency is not given to "Americanizing" the Hispanic community as it was to the turn-of-the-century immigrant, the simple answer is that the East Coast does not directly abut Central Europe as California, Texas, Arizona, and New Mexico abut Mexico. Americanization, at least as it was conceived then, is simply not practicable. The ties of culture, and language even, cannot be that decisively broken. Nevertheless, of the three chief obstacles to assimilation—poverty, language, and culture— the last is certainly the one most easily lived with. Indeed, most Americans would think today that differences of culture were positively valuable and worth keeping. About 60 percent of those Hispanics legally residing in the United States are of Mexican origin. Most of the rest are from Cuba or Puerto Rico.

Mexican-Americans or other Hispanics make up about a fifth of California's population and a fifth of Texas's. In the booming California economy, many have done well and moved up the economic ladder, suggesting that prejudice is not an inevitable barrier to their success. The same is true in Texas, though a Hispanic middle class of any size is emerging more slowly.

To ask the Chicano picking vegetables outside San Antonio or working in a car wash in San Bernardino to love his temporary or adopted country is asking too much. Many Mexican-Americans come from poverty to work hard in America for little return and without security. They are easily exploited as domestic servants, in sweatshops, and in the fields. Throughout the Southwest, the wealthy have an interest in a flow of cheap labor from the south. It matters little to them if the labor is documented or not. Indeed, if it is not, the workers can be made more pliant. In the Southwest and in Texas, the powers that be are not at all sure there is a "problem" with undocumented workers. In their eyes, why should there be? Chicanos are paid little; they pay sales taxes and income taxes.

For Chicanos this exploitation of their people is not a folk memory but a continuing cause of resentment against the society, which is shared even by those who have risen into the American middle class.

So much was obvious even in the play *Zoot Suit* by Luis Valdez, when it was put on at a theater in Hollywood. The play tells the Second

World War story of the Sleepy Lagoon Bar, where young Chicano patrons in shiny zoot suits—knee-length jackets with wide lapels and heavily padded shoulders, tight cuffed trousers, and watch chains long enough to brush the ground—were attacked and savagely beaten by American servicemen. The servicemen were not punished or even criticized. The *Los Angeles Times* assumed that they were behaving as any red-blooded American male should when confronted by such outrageous eccentricity.

The Chicanos in the audience were not ready to see this as a period drama. Their anger was palpable. The police in Southern California, they believe, still treat Chicano suspects with casual brutality. For many of them, Luis Valdez's play spoke to today.

Chicanos have a strong culture. They tend to marry within their own community. When a Hispanic marries "out," it is often the Anglo who is assimilated, or at least taken into an extended Spanish family. Hispanics keep Spanish names for their children, and do not bother to Anglicize their last names. They have remained generally Catholic, although some have defected to Pentecostal or charismatic denominations. They have stuck to traditional diets. Above all, they are proud of their language. This, not their commonly dark skins—betokening Indian ancestry—is what could threaten to keep the many poor among them out of the American mainstream.

Divided though they are, it is difficult to imagine the American people without a single common language. Opinion has wavered on whether bilingualism is a good or a bad thing. Congress, in 1974, passed a bill favoring those who wanted Spanish maintained. This was taken, however, as a discouragement to learning English. Since then, opinion has swung back to treating the learning of English as a priority, even if this need not mean—with a Spanish-speaking continent next door —forgetting the original language in the process, as it has meant for so many other hyphenated Americans.

Puerto Ricans are like many of the poorer Chicanos. Only one in twenty has completed college. Perhaps because they are disproportionately young, they are concentrated in the most menial jobs, such as busboys, dishwashers, food counter workers, amusement park attendants, welfare and health aides, hospital orderlies, cleaners, and janitor's assistants. During the 1970s, many went back to Puerto Rico even though times were bad there as well. The issue of status for Puerto

Ricans is not assimilation but something more specific: Should Puerto Rico become a state or remain a commonwealth? Among the more educated younger Puerto Ricans in San Juan, the movement for statehood has grown. Only a small minority favor independence, so Puerto Ricans, who are American citizens, will not have to make a choice of nationality. Whatever happens, there is little question of fully breaking ties with the mainland.

The Cubans, many of them middle-class emigrants from the revolution, show in large numbers the same drive as Asian parents in spurring on their children to achievement at school and college. Miami, their stronghold, has become a bilingual city. Cubans who arrived twenty years ago with virtually nothing have climbed the traditional entrepreneurial ladder, from working odd jobs and opening small stores, to owning gasoline stations and undertaking parlors, to running banks and insurance businesses. A few of the older Cubans still harbor dreams of a return to a Cuba without Castro, but many of the younger ones are making too much money in America to much care, and besides, like many exiled Cubans, they are secretly proud of Castro for having put Cuba on the map. Despite an appalling crime rate, Miami is becoming a financial center for the Caribbean. Cuban-Americans, comfortably American but holding on to their Latin ties, are enjoying the prosperity.

Resentful at watching Cubans leapfrog past them, Miami's blacks rioted in 1980 after the acquittal of policemen accused of killing a young black businessman. Fifteen people were killed and much of the black ghetto in Miami was razed. That same year it was reported that while one white American in ten was living in poverty—as officially defined—the numbers for Hispanics and blacks were one in four and one in three, respectively. Black Americans seem to have won the legal struggle to be accepted, but huge obstacles remain to erasing their poverty.

While laws by themselves do not remove prejudice, signs are appearing among a new generation of white Americans that there is less hostility and fear. No visitor to the South can avoid being struck by the extraordinary changes for the better that have occurred there in only twenty years. The two races no longer live visibly separate lives.

For politicians in the South, backsliding on racial progress was made increasingly risky by the Voting Rights Act of 1965, although some of its provisions were endangered under the Reagan administration. The act put an end to such evasions as that used by Forrest County, Mississippi, which declined to register blacks as voters because they could not answer satisfactorily the question: "How many bubbles are in a bar of soap?" In 1960, three-fifths of the voting-age whites in the South but only just over a quarter of the blacks were registered to vote. By 1976, it was just over two-thirds of the whites and just under two-thirds of the blacks. Andrew Young was able to say: "It used to be Southern politics was just 'nigger' politics—a question of which candidate could 'outnigger' the other. Then you registered 10 percent to 15 percent in the community, and folks would start saying 'Nigra.' Later you got 35 percent to 40 percent registered and it was amazing how quick they learned to say 'Nee-grow.' And now that we've got 50 percent, 60 percent, 70 percent, of the black votes registered in the South, everybody's proud to be associated with their black brothers and sisters."

Ebony, the glossy magazine for upwardly mobile blacks, has listed Southern cities among the ten best cities for blacks in the United States. Talented blacks no longer leave the South in large numbers. Regional emigration now flows into the South and many blacks in the North are returning. In part this reflects a less distant relationship between the races there. The white Southern claim that people in Dixie like blacks as individuals but not as a people while Northerners like blacks as a people but not as individuals has some substance.

Late for the horse races in New Orleans, a visiting banker from Philadelphia was rescued by a porter at his hotel in the French Quarter, who arranged for him to squeeze into a taxicab already occupied by three local bettors. The cab was driven by one of those gray-eyed Southerners with a menacing slow drawl, in which every seemingly lazy racial epithet is really an attempt to goad the squirming listener into daring to disagree. On the way to the track, the bettors told racist jokes far crueler than the Amos 'n' Andy putdowns. Yet when they got to the races, they immediately fell in with several black bettors. Race tips were swapped, big winners bought beers for everybody, and good-natured teasing kept all but the sore losers jolly until it was time to go home.

What is so baffling is that the greatest black progress has been made in intangibles. Attitudes have changed, to be sure, and this is a profound change, but hundred of millions of dollars spent since the middle of the 1960s have not pulled black Americans out of last place in terms of housing, schooling, and poverty. There are, however, some signs of progress. Nearly 60 percent of black Americans over age 25 in 1975 had less than four years of high school education. Among blacks 20–24, the corresponding figure had fallen to nearer 30 percent. But the overall picture remains bleak.

Unemployment among blacks is twice as high as among whites. Black median family income in 1980 was $12,674—it was $21,904 for whites—the gap having closed slightly since the early 1970s. Blacks, indeed, may no longer invariably be "last hired, first fired," but there is ample evidence to support the claim of black politicians that hard times hurt black Americans harder. Joblessness for black teenagers in the late 1970s seldom fell much below 35 percent, double the rate it used to be in the more prosperous 1950s. About 18 percent of male-headed black families, and some 55 percent of female-headed black families, were in 1974, even before the onset of the worst recession since the 1930s, living on incomes judged below the poverty level according to federal standards.

In 1954, the Supreme Court cut the thread by which so much legal discrimination against black Americans was tied. In *Brown* v. *Board of Education*, the Court rejected as unconstitutional the doctrine of "separate but equal." Slowly, other decisions followed. The Civil Rights (1964) and the Voting Rights (1965) acts consolidated legal protection for blacks against discrimination by whites. These came only after the fiercest pressure from the civil rights movement, in which whites, as well as blacks, were killed. The second piece of legislation, to ensure that blacks effectively disfranchised by local practice should be able to register and vote, came as the first ghetto uprisings began.

But what exactly was won? Segregation as it was practiced in the South has gone. Black Americans, like William Coleman, Patricia Harris, Andrew Brimmer, or Franklin Thomas, can now be found at or near the top of many professions. They sit in the board rooms of banks and businesses, and are not always there merely as tokens for appearance' sake. There are no black senators, but a number of black politicians in the House form the Congressional Black Caucus. As important, blacks appear matter-of-factly in television and advertising.

For middle-class blacks, a minority within the minority, the last twenty years have been a liberation indeed, but the benefits of change still elude the black poor.

Recent years have given American optimism several large dents. Strong parts of the economy are facing unexpected problems of growth. Americans wish the weaker parts would grow as they once did. Doubts are seldom publicly voiced, for politicians who say such things are not popular. Messengers without good news seldom are. Listen to upbeat politicians and to the Babbitry of small-time businessmen, and Americans, one would think, are still engaged in a glorious game where nobody needs to be a loser, where people climb up ladders and hardly anybody ever needs to take a step down. "We are too great a nation," Ronald Reagan said at his inauguration, "to limit ourselves to small dreams."

Americans used to believe this more confidently than they do today. During the depression of the 1930s, the British and the French were gripped with a spirit of retrenchment. People had short horizons and the assumption was shared that gains could be had only at the expense of others. Americans, by contrast, were more positive and expansionist, even though the depression in America was deeper. The whole thrust of New Deal policy, if not its effect, was toward raising purchasing power. Only the most smug Americans are sure nothing has changed.

Fuel shortages and higher fuel prices in the 1970s were an obvious symptom for many Americans that something was wrong. It was also, too hastily, assumed that America might be running short of raw materials or at least too dependent on uncertain suppliers from overseas. Actually, the United States has more breathing space than any industrial rival when it comes to natural resources. It has a much larger farm, mine, and energy output than, for example, Japan, a country the size of California that was exhausted thirty years ago but is positively bouncing about its future today.

Another symptom was the growing lobby that questioned the costs of economic growth, notably environmentalists, although doubts about growth were broader than this. The late economist Fred Hirsch wrote about them in a book called *The Social Limits to Growth*. His main idea may be illustrated by recalling the world's most famous maritime disaster.

When the *Titanic* sank off Newfoundland in 1912, almost all the women and children in first class were saved. So were many of the men. But many men, too, were lost, such as John Jacob Astor and the young Harry Widener, who had been in Europe buying books. In second class, most of the women and children, again, were saved, but most of the men drowned. In third class and steerage, almost everyone went down, regardless of age or sex. As there were too few lifeboats on the sinking liner to go around for the unfortunate passengers, a seat on one of them was what Hirsch would have called a positional good. Getting a seat was only any use if others did not clamber on and swamp the boat. A seat's value was directly dependent on others' not having one.

Pointing out that if everyone stands on tiptoe nobody sees any better—except the privileged in the first row, he could have added, who always see well—Hirsch argued that in an affluent society, the value or satisfaction of attaining many of the most desirable goals in life is diminished if too many others realize the same ambition. Just as a bachelor's degree ceases to be a passport to a prestigious or high-paying job when so many students obtain one that the minimum qualification for a desirable job is consequently raised to a doctorate, so a cottage on the ocean or on a forest lake bought for quiet and solitude provides diminishing satisfaction if others are allowed to crowd in.

It is by now obvious that a large and growing number of middle-class Americans have implicitly decided that the quality of their life is threatened by congestion and that the threat must be repulsed. In long-settled, relatively heavily populated places like the Northeast, where a solid phalanx of weekend beach properties keeps the less well-to-do away from long stretches of the seashore, this is by now such a commonplace as to pass almost without comment. What is newer is the way that those who have made good their escape from crowded, polluted parts of the country, or from deteriorating inner cities to small country towns, are protecting their turf. Their aim is not so much to keep up with as to keep out the Joneses.

"Come but don't stay" is the uncompromising greeting for visitors to Oregon. In King County outside Seattle, Washington, voters agreed in a referendum to purchase farmland as a cordon sanitaire between themselves and suburbs that had otherwise threatened to engulf the greenbelt. Zoning laws are rising up everywhere to outlaw high density, as residents seek to prevent greedy neighbors from selling their land to whom they please or from splitting it into three or four separate plots to bring in more money. Moratoriums that would hinder or stop dead any further development are not uncommon in and around Los Angeles—an area that often leads the nation. More than they used to, Americans are also beginning to weigh the prospect of more money in an ugly place against less money in an attractive place and to decide that the scenery is worth more than the financial difference. Such a man is Andrew Safir, chief economist for the state of California, who shares an incomprehensible national prejudice that New York—one of the world's most splendid cities, and the capital of the United States in almost everything other than politics—is an ugly city. Ignore this prejudice. What counts is the trade-off that he and others in places like San Francisco have made in deciding to curtail their ambition for more money.

Safir explains: "Salaries in the Bay Area reflect the quality-of-life differential. In New York you work in a filthy environment so you can buy a house in the Hamptons or Vermont to get out of the crap you're living and working in. The easier thing to do is to benefit from an attractive environment directly, as we do here. In fact, nonpecuniary income in the form of nice surroundings is a better bet than pecuniary income, because it can't be taxed and isn't subject to inflation." Economists used to rate this an un-American idea.

The agnosticism many Americans feel about economic growth is a big change in a country where it has always been felt that economic growth would solve more problems than it created. In the present climate, however, doubts about the desirability of overvigorous economic growth have taken at least a temporary back seat to the question of whether there is to be enough economic growth to keep the country stable. Uncertainty about the economy has deep political consequences, especially since the economy for the first time since the 1930s has become the major national issue which eclipses all others and since social divisions Americans can cope with in good economic times grow more threatening in bad.

If, as this book will argue, Americans need to invest more in their industries to keep them competitive, and, quite generally, spend less today in order to be solvent tomorrow, how are the sacrifices to be apportioned? Many Americans enjoy one of the most successful societies on earth. America is open, free, and rich. It is also deeply unequal.

Economic growth from World War II until the early 1970s made it possible for government to reduce some of the inequality or at least dampen its social effects.

The difference government has made is easily appreciated by looking at some income distribution figures, before and after both taxes and such so-called transfers as social security benefits, food stamps, public housing subsidies, Medicare, and so on are taken into account. Beforehand, in ranking working Americans by their earning power, the top two-fifths in 1976–1977 got 76.2 percent of the total personal income. The middle fifth got 16.3 percent. The bottom two-fifths got 7.5 percent. Unequal indeed. After progressive income taxes and social transfers were taken into account, however, a big change occurred, at least between the well-off and the poor. The top two-fifths' share of total income was cut by 11.5 percentage points, most of it coming from the best-paid. The bottom two-fifths increased their share thanks to government transfers by 11.2 percentage points. The middle fifth's position was improved, but by almost too little to count.

Among an electorate that is disproportionately middle class because the less well-off Americans fail to vote their numbers, the political support for this kind of government program has crumbled, with the side effect that confidence in the federal government has also badly weakened. The conservative revival of recent years could be encapsulated in the *mea culpa* heard from many Democrats eager to placate the new idols of the right: "We paid too much attention to equality and not enough to efficiency."

Americans, it has often been observed, are not a class-conscious people. Work is done in skyscrapers but Americans tend to live in bungalows with no upstairs, no downstairs. Americans, if asked by pollsters what social class they belong to, say, without thinking, "middle class." The term means almost the same as "ordinary." To say one is middle class is to say, in America, that one is neither a Mellon nor drawing Aid to Families with Dependent Children. The term is an exclusion of extremes. If the pollsters' questions are artfully enough put, the same American who says he is middle class will sometimes proudly claim to be working class as well. In a television speech on taxes; Reagan included Americans earning anything between $15,000 and $60,000 a year as "middle class." *U.S. News & World Report* asked not so long ago: "Can the US close the gap between the haves and the middle-class have-nots?"

Further confusion arises with the decline of blue-collar—that is, manufacturing—jobs, which now account for only about a fifth of all jobs. These have traditionally been thought of as working-class jobs, while white-collar jobs were middle class. Now that, leaving out construction and mining, white-collar jobs account for three-quarters of the nonfarm labor force, is this not another sign that Americans are, indeed, all becoming middle class? It might be if in America's new, mature service economy all jobs were well paid and carried high prestige. They do not. There are doctors and lawyers at one end, hospital porters, supermarket checkout clerks, and office cleaners at the other.

This lack of class consciousness is not a mysterious gift of national character, but the product of circumstances. Regional separation, ethnic and racial divisions, above all economic success, have worked against the setting of hard class lines. Regional, ethnic, and racial divisions have, fortunately, grown much smaller. Even as to racial prejudice, the success of middle-class blacks suggests that the main obstacle to advancement today is as much poverty as color. The job of keeping Americans indifferent to class thus falls more and more squarely on the performance of the economic dynamo. If this is to be kept turning only at the expense of efforts to reduce inequality, what is the way out of the box?

2

LIVING OFF CAPITAL

Business and the Economy

As SEEN through the eyes of American industrialists, the United States is not so much stable as stuck. In 1980, for the first year ever, Japan manufactured more cars and trucks than the United States. Japan also, again for the first time, topped American production of crude steel, by turning out 123 million net tons against 112 million in the United States. For Americans these figures were shocking. Years ago, when "Made in Japan" meant cheap imitation, the story was commonly told of a Japanese town that had renamed itself Usa to overcome this handicap. Today it is very difficult for Americans to think of Japan as a Hertz and of their own country as an Avis that must try harder because it is number two.

Americans, though, may have to grow used to the idea of Japan forging ahead, dependent as it is on foreigners for food supplies and for 99.5 percent of its oil. The Japanese routinely invest a larger share and consume a smaller share of their national income than do Americans, and with each year that passes, this habit serves to make their competitive edge in world markets even sharper. The Japanese show no sign of complacency. Reagan administration economists were dismayed to read, only a few weeks after getting their feet under their desks in Washington, a calculation by Peter Peterson, chairman of the board of the investment bank Lehman Brothers Kuhn Loeb and a former secretary of commerce, that Japan, with an economy half the size, had achieved the "extraordinary landmark" of spending more on new factories, machines, and tools than the United States.

While the average American does not follow investment and industrial output statistics with the same anguished fascination as economists and industrialists, the sense that America is experiencing a national economic decline is by now widespread. The country's pinched circumstances are seen in the relative loss of public interest in the high drama of foreign affairs and the much greater interest in bread-and-butter issues. Economic news that was once relegated to the back, business section, pages of the newspapers is today carried prominently on page one. Consumer price, unemployment, and interest rate stories often lead off the nightly news on television. The country's reduced circumstances are also seen in the way American Presidents are called upon to explain and to defend their country's fiscal and monetary policies at economic summits to the leaders of nations that a generation ago were dependent on Marshall Plan aid. The American public is as much puzzled as it is vexed by the change. Perplexed that the land of Henry Ford is left with car companies crippled by arthritis; that the land of Carnegie and Frick has to introduce trigger prices as a protective defense against foreign steel; that America's television sets, cameras, and typewriters are made increasingly, and sometimes exclusively, by foreign companies.

Whatever other accusations can be hurled at Americans, they cannot be accused of complacency. Their self-criticism has been remorseless during a seemingly unending series of large economic setbacks that began in August 1971, when President Nixon severed the dollar's convertibility into gold to prevent a landslide of the mountain of dollars held abroad from carrying away Fort Knox. For years economists had known that as the world's economies became more interdependent, the sovereignty of nation-states in economic policymaking was being whittled away. A failed harvest in the Soviet Union could force up bread prices in the United States. A credit crunch masterminded by the Federal Reserve Board in Washington could put people out of work in Dortmund, West Germany. A change in Paris fashions could bring big profits or losses for New Orleans cotton traders. For most people, economic interdependence remained an abstraction, the sort of words that cluttered up diplomatic communiqués, until the forced devaluations of the dollar and until, much more dramatically, the 1973–1974 oil embargoes. Because of events beyond their shores, over which they had little influence, Americans were forced to line up, sometimes for hours, for gasoline only then to be told they could have only five gallons or five dollars' worth or, even more infuriating, find that the gasoline had run out before they reached the head of the line.

Americans since then have engaged in an orgy of self-examination. Their economists have heavily underlined their calling's reputation as a dismal science. Lester Thurow of the Massachusetts Institute of Technology notes that seemingly insoluble problems are emerging everywhere—inflation, unemployment, slow growth, environmental decay, irreconcilable group demands, and complicated, cumbrous regulations. Herbert Stein, a former chairman of the White House Council of Economic Advisers, intones that whereas consumer prices rose at an average rate of 1.3 percent a year from 1960 to 1965, they rose at an average annual rate of 6.6 percent from 1965 to 1980, and of 9 percent from 1975 to 1980. He twirls his worry beads, too, about productivity, which increased by 3.7 percent a year from 1960 to 1965, by 1.6 percent a year from 1965 to 1980, and by only 0.9 percent from 1975 to 1980. Felix Rohatyn of Lazard Frères is as grim. "The United States today is challenged not only by foreign competition in its basic industries; it also depends on highly unstable countries not only for its basic energy supply, but also for the strength or weakness of the dollar."

In some ways these and most other Americans are rich people crying their way to the bank. The United States economy has not declined in actual terms but only relatively—and part of this relative decline was inevitable, even desirable. In 1950, the United States accounted for nearly 40 percent of the world's gross national product, and thirty years later, for around 20 percent. This towering strength in 1950 was both artificial and transitory. Europe and Japan, formidable competitors in the 1930s, stood in ruins. Many third world countries were still undeveloped. The halving of America's total share of world production occurred as Japan and Europe recovered from the devastation of World War II and as several backward countries, led by South Korea, Singapore, Mexico, Brazil, and Taiwan, started to industrialize by exploiting their low-wage advantage in labor-intensive industries.

The United States during recent years has still enjoyed, and improved upon, an enviable standard of living. Visitors from Western Europe, even today, continue to gape at college students with electric typewriters, children with home computers, FM radios in rental cars, ten-speed bicycles, jogging uniforms, eye clinics for pets, computer chess sets, and refrigerators as big as Volkswagens. Foreigners, too, are still impressed by the everyday efficiencies of American life, especially when it comes to keeping a scattered people in touch with each other: smoothly working long-distance telephones, easily rented cars, and hop-aboard commuter air shuttles. American scientists routinely accept the biggest share of Nobel prizes in their disciplines and can take credit for more than half of the important technological innovations made during the past thirty years. Polio vaccine, oral contraceptives, the transistor, the nuclear reactor, and recombinant DNA technology are all products of American scientists. And the country has much greater resources in land and minerals than all advanced industrial countries other than Canada and the Soviet Union.

Yet Americans have quite rightly concluded that none of this is enough, not simply because others are catching up. The fact that it took seven Japanese to produce as much as one American worker in 1950, while today in many industries, like cars and steel, the Japanese are as or more productive than their American counterparts, is not in itself either alarming or suprising. The heavily worked Japanese are the envy of bosses almost everywhere. Thomas Murphy, until recently chief executive of General Motors, spoke for French and British industrialists as much as for American ones when he said: "The workers of Japan are motivated by a relentless work ethic. As a nation, they are prepared to work harder—and even cut corners—to keep goods flowing abroad." What, instead, is the real cause for dismay is that Americans are doing less well by the very standards that until recently they themselves set.

Within the past decade and a half, the United States has slipped from a better than 3 percent a year improvement in productivity, as measured by output per man-hour, to a place where the yearly improvement is, as often as not, below 1 percent. The trouble is less with manufacturing. Labor productivity there continues to improve at a respectable rate. The problem arises because manufacturing jobs are a declining share of all jobs. In America's fast-maturing, late-capitalist economy, the new jobs more and more are white-collar and service jobs of low productivity. Though the living standards of American families have continued to rise, much of this is due to the creation of two-income families as wives go out to work. Some of the gain, for the families concerned, is illusory. As many of them have discovered, two incomes do not come cheap. It means higher transport costs—sometimes a new car and nearly always higher fuel or fare costs. Meals and clothes cost more as the working couple has less time to shop around for bargains, eats out more often, and finds the second job means more wear and tear on more expensive clothes. Add in the cost of child care and of outsiders to carry out tasks in the home that a working couple cannot spare that time to perform, and such extra expenses can quickly eat up half of the second paycheck.

Inflation has picked away at this scab of dissatisfaction. After ranking during the Eisenhower, Kennedy, and early Johnson administrations alongside Switzerland and West Germany as a low-inflation country, the United States, when not in a slump, has so deteriorated in price performance that it finds itself bracketed with high-inflation countries like Britain, Italy, and France. The damage this does to national morale is recognized by economists of the right, left, and center. People take home paychecks that are larger than they ever expected to earn, yet find that far from being rich, they still have to struggle to make ends meet. They feel cheated.

Interest in finding a way out of this thicket is intense. Two serious books by American academics on why the Japanese are so successful were 1981 best-sellers—*Theory Z: How American Business Can Meet the Japanese Challenge* by William Ouchi of the University of California at Los Angeles, and *The Art of Japanese Management* by Richard Tanner Pascale of Stanford and Anthony G. Athos of Harvard. American economists, undeterred by their profession's multiple failures, continue to offer maps that promise to lead the country on to the gently rolling hills of noninflationary growth. They are, though, faced with a particular handicap: something called the American economic system. Ask a person in Paris, London, or Bonn what economic system is peculiarly French, British, or German. If they understand the question at all, they will be at a loss for an answer. A country or nation is one thing to them, a particular economic system is another. Political parties define themselves by offering alternative visions of how the economy ought to be organized. Not so in the United States. Free enterprise is the American way. Serious doubts about this system are taken as a symptom of disaffection, not to say disloyalty. There is, of course, huge room for disagreement about what exactly free enterprise means.

Americans know that for practical purposes, the economic freedom they talk about is immensely complicated, managed, and partial. But most American economists nevertheless feel a need to demonstrate that their ideas are within the American economic tradition—a requirement that constrains economic thinking.

The debate is not as ragged as it appears. The economic problem solvers can be divided into four broad schools. On the right is the free-market school, occupied by capitalist fundamentalists who want to go back to the basics of very limited government and fierce but fair competition—or rather move on to these, since they have never fully been tried. Since the simple answers they provide for complicated questions attract a large reading public, prominent in their ranks are the authors of several recent best-sellers, some who are well-known economists, some simply popularizers: William Simon *(A Time for Truth)*, Robert Ringer *(Restoring the American Dream)*, Milton and Rose Friedman *(Free to Choose)*, and George Gilder *(Wealth and Poverty)*. Fundamentalist economics was the gospel Reagan brought to Washington. It is split into a monetarist church, keen for sound money, and a supply-side church, emphasizing economic growth. Jude Wanniski, a puckish intelligence who favors a return to the gold standard, is the guardian of supply-side doctrinal purity. Jack Kemp, the straw-haired former quarterback now a Republican congressman from Buffalo, is this church's most photogenic deacon. Among the more eccentric acolytes of the back-to-basics right is Art Laffer, the inventor of the Laffer curve, which purports to show that any given amount of tax revenues can be produced at two levels of taxation, one high, the other low. Strong in the universities are members of the rational-expectations group of economists, who have an extraordinary faith in the clairvoyance of the financial and commodities markets.

At the other side of the political spectrum are the descendants of the New Deal: liberal Democrats, Keynesians, and venerable figures like John Kenneth Galbraith, Robert Heilbroner, and Walter Heller. This school is as strongly for wage and price controls as the free marketeers are against them. Most of its members have labored as top government economists in Washington, and they hold to the opinion that full employment and low inflation can be won by wise rulers enlisting the help of enlightened business and labor leaders. *The New York Review of Books* is a favorite outlet for their articles, although

Heller writes in the *Wall Street Journal*, a lone liberal economist there.

These two schools, the capitalist fundamentalists and the old New Dealers, would commonly be thought right and left, conservative and liberal, respectively. This distinction obscures the less obvious point that both are alike in taking a narrowly economic approach. This is not true of the other two groups: the neoconservatives on the right, and on the center left, the social-limits-to-growth school.

When it comes to economics, neoconservatives believe strongly in business, but they are not doctrinaire believers in free enterprise, not least because they are not exclusively, or even mainly, interested in economics. They are social critics, united as much as anything by a common target: the loathed liberal intellectual. While they believe in the old American virtues of hard work and self-reliance, they are ambivalent toward capitalism. They want respect for tradition, for authority, for the family, for institutions, above all for business and industry, which liberals, they feel, have scorned.

These neoconservatives and the social-limits-to-growth people have a controversial assumption in common. Both believe sociology and economics are inseparable. They differ in the conclusions they draw from this assumption. The neoconservatives tend to think the American economy has grown slothful because of changed American attitudes—greater interest in buying than in producing, a loss of respect for authority and expertise, too much attention to the claims of politically active blacks and women. Government is blamed for weakening the self-reliance of the American people by playing sugar daddy and nanny. Their economic philosophy might be summed up as Business Knows Best.

The social-limits-to-growth school is less quick to find villains. Its representatives are Tibor Scitovsky and the late Fred Hirsch, with a subgroup led by Lester Thurow. Jerry Brown is the politician who seems instinctively to have caught their message. These economists are saying that the promise of constantly rising prosperity leading to a sense of well-being for all can no longer be delivered. As Thurow has put it, America's economy is coming closer to being a zero-sum game. If the problems of high energy costs and inflation are to be beaten, many Americans will be required to suffer economic losses as huge sums are redirected out of consumption into investment. Society as a whole may be better off as a result, he argues, but this will be little immediate consolation to the losers in the game.

If there is one theme that is apparent in all four groups, it is nostalgia. For each of them describes a country whose economic past is to them in important respects better than the present. The capitalist fundamentalists look back to the days when Calvin Coolidge could say, with some accuracy, "the business of America is business." The descendants of the New Deal bemoan the rise of callous self-interest. The neoconservatives sigh over an abandoned sense of contentment in family and work. The social-limits-to-growth school looks back to when the main distributional task of society was to share out the winnings, not to apportion the losses.

American economists are united on at least one other issue. This is their frustration over a political system that seems increasingly unable to form a coalition to get necessary but unpopular economic reforms passed into law. Tax decreases sail through. Measures that threaten to hurt any powerful constituency are becalmed or shipwrecked in Congress. No matter, say, that the thorough exploitation of coal reserves of Montana will strengthen the American economy and the nation's foreign policy by making the United States less reliant on oil imported from OPEC countries. If the Indians and ranchers of Montana reckon the new coal mines will lower the quality of their lives, woe betide the representative who gives the national interest priority over the parochial interests of Montana. Come election day, that representative will be searching for alternative employment.

The eagerness of representatives to please and appease has blocked taxes that economists of the right, left, and center have supported as in the national interest. Underpriced gasoline is one example. The United States accounts for 5 percent of the world's people and nearly half of the world's consumption of gasoline. A large encouragement for Americans not to use less is that even when Congress, after seven years of foot dragging, finally agreed to oblige American motorists to be charged the world price for oil, it balked at the idea of depressing consumption further by increasing gasoline taxes. The federal tax on gasoline remains a tiny 14 cents a gallon, versus anything from $1.25 to $2.00 in other industrial countries, and most of the 14 cents goes to the highway trust fund to finance road maintenance and construction.

Economists and business leaders of all stripes regard this as a mistake. Felix Rohatyn rages against the "cowardly avoidance of taxing gasoline at much higher rates." Peter Peterson warns about the "Vietnamish" alternatives to energy conservation. Higher taxes on gasoline may be in the national interest, but elected representatives are sure that support for such an unpopular measure will cost them votes and so possibly also their jobs.

Tax changes that win more votes than they lose, on the other hand, have no difficulty in getting passed into law. The American tax system can, as a result, be accurately described as second to none in complexity. Lobbies for special interests have succeeded in winning exemptions, incentives, deductions, and exclusions that make tax accountancy a profession for people with creative minds and vivid imaginations. The system provokes court battles where taxpayers defend their returns against the IRS. Summaries in the *Wall Street Journal* are evidence of splendid, often astonishing originality in the creation of tax returns.

A Colonel Imhoff, former member of General Douglas MacArthur's staff, claimed that he and his wife used half of the fifteen rooms at their house in Merion Station, Pennsylvania, in producing their investment income. One of their tax claims, rejected by a court in 1979, was for "a dental bill for a miniature poodle who was a part of the internal security system." An ex-congressman from Louisiana, James Morrison, claimed, also in vain, $61,000 in charitable contributions for giving his files, mainly letters, to a university. The Fifth Circuit U.S. Court of Appeals wrote: "Our wonder at the claims of taxpayers never ceases; it surely must be true that hope springs eternal in the breast of man."

Glenn Young of Sapulpa, Oklahoma, was also declared a loser by the courts. Young refused to cooperate when Conrad Carson, an IRS agent, came to his law office to audit his tax return. When a summons was put on his desk, the eighty-four-year-old Young kneed Carson and hit him with a fist. Put on trial for assault, Young asserted he ought to have kicked Carson "harder and quicker and longer." He appealed a $3,000 fine. While the Tenth Circuit U.S. Appeals Court found Young's brief "hard to follow," it inferred a claim that Carson's visit did not qualify as an official one because the summons was improperly served. The court rejected this and other arguments showing "general dissatisfaction" with the tax laws and the IRS. In upholding the conviction, the court decided: "Good faith belief in the propriety of his [Young's] action is not a defense to the crime."

Not everyone loses. Brigham Young University emerged victorious when the IRS audited 162 returns showing gifts to the Mormon institution of art, silver mine claims, and other property valued for tax deduction purposes at $16 million. Every single deduction, by IRS reckoning, was excessive. It revalued the gifts at $1.5 million and told the university to hand over a list of all its other donors so it could investigate them, too. When the university refused, a federal judge upheld its defiance.

This entertaining litigation adds to the joy of the nation. It also serves to underline a serious criticism made of the tax system. For the intricate system with countless loopholes shows that however hard it is to make changes in the general interest, lobbyists for powerful or parochial special interests have too often got what they wanted. The country is the loser. It is now close to uncontroversial that an important reason why America's productivity performance is lagging is insufficient investment. Not only economists and corporate executives but labor leaders, like Lane Kirkland of AFL-CIO and Douglas Fraser of the United Auto Workers, agree that America's business investment, running at about 10 percent of the gross national product, must be pushed up to something closer to Japan's 17 percent of the gross national product if the country is not to become a second-class political and economic power by the twenty-first century. Changing the tax system so that it encourages the diversion of an extra $150 billion a year or so into investment to appreciably narrow the American-Japanese gap has proved an almost impossible task. American taxes still have a bias toward consumption and tend to favor borrowers over lenders, spenders over investors and savers.

Perhaps because increased business investment has proved so difficult to generate and the tax system so difficult to reform, exaggerated emphasis has been put on finding other, secondary, causes of America's relative economic decline. A favorite scapegoat among bosses and in a predominantly conservative press is today's worker. The belief that today's Americans are letting the country down by not working as hard as their parents and grandparents is widely propagated and has broad currency, particularly in the older generation. The truth is that the big gains in productivity are not achieved by working people harder—by assembly line speed ups, shorter coffee breaks, longer hours. They are achieved by people working smarter. America's productivity growth rate is lagging mainly because too much of the national income goes into consumption and too little into investing in research and in more efficient factories, machines, tools, and technology.

Yet when Edward Denison, a respected economist, had a 212-page study on America's productivity published by the Brookings Institution, laymen were exasperated by his apparent obtuseness. Denison started receiving long-distance telephone calls in which he was informed, usually with the patronizing air used in speaking to children and the simple minded, that the cause of the trouble is clear. "People don't want to work anymore." Sometimes the comment was more pointed. "Young people don't work like we did at their age." Without doubt, this is the leading popular explanation for the country's economic woes. Denison is skeptical about it, as are nearly all economists who have studied productivity trends in this or other advanced industrial countries. In every age and in every country going back to Biblical or Confucian times, the older generation has had a self-congratulatory tendency to see members of the younger generation as loafers unwilling to work as hard as their parents and grandparents did before them. This is true even in Japan, whose hivelike workers are famed for humming company songs during their lunch breaks. Thus, as Denison has triumphantly noted, *Mainichi Shimbun*, the Tokyo newspaper, asserted in an editorial published shortly before his study appeared:

> Opinions have been expressed at offices and factories that today's people are not eager to work. The view is not anything new. Every generation seems to say the same thing about its youth. Still, young people must seriously ponder the allegation. . . . We . . . exhort the newly employed young people to tackle their work with due seriousness. A government survey shows that two-thirds of today's youth want to live a carefree life to their personal taste outside concern about work. If they want to take a job, however, they are required to care more seriously about work. A switch is needed in their life-style concept.

Just as this allegation of laziness against young Japanese seems ridiculous to Americans, so do allegations that young Americans are lazy seem ridiculous to non-Americans. Americans work very hard. The workweek of people employed in manufacturing has remained constant at around forty hours, slipping slightly in economic slumps, increasing slightly in economic booms, for the past thirty years. When ordinary working hours are reduced, Americans do not take time off. They work more overtime, or moonlight in a second job. Their vacations are astonishingly short. For Americans, two or three weeks' paid vacation a year is a common arrangement, while five and even six weeks' annual leave is common in Europe. Paris is a ghost town in August. The German Steel and Metallurgical Union has calculated that during a recent three-year period, Americans in the metallurgical industries worked an average of twenty-four hours more a month than Belgians or Germans.

While single answers to a complicated economic question like a slowdown in productivity are rightly viewed with deep suspicion by economists, it does seem that in seeking clues on ways to solve the problem, the country ought to look harder not at the alleged decline in the work ethic, but at American corporate management. Lack of productive investment undoubtedly explains much of the lag. But is it not also possible that America has become less successful because the venerable corporations that dominate the heights of the American economy are not being run in the best way by the best people? That weaknesses in American management have contributed to the nation's relative economic decline? That businesses are investing in the wrong things as well as not investing enough?

Before looking at the large mature corporations that dominate the Fortune 500 and the American economy, it is as well to remind ourselves of the energetic presence of American entrepreneurs. As self-made men—there are few women in their ranks—they are heroes of American folklore. They have created the businesses they run. Their success is lionized by admirers from Ralph Nader to the managers of blue-chip corporations. While inspirational backyard-shed-to-AAA-credit-rating stories about entrepreneurs are a repetitive feature in business magazines, the readers are never bored. American executives who enjoy, as Dorothy Parker might have put it, the security of the corporate marriage bed may envy the self-made entrepreneurs and the rough and tumble of their bachelor couches, but they do not want to change places. In settling for a salaried career, the corporate executives explicitly reject the chance of making the large private fortune that is the mark of a successful entrepreneur. Many do make millions on salaries and benefits but are unready to gamble for more. They are still free to fantasize. In thinking of themselves as footloose entrepreneurs, they are like dentists and doctors playing cowboy, who turn up in Stetsons at the feedlot to inspect their tax-shelter cattle, or like Pentagon clerks playing soldier, who trade in the family Chevelle for a jeep. To found a small business and then to expand it into a large, successful corporation takes guts and enthusiasm and very hard work—from oneself and others—as well as luck. It is a residual strength of the American economy that it throws up so many risk-takers with an insatiable drive for success. In several Western European countries it is much more acceptable to inherit than to make money. Britain, most strikingly, labors under a class system that ranks landed gentry, financiers, senior civil servants, and members of the professions far above self-made entrepreneurs, thus virtually guaranteeing industrial failure.

Americans, in contrast, admire success, particularly when it is preceded by a long struggle against long odds. Those harnessing science and industry are particularly admired. These are men like Henry Singleton, a loose-limbed, taciturn Texas engineer, who left Litton Industries to build Teledyne, his own exceptionally successful conglomerate based on high technology; or Peter Sprague, the founder in 1965, at the age of twenty-five, of National Semiconductor, after he studied, successively, at three of the finest institutions of higher education in the world —Yale, Columbia, and the Massachusetts Institute of Technology; or men from the older generation like William Hewlett and David Packard, encouraged while students by Stanford's Frederick Terman, a leading engineer, to found the first of California's big electronics firms. Such advanced-technology entrepreneurs, most of them holding doctorates, are thick on the ground in the Silicon Valley outside San Francisco, along Route 128 outside Boston, and in the Research Triangle Park in North Carolina. Their plants do not cause pollution. They provide good clean work and offer the prospect of quick promotion in fast-growing businesses to highly qualified staff. In short, they offer the sort of investment and jobs that every locality cries for.

Even in America it is a mistake to think that new money carries exactly the same prestige as old money. Americans can be as snobbish as any other people. Haroldson Lafayette Hunt, the Texas oilman, was so irked by the Texas preference for old money made from cotton or cattle to new money made from oil, he sought refuge in a fictitious family tree. Hunt came to believe he was a direct descendant of the Reverend Robert Hunt, chaplain of Captain John Smith's Jamestown Colony. As his biographer has remarked, the claim was impossible since the Reverend Hunt left no children. Meyer Guggenheim, the mining magnate, also wanted a higher social standing. Guggenheim moved his family from Philadelphia, where Main Line families kept their distance from newcomers, to New York to win acceptance. The wealthy German-Jewish families of Manhattan were not as welcoming as the Guggenheims had hoped. The others had made their money in banking and finance, not by digging holes in the ground. To the mortification of Meyer and his wife, Barbara, who spoke her English with a thick Swiss accent, they were known as the "Googs." Like others, Carnegie, and Frick among them, the Guggenheims tried to root their new money in history by living in latter-day palaces.

The once thin distinction between old money and new is becoming much thicker as the old fortunes of America develop a patina. The Cabots of Boston, tending a fortune that dates back to rum, slaves, and opium, have long been treated as untitled aristocrats. As *Wall Street Journal* writers put it in *American Dynasties Today:*

> Money is the primary basis for social position in America. But it isn't enough. Status often depends on how old the family's money is, rather than how much there is. Top society in Dallas traces its origins back to cattle and cotton money and sneers at nouveau riche oil millionaires. In Detroit, lumber and mining fortunes are considered more respectable than automobile fortunes. In Boston, the trick is to trace money back to a daring sea captain.

If attention to such differences is more common in America than is often supposed, and much more noticeable than in West Germany, say, where the existing social order was overturned by war, it is not yet anything as pervasive as in Britain. Babson College, a business school in Massachusetts, is doing its bit to keep it that way. A few years ago, it asked several members of the business press, including Malcolm Forbes, the proprietor of *Forbes* magazine, Bernard Alexander, the publisher of *Business Week,* Robert Bartley of the *Wall Street Journal,* and a British financial writer, to form a panel that would each fall choose four or five business people for the college's Academy of Distinguished Entrepreneurs. The decisions are made over a slow lunch and good claret in a well-padded setting—a wood-paneled room at the midtown University Club of New York one year, the florid dining room of Malcolm Forbes the next. The judges get biographies of possible winners from Babson College. They are also free to suggest names of their own.

The custom is for each judge to put forward a name and then try to persuade the others, until they are agreed on four or five winners.

Sometimes the selections are argued only on the candidate's merits. This was the case with Frank Perdue, who turned a Maryland chicken farm into the biggest poultry processor on the Chesapeake Bay's Eastern Shore, and amassed a $100 million fortune, by feeding his birds something that turns their skin yellow. The substance is said to be xanthophyll, a yellow coloring matter occurring with chlorophyll in plants. Whatever it is, the birds' color lets them command a premium price in the Northeast, where shoppers apparently think a yellow chicken is tastier and more nutritious than a white chicken. The feeding regime is supported by an advertising campaign of great flair. Frank Perdue, who looks and sounds like his fowls, with his beaked nose and high-pitched, clucking voice, appears in television commercials to boast: "It takes a tough man to make a tender chicken," or "My chickens eat better than you do."

Nothing was said about either Perdue's race or his sex as the judges pondered the pros and cons of choosing him for the Babson Hall of Fame. Perdue had come as a spectator to Babson College's award presentation in an earlier year. Did making himself obvious disqualify him? On the contrary, the judges decided. In turning up he was showing the commendable pushiness of the self-made man. The judges were not giving an award for bashfulness. Broiler chickens, all the judges agreed, were bland and unappetizing. Against this, Perdue had cleverly exploited an "advance" in breeding science and helped make chicken a cheap everyday meal instead of a Sunday treat. In 1940, it took from twelve to fourteen weeks to produce a four-pound chicken and the bird ate four pounds of feed for each pound of weight it gained. Today the same size bird is raised in less than eight weeks and eats less than two pounds of feed for each pound it gains in weight.

However, the American tradition of a balanced ticket runs strongly through even such exercises as the lunch of the Babson College judges. None of the judges is really expected to select entrepreneurs for the Hall of Fame on the basis of merit alone. Though sex and color were not a factor when Perdue was being talked about, they were certainly taken into account when the judges chose Diane von Furstenberg, the Belgian-born New York "Princess of Fashion," and Berry Gordy, a black songwriter and ex–assembly line worker from Detroit, who founded Tamla and other record labels to market the "Motown sound" of Smokey Robinson, The Supremes, Marvin Gaye, The Vandellas, The Four Tops and many, many more. The judges decided that though the overwhelming majority of entrepreneurs were white men, it was necessary to search out blacks and women worthy of the award. This, they reasoned, would provide "minorities" with entrepreneurial heroes and heroines to look up to.

The entrepreneurs are by now an important tributary rather than part of the mainstream of American business. A half century has passed since Adolf A. Berle and Gardner C. Means wrote their famous book, *The Modern Corporation and Private Property,* in which they concluded that the ownership had been divorced from control in the bulk of American business. Today the vast majority of the country's leading financial and industrial corporations are run by employees rewarded by salaries and bonuses—people who are paid to manage and are fired by the directors if they fail to measure up to expectations.

This does not mean that the vast fortunes amassed by the great captains of industry have been dissipated in the legendary manner of shirtsleeves to shirtsleeves in three generations. Leaf through the records of shareholders of the largest corporations and it is quickly obvious that while the inheritors have withdrawn from active management into passive investment, some of the heirs to tycoons' fortunes remain very, very rich. At the start of 1981, the Mellon family interests still owned 20 percent of Alcoa, 20 percent of Koppers Company, and 11 percent of Gulf Oil. The du Pont family interests owned 35 percent of Du Pont (some of the family use a small *d;* the business capitalizes), 19 percent of the Charter Company, and 7 percent of General Motors. All this, as one of the younger Rockefellers, who ought to know, commented, "will buy a helluva lot of chopped chicken liver."

There is a big difference between owning a big chunk of and

actually running a corporation. As heirs in charge of family enterprises, David Rockefeller of Chase Manhattan and Henry Ford II were almost the last of their breed. Eventually both, as senior citizens, did voluntarily but reluctantly agree to hand over to professional managers, to Willard Butcher at Chase and Philip Caldwell at Ford, though not before enjoying the full satisfaction of running personal fiefdoms. In his dealings with his most senior employees, Ford was just as imperious as the most arrogant of the old robber barons. At least five men who at one time or another acquired the status of Ford's right-hand man in the company suddenly found themselves shoved out of work. The boss was blunt. In sacking Lee Iacocca in 1978 as president of the Ford Motor Company, a position Iacocca had held for more than seven years, Ford was reported to have said simply: "I just don't like you." Public relations men later claimed that Ford had really been more tactful. They got a skeptical hearing. The style sounded right. When Ford moved in to take control of the company from his grandfather's henchmen thirty-five years earlier, the young man had carried a gun to work each day.

It remains possible in America to build a Ford-sized money mountain, as Daniel Ludwig has demonstrated. A loner who dropped out of school in the eighth grade in South Haven, Michigan, he is, by most reckonings, worth more than Howard Hughes, J. Paul Getty, or H. L. Hunt ever were. He owns, among other things, the largest fleet of ocean liners in the world, 2.5 million acres of loss-making forest in Brazil, a one-million-acre cattle ranch in Venezuela, an oil refinery in Panama, iron deposits in Canada and Australia, potash deposits in Ethiopia, the largest solar-evaporation salt plant in the world, on Mexico's Baja California peninsula, insurance companies, savings and loan associations, and hotels. Ludwig's holdings are estimated at about $3 billion, all of it his. After falling out with a partner long ago, Ludwig has gone without partners or stockholders.

Nevertheless, without demeaning Ludwig or the lively entrepreneurs who contribute so much to America's business vitality, they are in the margin, even if they do more than their share in creating jobs. The big corporations whose investment, marketing, and employment decisions have the heaviest immediate influence on the nation's prosperity, or lack of it, are run by professional managers who rarely own more than a fraction of 1 percent of the corporation's stock. And all the signs are that the corporations they head are destined, through mergers, takeovers, and other forms of amalgamation, to grow even bigger and more dominant during the next few years. The Reagan administration's assistant attorney general for antitrust, William Baxter, a Stanford Law School professor, acted as his master's voice in letting business know he would be lenient, even permissive, in his interpretation of antitrust merger laws. The treasury secretary, Donald Regan, agreed. Just as Du Pont, the country's largest chemical company, was about to absorb Conoco, the country's ninth-largest oil company, he said, disarmingly: "Our economy is growing and the world is growing. So why shouldn't companies grow!" Many economists who once backed strict antitrust merger enforcement have come around to their way of thinking. Readings of laws dating back to the trust-busting days of the Taft-Roosevelt administration, they believe, are in need of a complete overhaul. Through concentration, big business in America is poised to grow ever bigger, the burden of decision, if not true control, vested in fewer and fewer hands.

Commanders of the giant corporations at the economy's heights are so different from each other that it occasionally seems there are no rules, only exceptions. At one extreme are the chief executives of businesses that are as much bureaucracies as is any great department of government. General Motors is such a business. It is known to its executives simply as "the Corporation," just as executives at AT&T talk of "the Business" and CIA workers of "the Company" or "the Agency." Elevators at GM's headquarters, on a featureless boulevard in midtown Detroit, are fitted with both closed-circuit TV cameras and listening devices. Installed for the safety of the staff, these mechnical eyes and ears inevitably inhibit relaxed conversation. The most senior executives occupy a part of the fourteenth floor, where the atmosphere is still more forbidding. The hallways are deserted. Voices are kept low. Laughter is discouraged, since it suggests frivolity. All the executives wear dark suits, light shirts, and somber ties. The most important office, that of the chief executive, is a reward for decades of service to "the Corporation." The occupant is a man who has proved himself a super team player—without worrying eccentricity, willing always to subordinate his private life to "the Corporation," ready to work a twelve-hour day, to spend many evenings at GM get-togethers at the Detroit Club, where the main course is steak and where drinking by young hopefuls is monitored by seniors for signs of personal weakness. Layer upon layer of well-motivated bureaucracy insulates the fourteenth floor from junior executives in the divisions. John DeLorean, an intrepid defector from "the Corporation's" fourteenth floor whose sports car factory in West Belfast in the North of Ireland failed, and who was then involved in a cocaine scandal, knew all about the red tape as general manager of the Chevrolet Division. DeLorean has written of the frustrations of Tom Adams, the head of Campbell-Ewald, the advertising agency handling the Chevrolet account: "Under the existing system, Chevrolet advertising was approved first by the advertising manager, then by the regional sales managers, the assistant general sales managers, the general sales manager, the divisional general manager, and a similar set of management levels in the corporate marketing staff before going to the Fourteenth Floor. At each level, especially in the division, the advertising was picked apart, with specific changes recommended or ordered. I think a lot of the Chevy sales people felt that it was their job to make changes and suggestions, even though the process usually emasculated the division's advertising campaign. To adapt to this practice, the agency switched its priority from preparing advertising which it thought would be effective to devising campaigns it thought could get through the approval process."

At General Motors and at many other giant American corporations, the task of senior managers, and the test of a chief executive's success or failure, is to prevent the bureaucracy from stifling itself. General Motors employs more than 700,000; General Electric more than 400,000; IBM more than 300,000; AT&T close to 1 million.

In these and other corporations, where the way to succeed is to work exceptionally hard, to please superiors, and to demonstrate outstanding loyalty to the firm, any hint of a personality cult is discouraged. The chief executives are self-effacing and to the general public all but anonymous. The old barons of American capitalism were household names. Everybody knew about the triumphs and travails of John D. Rockefeller, Andrew Carnegie, Collis Huntington, Henry Clay Frick, the senior Henry Ford, and Andrew Mellon. Today it is a fair bet that fewer than one in one hundred Americans could name the head of Exxon, ranked by sales the world's largest corporation. Exxon employs 176,000 and in 1980 earned a profit of $5.7 billion after taxes. Its sales were $103 billion. Outside the oil business, its chief executive, Clifton Canter Garvin, is virtually unknown.

Read his curriculum vitae, and it is not hard to see why. After a chemical engineering degree at Virginia Polytechnic Institute, he joined Exxon at the age of twenty-six, in 1947. Then for two decades he kept his nose clean and his mouth mainly shut before starting to plod up the higher reaches of the corporate ladder. The mature, solid, publicly unknown Garvin was promoted from the president's executive assistant to vice-president, from executive vice-president to president, and finally to chairman of the board. With small variations on the theme, much the same can be said of the chief executives of many of the largest corporations. Not so many, however, that every American business leader can be shaded gray.

Men colorful enough to earn a profile in a mass-circulation magazine like *People*, not merely the stodgier pages of the business press, can still be found. The risk-chasing David Mahoney, who worked for five different companies before becoming chief executive of Norton Simon, is one. Mahoney loves being seen in the company of Hollywood, sports, and political celebrities and has a well-deserved reputation for being pitiless at work. When a manager confided his fear that he might fall a little short of his profit goal, Mahoney replied: "Then clean out your desk and go home." Donald Kendall of PepsiCo, a friend of Richard Nixon, also enjoys the center stage. His good-natured, elfin face is misleading. He is a driving boss who, in the words of an associate, employs people who would "rather be in the Marines than the Army." He has a thing about physical fitness. Pepsi employs four physical instructors at its headquarters in Purchase, New York. Employees spitefully volunteer that many more executives are to be seen puffing around the company grounds when Kendall is about than when he is off traveling.

Corporations also have distinct subcultures, which mold all who work for them, including the boss. IBM puts enormous stress on quick, efficient service to customers. It demands conformity from its employees and wants them to view their own interests and those of IBM as identical. In return, IBM is ready to go to great pains to make sure square pegs are fitted into square holes. ITT is less subtle. It is happiest with a ruthless chief executive so obsessed with profits that employees are seen as mini-profit centers rather than as men and women. Levi

Strauss and J. C. Penney are motivated by enlightened self-interest, assuming that customers will remain loyal if they get their money's worth. At J. C. Penney a store manager has been scolded for earning too large a profit. An overly fat profit is seen as unfair to customers and so against the chain store's interests. In recessions, employees at J. C. Penney are not laid off since the store believes loyalty is a two-way thing. Most of this would be regarded as sentimental softheadedness at Donald Kendall's PepsiCo, where the average executive tenure is ten years, versus thirty-three years at J. C. Penney. It would be found strange, too, in any of Rupert Murdoch's newspapers or the companies acquired by Thomas Mellon Evans, described by a congressman as "the corporate embodiment of Jaws, the great white shark."

The differences between the bosses of America's biggest corporations are nevertheless on closer examination less striking, and less important, than the similarities. When Arthur Louis of *Fortune* researched his book, *The Tycoons*, all but one of the 500 largest industrial corporations in America were run by men. The only exception is Katharine Graham of the Washington Post Company, which in 1980 ranked 406th, with annual sales of $660 million. She did not become chief executive through her own efforts. The top job passed on from her father, Eugene Meyer, to her husband, Philip Graham, and she inherited it when Graham killed himself in 1963. Katharine Graham, though, proved herself an exceptionally determined chief executive. The *Washington Post* established itself as the city's unquestioned leader in advertising, and helped push its evening rival, the *Washington Star*, out of business. Prejudice against women's getting the top corporate job is still very strong, despite a weakening of resistance to professional women in lower jobs.

Besides being male, the chief executives of the Fortune 500 are white. Again there is a single exception, and he is Chinese-American, not black. An Wang of Wang Laboratories got into the Fortune 500 by himself founding and then expanding this maker of small computers. Besides being both male and white, the overwhelming majority of chief executives are also Christian. This is no longer synonymous with Protestant. Catholics are today almost as numerous in the top ranks of American business as they are in the American population as a whole. They are particularly well represented in the car business. Catholics have always been entrenched in the top management of tire companies in Akron, Ohio. They have since made a breakthrough in the automobile business in Detroit. Henry Ford II is a Catholic. So are the past three chief executives of General Motors: James Roche, Richard Gerstenberg, and Thomas Aquinas Murphy.

Jews, though, are still on the outside looking in. Louis found four Jewish chief executives in the top 100 industrial corporations, but noted that three of these were entrepreneurs—Armand Hammer, the Russophile chairman of Occidental Petroleum; Austrian-born Charles Bluhdorn, then the head of Gulf + Western Industries, a conglomerate often called Engulf & Devour; and Leon Hess, the boss of Amerada Hess, the oil independent. This left Irving Shapiro of Du Pont as the only Jewish professional manager to have risen through the ranks to head one of the top 100 industrial corporations—a truly astounding statistic when measured against the success of Jewish businessmen on Wall Street.

It suggests that anti-Semitism is not entirely dead. Shapiro was given a head start by having friends in high places. He became friendly with Richard Nixon when both were making their names as anti-Communists. Shapiro served as assistant prosecutor in the show trial of the Communist Eleven under the Smith Act. All eleven were sent to jail in what many lawyers would now concede was a perversion of justice.

A more pertinent characteristic shared by most American chief executives is a great emphasis, often amounting to an obsession, on short-term profits. Perhaps because so many of them do not get the top job until they are well into their fifties, and perhaps also because their income is so often boosted by bonuses or stock options that are closely linked to profits, there is at most corporations an unwillingness by professional managers to look seriously ahead into the next five years, let alone into the next decade. As DeLorean says: "The people running General Motors today tend to be short-term, professional managers. They are in the top spots only a short time, less than ten years. In a sense, they just learn their job about the time they have to leave. So the concern at the top today is for the short-term health of the company. These professional managers want to produce a good record while they are in office."

The myopia at GM cost the country dearly. GM has traditionally dominated the market for big cars in America and when car buyers, around 1966, began to buy smaller cars, many of them imported, GM was slow to respond. Not because it was unaware of burgeoning demand for small cars. Instead, because it feared that if purchasers of its large cars were given the choice of a smaller car also made by GM, many would prefer the smaller car, on which profit margins were slimmer. When at last GM got around to making a small car in 1970, it produced a lemon, called the Vega. It lost some of its most loyal customers to foreign importers as Americans rushed to trade in gasoline guzzlers for gasoline sippers in the wake of the 1973–1974 Arab oil embargo.

A final shared characteristic is an unwillingness by business leaders to expose themselves to opinions that cause them discomfort, and this is something that is as true of self-made men as of professional managers, of Wall Street as of Main Street. Gathered together at business conventions, they are usually insulated from thoughts that could cause their blood pressure to rise. The purpose of these meetings, at piedmont spas or seaside hotels, is more to confirm than to challenge what they believe. A bestiary of opponents—the antinuclear movements, Ralph Nader, Barry Commoner, European socialists, environmentalists, small-is-beautiful economists—is ridiculed by speakers, to gruff applause. The targets are rarely given a chance to speak for themselves.

The annual convention of the Securities Industry Association attended by the top brass of Wall Street is typical. It takes place each year at the Boca Raton Hotel and Club, north of Fort Lauderdale in Florida. The architecture is pseudo-Spanish but the atmosphere is blue-chip WASP. An American flag flies beside the swimming pool. Kippered herrings are on the breakfast menu. The golf course is edged by an exotic selection of well-tended tropical vegetation—giant bamboo, night-blooming jasmine, thatch palms, lofty figs, satinleaf bushes, red silk cotton, and monkey puzzle trees.

The conventioneers are jocularly matey. Nicknames are de rigueur. Robert Gardiner, the head of Dean Witter, calls Robert Baldwin, the head of Morgan Stanley, "Baldy." Baldwin calls Gardiner "Stretch." They are out to enjoy themselves, at least so their clothes suggest. Men who customarily wear three-piece suits and black shoes are got up in white loafers and in floral shirts and in trousers that could have been made from curtaining material.

The speakers' programs offer almost nothing but reassurance and confirmation of conventional business wisdom. Their keynote speaker on energy at one recent convention was Clifton Garvin of Exxon. On the economy it was Ezra Solomon, professor of finance at the Graduate School of Business at Stanford, which vies with Harvard's as the finest business school. "Perspective on the 1980s" was up to William Simon, a former Republican secretary of the treasury and author of a free-enterprise polemic called *A Time for Truth*. On tax policy and capital formation, it was William Ballhaus, president of Bechman Instruments Inc.

William Simon, in particular, was fundamentalist. He told the Wall Street elite, before Ronald Reagan's election: "My friends, the sad truth is that here in the United States we have a government rolling out of control and careening crazily down its own road to socialism. . . . If a collapse does occur, the United States will, in my judgment, simultaneously turn into an economic dictatorship. So many citizens have been trained to see the government as economically omniscient and omnipotent, and to blame all economic ills on 'business,' that disaster could easily bring popular demand for takeover of the major means of production by the state. Legal precedent and ideological justification exist. It would take little to accomplish this transition. Therefore, political courage and public wisdom are our only hope for preserving the premier economy of the world, as well as our individual freedom." And so on. There was dutiful applause when Simon, known to his old colleagues at Salomon Brothers as "Simple Simon," sat down. It is lonely at the top and so easy to get out of touch.

The paradox is that American business leaders, and their Republican and Democratic allies in Washington, are not nearly as wedded to the dogma of free enterprise as they convince themselves and others that they are. To be sure, few of them want their country to go the way of France and Japan, where private industry and mercantilist governments work hand in hand. In these countries industrial policies are carefully crafted to offer maximum backing to the advanced-technology businesses that the French and Japanese authorities believe will keep their nations internationally competitive in the twenty-first century. America's advanced-technology enterprises, with a narrowing but still significant know-how jump on foreign rivals, are doing well. While

Pentagon contracts have greatly aided the modern high-technology sector, such American success stories as IBM, Hewlett-Packard, Wang Laboratories, and Teledyne have earned bumper profits without significant government support.

The belief of American executives in the free market falters instead when their particular business or industry is in trouble. Then its bosses and, less hypocritically, its labor leaders are quick to seek help from Washington. So long as the business or industry is a large one, it is rarely sent away empty-handed. Only for small businesses is bankruptcy the price of failure. Corner stores, dry cleaners, or antique shops may rise or fall on the efforts of their owners. Large businesses are tugged back from the abyss when Washington decides the political costs of letting them fail are too high to risk. Braniff International was allowed to go bankrupt but American Motors, Douglas Aircraft, Lockheed, and Chrysler have all in recent years been given a massive money transfusion by the federal government. When steel industry executives and trade unionists pleaded poverty before the Carter administration, a trigger price mechanism was introduced to protect them against foreign steel. When car companies complained to the Reagan administration that their profit margins were under intolerable pressure, the Japanese government was bullied by the White House into conceding "voluntary" quotas on exports of Japanese cars across the Pacific. Much relieved, Detroit celebrated by raising its prices. Ships built in America and crewed by American seamen are uncompetitively costly, so they have been cosseted by a law that prohibits foreign-flag ships from plying between American ports. Quotas, again voluntary only in the sense that the alternative is severe mandatory quotas, also restrain imports of Asian-made television sets, clothing, and textiles, to the immense relief of their hard-pressed competitors in the United States. In the railroad business, the profitable lines chug along in the private sector earning profits and dividends for their stockholders, while the loss-making lines are shunted off to become wards of the taxpayer. The railroad casualties so far, all of them effectively nationalized, include the Penn Central, the Reading, the Central of New Jersey, the Erie Lackawanna, the Lehigh Valley, and the Lehigh and Hudson River.

Felix Rohatyn is an embarrassment to most of his fellow investment bankers when he says: "To cries of interference with the free market system, I would point out that, at present, the price of our energy is not freely set, the price of our food is not freely set, the price at which we borrow money is not freely set. Although free markets are clearly desirable, the fact of the matter is that we do not live in a free market economy and never will; we live in a mixed economy in which prices and capital are subject to government influences and will continue to be so."

Administrations, Republican and Democratic, are unwilling to concede this publicly. Talk about a precedent being established is resolutely discouraged. Instead, every time the White House and Congress come to the aid of a stricken business, they make sincere acts of contrition and promise not to commit the same sin again. Though the Republicans purport to be more committed to the free market than the Democrats, the three most controversial rescues of businesses in the United States during the past quarter century have taken place under Republican administrations. The evidence is that Republicans find it even harder than Democrats to turn an unhearing ear to cries of distress from corporate America.

Oil was the Oliver Twist, begging the government for more help, in the 1950s. Cheap crude flowing in from the Middle East depressed prices in the United States to a level the oil companies described as ruinous. Oilmen wrapped themselves in the Stars and Stripes and sent in their Washington lobbyists to convince Congress that unless the flood of foreign oil was stemmed, American oil drillers would be driven out of business, leaving the country dangerously dependent on foreign oil suppliers. President Eisenhower endorsed their argument. In 1957, oil import quotas were imposed to slow the inflow of Arab oil. America had opted for what critics of the oil companies denounced as a policy of "drain America first." Instead of buying cheap oil from abroad while it was available and conserving more of its own oil reserves in the ground, the United States decided instead to divert the cheap oil to other countries. Amazingly, this policy was sold to the public as serving America's national security interests.

The oil industry did not rest content with the curbs on imported oil. To tighten the tap on the amount of domestically produced oil flowing into the market, and so through scarcity to harden prices, it persuaded the Texas Railroad Commission to continue to limit the oil that could be pumped. This, two-facedly, was justified by oilmen on the grounds of long-term conservation. The oil industry then had the best of both worlds. Playing the national security card, it had persuaded the federal government to keep out foreign oil and a regulatory agency to slow depletion of domestic oil reserves. The industry did not recant and become a born-again preacher of free enterprise until the OPEC cartel, by manipulating supply, began pushing up the world price of oil. The output limitations of the Texas Railroad Commission were then seen by oilmen as burdensome government regulations that inhibited the free workings of the market. The limitations were scrapped.

The rescue of Lockheed under the Nixon administration was also presented as an extraordinary exception to America's free enterprise system, justified only by the company's importance to national security. Lockheed's troubles were traced to the decision of the Defense Department in 1965 to negotiate for the C-5 military transport the first of its so-called total procurement contracts. These contracts were supposed to put a stop to habitual cost overruns on Pentagon hardware. When this new contract caused Lockheed huge losses, the Defense Department at first did not listen to pleas for its renegotiation. Then, at the beginning of 1971, Edward Heath's Conservative government in Britain reversed a decision of previous Labor governments to support struggling Rolls-Royce. This imperiled Lockheed, for Rolls-Royce was the maker of RB-211 engines for the Lockheed L-1011 airbus. When Rolls-Royce went bust, Heath's government decided against a rescue. The Pentagon and John Connally, the then treasury secretary, were appalled. Connally dressed down the economic minister at the British embassy, Sir Derek Mitchell, and quickly persuaded the British to reassess the costs of this hands-off policy. Rolls-Royce was an important defense contractor. The loss of jobs and balance-of-trade costs were, on reflection, conceded to be too great. The decision not to intervene to help Rolls-Royce was reversed by the British on the condition that the American side prop up Lockheed. The Pentagon paid out hundreds of millions of dollars to make good Lockheed's losses on its contracts for the C-5 and other defense equipment. The Senate, lobbied hard by Connally and by Lockheed's chief executive, Daniel Jeremiah Haughton, a slow-talking farm boy from Alabama with a sunny smile, agreed by a one-vote margin to underwrite the firm's solvency with $250 million in government loan guarantees.

A third great rescue, again described as an aberration that had no bearing on what had happened before or would happen afterward, was the $1.5 billion Chrysler bailout. The Reagan administration not only decided to go through with this rescue, arranged under Carter, but also agreed that Detroit should be able to increase prices and make a strong recovery from the auto slump of 1980 by slowing imports of cars from Japan. Top members of the Reagan team were split. In favor of quotas were the secretary of commerce, Malcolm Baldrige, a former chief executive of Scovill Inc.; the transportation secretary, Drew Lewis, a Pennsylvania adviser to failing businesses before he was recruited by the Republican National Committee; and the labor secretary, Ray Donovan, a New Jersey businessman. Opposed to quotas were the treasury secretary, Donald Regan, formerly of Merrill Lynch; the chairman of the Council of Economic Advisers, Murray Weidenbaum, a critic of government regulation of business; and the budget director, David Stockman, a former Michigan congressman.

The White House broke the impasse in coming out for quotas. The reasons were political, not economic. Ronald Reagan had all but promised quotas to win blue-collar votes in his campaign against President Carter. Talking about a need for Japanese export restraint, candidate Reagan had said: "This is something where I think the government has a responsibility that it's shirked so far. And it's a place government can be legitimately involved, and that is to convince Japan that *in one way or another, and for their own best interest* [emphasis added], the deluge of their cars into the U.S. must be slowed while our own industry gets back on its feet." The administration made the Japanese an offer they could not refuse. Either, the Japanese were told, introduce "voluntary" quotas on your car exports to America or *else* Congress, with a nod and a wink from the White House, will bring in far meaner mandatory import quotas. When the Japanese capitulated, the American public was promised this was a never-to-be-repeated deviation from America's free-market system. America's trading partners were assured that the Reagan administration was as passionately devoted to free trade as ever, that such a lapse from grace would not recur.

The pattern is clear. America has the habit but not the policy of chronic government intervention. As a result, the American industrial economy is being distorted in the worst possible way. Administrations of all political colors are unwilling to accept Lester Thurow's and Milton Friedman's truism that capitalism is a doctrine of failure. The inefficient are supposed to be driven out of business by the efficient in a free-market system. Neither are administrations prepared to introduce a coherent industrial policy, like that pursued by the Japanese and many European countries, notably France, which seeks to influence the flow of investment in the national interest. Interventions by government in the American private sector have no theme other than to keep alive an industry or a firm that has demonstrated its condition is critical.

The damage this improvisation does to the national economy is invisible but serious. Economists of all persuasions are nearly unanimous in agreeing that a main reason the United States has become an Avis rather than a Hertz is inadequate investment in new plant and equipment by business. Yet these ad hoc interventions by the administration and the Congress inevitably distort, without rhyme or reason, the inadequate business investment that does occur. Firms that would otherwise go out of business are made credit worthy by Uncle Sam's underwriting their bank loans. Industries that are internationally uncompetitive, like shipbuilding, are able to attract equity capital and sell bonds because government subsidies keep them profitable.

The conclusion is inescapable. The American economy will remain stuck, unable to achieve sustained growth, until at a very minimum an administration and a Congress come up with an industrial strategy. Such an industrial strategy will have, in order to work, to be fair and, more important, be seen to be fair. It will require that 4 percent or 5 percent of the national income be switched into investment, or at current levels no less than $150 billion, which means a substantial, if temporary, fall in living standards. An industrial policy implies that some at least of that investment will have to go through a 1980s equivalent of the Reconstruction Finance Corporation, which served the economy so well during the Great Depression.

In looking for evidence that such a policy could work, it is not necessary to peer across the Pacific to Japan or across the Atlantic to Europe. As Felix Rohatyn has noted, in 1975 New York was in a far more parlous condition than that of the national economy today. The city's bankruptcy was only averted by the state governor's and the city's labor and business leaders' putting together of a coherent austerity plan of shared sacrifices. Union leaders accepted a loss of jobs, frozen wages, and the investment of their members' pension fund money in financial paper issued by the city. Students at the City University were charged for tuition. Subway and bus fares were increased. Noteholders accepted a moratorium on the repayment of their city notes. City services were cut back: library opening hours, street cleaning, park maintenance. Banks, though nervous about getting their money back, lent the city more. Though the quality of life in the city suffered a decline, by 1981 New York City had a balanced budget—something the federal government has achieved only once in the past twenty years. The city's economy, while not exactly thriving, was on the mend. It is still possible that the federal government can put forward a similar national coalition to support a coherent plan for a revival of the national economy. Otherwise, the country will continue to muddle through until a crisis, like that in New York, breaks on a national scale.

Underinvestment is only part of the problem. Job satisfaction has fallen to its lowest level in twenty-five years. The self-employed are happier, but they are a small minority. Of the 105 million Americans who must work for a living, about 100 million of them, when they can find a job, work for someone else. Yet despite the decline in job satisfaction and the rising anger opinion pollsters detect about the country's economic failure, Americans are still unwilling to contemplate radical reforms. American business is spared European demands for nationalization or for worker directors. West Germany's postwar success is envied, but few wish to copy laws that require large companies in Germany to permit their workers to elect half the members of a supervisory board to oversee such strategic corporate decisions as plant closures and the siting of new investments. Americans, outside the steel industry, are also remarkably tolerant of the way corporations in basic industries—cars, aerospace, airlines, shipbuilding—routinely lay off blue-collar workers when order books slim. Few employees aspire to the job security won by unions in continental Europe, where laws on redundancy pay are so costly that corporations are deterred from handing out dismissal notices in anything other than a dire emergency, although the auto workers are now following the steelworkers in bargaining less for greater benefits than to keep their jobs. Japanese employment practices are seen as unimportable. Americans find it hard to comprehend an industrial system where redundancies are regarded by both bosses and workers as a serious breach of trust.

Even when the anger of American workers comes to the boil, they have tended to confine their demands to remedies for specific grievances. Only very recently have a minority begun to dabble in more fundamental reforms, which would give them more control of the organization of their work, or more wide-reaching national economic reforms. Thus, when the 550,000-member Communications Workers of America in 1978 launched a campaign to reduce job stress in the Bell Telephone System, its objectives, typically, were limited. There was no thought of demanding half the seats on the board of AT&T for worker representatives, or of public ownership of the telephone system. The demonstrations were directed instead against compulsory overtime, arbitrary absenteeism controls, and exacting schedules, derided by the unions as "timed potty breaks."

This reluctance to contemplate any fundamental challenge to the "American economic system" was noticeable even in the bitter strike by workers at the Vega plant of General Motors in Lordstown, Ohio, in 1972—a strike described as the "most dramatic instance of work resistance since the Flint sit-downs in 1937." Fed-up workers turned angrily against their plant. The plant manager complained: "We have had sabotage and we have had deliberate missing of work. . . . Slashing of seat covers, smashing of radios, scratching of instruments in the instrument panel, scratching of paint, tearing glove compartment doors, destroying or bending the gearshift levers, and various other things of serious consequence." General Motors was distressed. It had sited the plant in Lordstown to break new ground and to escape the chronic mistrust between bosses and workers in the old auto towns. When GM decided to switch the assembly plant to a small car called the Vega, after a bright star in the constellation Lyra, it knew it would have to achieve superproductivity to compete on prices with the Datsun, the Toyota, the Volkswagen Beetle, and other imports. The first Vega rolled out in the summer of 1970. It quickly proved the fastest-selling subcompact car made in the United States. Then someone took a look at the balance sheet. A contract strike by the UAW had interrupted the launch of the Vega and the car was not making a large enough profit. In October 1971, GMAD, the General Motors assembly division, famed for its cost-cutting efficiency, was sent in to take over the plant and boost profits. GMAD promptly "rationalized" an assembly line that was designed to turn out more than one hundred cars an hour. The time-and-motion study experts gave some workers jobs that two had performed before and took seven hundred people off the assembly line. A decline set in fast. GM had to send home workers on an eight-hour shift after only three hours' work, or just as soon as they had generated enough work to keep men in the repair division busy.

The workers complained of impossible work schedules, of having to put a part in one car as the next car came along and knocked into them. They retaliated by putting five electrical wires in a car engine when they were supposed to put in six, by putting keys down the gas pipe, or by deliberately denting fenders. By the spring of 1972, they were distributing leaflets in the area telling people not to buy Vegas. They were workers at the plant, they said, and knew the cars were a lousy product. The main complaint, especially from the younger workers, was that they were treated like machines, not people. Among them were hillbillies from West Virginia who left no doubt about how they could deal with "scabs" crossing picket lines. German- and Japanese-language slogans pasted up in the factory to instill in these workers the threat of foreign competition were seen as an insult. So were other GM posters, with such trite slogans as "Waste Not Want Not" and "A Fair Day's Work for a Fair Day's Pay."

A fertile recruiting ground for socialist organizers? Not in America, not in Lordstown. These same workers were scathing the plans of Senator George McGovern, the Democratic party's presidential candidate in 1972, for a steep tax on incomes above $200,000 a year. They found the idea un-American. If a man started his own business, they felt, he was entitled to keep the better share of the money he made. Some of the car workers looked forward to leaving the assembly line. They wanted to become small capitalists, to open a garage, a hamburger joint, a laundromat. Nor if one of them made a go of this would his fellow workers, remaining behind, begrudge him his success.

The workers were confirming a judgment made years earlier by Denis Brogan in *The American Character:* "By European standards, what is still more notable about American life is that competition, even by the new softer, more formally amiable methods, is the accepted way of life. So is the lavishness of the prizes; so is the acceptance of the fact that not everybody can answer the $64,000 question—and the absence of jealousy of the winners. This absence of jealousy, this conviction that the game is worth playing and the results not cooked, is one of the chief sources of American wealth, well-being and political stability."

Far fewer today would agree with the confident assertion of the last sentence, but Americans continue to demonstrate little class consciousness. Lane Kirkland, who inherited the presidency of the AFL-CIO from his mentor, George Meany, seeks collaboration with big business rather than confrontation. He grumbles about an irrational American attachment to laissez-faire policies and points out that more successful countries call in labor, business, and the public to deal collectively with national problems. Few listen. Kirkland is a Henry Jackson Democrat, against the Russians and for the New Deal, and like the senator from Washington State, he is as effective as Sominex is advertised as being at helping people relax so they can get to sleep.

The labor movement continues to lose influence under Kirkland, as it did under Meany. During the past quarter of a century, union membership has declined from over a third of the labor force to not much above a fifth. Even when labor apologists are given the benefit of the doubt, and the 7 percent of American workers who belong to employee associations are counted as union members, there is no denying the receding influence of the labor movement. In Congress, labor lobbyists are routinely taken to the cleaners by the Business Roundtable, representing the biggest of big businesses. The Reagan White House remains aloof from the AFL-CIO, treating it with the same disdain fellow conservative Margaret Thatcher shows toward the British Trades Union Congress. At the start of the 1980s, unions were losing more than half of their registration drives. Counterattacking employers are more often than not successful when decertification elections are organized to get rid of unions.

Labor leaders have so far shown themselves more skillful at explaining why the unions are losing members than at reversing the trend. Mobster Jimmy Hoffa of the Teamsters, murder-plotter Tony Boyle of the Mine Workers, and a few other "bad apples" are accused of giving unions a poor name. Unions, it is explained, have also lost members because industries moved South, where right-to-work laws reinforce an aversion to union organizers. The work of professional union busters, who make a living out of advising companies how to frustrate labor organizers, is another reason, or excuse, that is advanced for labor's retreat. Unions can take comfort that business still regards them as a positive threat and not organizations whose historical time has passed and who can be left simply to fade away.

Not all labor leaders are as complacent as the AFL-CIO bureaucracy or as collaborationist as the union official at Volkswagen's plant in New Stanton, Pennsylvania, who was quoted as saying: "Relations with the company are good and improving. . . . It's like a marriage— you have your ups and downs." Douglas Fraser, the recently retired head of the United Auto Workers (UAW), who talks out of the side of his mouth and looks a bit like a friendly frog, maintained his union's progressive reputation. Just as the UAW, under Walter Reuther and then Leonard Woodcock, led the way in supporting the civil rights movement, so Douglas Fraser was in the van of a campaign for worker directors. The Big Three car companies in Detroit tried to laugh it off as a bargaining chip that the UAW wanted to trade in for better wages and conditions. Chrysler found Fraser was not joking when, close to bankruptcy, it asked the union to agree to lower wages for its members at Chrysler than for those at Ford and General Motors. The union was willing to go along with this, but not before Chrysler agreed to Fraser's joining its board of directors. William Winpisinger, president of the International Association of Machinists and Aerospace Workers, is even more militant. He is one of the few leaders of an American union to label himself a socialist. Fred Kroll, the firebrand president of the Railway Clerks Union, is another activist. When the Reagan administration staged a blitzkrieg on social, health, and safety programs, Kroll fumed: "We should emulate our Polish brothers. We should shut this country down for a day or two with some militant acts. That's the way to bring the message home."

Nobody, it seems, was listening. Opinion pollsters routinely report that a majority of Americans want wage and price controls, anathema to the free marketeers who dominate the economic thinking of the Reagan administration, but otherwise there is little questioning of conventional economic wisdom on the part of the public. While the wages of many workers have during the past decade barely kept up with inflation, families have avoided hard times by many more women joining the work force. Families which would otherwise have been complaining of living standards that do not improve or threaten to fall have kept quiet because a second income lets them stay ahead of inflation.

This source of worker apathy in the past decade could easily become a cause of worker militancy in the 1980s. Most women are at work, so this one-time jump in the family income is over and working women have a real reason for grievance. In relative terms, they are no better off than they were forty years ago. Give or take a few percentage points, the average earnings of a year-round, full-time female worker have remained stuck at 60 percent of the average male's earnings since 1939. If the unions organize successfully in the burgeoning service sector where most women work, and campaign to correct this injustice, they stand to make a strong comeback, particularly if at the same time the policies of the resurgent Republican right provoke a backlash against the gutting of social programs. There is always the risk that the feminist movement and the labor movement could work at cross-purposes and weaken each other. It has happened before. Animosities between blacks and whites, and now between blacks and Hispanics, have fragmented the American labor movement and blocked the development of a working-class culture. The unions' challenge is to create a sense of solidarity between male and female workers. Whether they succeed or not, the mass entry of women into the labor force has already had a profound effect on American economic, social, and sexual life.

3

WOMEN AT ODDS
The Sexes and the Family

THE FACT THAT a woman earns only about sixty cents for every dollar made by a man, and that this ratio has not changed in more than forty years, is awkward both for the women's movement and for its opponents. All movements like to have at least an illusion of progress, and it is dispiriting to find that nothing, not even the Equal Pay Act, passed in 1963 over the strident objections of the National Association of Manufacturers and the U.S. Chamber of Commerce, has done anything to narrow the gap between the wages of women and those of men. Women with college degrees continue on average to earn less than male high school dropouts.

The gap is even more awkward for opponents of the women's movement—that coalition embracing such odd bedfellows as advocates of a retreat to traditional sexual roles and free enterprise ideologues reciting that wages are set most fairly by the free workings of the market. For it is hard for anyone, other than a misogynist, to believe that American women are worth only three-fifths as much as their male counterparts. Yet if opponents of the women's movement are forced to concede that women are not being paid their true worth because they are women, or alternatively that men are being paid above their true worth because they are men, then sexual discrimination must be admitted.

Attempts are made to weasel out of this box. Women are paid less, it is said, because their recent strong influx into the labor force has concentrated more of them into the low-paying entry-level jobs of inexperienced workers. Many women, it is also said, have child-caring and homemaking duties that deter them from the overtime and after-hours work that fattens pay packets and promotion prospects. While neither argument is baseless, the overwhelming cause for the discrepancy in wages remains the concentration of women in low-paying, dead-end jobs.

While other issues divided the women present, the fact of discrimination in the job market was pretty close to uncontroversial when delegates opened the National Women's Conference in a stuffy hall in Houston, Texas, in mid-November 1977, by intoning, in unison: "We are here, America, at last to move history forward for women."

This gathering of some two thousand women, outnumbered by five times as many alternates and observers, was both a triumph and a turning point for the women's movement from which it sprang. The conference, officially speaking, was America's follow-up to International Women's Year, held two years earlier. On signing the executive order setting up the commission that would organize the women's conference, President Ford gave official recognition to the aspirations of the women's movement. "Americans," he said, "must now deal with those inequities that still linger as barriers to full participation of women in our national life." Under pressure from the energetic, rasp-voiced commission chairman, Bella Abzug, then one of New York's best known and most persistent representatives in the House, Congress was even persuaded to cough up $5 million toward the cost of the conference itself and the preliminary meetings in the states to draft resolutions and pick delegates.

The conference was held in the Sam Houston Auditorium, a run-down building from the 1930s. This has a barrel ceiling, like a hangar or an armory. Art deco friezes decorate the walls. Above the stage hung the conference symbol, a white dove surrounding the sign that biologists use for "female" and astronomers for Venus. The smell of fried food gave the hall the air of an enormous hotel kitchen. There were no bars serving hard liquor, no bands playing college football songs, few husbands, and almost no lobbyists. These things, and the sex of the delegates, aside, the Houston conference had all the look of a national party convention.

The charge was heard that the delegations from the states were not representative of American women. Politically, this was correct. Despite efforts by conservatives, especially in Western and Southern states, to win representation to the Houston conference, right-wing and antifeminist delegates were in a minority. At most, they represented about a fifth of the delegates. In another sense, the Houston delegates —there were 1,981 by official count—were a representative cross section. There were women of every color, young and old, well-off women in expensively tailored clothes, and less well-off women in jeans or double knits. The big names of the women's movement—women such as Betty Friedan, Gloria Steinem, and Bella Abzug—were besieged for television interviews. So were battered wives, crippled women, and ordinary housewives. One commission member, the unassuming, unstarlike Jean Stapleton, who played Archie Bunker's wife on *All in the Family,* was greeted with warm applause when introduced on stage, the very symbol of long-suffering womanhood.

The Houston conference was a mingling of many currents. Eleanor Smeal, head of the National Organization for Women, represented the mainstream of American feminism. There were Republican politicians, like Margaret Heckler of Massachusetts, and Democratic ones, like Representative Shirley Chisholm of New York, one of the few women to have entered major presidential primaries. Three Presidents' wives were there, too. Lady Bird Johnson, dressed in red, who had been a loyal wife in an impossible job of her own, an admirer of Eleanor Roosevelt and a model for progressive women in her day. Betty Ford, in blue, unpompous and self-possessed, who admitted she drank under the strain of it all; she was not asked by reporters on the presidential campaign how often she slept with her husband, she said, but had she been, she would have told them: "As often as possible." Rosalynn Carter, in green, slim, pretty, shy, but tough enough in her husband's defense to be known as "the iron magnolia."

There were black, white, and Hispanic women. Coretta King, the widow of the civil rights hero, said that sexism and racism were "dual discriminations." Many of the black women at Houston, though, questioned how far they shared any broad interests with white feminists. Radical feminist groups, which took root in the late 1960s, when horizons were broader, came too. A wishful banner of theirs in the California delegation read: "Imagination rules the world." These groups doubted the use of working inside the system for gradual change. In them the fires of the radical women's movement still burned.

They brought to mind the heady days of 1970 when Robin Morgan could write in the magazine *Rat:* "Let it all hang out; let it seem bitchy, catty, dykey, frustrated, crazy, Solanasesque, nutty, frigid, ridiculous, bitter, embarrassing, man-hating, libelous, pure, unfair, envious, intuitive, low-down, stupid, petty, liberating; we are the women that men have warned us about." Those were the times when Jill Johnston could cause a rumpus during a New York symposium by ardently embracing her woman friend on stage; when Ti-Grace Atkinson was punched for saying that the Virgin Mary had been used; when Valerie Solanas, who became notorious for shooting Andy Warhol, wrote in her manifesto of the Society for Cutting Up Men that "to be male is to be deficient, emotionally limited . . . males are emotional cripples."

By the time of Houston, political theater of this sort was being discounted. Ridicule was too easy a weapon for opponents of a movement that, first of all, was asking to be taken seriously. From a six-foot-tall Carrie Nation smashing up saloons with an ax to feminists burning brassieres, caricature is something women who would break into public life have had to live with. At the famous, but ill-reported, women's protest during the 1968 Miss America pageant, several pieces of underwear, some wigs, and a few false eyelashes were thrown into a "Freedom Trash Can," but no bras were burned. Flags and draft cards were being burned at about that time, so it is not difficult to see how the symbol came to be created. In any event, once invented, it stuck.

Perhaps precisely because those who resent the entry of women into public life tend to lump them together as "women's libbers" or "bra burners," some delegates at Houston, especially some of the younger ones, hesitated about calling themselves "feminists" at all. After the high point of the women's movement, in the mid-seventies, among quite independent and capable young women it was noticeable how general this reluctance to accept the label became. Something similar happened after the great suffrage fight earlier in this century. Noting the change in a 1927 *Harper's* article, the writer Dorothy Bromley said: ". . . the feminist, new style, professes no loyalty to women *en masse* although she staunchly believes in individual women." The new feminist, she thought, was more interested in independence and work than in gestures such as "never darning a sock or keeping her maiden name."

Considering these many currents among the delegates, it was hardly surprising that there should have been plenty of conflict at Houston. Should there be a special government department for women? Bella Abzug, a liberal Democrat with a deep interest in welfare programs and protective social legislation, was for a separate women's agency. Women, more than men, are poor, dependent, in need, and under-unionized. As do all who rely heavily on social services, women suffer in a jungle of overlapping and often warring government agencies. Others, like Betty Friedan and Midge Costanza, were against a special department. An early supporter of Carter's in New York State, Costanza was the chief public liaison officer at the White House until she fell afoul of the Carter Georgians. To her and to Friedan, a special women's department would only encourage the notion that women in public life were a disturbing exception.

The dispute echoed old arguments that had long divided women. When Alice Paul founded the National Women's Party in 1923 and began campaigning for an Equal Rights Amendment, other progressive women opposed her. Their fear was that the call for women's equality could wipe out the special protections and health programs for women that only recently had been enacted. As Felix Frankfurter, then a law professor at Harvard, shrewdly observed, the campaigners for the early equal rights amendment catered more to the interests of professional women than to the needs of "millions of wage-earning women." This split in the movement—between middle-class and working-class women—has never been fully bridged. Nobody expected it to be bridged at Houston. The proposal for a special women's department died.

Homosexuality caused predictable trouble. There was strong backing for a resolution urging an end to discrimination against lesbians, but fierce opposition, too. Outside the conference hall, antifeminists waved placards which read: "If lesbians did not recruit, they would die out in a generation." Even inside, the issue was too strong for some delegates. One unsmiling woman held up a sign: "Keep 'em in the closet." Amid quickly stifled laughter from her listeners, a delegate from Oklahoma said: "God in heaven has never dictated whether we should be homosexual or heterosexual. We would never advocate stoning . . . so long as homosexuals keep their preferences private, like adulterers and adulteresses."

The lesbian question, said a Georgia delegate, had "always been an albatross round the neck of the women's movement." With this Betty Friedan strongly agreed. "For someone who grew up in Peoria, Illinois," she said, "I have trouble with this issue." Ellie Smeal drew an opposite conclusion: Lesbianism—or rather prejudice against lesbians —was something that affected all women. The resolution was "for all women," she said, "whose possibilities are restrained by the fear and threat of being called a lesbian." Her argument was well received, even if in terms of sheer numbers the lesbian caucus was a small force at Houston. For "dykey" is only one of the cruder slurs used against an independent woman—slurs that include "strident" or "assertive" as well as a further possible lexicon of pejoratives. The lesbian rights resolution was noisily put to vote and overwhelmingly carried. Afterward, the lesbian caucus celebrated at the Sheraton Houston to a band called Sweet Honey in the Rock.

Only on a handful of the delegates were the conservatives a force. The liberal majority outnumbered them four to one. As if to maintain its reputation as the most benighted state, Mississippi sent an all-white delegation. This included seven men, four of whom were members of the Ku Klux Klan. "We were told in church," according to a woman who had taken part in the Mississippi state meeting, "that the ERA meant the end of marriage, that schoolbooks would show pictures of people having sex with animals, and we've got to protect our children." On motion after motion, the conservatives were voted down. Only on the final day, when the main conference business was completed, did they walk out in protest.

These delegates were mostly white and lower-middle-class women from Bible Belt states of the South or Midwest. These were not the sort to smile when their moral arguments were padded by references to the Good Book. Many began as opponents of abortion in what became known as the "pro-life" movement. The "pro-life" movement, in turn, had grown into a "pro-family" movement, a potent backlash, broad in scope, aroused for the defense of children, church, and kitchen.

The leader of the antifeminists in Houston was Phyllis Schlafly, a conservative Republican who led the campaign against the Equal Rights Amendment. The strength of the reaction was alarming to the women's movement. There could be little doubt, by the time of the Houston meeting, that American politicians were a lot more scared of Phyllis Schlafly and her allies than of Bella Abzug and hers. Houston was a triumph for the women's movement, having been brought off at all. It was also a turning point. For by the time it took place, the movement was squarely on the defensive.

The program eventually agreed upon at Houston to advance the cause of women called for an end to discrimination against women in jobs, credit, and insurance, all areas in which recent years had brought some progress; more controversially, it called for public financing of abortions and for setting up federally funded shelters for battered wives; yet, as opposition to publicly supported child care was strong (an Ohio delegate likened it to "Hitler's youth camps"), the resolution on this was watered down; the conference urged that steps be taken to get women into top jobs, including judgeships, an issue to which most male politicians were, by then, paying at least lip service. Most of the program was, nevertheless, ignored by Congress and the White House when the time came to present it later.

Concerned that in this hostile climate the women's movement might overreach itself, some delegates wanted the conference to concentrate on the Equal Rights Amendment. "If the energy of this conference isn't transformed into efforts to ratify," said Betty Friedan, "then we'll have been had." The amendment was passed by Congress during the flood tide of the movement in 1972, washing over the opposition of the Mormons, the hierarchy of the Catholic Church, and the nation's favorite scold, jowly Senator Sam Ervin of North Carolina, who derided it as "the unisex amendment" and, in an echo of the old fight against civil rights for blacks, warned that since discriminations "are not created by law, they cannot be abolished by law." By the time of the Houston meeting, though, ERA was still three states short of the thirty-eight required for ratification; six states short if three had acted constitutionally when after first supporting ERA they changed their minds. So it remained, and its chances of ratification did not improve as the 1982 deadline for approval by the states approached. Opinion polls indicating that up to two-thirds of Americans who had heard of ERA supported it might have given the women's movement false confidence. Like all progressive social movements, it was caught in a conflict between the necessity for militancy to remain in forward gear and the necessity for moderation to win over the undecided, who are battened on by opposition from the right. Just as Tom Hayden and Jane Fonda fired up the committed to redouble their opposition to the Vietnam War at the same time they turned lukewarm supporters of the peace movement cold, so Bella Abzug, Betty Friedan, and Gloria Steinem were more effective in the role of the committed preaching to the converted than to winning over to their cause waverers with half an ear distracted by the carping of the antifeminists.

Houston itself might seem at first a very odd place in which to hold a women's conference. The city prizes that extravagance, restlessness, and ungoverned energy that American historical legend tends to associate with men, just as it puts little store by those thrifty, civilizing qualities traditionally expected from women. Houston has an unbridled, frontier character that its twin rivals to the north, Fort Worth and Dallas, long ago ceased to possess, let alone boast of. Despite their popular image, these two, by comparison with Houston, are settled, domesticated, and God-fearing.

Each vies with the other for which has the older money. Fort Worth grew up as a cattle town, Dallas as a railhead. They are Texas's link with the rest of the country. This is not just because of the cyclopean airport that occupies several thousand acres of scrubland in between the two. Texans in these cities are used to listening to what the North thinks. Houston, by contrast, is making too much money in oil and chemicals to much bother with outsiders, unless they come to stay, which they are doing at a rate of more than five thousand a month.

Houston is a sprawling new city off on its own near the Gulf Coast. Reaching it by air is still difficult even for the most resourceful user of America's twentieth-century Bradshaw, the *North American Pocket Flight Guide*. Houston never stands still long enough for anyone to count, but it is believed to have more than two and a half million residents. Of cities its size, none are farther below the Mason-Dixon line. One in every five Houstonians is black, one in ten Chicano. For them, Houston is the worst of North and South, Dixie racism in an urban slum. Left to its own devices, Houston does without restraints felt necessary elsewhere. Its lack of planning produces brilliant single buildings amid empty lots; its repetitive grid of suburb and freeway resembles Los Angeles, ironed flat, with the sea and mountains removed. Houston is in the running every year, when the crime figures are collected, for the title "Murder Capital, U.S.A." Houston's violence, the visitor feels, is bred less from frustration and resentment—as is the violence, for example, in Detroit or Saint Louis—than from lawlessness and lack of controls.

In Dallas, one senses the watching eyes of the city's innumerable churches. Towering over Houston is the Exxon Building, topped by the Petroleum Club. Nobody there is watching, one feels, since they are much too busy making money. Working to make money and putting money to work to make more money are what Americans prize above all things. No sin is graver in America than idleness, no punishment worse than being without work, no condition more despised than dependence. To call Houston "male-dominated," let alone "male," would beg many questions. In 1981, the city elected the financial controller, Mrs. Kathy Whitmire, as mayor, suggesting city politics was not exclusively or straightforwardly under the thumb of men.

To the extent, though, that Houston typifies a raw American respect for making money, then it was, after all, perhaps the right place to begin to reflect on the condition of women in America. For until the American veneration of hard work and contempt for indigence is understood, one cannot grasp the ambivalence with which women in America have traditionally been treated.

Early visitors noted how quickly after independence the land-rich country threw off the British legal tradition of passing property from father to eldest son or, in the absence of a son, to the closest male blood relative, and how American parents divided their property equally among their sons and daughters. American women struck Tocqueville as strong, self-confident, and able. Unlike their European counterparts, they were given great freedom and were expected to control themselves. Along with other observers, he noticed the ease with which young American women traveled about unescorted, the respect generally paid them, and the severe penalties for rape. Yet he observed, too, that their freedom was confined "within a narrow circle of domestic interests."

The Argentinian traveler Domingo Sarmiento contrasted the freedom enjoyed by unmarried women with the "perpetual prison" that awaited them on marriage. The vigorous, half-deaf English abolitionist, Harriet Martineau, had no patience with the courtesies and deference shown to American women by American men. "Indulgence," she said, "is given her as a substitute for justice."

Higher living standards, better health, more home appliances, and less back-breaking work all slowly changed the lot of American women. As women came to enjoy the spending of household money, they began to be wooed as consumers. Yet they remained, exalted and abased, within their own domestic sphere. Women were looked up to as the civilizers of a frontier nation and as moral custodians in the home. For practical purposes, they were excluded from business, politics, and labor. When women did break into public life late in the nineteenth century, it was as the scourge of bottle and brothel.

Women's sphere, it is true, extended beyond the home. It included the school board. (In Kentucky, as early as 1838, women had the vote for school matters, and several other states followed this by the 1880s.) It ran to the church, to the hospital, to the library, to the museum, and to the art gallery. The tasks involved were either extensions of what women did at home or considered notably feminine, one reason that treating the arts as effeminate took an unusually long time dying in America. And when, much later, middle-class women did begin to leave the home and join the labor force in large numbers, their work, tending, as it did, to concentrate on the "nurturing" jobs, such as teaching and nursing, did not compete directly with men's.

This tidy doctrine of two spheres has been thrown down. Women were once exalted as guardians of the home but debased for their dependence and their exclusion from the world of proper work. This attitude could not survive one of the biggest social changes in modern America: the massive movement of women in recent years into the labor force. The proportion of women at work has grown, at varying paces, throughout the century. Today, more than half of American women over the age of sixteen are in jobs or looking for work. It would be extraordinary if the old rules for thinking about women and men did apply. Nothing agreed upon has emerged to take their place. To feminism and its supporters, the division of sex should be stripped away; at the very least, for them, men and women should share equally the inequalities of money, race, or background. To the conservative reaction, the old ideas of a masculine and a feminine sphere still exert a considerable pull. To them the quandary is sharp: Should women be praised now for their industry or damned for their man-hating destruction of the hearth?

"Women's rights are as American as apple pie," said a delegate at the Houston conference. Her words would have surprised the drafters of the Bill of Rights. American women played a remarkably small public part in the affairs of the early republic, and even their recorded private influence was small. New Jersey allowed women taxpayers to vote under its first state constitution, but this was exceptional, and may have slipped in by mistake. The right was withdrawn in 1807. Perhaps recognizing how long and how hard women's rights had had to be fought for, the speaker may have intended her words ironically.

Throughout the conference there were passing historical references, of an emblematic sort, to earlier feminists. The chairman's gavel was used originally at a women's franchise meeting in Washington eighty-one years previously by the famous temperance and suffrage campaigner Susan B. Anthony. In Houston, at one point, an elderly delegate from Florida went up on stage and was introduced as Anthony's great-niece. The delegates cheered wildly, in sentimental homage to the past. Had other descendants been rounded up, there could have been an instructive historical tableau of early feminism.

There were the Grimké sisters, daughters of Southern slave owners. They became Quakers, freed their slaves, and preached emancipation. There was Elizabeth Cady Stanton. On her way to the antislavery convention in London in 1840, she sat opposite a fellow passenger who lectured her about the natural inferiority of women while she beat him at chess. At the convention, she and Lucretia Mott, the organizer of stores in Philadelphia that sold only stuff made and grown by nonslave labor, were not, as women, allowed on the floor. Returning to America, they began campaigning not just for slaves but for women. Their draft of the Seneca Falls Declaration of Rights and Sentiments in 1848 amended Jefferson: "All men and women are created equal."

There was Lucy Stone, briefly a student at Oberlin, the first college to admit women and blacks. She spoke for the Anti-Slavery Society and founded the *Women's Journal.* When she married, in 1855, she kept her maiden name. Then there were the Claflin sisters. Tennessee was a spiritualist who made a small fortune as a stockbroker with the help of railroad tycoon Cornelius Vanderbilt, who dabbled in the occult himself. Her weekly paper supported woman suffrage, free love, and socialism. Her sister, Victoria Woodhull, was the first woman to try for the White House. She ran in 1872, with Frederick Douglass as her vice-presidential candidate, for the People's party.

Charlotte Perkins Gilman, among a later generation of feminists, was one of the first to think hard about women and work. She was a protégé of Lester Ward and was influenced by the Fabians in Britain. Her study of women's work inside and outside the home led her to believe that women could only be equal with men when housework was fully socialized. For middle-class women, at least, freedom of sorts from housework was about to come with Heinz's canned food, the Sears catalogue, and the vacuum cleaner. Another great liberation for women was the nineteenth-century drop in fertility. This fell, from 1800 to 1900, by a half, relieving American women of the dangers and burdens of unlimited childbearing. Together these changes made possible the first wave of feminism by giving middle-class women at large something they had not had before—time.

Their targets were the brothel and the saloon. The first threatened women's self-respect, the second their livelihood. The social purity movement campaigned not simply to regulate prostitution, as in France, but to abolish it altogether. War against the second-oldest profession had mixed results. The clearest and most lasting, if legend is to be believed, was the closing of New Orleans's red-light district, which sent jazz upriver to Saint Louis and Chicago. Of far greater effect was temperance. The Woman's Christian Temperance Union, founded by Frances Willard in 1874, grew to enormous weight. There was already a convert in the White House. "Lemonade Lucy," the wife of President Rutherford B. Hayes, served no alcohol at official dinners. Waiters would sneak it in inside frozen punches, but the secretary of state still refused to invite diplomats to Lemonade Lucy's dry functions. The temperance movement was Republican, anti-Democrat, and anti-immigrant. As the movement grew, it did not always look favorably on woman suffrage. When Susan B. Anthony addressed the WCTU in 1881 on the franchise, many of its more conservative members left in protest.

Yet the streams did join. Not least because the chauvinist undertones of the temperance movement extended to arguments for giving white, American-born women the vote. "Think of Patrick and Sambo and Hans and Ung Tung," wrote Elizabeth Cady Stanton, "who do not know the difference between a monarchy and a republic and who never read the Declaration of Independence or Webster's spelling book, making laws for Lydia Marcia Child, Lucretia Mott, or Fanny Kemble." Susan B. Anthony showed indifference to principle in selecting a printer for her newspaper *Revolution*, with its famous motto: "Men their rights and nothing more; women their rights and nothing less." Though the newspaper supported efforts to unionize women, it was, to save cost, produced at a nonunion printing shop that employed scab labor.

Largely as a stunt to attract national attention, Wyoming Territory granted women the vote in 1869. Colorado, Idaho, and Utah followed in the 1890s, the latter to maintain Mormon supremacy. Eight other states, mainly in the West, but including New York, followed by 1917. Extravagant claims were made on both sides. The head of the Aero Club of America warned that woman suffrage would mean "the dilution with the qualities of the cow, of the qualities of the bull upon which the herd's safety must depend."

When a reluctant President Wilson finally agreed in 1918 to give his backing to the suffrage amendment (he had for some time considered the women's vote as a matter for the individual states), this was the overdue success for a waning movement. Few women voted at first. Women's lives did not greatly change. Elizabeth Cady Stanton had always doubted how much difference the franchise for women would make on its own. By the time the Nineteenth Amendment was ratified, in August 1920, its immediate predecessor, banning the manufacture and sale of alcoholic beverages, was already in effect. A younger, equally independent-minded generation of young women was coming to the fore. They were not at all sure what to make of these fruits of nineteenth-century feminism. What they were chiefly after was a drink.

And a husband. After the war, the model for women became the wife-companion. Marriage manuals began putting a new emphasis on romantic love. Children, for the first time, came to be seen as problems. Parents were encouraged to turn to professionals on how to cope. Marriage, Americans were told, was for love and sex. Colleges opened their gates to women. By 1920, two-fifths of graduates were women, although most of these had degrees in domestic science and child rearing. Sororities flourished. The pressure of extracurricular activities (which meant just about anything) was on women to become interesting wife-companions. Sociologists went to Nebraska to study dating rituals. The change was reflected in magazine advertising. By 1931, there were more advertisements in the *Ladies' Home Journal* for cosmetics than for food. As an article on "Our Booming Beauty Business" in 1930 began: "The average American woman has sixteen square feet of skin."

All this was liberating in its own way. The grandmothers of the progressive woman of the 1920s railed against the saloon; her mother marched for women's franchise. She asserted her independence by smoking, drinking, and lifting her hemline, by turning herself into the "sexual object" her daughter or granddaughter would come to deride.

Another current was flowing at the same time. Women were entering the labor force in large numbers. This slowed with the Great Depression, but it did not stop. "Get the men back to work" was the order of the day in the 1930s. Women's jobs came second. In 1932, a standing order was promulgated imposing dismissals in federal jobs on spouses first. Three-quarters of those laid off were women. During the New Deal, public day care centers were established, in a limited way, but this was more to give sacked teachers jobs than to encourage women to leave the home and work. "Rosie the riveter" became a national symbol when the Second World War sucked women into industrial work. The coming of peace did not, as is often thought, mean a drop in the female labor force. Between 1940 and 1950, the proportion of women in the labor force increased, from 27 percent to 31 percent. After the war, about 2.25 million women did leave the labor force to return home, as the demobilized veterans returned to claim their old jobs. Yet 2.75 million new women workers came into the labor force in this period. While the traditional pattern of sexual segregation returned, with men doing men's work and women doing women's, the number of women in the labor force continued to climb.

For women, however, the postwar period is thought of as a time of babies and suburbs, not jobs. Up to a point, this is true. The years between 1946 and 1964 were prolific. In 1946, the birth rate (for women aged fifteen to forty-four) jumped to its level before the Great Depression. It continued to rise, peaking in 1957 and falling off in 1964, after which there was a sharp drop. In 1957, American women were producing children at a rate not matched since before World War I. This rate, stretched theoretically over women's childbearing years, would have been almost enough to provide the average American family with four children. This highly unusual population increase was coupled with another very important social change in American life that bore with particular directness on women. This was the rapid growth of city suburbs. In fact, two-thirds of the population increase between 1950 and 1960 occurred there. Not all of this increase, of course, was due to suburban births. Many families were moving to the suburbs as well.

Suburbs were underwritten by conscious government policy to boost the construction industry as a hedge against a second economic depression, which was widely feared with the return to a peacetime economy. This policy involved federally guaranteed, low-cost mortgages and the federal sponsorship of a massive highway building program. Families flocked to the suburbs for many different reasons, but the appeal of better family life, with a privacy unheard of for most Americans, undoubtedly played a large part. Real estate agents advertised houses with large master bedrooms, where away from the children, husbands and wives, or whoever, encouraged by greater frankness and enlightenment, could lead ever more adventurous sexual lives.

The suburbs quickly became a governing symbol of modern American middle-class life, filmed, written about, and analyzed. The more prosperous suburbs were in many respects a triumphant American success, providing those who already lived in them with widely undisputed status and those who did not with something to aspire to. For Americans who wanted to live there but could not afford to, suburban life was to be envied. For Americans who did live there, as the early critics of suburban life copiously pointed out, the besetting sin was complacency. Yet were not those who enjoyed suburban living right to be content? For women especially, the suburbs seemed to offer the opportunity, postponed by depression and world war, to become the ideal wife-companion. What the American young woman of the 1920s was abruptly cheated of, her daughter, in the 1950s, would be able, in unimagined abundance, to enjoy.

This is not quite how it turned out. The housewife maturing in the suburbs was also the granddaughter of the suffragette. Successful and attractive as they were, the suburbs, both in legend and in fact, became the origin for the second wave of modern feminism. As women without jobs spent days as well as nights in the suburbs, it was not difficult to see that women were somehow at the center of the suburban predicament. Late in the 1950s, a graduate of prestigious Smith College, sensing a puzzling but pervasive dissatisfaction among her friends, began interviewing classmates from 1942. The result was a book that did much to set the intellectual tone in which the 1960s women's movement grew. *The Feminine Mystique*, by Betty Friedan, came out in 1963. In it, the author argued that the model of the wife-companion had failed, both in the bedroom—with Freudian psychiatrists taking, indirectly, much of the blame—and in the nursery too, where "the curse of lack of self-direction and self-satisfaction in the mother would be visited on the children." The book was written with the preoccupations of middle-class women in mind. In many senses, this was not a political book. The concerns were personal, individual, rather than social. Yet Friedan's answer to her subjects' predicament was in the feminist tradition: Take charge of your own life. In practical terms, Friedan argued, this first of all meant going out to work, although she has lately seemed to have changed her mind. The argument had come full circle. Elizabeth Cady Stanton and those other early feminists who argued that the suffrage alone would not much change women's lot seemed to have been proved right. The time had come for their granddaughters to pick up where they had left off.

Looking back from the Houston women's conference, an observer could find plenty of evidence to suggest that the lot of American women had changed considerably in the ten years or so since the postwar women's movement began. A precise date for this would be a fiction, but a convenient reference point is the founding of the National Organization for Women in 1966. To the eye and ear, the most striking change was a sweeping rectification of names. In the space of a few years, the vocabulary of the sexes radically changed. Efforts were made to purge speech and writing of gender-specific words and replace them with gender-neutral ones. Considering how languages resist, this purification in the name of women was astonishingly successful.

Old gender-specific terms such as "chairman," "stewardess," "housewife," and "husband" had to compete with "chairperson," "flight attendant," "homemaker," and "spouse." Early Quakers, it is said, rejected "Mr." because it was a contraction for "Master," and calling each other "Master" offended their egalitarian sensibilities. By a similar token, "Mrs." and "Miss" were rejected for telling more about the bearer's marital status than the uninformative "Mr.," applied to bachelors and married men alike. "Ms." was coined to repair the discrimination, gained partial currency, and in 1972 became the name of the most durable of the feminist magazines. The prefix "Ms." was included, the same year, together with the new term "liberated woman" and the overarching notion of sexism, in an American Heritage dictionary for schools. In 1973, the Government Printing Office in Washington accepted "Ms." as an alternative title and a year later the book and magazine publisher McGraw-Hill, aware of its market, put out a nonsexist stylebook for copy editors. Maiden names became an issue again. Teresa Shoemaker took hers all the way to the Supreme Court of Washington State, which allowed her to keep it. The battle of words produced some powerful sponsors. United Technologies, a conglomerate whose subsidiaries employ many women, bought expensive advertising space in papers and magazines in 1979 to deliver a small homily against using the demeaning word "girl" to describe a woman.

The term "sexism" was derived by analogy with "racism," to mean prejudice on the grounds of sex. A similar transformation occurred in the late 1960s with the way Americans spoke and wrote about blacks, as the term "Negro," in print at least, virtually vanished. Later, the term "gay" widely replaced "fag" or ruder variants as a spoken alternative to "homosexual," although when it came to the printed word, the battle lines were drawn. The University of Chicago Press, something of an authority in matters of style, included the word in the title of a history of homosexuality in Christianity. The *Wall Street Journal's* stylebook rejects the term, except in quotations. It is tempting for practical-minded Americans to dismiss such changes as so much talk. In a sense, they are. Habits of thought change more slowly than usage. Nonetheless, without such terms as "sexism," victims of the prejudice, male or female, could hardly begin thinking about, let alone remedying, sexual discrimination. When Betty Friedan first wrote, she called it "the problem that has no name."

As remarkable as the baptism of the problem was the speed of its recognition, once named. *Time* and *Newsweek* did cover stories on the women's movement in 1971. Two years later, Dr. Benjamin Spock denounced sexism and issued a new, nonsexist edition of his best-selling manual on raising babies, an American standby since it first appeared twenty-seven years earlier. *Time* celebrated the year of the woman in 1975 by making women its "Man of the Year."

There was more graspable change as well. Women began breaking into male preserves at work. Eleven women were ordained into the Episcopal Church. Sally Priesand became the first woman rabbi. The Navy got its first female helicopter pilot, the astronauts their first female trainee, and the nuclear power industry its first female engineer. Janet Guthrie raced in the Indianapolis 500 and Beverly Sills refused to sing at the Met in New York until Sarah Caldwell was invited to conduct. Shortly after his election, President Reagan fulfilled his pledge to nominate a woman for the Supreme Court; Sandra Day O'Connor assumed the bench soon after.

Women also began standing on their own in politics. The "widow's mandate"—that tradition by which the only dependable road for women to enter politics was in taking over a job from a dead husband —was no longer as strong as it had been. In 1972, Shirley Chisholm ran for the Democratic nomination. Ella Grasso of Connecticut later became the first woman elected as state governor in her own right. The Democratic party felt the tide. In 1972, 40 percent of the delegates to its convention in Miami were women, as against 13 percent at the tumult in Chicago four years earlier. By 1980, this had risen by party rule to a statutory 50 percent. Women everywhere are less an exception in politics than they were, although their representation nationally is still pitifully small. In the three and a half decades after the Second World War, the number of women in the U.S. Senate was never more than three; in the House of Representatives never more than twenty. Yet in the states, where many political changes in the federal system often have their start, there are signs of more rapid change.

Differences in the voting behavior of men and women have changed since the early days when women won the vote. After 1920, women did not initially vote their numbers. Though still measurable, the gap between men and women voter turnout has narrowed apprecia-bly. Women remain notably more "dovish" than men in poll answers and voting preferences. This not only bears out thousands of years of folk wisdom, but reflects the fact that social spending, usually in competition for money for the military, tends to help women as a group more than men. In the Vietnam law and order election of 1972, women voted more heavily than men for Senator George McGovern, the losing Democrat. In 1980, they voted less heavily than men for Ronald Reagan. This admittedly important distinction aside, the differences in political attitudes between men and women as a whole are rapidly shrinking.

Much of the recent progress for women's rights has been entrenched in law, although, as much of this law is court-made, how deeply entrenched it is remains open to future courts to decide. Courts have ruled that companies cannot refuse to hire women with small children unless they do the same for fathers; that women cannot be summarily excluded for their sex from jury duty; that the armed forces cannot peremptorily discharge a pregnant servicewoman.

The legislative high point for the women's movement came during the Ninety-second Congress, between 1971 and 1973. Besides voting for ERA, Congress extended the Equal Pay Act to the professions, empowered the Equal Employment Opportunities Commission to sue in court against sex discrimination, and prohibited sex discrimination in schools or colleges getting federal funds. A child-care bill was passed by this Congress, to give help to less well-off women, but this was vetoed by President Nixon. Removal of restrictions on credit enabled women who could afford it to take out their own mortgages far more freely than in the past. By 1980, women by themselves had become a significant share of the property-owning market. Builders even began putting up specially designed houses for single women with children, to share with others in the same position.

A new executive order required businesses with federal contracts to start preferential hiring of women and racial-minority employees, the effective beginning of affirmative action. There were many landmark sex-discrimination cases, including a successful challenge to Corning Glass Works. The men's bar of the Biltmore Hotel in New York was opened to women. Hiring at *Newsweek* and the American Stock Exchange was made more open to them as well. Most famous of all, perhaps, Ma Bell—AT&T—made a $75 million settlement for women employees, including some $20 million in back pay, with the Equal Employment Opportunities Commission (EEOC) and the Labor Department. *Reader's Digest,* a much smaller company, was obliged to pay $1.5 million. Other businesses quickly got the message and began to improve hiring practices. Yet in other ways, the EEOC was judged a failure, for its huge backlog of cases, its slowness and ineffectiveness, a curious criticism of a small federal agency doing its best to bend large social forces simply by legal writ and often with almost no political support.

These several changes for American women were welcomed by many and greeted by others with ridicule or resentment. To think that the lot of American women has irrevocably changed because of them would be as misleading as to treat the second wave of feminism as simply a passing fad. For underlying these changes is a transformation in the pattern of women's work that ensures that the old American ideas about men and women must be replaced, even if there is still sharp disagreement about what the new ideas should be.

Women's work causes strong passions. Early on in the modern women's movement, work outside the home tended to be offered as an escape from the emptiness of housekeeping, a release from the inferior sphere of women, and an entry into the respected, male world of real production. By the opposite token, women's work, for antifeminists, threatened to loosen America's already worn family patchwork, jeopardizing motherhood, children, and eventually women themselves. The one side tended to exaggerate the liberating effect of women's work, just as the other greatly overplayed its corrosive power.

Both also made the bigger mistake of casting the transformation of women's work as a matter of individual choice rather than as the result of broader economic pressures. There are some fortunate women for whom taking a job or not is a marginal proposition. It is such women that profeminists like Betty Friedan and antifeminists like Midge Decter seemed to have in mind when they alternatively cheered and jeered these women's preference for a job to the home. For the great majority of women pouring willy-nilly into the job market in the past years, going out to get a job was neither a matter of whim nor something to spite their men, put into their heads by feminists, but the simple, all-American question of earning a living.

To see how radically the pattern of women's work has changed, it is necessary to look at some figures. In the five years after the 1975 recession, the American economy produced 12.1 million jobs, more jobs then there are in Sweden and Australia put together. Of these new jobs, women accounted for 7.6 million. Women's share of the labor force has grown accordingly. In 1950, women made up less than 30 percent of the adult labor force aged sixteen or over. Thirty years later, 43 percent of the adult labor force was made up of women. Put another way, in 1950, two out of every three women stayed at home and did not work for a living. By 1980, one woman was out at work for every one at home—startling figures when it is realized that many of those at home were past working age or only temporarily out of the work force, to care for small children.

As every woman who works knows, this way of putting it is still not quite right. For a woman at work does not cease to run a house. She must look after either herself alone or, more frequently, her working husband and children, too. The essential fact to grasp about modern American women is not simply that they work, but that they overwork. Women are today's workaholics, quite as much as are office-drunk male executives. Nor is the affliction self-imposed. As the Stanford historian Carl Degler, in *At Odds: Women and the Family in America from the Revolution to the Present,* puts it: "Women's work . . . is still shaped around the family while the family is still shaped around the work of men." Women are being pushed out to work, yet they do not thereby lose their responsibilities to children, family, and home. This is their true predicament. Women's work, to use Degler's phrase, is "at odds" with the family. Conservative antifeminists seem to hope the matter could be solved by women's returning to their traditional roles. Some feminists are reluctant to accept the family/job problem as a genuine dilemma, since this might discourage women from working. Others frankly recognize the predicament but argue that the way out is through a greater sharing between men and women of the burdens of the home.

How did women's work come to be at odds with the family? Traditionally, young American-born women worked before marriage, after which they left the labor force often for good or until their husbands died and they were obliged to support themselves. This at least was the standard pattern of work for white women, other than immigrants. Whether under slavery or in the free labor market, black married women have always worked. Unlike white women, they could not rely on large enough incomes from their husbands to support themselves and their children. For white women, life was more fortunate. In 1890, for example, less than 14 percent of white women in the labor force were married and more than half of them were under age twenty-four. Throughout the twentieth century, the proportion of married and older women in the labor force has grown. The results of this important shift are clear. By 1970, two-thirds of all women in the labor force were married and only one out of every four was under twenty-four.

More recently, there has been an even more startling change for women of peak childbearing years (25–34). After the Second World War, women in this age group tended to leave the labor force. Between 1950 and 1960, the proportion of 25–34-year-old women in the labor force fell from 22.3 percent to 17.8 percent. The share of women 20–24 fell as well. This fits the earlier account of many women leaving the labor force to have children, while other women, in rather larger numbers, took their place in the labor force, if not in the same jobs. The large growth in the female labor force at this period was in women forty-four years old and over.

This pattern changed in the harder economic times of the past decade. Whereas in 1960 less than 30 percent of the women in the labor force were between twenty and thirty-four, by 1980 this childbearing age group accounted for more than two-fifths of the women at work or looking for a job. Not surprisingly, the number of young women with young children who were working rose as well. In 1960, the proportion of women at work with children under six years of age was below 20 percent. By 1980, this was 43 percent. In that year, more than half of all women with children under seventeen were at work.

The transformation of women's work that underlies the second wave of feminism could be summarized in the following way: At the beginning of the century, getting married, having children, and growing old were all protections for women against having to go out and work for themselves. By the last quarter of the century, these three protections had each been slowly stripped away. In the first half of 1980, two-thirds of all women 20–44 were in the labor force; three in every five women 45–54 were at work or looking for it; and despite earlier retirement for women, two in five women 55–64 were still in the labor force.

These are patterns common to most Western industrial countries, yet certain American peculiarities of attitude color how the transformation in women's work is treated. The leading peculiarity is the American belief, to which American women are no longer immune, that the path to salvation is through a paying job. This prevailing idea makes it very difficult to see that there may be people—mothers and housewives, perhaps—who would ideally prefer not to go out to work but do so because they have to. If work is salvation, then work is desirable. Nobody must be forced to do what is desirable. Women who go out to work, therefore, do so because they want to. That is the logic, give or take a premise or two, of work-conscious America.

The arguments about women's work could be put on a more realistic footing if its often unappealing, second-rate character were better appreciated. For most women, the passage from home to work is full of costs. Children must be taken care of, there is less time in the house, less time with one's husband. Daily life becomes an exacting logistical test. Nor is work itself all that it is sometimes made out to be. To understand the transformation in women's work one must also grasp the kinds of jobs that have recently been taken by women. Job for job, women remain second-class workers compared with men.

As against men, women are still very badly paid—particularly undereducated women. Even more striking is the fact that women today are more tightly segregated into a few categories of job, thought to constitute "women's work," than the few who worked were at the beginning of the century. Women, being less well trained, have, on the whole, fewer skills than men that are easily marketed in the labor force. Their work outside the home for pay is still remarkably like their unpaid work inside the home. Women are concentrated in "nurturing" jobs, if one includes as such secretarial work which involves looking after a boss. They continue to account for at least seventeen out of every twenty workers in nursing, elementary school teaching, secretarial work, and waiting on table. These, moreover, are just the sort of low-paid, service-sector jobs that have expanded most in recent years. As the population ages, demographers expect fewer elementary school teachers for the young and more nurses for the old. There is little reason to believe the pattern of sexual segregation in employment, separate and unequal, will much change.

This surprisingly constant pattern is masked by the breaking up of certain male professional near-monopolies. If the overall picture for American women is at best mixed, for professional women the past couple of decades have been good. In 1960, 16.4 percent of accountants, 3.3 percent of lawyers and judges, and 6.8 percent of physicians were women. By 1980, the corresponding figures were 36.2 percent of accountants, 12.8 percent of lawyers, and 13.4 percent of physicians (as against 75 percent of physicians in the Soviet Union, where, outside politics, sexual equality is more advanced than in capitalist countries). Yet even among professional women, there is a long way to go. Pay, on average 60 percent of men's, is not significantly better than for women workers in general. The higher women reach in the professions, the harder the going becomes. One notable difficulty for a young woman professional is that her peak childbearing years coincide with that period in a career when the smart prospects in a profession are moving on to the fast track. Such young women can be heard discussing whether it is psychologically better for a small child to have the mother in attendance in the first or the second year. It is taken for granted that the aspiring professional can take only one year off from work. The question is to pick which year is most helpful to the child.

Also, it is said that even the brightest women, by reason of steady conditioning, are often less ready than their more aggressive male counterparts to take the risks—in their thinking or their business dealings—that a highly competitive, free-market society especially values. There may be something in this, but not much. Taking risks is how free-market apologists like to think modern capitalists act, but the behavior of the large corporations does not bear them out. General Motors, Chrysler, and Ford were timid about bringing out small cars, the big steel companies about introducing new technology, until they had to. It would be hard to persuade even the simpleminded that only one of Fortune's 500 largest industrial corporations is headed by a woman because women are reluctant to take risks.

Despite these real and assumed handicaps, the role of professional women has altered. Indeed, as college-educated young women have begun to try the professional rat race, there are young men beginning to question whether it is really worth it. A noble few stay home to mind the house and the children while their wives go out to work. To the extent that men and women in this relatively privileged group are able to feel less imprisoned by the social presumptions of their gender, this is a genuine, if limited, step toward greater equality. Just as it is wrong to deny the real change that has swept over America during the past twenty or thirty years for middle-class blacks, so it is foolish to deny that professional women have made great strides. The change is not likely to be easily reversed. The great creative mirror of America that shows it as it would like to be—television advertising—has in recent years retouched the portrait of the American woman. There are still smiling actresses mopping floors and washing collars, but there are plenty of working women, by no means all pretty and lithe, out and about, looking after themselves. That itself is a big difference.

Still, it is important to bear in mind how relatively small is the group of women being talked about. Of some 43 million women in the labor force in 1979, 6.5 million had professional or technical jobs. Not so bad, it seems, until on closer inspection it turns out that 3.4 million of these were either nurses or teachers. High-paid professionals—physicians, lawyers, and so forth—accounted for only 7 percent of the female labor force. If judged by the increase in the opportunities for success of a few, then American women, in the words of the well-known cigarette advertisement, have "come a long way" at work. Women in good jobs, for example, are finding that seniority pays off. But judged by the sterner test of equality, women's work in America this century has seemed in quality, though not quantity, surprisingly resistant to change.

By repute, women workers are likely to report sick, miss work, or call in to say they must stay home to mind the children. Knowing this, many women are particularly anxious that their job must be seen to come first, the house and its duties second. Men, but not women, can be counted on to answer the boss's call first, or so it is commonly believed. As the need for women to work has grown, so has the pressure on women to conceal, if not decry, the pleasures of the house as petty and second-rate.

This distortion would probably have occurred even in the absence of a women's movement eager to create, especially for the aspiring middle-class woman, a sense of professional self-esteem. Nevertheless, antifeminists like Midge Decter and George Gilder, who are inclined to see working women as cakewinners rather than breadwinners, have used the degraded status of housework as a stick with which to beat the women's movement. They blame the movement for fostering a climate in which women are encouraged to think that minding the house is inferior to taking a job.

How rewarding is running a house? In terms of cash, not at all.

Housework is unpaid. Yet cash is not everything. Keeping house is full of pleasures for the keepers and the kept. Americans are a hospitable and house-proud people. Travelers who despair of finding a decent hotel or a good meal quickly discover that the best place to be entertained is in Americans' own homes. It is strange that swirling against the tide carrying women into the labor market is a torrent of culinary and decorative advice washing daily onto the breakfast table from newspapers' "Living" or "Home" sections, which encourage today's Americans to try to recreate a manner of living that passed with the Gilded Age, the household servant, and the garden-grown vegetable. This is a curious reversal in the evolution of American housework, which points, generally speaking, in the direction of ever more unlikely and ingenious mechanization. There were warnings of a countertrend in the 1960s when Stewart Brand's democratic and populist *Whole Earth Catalogue,* pushing today's Americans even further back in time, offered its readers advice about how to make their own clothes, teach their own children to spell, or can their own fruits and vegetables.

By and large, American housework has been a story of mechanical contrivance. Gadgets of the kind Richard Sears began advertising in his 1894 catalogue not only freed housework of much of its drudgery; they also replaced the household servant as surely as McCormick's reaper replaced the field hand. The proportion of household servants, having peaked in the 1870s, fell sharply in the first two decades after 1900. The American kitchen became the envy of the world.

How much time did the gadgetry really save? And more important for women, whose time was it? Running a house, even with the most lavish array of modern devices, is still time-consuming, as John Robinson's 1979 study of housework conducted for Cleveland State University indicated. This survey also underlines that in America it is women, not men, who bear the double burden of overwork. The survey recorded hours of housework done each week by working men, working women, and women at home who did not go out to work. The time spent on housework by the housewives fell, according to the study, from an average of fifty hours in 1965 to forty-four hours in 1975; for working men, shamed perhaps by the mood of the times, it crept up from nine to ten hours; for working women the load fell by five hours, but in 1975, the average working woman was still doing twenty-one hours, more than twice as much as the average working man.

The burden of women's double work is hardly new. Charlotte Perkins Gilman, the early-twentieth-century feminist, thought that women would not be free to compete equally with men until housework was socialized. She was right about the problem but, as far as America goes, wrong about the probable solution. The route of government action is just about the least likely to be tried. So far, almost all efforts toward the limited goal of federally funded child care have come to naught. This does not necessarily mean the future is entirely bleak.

Kathleen Newland, the author of several studies of women's lot worldwide, thinks it is a mistake to underestimate the fluidity of American society, its openness to new ideas, and its readiness to improvise. Some men, she points out, are already sharing the burdens of housework more equally with women, with no obvious inducement or pressure from government. About half of all Americans today tell pollsters they believe the most "satisfying" marriages are those in which both the husband and the wife work and both share in child rearing and housework. If they mean what they say, and the fashion has become a habit, women themselves could be surprised by the speed of change once it comes. Even if it happens tomorrow morning, the change will be overdue. The pressure of work, housework and overwork, is perhaps at least partly responsible for women's taking 80 percent of the amphetamines prescribed by doctors, two-thirds of the tranquilizers, and three-fifths of the barbiturates.

The leader of the antifeminists at Houston, Phyllis Schlafly, is a crisp public performer with obvious political talents. Displaying a keen sense of how best to annoy her opponents, she publicly made a point of thanking her husband, a Saint Louis lawyer, for giving her permission to leave home and organize the counter-rally. Despite this deliberately irritating piece of political theater, Mrs. Schlafly's place is not at the sink and never has been. Her whole career as the defender of the American housewife is something of a paradox. She led the counter-attack against the Equal Rights Amendment and the women's movement, whose followers she derided as "Typhoid Marys carrying a germ called lost identity." And yet, with the political signs reversed, Mrs. Schlafly is the very model of what many independent-minded middle-class American women aspire to. As a former leader of the National

Organization for Women told *People* magazine: "If I had a daughter, I'd like her to be a housewife just like Phyllis Schlafly."

Mrs. Schlafly is a Midwestern Republican conservative of the type that used to make Eastern Republicans' teeth grate. She was born in Saint Louis. The engineering business her father worked for went under in the Depression. To help the family through, her mother worked at women's jobs in the local department store, the school, the library, and the art museum. After Catholic school, the young Phyllis Stewart went to Washington University, worked in an arms plant during the war, and later won a scholarship to Radcliffe. Back home, she went to work for a bank. She attracted the attention of a wealthy lawyer, Fred Schlafly, interested, like her, in conservative politics. They married and had six children. Most are now grown. When Phyllis Schlafly is out crusading, a housekeeper looks after her husband and their twelve-room house across the Mississippi from Saint Louis. During their engagement, Fred Schlafly wrote a doggerel verse for her: "Cover girl with executive know-how/You don't desire a home now/-For *Küche, Kirche* and *Kinder*/Will surely a career hinder."

Mr. Schlafly could hardly have been more wrong. From this traditional female trinity, Mrs. Schlafly fashioned a highly successful political career. To begin with, however, she concentrated on the large, male subjects, such as defense and Russian subversion. During the great anti-Communist fear, she did research for Senator McCarthy, and later a radio program, *America, Wake Up!*, which was not a breakfast news program but warned of the perils of creeping socialism. Convinced that Robert McNamara, the Ford boss President Kennedy appointed to modernize the Defense Department, was undermining American forces, Mrs. Schlafly collaborated with a retired admiral to write a book attacking the "gravediggers" at the Pentagon. This was one of several books in which she scrutinized public figures to the left of Senator Barry Goldwater, her political idol. The best known is her campaign book for Goldwater, *A Choice Not an Echo*, which came out in time for his disastrous 1964 presidential campaign. Like many conservative Republicans, Mrs. Schlafly seemed to have taken a historic wrong turn. In 1967, she lost her attempt to become president of the National Federation of Republican Women. She left to form her own group, The Eagles Are Flying, at a moment when one might have thought that her brand of conservatism had had its day.

"The sweetheart of the silent majority," as her biographer calls her, was only just beginning. The growth of the women's movement and the congressional passage of ERA gave her the targets she had been waiting for. As civil rights protests and antiwar feeling died away, the conservative reaction found a new focus. At first, Mrs. Schlafly failed to grasp the potential of the women's movement. She was preoccupied with berating President Nixon and his national security adviser, Henry Kissinger, for selling America out, as conservatives saw it, to the Russians. On this, Mrs. Schlafly was a little ahead of her time. Mainstream opinion then supported détente with the Soviet Union. Her attacks on it seemed quaint. Her husband suggested that she turn her attention to the women's movement and ERA. All fell into place, and Mrs. Schlafly's crusade against modern feminism began.

The arguments Mrs. Schlafly publicized against ERA with such success were simple, some would say simpleminded, but they were potent. Two of those most frequently used were that women might be drafted if the amendment succeeded and that women would be equally responsible for the finances of the house (even though many states have laws that place liability for a couple's debts on whoever best can pay). These arguments were really beside the point. Mrs. Schlafly's appeal did not rest on persuasive skill so much as on her ability to voice a mood. ERA, like abortion later, was to her followers a symbol, a shorthand, a convenient abbreviation for a small world of prejudices, principles, and resentments.

The counterfeminists were not without more solid intellectual defenses. Midge Decter, an editor and a writer from New York, wrote a fierce polemic, *The New Chastity*, published as a book in 1972, against the women's movement. Decter and her husband, Norman Podhoretz, the editor of *Commentary*, were among the New York group that led the intellectual Thermidor known as neoconservatism. Often more biting than clear, Decter's book mocked, harried, and attempted to expose humbug in women's liberation. It contributed strongly to the intellectual climate in which, at the end of the 1970s, women's liberation found itself on the defensive.

The core of Decter's argument is that the true grievance of the women's movement was not that women are "mistreated, discriminated against, oppressed and enslaved," but that they are women. Decter agreed with the women's movement credo that housework was never-ending, but she denied that it was empty and unfulfilling. The true complaint the movement had against the work was not that it was too demanding, but that it was too monotonous. As for sexual relations with men, Decter argued, the women's movement exaggerated the significance of the clitoral orgasm and the supposed dispensability of men, a point that many women's liberationists could have readily agreed with. The true sexual complaint of the women's movement, according to Decter, is that women nowadays are having to bestow sexual favors on men without in return getting the power American women in the past are supposed to have enjoyed of civilizing and controlling them.

To women at work Decter says, in effect, that they should not complain if they find the competition with men difficult and caring for the house on the side taxing, since they are volunteers with no need to work. As for children, she believes that it is women's peculiar destiny to bear them, "their one irrevocable act." The claim of feminists to be victims, she wrote, was really a fear of freedom, the claim that womanliness is imposed by men is a failure to acknowledge their dependence, and the claim that femininity arises from a bad and meretricious culture is an expression of the feminists' self-hatred.

Decter used the technique, expected in a polemic, of pillorying her opponents' weakest arguments rather than attacking their best ones. Nevertheless, she helped to assure feminism a place as a target for intelligent conservatives.

Curiously enough, Decter offered no competing model of her own for the modern American woman. This task fell to a writer, Marabelle Morgan, with no intellectual pretensions whatsoever. Her book, *The Total Woman*, was an extraordinary popular success when it first appeared in 1972 and quickly ran through several paperback editions. By the end of the decade, it had sold more than three and a half million copies, in hardcover and paperback. This defense of tradition relies on the proposition that women are under no pressure to marry, but should, if they do, submit to their husbands. The husband's job is to command, the wife's to obey. Biblical references are supplied in support. "There was no laughter in the Abraham home," Mrs. Morgan wrote, "until Sarah adapted." She goes on: "It is only when a woman surrenders her life to her husband, reveres and worships him, and is willing to serve him, that she becomes really beautiful to him."

Her book is written in short sentences. The language is often cloying (sexual intercourse is called "sweet communion") and bathetic (a description of the author nodding off in a car after supper in Miami Beach while her fiancé proposed to her runs: "My full stomach and the hypnotic rhythm of the waves put me to sleep"). The book assumes that its readers are white suburbanites whose husbands all have office jobs. From the book's central purpose none of this detracts in any way. The contrived artlessness of its tone cannot disguise the fact that it is an extremely cleverly wrought and surely aimed counterfeminist tract.

Much of the book is sensible advice to wives about coping with their lot, assuming that that is what they have chosen to do. It entails learning to manage a husband. Of the book's 225 pages, all but 35, an afterthought about children, are devoted to this. Mrs. Morgan takes two not wholly consistent lines of attack. One is to say that since wives cannot usually change the facts of their marriage (it is an unequal deal, she seems to agree), the best thing to do is to change their attitudes to these facts. Norman Vincent Peale's authority is cited for the power of attitudes to alter facts. This leads Mrs. Morgan to the main piece of advice, known as the "Four A's": wives, she believes, should "accept, admire, adapt and appreciate their husbands."

What Mrs. Morgan presumably meant to write was "adapt to," since it is wives, not husbands, who, on her score, must do the adapting. As one reads on, though, it becomes clear that the slip was unwittingly intended. For running throughout Mrs. Morgan's book is a more manipulative and less submissive message. In all this it is not very difficult to recognize a modern variant of old wisdom, handed down from mothers, aunts, or grandmothers, about managing husbands to wives' advantage. The steps Mrs. Morgan recommends to please husbands are seldom offered without the prospect of certain reward in sight. Contemporary American marriage, as it emerges from the pages of *The Total Woman,* is a constant, unequal struggle in which the wife can never hope to win in open combat, but must continually resort to guile in order to extract what she wants from her remote and reluctant husband. In its view of American marriage, then, *The Total Woman* does not greatly differ from the picture offered by the women's movement of an unequal partnership.

The resourceful and positive-minded Mrs. Morgan also ran a class for adaptive wives. In one of the sessions she advised her pupils to stir their husbands' sexual interest, when it flagged, by greeting them on their return from the office in outré clothes, or perhaps in nothing at all. One graduate followed her advice, she recounts in the book. On her husband's homecoming, the woman "appeared in a sheer lace gown. Her husband was speechless when he opened the front door. The surprise element took him completely off guard. . . . The evening was not only lots of fun, but he also suggested a cruise to Nassau the following week."

The growth in the women's movement coincided with a decline in the birthrate and with a relaxation of sexual and social morals. While both changes occasion excited argument and reaction, it is the more liberal, or looser, moral code that in recent years has done more to push many traditional Americans a bit off balance. Daniel Yankelovich, the indefatigable pollster, has spoken about the shock that Americans, brought up in a country where a booming economy and a restrictive culture were taken for granted, are experiencing in adjusting to a country with a wide-open culture and a restrictive economy. Those who have left to live abroad for a few years have no difficulty in agreeing. The changes they notice on their return often startle them.

An admittedly extreme example is Jeremiah Denton from Mobile, Alabama. On July 18, 1965, three days after his forty-first birthday, he was shot down in Vietnam while leading a group of twenty-four aircraft from the U.S.S. *Independence.* The Vietnamese took him prisoner and he was not released until he was forty-eight years old, having spent seven and a half years in prison camps, four of them in solitary confinement. As a POW he got "as religious as hell" and on his return home in 1973 he said simply: "God Bless America." He quickly found the America he had left was not the America he had come home to. Cinemas were showing X-rated movies of the sort he associated with Scandinavian red-light districts. Pornographic magazines were stacked within easy reach of children in drugstores. The yellow pages accepted advertisements for "outcall massage services." The ever curious Phil Donahue talked about sexual variation on his national television show. A CBS television interviewer calmly discussed with a family from Tacoma the father's incest with a daughter.

Shaken by what he saw as wide-ranging contempt for the "American way of life," Jeremiah Denton resigned his commission in the

United States Navy to organize a group called Coalition for Decency. Though a Catholic, and a critic of the inability or unwillingness of the mostly Protestant Moral Majority to attract black support, he won the backing of both the Moral Majority and its moving spirit, Jerry Falwell, when he ran for and was elected to the United States Senate from Alabama in 1980. Denton is far to the right of mainstream opinion in America. So far to the right, indeed, that many who knew him were not surprised when he was reported—inaccurately, he insists—as saying that the death penalty should be introduced for adultery.

Many of those ready to hail the country's sexual liberation as, on balance, a good thing remain disconcerted by openness about homosexuality. The American Psychiatric Association's removal of homosexuality from its central diagnostic manual of psychiatric illnesses was easy for the broad-minded to tolerate. So was a recommendation in an article in the association's journal that male chauvinism should be included in the same manual, as a treatable complaint. The estimate by sex researcher William Masters that as many as 21 million Americans are homosexual and that one man in three and one woman in five has at some time had homosexual experience causes no surprise thirty years after the publication of the first of the famous Kinsey surveys in 1948. Yet homosexuals still find themselves between acceptance and rejection, and straight America still does not know what to make of Christopher Street in Manhattan, the main street of a gay ghetto, or of Castro Street in San Francisco, where heterosexual men are taken aback to be mocked, usually good-naturedly, as "breeders."

As franker grandparents remind young Americans, the upheaval in social and sexual manners that goes under the general heading of "permissiveness" has, of course, been going on for a long time. It began for the well-off in the 1920s, if not before, and for the rest of America after the Second World War. Cars freed couples from parents' sofas, as attested in a famous Peter Arno cartoon. Contraceptives and penicillin meant that sex unwed was less reliably its own punishment. Though moral change has undoubtedly accelerated in recent years, some of this sensation of speed comes not from people behaving differently but from a new and generally healthy reluctance to conceal what has been going on. In a country where the majority is settling down, a bit older and a bit wiser, despite the Moral Majority, the old inhibitions are giving way to a new, different-strokes-for-different-folks tolerance.

Not all Americans are comfortable with, or ready to tolerate, the relaxation of morals. There are traditionalists convinced that all this is the sign of sickness in American moral and domestic life. They can find plenty of other, for them, symptoms as well. Almost everyone knows that figures for divorce, venereal disease, illegitimacy, teenage pregnancy, teenage alcoholism, teenage drug-taking, and teenage suicide have been rising. Traditionalists feel strongly that they have a case that needs answering and their complaint has been well received among many of the same Americans who listened to George Wallace's antibusing messages and applaud the sometimes crude campaigns waged against Washington by those who seek relocation there through election to the Senate, the House of Representatives, and the White House.

These voters, worried almost as much by the relaxation of morals as they were worried earlier by the relaxation of discrimination against blacks, have tended to be blue-collar, lower-middle-class whites with children in public schools, where delinquency rates rise as test scores fall. Liberal politicians, they came to feel, were too soft on blacks, with whom they had little direct contact, and out of touch with ordinary Americans like themselves. As likely as not Democrats who had grown up in pro–New Deal homes, these parents began to resent government regulations that interfered with their children. Busing for desegregation and the constitutional ban on school prayer made them angriest, but their feeling spread to many areas where it was felt that the government, in pursuit of welfare programs, was treading on the private sphere.

Toleration of homosexuals, especially homosexual teachers, was irksome to the less broad-minded. This fear was effectively played upon in Anita Bryant's successful "Protect America's Children" campaign in Dade County, Florida, the same year as the National Women's Conference in Houston. A Miami initiative protecting local homosexuals from various forms of discrimination in hiring and housing was defeated, as were several similar ordinances elsewhere. That American determination to make sure that schools were not teaching their children anything parents thought wrong reared up with an increase in the censoring of school library stocks and with the demand by religious fundamentalists that the Bible story of creation be given equal time in school science lessons with the theory of evolution.

These drifting, separate, and often contradictory sexual, racial, and educational concerns needed a unifying theme. The symbol of the American family, which suggested the "pro-family" catchphrase, did the job perfectly. A weakening of the American family became the popular diagnosis that unified and seemed to explain these sometimes bewildering symptoms. A return to traditional family values was the widely advertised cure.

Today is hardly the first time that America has suffered a scare about the future of the family. This has happened periodically in the past. There was a similar alarm at the end of the last century, when America was completing its transition from a rural, agricultural, and Anglo-Saxon country to a nation of big cities, industry, and new immigrants. Then, as today, the symptoms were a rising divorce rate, an upheaval in morals, an opening of jobs for women, and a falling birthrate, at least, as Teddy Roosevelt put it, among women "of the higher races." Then, as now, there were tensions, not only between men and women, but between black and white. Then, as now, the American family was used as a code term, as loaded with political meaning as the American flag.

Considering only this symbolic freight it carries, it was hardly surprising that a strong defense should have been mounted on the family's behalf after the rough press it had been getting in America for several decades. The leading character in this drama, the model "nuclear" family, is, strictly speaking, neither traditional nor representative. If historical demographers were forced to pick a single traditional type of American family, it would be the big farm family, although black families, immigrant families, and even old dynastic families still found in the South and New England are all different and all equally traditional. Even today, while it is true that most Americans spend part of their lives in a "nuclear" family consisting of two parents with children, this model family, at any moment, represents less than half the different family households. When the family is argued over, nonetheless, it is usually the nuclear family Americans think about. This family model has undoubtedly taken a beating in recent years from progressive social critics for the cramping and even destructive effects on its members. Such ideas, previously confined to a fairly small stream of critical sociologists and psychologists, had by the early 1970s gained fashionable currency, in the work, for instance, of the American Paul Goodman, the Scot R. D. Laing, and the Englishman David Cooper. Their ideas seemed to underwrite the experiment in communal living, which in turn gained wide publicity. Television, whose stock-in-trade was the soap opera and the marital comedy, also gave the institution of the family a newly critical eye. The Loud family of Santa Barbara caused a national stir in 1971 by virtually talking itself to pieces for the camera in a series aired two years later on public television. Parody followed documentary by mid-decade as *Mary Hartman, Mary Hartman* mocked daytime television's soap operas. This minor American art form, the soap opera, does not itself show family life at its Norman Rockwell simplest, it is true. Like Jacobean tragedies without the numerous and bloody deaths, the "soaps" are full of passion, jealousy, betrayal, and revenge. Yet the prevailing rules of marriage and the family, while repeatedly broken by the characters, are never themselves questioned.

To more traditionally minded Americans, all this has been hard to take. Beleaguered, they were relieved when an attack was mounted on the model American family from the opposite direction. Far from criticizing it for being too strict, too emotionally confining—an idea dear to psychiatrists carried over from Western Europe—the new attackers challenged the American family for being too loose, too democratic, and not authoritarian enough. This charge is an old one. Tocqueville thought that the family, in America, did not really exist, so weak was the authority of the father over his children. Geoffrey Gorer was one of many more recent foreign observers who noted the tyranny of the child in the American family, the weakness of fathers, the phenomena known as "momism" and "teenism."

Indeed, few foreign ideas of America are more deeply held than the image of the American child as a large, noisy, spoiled brat, a "gimme" kid, whose messy room is full of gigantic toys, who seldom says "please," and never stands up in the presence of his or her elders. The image, while correct in all its particulars, is also sour and partial, for it misses the two most important things about American children. One is their great energy and self-confidence. The other is the fact that it is difficult to imagine anyplace in the world where it would be more fun to be a child, at least a child who is well provided for. As families have grown smaller, parents have been able to devote more and more time and affection, perhaps too much, to ever dwindling broods.

Houses and apartments grown less crowded have enabled children to have their own rooms.

American childhood is not only indulged but protracted. Adolescence in a middle-class home can last into children's mid-twenties or beyond. Discipline by parents is lax. Parents and children in America coexist on an equal footing, eating together, playing together in the park—a rare sight in Europe—and most strikingly of all, dressing alike. In Europe, parents dress their children up on weekends to look like little adults. In America, on weekends, parents dress down to look like their children. The prevailing childishness of much American mass culture, including the fast-food franchise, owes much to this family democracy and to the fact that children are an important part of the consumer market. Teenagers have a large discretionary income, much of it earned by themselves. Perhaps as a residue of farm America, many young Americans are used to a daily round of chores and local jobs that are disciplines of their own. The spending of money itself gives American children a certain independence.

Family democracy is being underwritten more and more in the law, as courts look favorably on claims for children's rights. Parents no longer have sweeping power to prevent their children from getting necessary medical care. Nor can they interfere as easily as they once could with a child who wants to get contraceptives, although the Right is trying to change this. Parents can still take children's earnings in return for the child's presumed right for parental support, although several states, including New York and California, put certain obstacles in the way of parents who would do this unfairly. Illegitimate children can now claim considerable rights from their natural fathers. It is an old legal presumption that children and parents cannot sue one another. Nevertheless, the California Supreme Court has abolished the parent-child suit immunity rule and thirteen states, in certain instances, allow children to sue their parents.

By almost any measure, the material lot of American children has steadily advanced, although black children's health, while greatly improved itself in the past two decades, still lags badly behind white children's. Child abuse is more uncovered and discussed than before. Whipping or beating is all but forbidden in schools. It is to all outward appearances great to be an American child. But do Americans look back on their childhoods and think: That was the right way to bring up children?

One contemporary critic who answers a resounding No is the historian and essayist Christopher Lasch. His diagnosis borrows heavily from the work of psychiatry and from earlier social theorists, such as Theodor Adorno, whose study of the origins of fascism led him to ask if over-tolerated children did not risk growing up into rigid, intolerant adults. If Lasch's diagnosis is correct, the modern American family is not a horse on which even the traditionalists would want to put much money. To Lasch, the American family is unable to produce the mature, independent-minded, and self-sufficient adults blessed by Protestantism and required for capitalism. Instead, the tolerant, permissive, and democratic American family produces a characteristic personality type, he believes, which shuns competition, fears success as much as failure, and craves to be led. This reading of the matter is supported, he would add, by the Pied Piper appeal for so many young Americans of religious sects such as the Unification Church of the Reverend Sun Myung Moon.

For most followers of the conservative pro-family movement, ignorance of such tangled matters is bliss. Traditionalists say, besides, in their bluff way, that what American families need is a crack of the patriarchal whip. The Family, capitalized, appealed to conservatives as an issue for straightforwardly political reasons as well as for those having to do with symbolism and the character of the children it produces. Because so many liberal Democrats had developed family policies of their own over the years, the conservative "pro-family" slogan was a convenient means of both knocking liberal Democrats and sounding the cry to get the government out of Americans' private lives. Family policy is by no means a monopoly of the right in America. Senator Daniel Patrick Moynihan of New York took an early interest in it, as did Walter Mondale. While working in the Nixon administration, Moynihan championed a guaranteed annual income for the poor to replace a system of welfare payments that arguably encouraged the breaking up of recipient families. Mondale was the Senate's leading supporter of federally supported child care in the early 1970s. Like Moynihan's, his efforts failed.

Jimmy Carter, with a good ear for popular tunes as a campaigner, picked up the "defend the family" theme as well. At a speech in Manchester, New Hampshire, and at another, in Denver, before the National Conference of Catholic Charities, early in his first presidential campaign, Carter laid out the theme that he was to return to often in 1976. This was that "the American family is in trouble." The evidence he offered was the familiar statistical litany of marital decline. Carter listed the findings that two out of every five marriages in America were ending in divorce; that one in eight children was born illegitimate; and that one child in six was living in a single-parent family.

Carter the candidate pledged to make "family policy" a high priority in his administration. During his term, a White House Family Conference was indeed called. As a token of governmental decentralization, four companion meetings of the conference were held in cities across the country. Despite the fanfare, the conference was not judged a success. As with so many other of President Carter's ventures, delegates came away from the conference as puzzled as when they arrived about what the policy really consisted of. Much of the confusion over family policy serves a purpose. In his book *The Futility of Family Policy*, Gilbert Steiner of the Brookings Institution traces how the code term "the family" is used by different politicians and the lobbies they represent. To some, family policy is a useful cover for promoting improved welfare programs for the poor; to others, it is a way of promoting federal child care without saying so out loud; to still others, it is an effort to look at government social policies as a whole and to judge how they help or hurt the American family.

In this last group, conservatives and Catholics are notably strong, and for them there is one "family" issue which brooks no confusion and transcends all others, and that is abortion. Of deep concern to many Catholics, who regard the 1.5 million abortions performed in America each year as, literally, murder, the anti-abortion cause also corrals many conservatives. Two days after Ronald Reagan was inaugurated, he met with a group of right-to-lifers in the Oval Office. Dr. Jack Willke, president of the National Right-to-Life Committee, said afterward: "It was a signal, because we were the first citizens' group in the White House. The one historical parallel is when the civil rights leaders were brought into the White House under Kennedy." Another bone was thrown to this pressure group when President Reagan named Richard

Schweiker, a dedicated foe of abortion and his running mate in the 1976 presidential election campaign, as health and human services secretary.

Those Catholics and conservatives who are against abortion want the federal government to do something to stop it. The federal government, at least in the shape of the federal courts, is already involved. Since 1973, neither Congress nor the states have been constitutionally allowed to prohibit abortion in the early months of pregnancy. The Supreme Court's historic decisions in *Roe* v. *Wade* and *Doe* v. *Bolton*, in which women lawyers, Sarah Weddington and Marjorie Pitt Hames, argued for the plaintiffs, effectively removed the power of states to restrict the practice of abortion, making it a matter for patient and doctor. This liberalization had prompt effect. In the five years that followed, the measurable abortion rate per 1,000 women of childbearing age rose from 16.5 (at the end of 1973) to 28.2 (at the end of 1978). There were already liberal abortion laws in many states. The most obvious result of the Court's legalization was to make it unnecessary for women seeking abortions in restrictive states to go across state lines or to an illegal practitioner. It was the abortion rate in previously restrictive Bible Belt states of the South and Midwest or in heavily Catholic states like Massachusetts that rose most sharply, making the matter all the more contentious.

To opponents of abortion such as the Catholic Church, the changes were intolerable. In 1975, its *Pastoral Plan for Pro-Life Activities* was approved by the National Conference of Catholic Bishops. Respect Life groups were set up in Catholic parishes across the country. Ellen McCormack, a Catholic housewife from Long Island, ran for President in 1976 as a single-issue, anti-abortion candidate. With the help of the new public campaign financing laws and a Catholic-backed fund-raising drive, she attracted great publicity. By 1981, the anti-abortion movement had grown into a powerful national force. It had a hand in defeating several liberal Democratic senators in the 1980 election as well as in electing Ronald Reagan, rated sounder on the issue than Jimmy Carter. The National Right-to-Life Committee, a nondenominational group including Catholics, Jews, Protestants, and atheists, by then claimed thirteen million members. Anti-abortion was a leading theme, too, for the New Right and the Moral Majority. They made uncomfortable bedmates for a Catholic Church anxious that the anti-abortion cause should not be discredited as a quixotic far-right crusade.

The quarrels between the pro-life anti-abortionists and the pro-choice pro-abortionists recall in many ways the long quarrel of two rival political cultures, Wets and Drys, over prohibition, though the abortion controversy goes deeper and is even more intractable. Some light is shed on why it broke on the nation when it did by remembering the family background to the quarrel: a steadily falling birthrate during the late 1960s and early 1970s. This was disturbing for many Americans. While few any longer think a strongly rising birthrate is a reliable sign of national health, many still sense that a sharp drop means something is wrong. Conservative apologists have fed the mood. Michael Novak, the Catholic columnist, says that in the individualist climate of the 1970s, having children was "an act of courage." Midge Decter argues that childbearing is women's destiny.

The issue cannot, however, be fully understood without some sense of the economic importance Americans have at different times given their children. In farm America, children worked. In a huge country with plentiful land, large families were at a premium. Children were an asset that paid off directly even if big families were a dangerous toll on the women who bore them. The farm family was a workable economic unit. In industrial America, "the bourgeois mind," as Christopher Lasch put it, "considered children hostages to the future." Children were treated as investments and their value was expected to pay off over time.

In today's brittle economic climate, children are coming more and more to be viewed as an economic liability, to be expensively provided for and trained for an uncertain job market, without the promise of any return to the parents in their old age. Before, parental love was able to express itself in the practical-minded desire to give children a better life than their parents or grandparents had enjoyed. This driving motive was particularly important for immigrant parents, as a partial recompense for uprooting from the Old World and as an unarguable token in the new one of success. Precisely because this economic calculus is going against children, traditionalist conservatives are especially anxious about policies that further encourage having fewer of them.

The change in the birthrate in the past two decades has been remarkable. At the peak of the nineteen-year post–World War II baby boom, women were having children at a rate that would have ensured the average family four children if maintained over a normal childbearing life. By 1972, the year before *Roe* v. *Wade,* this fertility rate had fallen by more than half, to 1.8, below the level at which a population reproduces itself.

Women having fewer children, generally speaking, is a sign of improvement and modernization. In a vast, labor-short, and underpopulated continent, having large families made sense in the last century, at least in strictly economic terms. That has all changed. It would not be difficult for Americans today to agree with what Margaret Sanger, the American advocate of birth control, said fifty years ago: that breeding too many children was wrong. Having fewer children suggests more interest in children, not less. With a few periodic jumps, including the postwar baby boom, the birthrate has fallen in this century. Yet the increase in child-rearing manuals, the wide acceptance of child psychology, the growth of a baby products industry, the diffusion of more enlightened child-raising practices, all suggest that fewer children means more attention is being paid to each.

Despite its decline, the birthrate has a long way to fall, for all conservatives fear. The proportion of women giving birth to a single child or to no children at all has hardly increased in the last several decades. According to survey polling, the vast majority of American women still want to have one child at least. The American Society for Non-Parents, which originated in Baltimore, has made predictably little headway. The whole subject tends to invite despondency, all the same. Reflecting on "The Decline of American Domestic Manners," Elizabeth Hardwick wrote recently in *Daedalus:* "One thing looms out of the shadows: the reluctance of so many *promising* young people to have children." Promise aside, there is a very practical question here. Who will pay today's young people's pensions when they grow old?

National birthrate statistics do more to conceal than reveal an answer. While they show that Americans are still more prolific than, for example, West Germans, not all Americans are equally prolific. Birthrates for white American women are lower than for black and Hispanic-American women, one reason for a racist undertow in the whole argument about fertility. But the real puzzle is this: When the birthrate was falling fairly rapidly, in the late 1960s and early 1970s, the older members of the postwar baby boom generation were themselves reaching the age at which they should have been having children.

The proportion of childbearing women in the population was rising fast in this period. The baby bulge should have become a young-mother bulge—or so every conventional demographer would have expected. For usually when the share of childbearing women in a population goes up, the birthrate goes up, too. Startlingly, the opposite occurred. The American birthrate continued to fall.

A California friend, on hearing there were to be observations in this book about American marriages, produced the following diary entry:

Michael and Jane drove up from Sacramento to Reno today to get married. S. and I went with them. They wanted us to come along for the ride and be witnesses. There was a storm in the mountains. Driving Route 80 in February takes snow chains. Ten miles short of the summit, their Dodge van started to skid. Michael stopped the van. We all helped put on the chains. Ten miles further down the highway, Michael stopped again to take them off. As we drove down into Nevada, there was sunlight coming up from below. The snow on the mountains looked purple. Coming off the snowline, the freeway cuts through the steep eastern bank of the Sierras. Billboards began to come up and, almost suddenly, the mountains gave way to high desert.

Reno sits there flat in a scrubble plateau. Michael and Jane stopped at the Chapel of Promise, a wedding advice bureau on the edge of town. They wanted to know where they could get married most cheaply. Jane's quit her nursing job and Michael is teaching school more or less for free as best I can make out. Jane has been through all this before. She was married when she was eighteen. An army husband. They went to Reno because of the California blood test laws. This time Jane wanted to get married outside Reno. On the drive up she imagined knocking on the door of a country JP, getting married in the kitchen, while the wife cooked everyone something to eat, just like in a Preston Sturges movie. Nobody else much liked the idea. Michael and Jane needed a marriage license. They drove to Washoe County Courthouse. This is more famous for divorces, and Marilyn Monroe in *The Misfits*.

Despite its casinos, Reno is like so many other small western towns, a few tall buildings in the middle of a grid of two-story shopfronts and bungalows. Jane noticed a sign which said "Free champagne for wedding parties." Nobody would decide whether to spend money for a drink.

Michael, who said very little all day, wanted to get the license. These were issued in an upstairs room at the courthouse, the size of a small post office. It was already seven in the evening, but licenses are issued until midnight, with a special charge after office hours. A couple of clerks, high on grass, took down Michael and Jane's details. They introduced us to the registrar, a thin, genial-looking man with a red face and curly gray hair. He lined us up across from his desk. Instead of a few perfunctory words, he delivered a long sermon about the duties of man and wife. Michael and Jane then exchanged vows. Michael asked me for the ring. His hands were still black from the snow chains.

When the registrar was done, Jane burst out, telling him how unexpectedly beautiful the ceremony had been. She rushed up to embrace him. Later, Jane said she had done this to see if he was really drunk. The registrar sat down at his desk and opened a drawer. He pulled out a thick plastic bag full of soap, shampoo, and toothpaste. "Here's your happy homemaker kit," he said, beaming, and began to write out the marriage certificate. "You know," he said with pride, "there are sixteen wedding chapels in this town but we find we're overall the most popular place. We still do thirty percent of the business."

Fredrika Bremer, the Swedish novelist who visited America in 1849, wrote of attending a wedding where the bride was already in her traveling costume:

> This marriage ceremony seemed to me characteristic of that haste and precipitation for which I have often heard the Americans reproached. Life is short, they say, and therefore they hurry along its path, dispensing with all needless forms and fashions which might impede the necessary business of life and perform even this as rapidly as possible making five minutes suffice to be married in.

Everyone knows that Americans get divorced more readily than almost any other people, with the possible exception of the Swedes. Perpetual optimists that they are, Americans also marry and remarry at a furious rate, an important fact about them that is less widely appreciated. For all the hand-wringing about divorce and the future of the family, the proportion of Americans reaching the age of fifty without ever marrying is now at its lowest point since reliable marriage statistics were first collected.

Divorce is America's great contribution to marriage. Divorce became the obvious expedient once better health meant that early death could no longer be waited for to release partners from bad marriages. It is quite fitting that Jane should be married in the courthouse where Marilyn Monroe, in the film, was divorced. It is not odd that the most conservative President in recent memory, Ronald Reagan, should be the first to break the prejudice against a divorced man occupying the White House. Twenty years before, this was reckoned an impediment to Nelson Rockefeller.

Americans may sometimes marry in haste, but they make a cult of marriage: ". . . religious communities and trading nations entertain peculiarly serious notions of marriage," wrote Tocqueville. So seriously did a couple in New York take marriage that, in a spirit of sexual equality, they rewrote the marriage contract. Their vow observed the rule that all contracts, in time, get longer. It laid down as a general principle that for better pay or worse, their time and work was equally valuable. It also spelled out a very detailed roster of weekly household chores, including caring for children-to-be. American eagerness to marry has much to do with a national wish to spell things out, to get things straight, to make explicit what elsewhere would be suggested. For a long time, two Americans meeting were both quite likely to be speaking English as a second language. With so many Americans on the move, besides, in the morning one or the other might be gone.

Far from rushing to the business of life and dispensing with forms, as Fredrika Bremer suggested, Americans keep old forms in new technologies, without the slightest trace of self-consciousness or any sense of incongruity, whether it be dial-a-prayer, the drive-in mortuary, or the computerized dating service. What is preserved is the ritual. So seriously do Americans take marriage that, as Cole Porter might have said, even gays do it.

With the cult of marriage goes a horror of singleness. America was not meant for single men or women. Protestant at birth, it lacked that tradition of celibacy—monastic or worldly—that colored European life, especially intellectual life, long after the Reformation. The difficulty of being single in America is not simply that builders, real estate agents, refrigerator manufacturers, supermarkets, psychologists, and advertisers tend to assume that all Americans are or will be married, although this does produce minor irritations. The problem is that America is a marriage-based culture, revolving around the home and the family. To be single, in America, is to be different, to stick out, and as young Americans learn early in school popularity contests, to stick out too much is a disadvantage. The great fear, in America, is to be alone and dependent. This not only determines American attitudes to women. It affects men and women alike. "The nightmare of American life is to be left dependent and helpless," wrote Max Lerner, an American patriot if ever there was one, in *America as a Civilization*, "a greater nightmare than failing to help others when they need help."

4

DEMOCRACY AND ITS DISCONTENTS
Politics and Government

WHEN RONALD REAGAN was running as a "citizen politician" for governor of California in 1966, on a platform attacking welfare rolls, high taxes, and bureaucrats, Louis Harris, the pollster, took a sounding of Americans' attitudes toward their government in Washington. More than two-fifths of those polled, Harris found, rated their confidence in it "high," not bad considering how low its reputation was soon to sink. Four days after Reagan was elected President, in November 1980, on the promise to "take government off the backs of the people" and make them "free again," Harris ran a poll that asked the same question as before. This time, the share of those with "high confidence" in the federal government had fallen to 17 percent.

If such findings sound artificial, there was an even more convincing sign of political disenchantment. It was not much remarked on at the time, astonishing as this may be, since it has come to be taken for granted. Barely half of those eligible to vote—53 percent, to be precise —actually bothered to do so. Of these, just over half—51 percent— went for Reagan. This Republican "landslide," magnified by unexpected victory in the Senate and astutely turned, in the first few months of the new administration, into a "mandate for change," was set off, in other words, by little more than a quarter—27 percent—of the American electorate.

This is not a partisan debating point. The same was true four years before. The quarter of the electorate that went for the Democrat Jimmy Carter was very slightly larger than the quarter that stuck with the Republican Jerry Ford. There are plenty of answers, none wholly convincing, given to why Americans should vote in such fewer numbers than, say, Europeans. One reason may be that like the Swiss, the exception in Europe, Americans hold a prodigious number of elections. It is exaggerating only a bit to say that in America the polls never close and that there is always someplace where votes are being counted. Another reason may be that the young vote less than the old. Until recently, the population was disproportionately young. Enfranchised 18–21-year-olds swelled the electorate in 1972. As the population ages, Americans may vote much more. The signs do not suggest this. The sociologist Herbert Gans did a study for Peter Hart Associates, a polling firm, of voters who sat out the 1976 election. Their commonest reasons for not voting were simple. Politicians, Gans was told, do not do what they say they will, and the choice of parties makes virtually no difference.

The silent abstention of half the nation's potential voters needs to be kept in mind when one watches the dazzling and furious spectacle of American politics. As the contenders slug it out in the ring, half the crowd have turned their chairs away and are sitting, arms crossed, looking in another direction. Nobody really knows what would happen if they decided to take an interest in the fight. Maybe they would split fifty-fifty and root like the rest of the crowd. Perhaps more would go for the underdog. Some might start tossing chairs into the ring. It is possible to do little more than guess. The likeliest supposition is that most nonwatchers would stay turned away. Whatever the case, making book on American politics needs a large margin of error. Take the 1980 election again. The results were quickly raked over to see if they ushered in a new Republican era, as Franklin Roosevelt opened the Democratic age half a century before. While this was asking to see the future before it had happened, there were clues. The Republican triumph was a sharp reminder of conservative resilience in a country where only politicians of the center were supposed to succeed. Yet the right was only a part of Reagan's support. Middle-of-the-road Republicans and Democrats voted for him as well. Was the quarter of the electorate Reagan won a sure foundation for a lasting Republican, let alone conservative, majority?

Elections make most sense retrospectively. They are less reliably signs of things to come than judgments on what has gone. This is particularly true in America, where the one sensible thing to expect from politics is the unexpected. The 1980 election was, most obviously, a verdict on Carter. By winning only five states and the District of Columbia outside his native Georgia, Carter showed that his unpopularity knew no regional bounds. Reagan's election pointed back to the past in several further senses. His victory stemmed from Carter's failures, but only some of these, and not the most important ones, were Carter's own. The job that Carter had to handle has been growing more and more difficult, as his four predecessors' failure to master it suggests. These successive failures all encouraged ever-wider expressions of disenchantment with the federal government. The two fed on each other, so that campaigning from the White House ceased to be a crushing advantage and became a positive liability. This made the job of candidate Carter in 1976 and candidate Reagan in 1980 all the easier, their job as President all the harder.

After witnessing these presidential difficulties for himself, inside Carter's White House, the well-known Democratic lawyer Lloyd Cutler came forward to suggest sweeping constitutional changes, the better to let Congress and the President govern instead of fighting each other. Sympathy for the idea was matched not so much by the overcautious feeling that rewriting ground rules was unwise as by the belief that a modern President's troubles are not at root institutional at all. The elaborate constitutional clockwork set up by eighteenth-century men of wealth alarmed more by too much government than by too little has normally tended to run down and stop without the driving wheel of a major political party capable of operating in Congress and the White House as a governing majority.

Between McKinley's election in 1896 and the onset of the New Deal, the Republicans were a majority of this sort, save for the interlude of the Wilson administration, the beneficiary of a Republican split. From 1933 until the late 1960s, the Democrats took the Republicans' place. Then things came unstuck. Neither party managed to hold voters from election to election or keep together governing majorities with any conviction. Neither seemed able to act as dependable brokers between competing economic interests or between the needs of corporate America and those of ordinary Americans. Inflation ravaged the political capital of both parties indiscriminately. Neither party seemed willing or ready to face an inescapable question: Who is to make sacrifices today, so that America will make investments in its social resources for the future, instead of spending them today? The President's institutional problems—with the public, within his own straggling administration, and with Congress—are real enough. Yet they are symptoms, at the most exposed point, of trouble in the political system at large.

Reagan profited directly from Carter's failure and less obviously from the decline of the old New Deal–Fair Deal–Great Society coalition that had held together the Democrats so long. Without this decline, even a more polished operator than Carter would have had to struggle. Reagan's own conservatism, of course, also pointed to the past, as did that of his most loyal followers. In the campaign in 1980, his most powerful images of what America might be were drawn from how it was, or rather from how it was imagined as having been. Restoration—of past respect, past prosperity, past freedom—was the theme of Reagan's inaugural address. Restoration implies loss, and the sense of loss underlying Reagan's conservatism might be called the politics of regret even though it is so superficially upbeat. For there is almost nothing in America's lost past that cannot be recovered, Reaganism implies, by cutting the guy ropes with which Lilliputian bureaucrats have tied down the American Gulliver.

During the election campaign, a whole landscape of American myth was condensed into a single stunning image of Reagan, which became an unofficial electoral icon, popping up everywhere on posters, buttons, and television screens. The image was of a hale, lean, and smiling man, wearing a Stetson hat and an open-necked denim shirt, with his face turned to the distance, eyes slightly narrowed, fatherly and defiant all at once, a ranger, a herd boss, a wagonmaster, or a cavalry captain. Curiously enough, Jimmy Carter's advertisers had been successful four years before in exploiting an equally agrarian theme. In television appeals, Carter was shown in baggy dungarees, kneeling on the brown earth of a peanut field and letting a small sample of the crop run through his hands, a provider, cultivator, man of the soil.

The image of Reagan gave off the optimism and confidence that Americans like in a President, while that of Carter, by contrast, suggested contrition and humility. Different as they were, each called up a less crowded and less tangled rural society that was already becoming a memory for most American grandparents. Herdsman and Planter:

strange images for the leaders of a late-industrial superpower. Stranger still, considering the complexity of the President's job at home today. This is to attempt to lead a new governing majority—assuming one can be created—which is able to keep returning, as its members jostle each other and shout for attention, to a simple political challenge: Which interests must spend less today so that the economy will remain solvent tomorrow?

Americans glorify and sentimentalize their Presidents once they are safely dead. Newly defeated or freshly elected ones they treat with unrelieved brutality. Few modern Presidents expect to leave office with their popularity intact. Decent obscurity on a handsome government pension is the best to hope for. After the briefest "honeymoon," new Presidents glumly or desperately watch domestic confidence drain noisily away as Congress and the press pull out the plug from their little basin of goodwill. Exaggerated disappointment follows artificial hope and anticipated failure brings on the real thing. As a smiling Ronald Reagan took the oath of office on the west steps of the Capitol under an unseasonably warm January sun, his three closest advisers looking on, Ed Meese, James Baker, and Mike Deaver, had they spared a thought for the political fate of Reagan's five immediate predecessors, would have found few reasons for rating highly their man's chances of breaking this dismal pattern. For none of the five was a success, all having begun or ended unpredictably, and most of them badly.

Eisenhower was the last President to complete what had come to be thought of as the standard two four-year terms. In the next two decades, 1961–1981, there were five Presidents, and the sixth, Reagan, took office ten days shy of his seventieth birthday, making him old for a second term. Not since 1877–1897, when five weak Presidents threw open the federal government to the financial and industrial robber barons, or 1841–1861, when seven Presidents stumbled over themselves to civil war, has the revolving door at the White House turned so fast. The Oval Office seems again to be more a predicament than a seat of power, those in it less shapers of events than victims of circumstance.

The trouble appears to lie as much in the job as with its holders. Weak Presidents are no more capable of making today's federal government budge at all than strong ones are of leashing its formidable powers. Kennedy's New Frontier was never crossed. Johnson over-reached his strength and undid his best achievements. Under Nixon, the "imperial presidency" inherited from the Democrats grew even less responsive, still more secretive, and in the end criminal. Ford and Carter, two weak but fundamentally decent Presidents who followed and who had, after Vietnam and Watergate, only to bring off a modest job of dignified mopping up, nonetheless managed to etch into the office their own marks of frustration or failure. This sorry list is bracketed by two presidential shootings—Kennedy dead, Reagan badly wounded—saying less about politics or the presidency than about America's absurd gun laws, but bolstering all the same the forgivably mistaken impression that political leaders in America come cheap.

This sketch of the White House melodrama is deliberately over-drawn. The news was not all bad. There were normal, workaday periods at the White House over the twenty years, when budgets or farm subsidies were talked about and when the prevailing tone was set more by think tank study papers than by *The Duchess of Malfi*. Presidential talents and weaknesses did vary. Before taking office, Johnson had mastered Congress, Nixon foreign affairs, Carter every briefing book his aides took down to him in Plains. Circumstances varied, too. Johnson enlarged and Nixon would not cleanly end a bitterly unpopular war. Some had fairly easy, some difficult, economies to deal with. Nixon and Ford faced Congresses of the opposite party. Each President inherited another's and handed on his own difficulties. The very standard of success—or at least of disasters avoided—against which the five are so readily set, Eisenhower of the winning smile and modest golf handicap, did not preside over the eight tranquil years of revisionist legend, although he did spare himself much trouble, notably on race relations, by storing it up for the Democrats.

Assuming Reagan's men had pressed the question this far—and there was plenty else, including the complacency of winning, to fill their minds—they might have further reassured themselves that five is a small sample and that the future is not exactly like the past. "Let us begin an era of national renewal . . ." the new President was saying. "We have every right to dream heroic dreams." Yes, indeed, the advisers would have comfortably concluded to themselves, things with this President, so evidently relaxed and at ease with himself, would be different.

Even at that moment, however, certain things about the White House which do not change—its theatricality, its blocking marks, center front, on the global stage—were distracting the listeners below. The outgoing President's advisers had spent a gloomy morning in the Oval Office, not knowing if Carter was to get a last token of compensation for his humiliating defeat. Would the captive Americans, the silent chorus of the 1980 presidential campaign, leave Iran during Carter's presidency? As the grandfather clock in the Oval Office ticked toward noon, Jody Powell and Hamilton Jordan, Carter's closest aides, had walked to the globe beside the President's desk to measure the distance from Teheran to friendly airspace over southern Turkey, in order to see if there was still time. There was no tape, so they had measured the distance with their thumbs. The chances had looked poor. Carter had driven up to the Capitol with Reagan, the traditional display of unbroken command, and then had flown off to Plains, still not knowing if the captives were free. So as Reagan was winding up his inaugural address, a reporter on the thawed grass below the Capitol steps began passing word from his transistor radio that the American captives had flown safely out of Iran. No writer of melodrama would have dared invent the scene.

Accept that each presidency is different. Agree that a President's troubles are exaggerated. Concede that the office is distorted by the very attention it gets and by its consequent staginess. The President's job, at the best of times, is still famously if not impossibly difficult. Truman likened getting anything important done from the White House to "pushing a damp noodle across a table." When Eisenhower was elected, Truman sympathized. "Poor Ike," he said. "He won't know what to do. He'll say, 'Do this, do that!' and nothing will happen." Johnson vented his frustration just as pungently. "The only power I've got is nuclear," he liked to say, "and I can't use that."

There was truth in that remark. Presidents are long on power to destroy or disrupt, short on usable authority. They can blow up oil fields, let the dollar sink, seize foreigners' assets, start trade wars, defoliate jungles, incinerate cities. Even if his formal power is disputed, a bold President can act first and wait for Congress or the courts to challenge him afterward. This sort of clubfooted action is better threatened, though, than carried out, for it gives the President all the power of an elephant in a canoe. To do the things he will be blamed for failing to do—bring prices down, find more jobs, keep America strong, at peace, and talking with the Russians, in that order—the President's powers are very limited.

They are limited, first of all, because they are shared. Presidents are responsible for managing a $3.5 trillion economy by means of a $700 billion plus federal budget without fully controlling central credit creation, the job of the Federal Reserve, and without the effective power to raise and lower taxes. That is up to Congress, which is often of a different party from the President or even itself divided, party discipline at the best of times being slight.

The power of the President, as head of the federal government, is shared with fifty states, the largest of which—California, New York, Texas, Pennsylvania, Illinois—would each make a medium-sized country. When the British and the French were trying to secure landing rights for a supersonic passenger jet at New York, they could seldom keep in mind that this was also a local, not simply a federal, matter and could not understand why Ford, who was President at the time and whose administration favored letting the plane land, would not interfere on their behalf. It is easy to confuse "big government" with the federal government. The number of government jobs at all levels is roughly sixteen million, of which less than a fifth are federal. Up to 1981, when the number began falling—for only the second time since the New Deal—the greatest growth in government employment came at the state and local level. "Big government," more and more, has become a mishmash in which mayors, state governors, and administrations in Washington overlap, collide, and cooperate without tidy lines of authority, as initiative flows back and forth among all three.

Presidents conduct a diplomatic orchestra whose leading players—the secretaries of defense and state, the national security adviser, and the director of the Central Intelligence Agency—often each choose their own key. Even when these players do harmonize and the White House finds the theme in its foreign policy, the Senate is there with "advice" but not necessarily "consent," to make sure the President does not get carried away by his own music. This interference, as it is seen and lamented by professional diplomats and never fully understood by foreigners, was once the privilege of the old Republican isolationists, but in recent years it has been notably bipartisan.

Liberal Democrats in 1975 succeeded in suspending funds for secret

American operations in Angola. Ultraconservatives in 1981—led by Jesse Helms, a senator from North Carolina whose curiosity about the world at large rivals in shallowness his interest in modern thinking of any kind—held up Senate confirmation of Reagan's top appointments to the State Department for several months, until the ultras' clients could be found jobs at the department as well. Most damaging of all for the President's authority, after Carter and Brezhnev had signed the second strategic arms limitation agreement in Vienna, the Senate, as a body, failed to act on its ratification, discouraged by Henry Kissinger, among others, who as secretary of state had complained loudest about congressional meddling in foreign affairs.

It takes two to have this tug-of-war. After World War II, Congress, impressed by the urgencies of the cold war, got into the habit of giving Presidents ever vaguer authority in foreign affairs. Then, chastened by Vietnam, Congress tried to win some of this authority back, with such legal restrictions as the Case Act and the War Powers resolution. These constrain Presidents only if Congress wants Presidents held to them. Besides, they are symptoms more than causes of presidential weakness in foreign affairs, which lie as much in the White House as in Congress. For Congress gets drawn deepest into foreign affairs to correct an idea that grips most Presidents at one time or another, one best expressed by Kennedy to Nixon shortly after the Bay of Pigs. Talking of managing foreign policy, Kennedy said: "Who gives a shit if the minimum wage is $1.25 or $1.50? This is what matters." Congress is there to remind Presidents, who forget, that diplomacy cannot be pursued at any price, that superpowers, to remain powers, must stay solvent, and that Presidents who keep American commitments at home and abroad in balance normally get the freest hand from Congress in foreign affairs.

Presidents yearn for more power, secondly, when faced with the excessive, often conflicting demands made on them. They are told that Americans want cheap, plentiful gasoline, clean air, and efficient industries; low interest rates, low prices, and high employment; a strong, well-respected country in which the young do not have to go off to fight; a President who is open and decent like Carter or Ford, but also forceful and decisive like Nixon or Johnson; less government red tape and spending for programs that help others but more subsidies for themselves; a tax system that gives to the poor and does not take from the rich, while permitting the middle class, to which most Americans believe they belong, to hold its ground. Some or all Americans want some or all of these things most of the time. Meanwhile the rich and the powerful, thanks to more fully funded lobbies and to superior political networks, are in a better position at the "great barbecue" of American politics to "get theirs" and keep it—as the handing on from generation to generation of great wealth and influence by grand families or, much more important today, by grand institutions, attests. Ordinary Americans, all the same, can organize themselves as well to press for their share, and the government, particularly the President, must at least appear to listen to claims from every side if the present system is to work democratically at all.

There is absolutely nothing new in saying that Presidents must make difficult choices. What is new is a growing loss of points of support that Presidents used more confidently to rely on to help make their choices, once taken, stick. This slinking away of possible allies and breaking up of institutional furniture on which Presidents can lean naturally discourages all but the bravest or most innocent from taking hard decisions—whose current income is to fall to restore the stock of social capital?—in the first place. The two major parties have weakened considerably, not so much as organizations—never a strong point—nor as campaign labels and loose electoral alliances, for which they still passably serve, but as governing coalitions of men and women ready to bury particular views if not for the party line at least in the promise of future jobs.

To make matters worse, Congress is now as fragmented and unpredictable as it has ever been, without even such old obstructions as the Southern Democratic committee chairmen to serve as landmarks. The President is thus left navigating pilotless in a fog, either plotting a course himself with help only from his own small circle of advisers, or, more probably, simply drifting toward election day, which comes around at a time over which he has no choosing. When it does come, and the unachievable has not been achieved, the fog lifts, each member of Congress is found safe at port in his district, and the President is there for all to see, beached under a clear sky, dejectedly taking the blame.

This may seem unjust. Presidents share too much of their limited power for them accurately to be said to be in charge. There is, however, in the American system no other single figure to blame. While it is possible to search the Constitution for a head of government without finding one, the President is the only remotely plausible modern candidate for this role, not the Speaker of the House, not the Chief Justice, not the majority leader of the Senate, although Sam Rayburn, Earl Warren, and of course Lyndon Johnson were politicians of presidential weight.

Any rising sympathy for the President or indulgence toward the office should be muted, also, by the consideration that this dilemma of responsibility without true power is greatly of his own making. To depersonalize the matter, the dilemma arises from the logic of the modern presidency. Since Franklin Roosevelt, the presidency has expanded its reach by appealing more and more over the heads of the members of the House and Senate, directly to the voting public. Since Eisenhower, a Republican by adoption who did little for his party, Presidents have mounted reelection campaigns independently of parties, on their own from the White House.

This perversity—the attempted strengthening of the President's office which leads inevitably to its weakening—reaches a pitch in the antipolitician, a familiar enough figure in American politics. Today's antipolitician not only runs for President independently of Congress and party, but attacks the federal government he seeks to lead, and continues to do so once in office. This technique, made familiar by both Carter and Reagan, is most transparently a way of trying to escape the dilemma of responsibility-without-power by seeming to step out of the White House even while in it. It may also be seen, high-mindedly, as an effort to diminish expectations of what government can deliver and to check its budgetary growth.

Coolidge was past master at what he called the do-little style of government. "A remarkable man, a *really* remarkable man," harumphed H. L. Mencken. "Nero fiddled while Rome burned. Coolidge only snores." Silent Cal got away with it, though, partly because the White House press liked the long holidays he took, partly because he had the good sense, despite second thoughts, not to run again in 1928, just before the great crash, and partly because government at all levels then accounted for less than 9 percent of the gross national product. Today government takes in more than three times as much, the federal government alone more than 20 percent of the GNP, and so the spectacle of Presidents belittling the vast government they lead is correspondingly less persuasive.

The current style, all the same, is for Presidents to heave rocks at their own windows. Reagan chose Coolidge as the modern predecessor he most admired and had Coolidge's portrait hung in the White House in place of Truman's. Carter looked up to Truman, but he, too, subscribed deep down to the less-government-is-better-government philosophy. "Government cannot solve our problems," he told Congress in 1978, an odd thing to say for a man who was asking it for more than a half trillion dollars to spend the next year. "When the city of Chicago burned down," countless Republican audiences heard Reagan say on the campaign trail over the years, "the people of the city didn't write to Washington for help. They rebuilt it themselves." "Government is not the solution . . . government is the problem," Reagan said in his inaugural address. Both Carter and Reagan played successfully on business or public dissatisfaction with government to get elected. Once in office, willy-nilly, they became its target. They were outsiders and became insiders, anti-Washington candidates who became, with success, the very symbol of Washington.

The President's task has been shown to be difficult, but not impossible. The worst could be avoided and accomplishments achieved if three very hard but rudimentary tasks—preventing the public support that elected him from slipping away, organizing and running a vast administration, and dealing successfully with Congress—were brought off successfully. Keeping public support used to be a matter of holding together an electoral coalition with the help of state and city barons of the President's party. Now that President and party are often at arms' length, independent voters legion, and ticket splitting at the polls common, keeping public support has become more and more a matter for the President and his entourage alone.

To hang on to popularity, most Presidents have stage managers who mount appealing political theater. Hoover took advice from Freud's nephew, public relations expert Edward L. Bernays, the original presidential "media adviser." It was a young Bernays, so the story goes, who recommended that Tomáš Masaryk to announce the foundation of the Czech republic not on a Monday, as originally planned, but on a

Sunday, a slow news day, when it would get most attention. Roosevelt knew the importance of modern communications to propaganda. He flew to Chicago to accept the Democratic nomination and originated the fireside chat. Nixon rescued his early career with the brilliant, if fascinatingly repellent, "Checkers" speech. Kennedy made a habit of televised press conferences.

Reagan has an astute team of media advisers and pollsters who try to shield him from the effect of hard or unpopular decisions on the public mind and associate him only with successes. Reagan's own talents are considerable. His first job was with an Iowa radio station, where he simulated live coverage of baseball games from telegraphic summaries. His timing, perfected during years of touring General Electric plants to give talks about Hollywood and free enterprise, and his one-liner jokes, perfected among wealthy California businessmen at the Bohemian Club's "summer high jinks," as they are known, in the countryside north of San Francisco, made him an unmatchable political communicator on television.

Not all Presidents are as talented. Ford's performances were stumbling—literally—and wooden. "So dumb," Lyndon Johnson had cracked about him, "he can't walk and fart at the same time." The language came no more easily to Ford than it had to Eisenhower. "If Lincoln were alive today," Ford told an audience, "he'd roll over in his grave." "Disgustingly sane" was Ford's description of himself, and he probably was the most ordinary, unpresuming man to have the job since Warren Harding. This made it very difficult for anyone, including his political opponents, to dislike him. His ordinariness was put to good use after Nixon, and the day he took over from his disgraced boss, a point was made of letting the photographers snap him preparing toast for the family breakfast.

Carter was a skillful campaigner, especially in small groups, but as a public performer on the presidential stage he never managed to shake what his own campaign manager called his "weirdo factor." A naval engineer by training, Carter tried to win over others too much by argument and detail alone. There was hardly an inch of actor in him. To talk to directly, Carter was aloof and intense by turns, careful with words and sure of his own correctness. More than any of this, the listener was struck by his physical slightness, as if he were all ever-turning brain and determination. Carter could walk into the gilded, mirrored East Room of the White House for press conferences and reach the podium before he made his presence felt.

Carter tried fireside chats and a televised "phone-in" with Walter Cronkite—then anchorman for the CBS Evening News and una-nointed television co-President—during which, it was said, more than a million people called to speak with the President. Such efforts at direct communication were a losing struggle. Carter could never erase from the public mind, once he had let them be implanted there, two images of himself: dropping senseless in a marathon among runners half his age and, every cartoonist's dream, taking a paddle to a hissing rabbit that had swum up to the boat from which he was fishing. His pollster, Pat Caddell, had warned him, in a famous if awkwardly ex-pressed memorandum, against substituting "substance for style." Carter was better than he made himself out to be, but not enough better. Bad communicators can hide achievements. The best com-municators cannot, for long, hide incompetence.

All these Presidents tried and failed at the first presidential job: preventing the public support that elected them from slipping away. Avoiding this is complicated by continuous assessment of presidential performance in opinion polls. Successful as Reagan was, for example, with Congress during his first year, as of March 1982 he stood lower in the polls than Carter had after twelve months in office. Congress cannot unseat a President, short of impeachment, and a Congress's refusal to pass bills is not a decisive test of a President's popularity. Voters get a chance to judge only once every four years. In between, the polls, wavering and unsound as many think them, are frequently consulted to discover how the President is doing. As the machinery grows fancier—the Qube television system in Columbus, Ohio, which allows viewers to "talk back" to the broadcaster, is a pointer to where political communications may soon be headed—opinion soundings are likely to grow even commoner, quicker, and more credited. Dips in a presidential rating are met grimly at the White House. "Just give us the numbers," Kennedy used to say impatiently to Lou Harris, who always wanted to caution the President against reading too much into his polls. "We can work out what they mean." Slippage in the polls tends to be reinforcing in such an atmosphere and Presidents come under pressure to recover lost ground—which may not be lost at all—

by dramatic gestures, especially abroad, as the *Mayaguez* incident, the Iran rescue mission, and the Gulf of Sidra action attest.

Further complicating the President's task of keeping public support are the new primary election rules. Because of these it is much easier for a candidate of his own party to mount a credible challenge to the President's renomination, which used to be more or less taken for granted. Ford from Reagan in 1976 and Carter from Edward Kennedy in 1980 faced serious challenges that split their parties and preoccupied them for the better part of a year, until their ultimate defeat in the general election. This inability of Presidents any longer to count on near-automatic renomination drains their authority with Congress, their party, and the public. Efforts among Democrats, weakened most by the primary system, were under way in 1982 to reform the rules once more, this time to give party loyalists a greater say again in which candidate is nominated. It was still true that besides their other two tasks—organizing and running a vast administration and dealing with Congress—Presidents must from the day they enter the White House pursue an unending campaign.

Organizing and running a vast administration, the President's second task, is managing the unmanageable; yet Presidents must still try. Today's Presidents promise to get the federal government under control or at least to check its growth. Carter called it a "horrible, bloated bureaucracy." Reagan, on the stump, told audiences he liked "to fantasize what it would be like if everyone in government would quietly slip away and close the doors and disappear," and, he had decided, "... we would get along a lot better than we think." Like all Presidents, both discovered that the federal government is ally as well as enemy. The Office of Personnel Management reported that as of January 1981, the federal government employed some 2.9 million persons, all but 55,000—in Congress and the courts—working for the executive branch. This included 884,000 military personnel in the Department of Defense and 655,000 in the now independent Postal Service. About 300,000 of all these federal workers are in Washington. The rest are scattered abroad or in the states, administering federal programs—a political tool, if the White House will use it, for currying favor in particular regions and districts.

A.A.-F

For a President, putting together an administration is like trying to erect an Egyptian pyramid from the top down. At its peak, the executive branch has no permanent civil service; there the merit system ceases to apply and Presidents have an immediate job on taking over of filling some two thousand patronage positions. These are not mere postmasterships or minor posts. Several hundred are the most important positions in the big departments and agencies. Washington lacks the advantages—and the disadvantages—of an organized, stable governing elite like the Whitehall mandarins or French *Énarques* at the top of a career civil service to carry over from government to government. The Washington best-seller during any change of administration is the "plum book," a yellow-covered document put out by the Committee on Post Office and Civil Service in the House of Representatives under the title "United States Government Policy and Supporting Positions." In its 135-odd pages are listed all the leading political positions, along with their salaries, in the departments, agencies, and boards. For the gentlemen-in-waiting, these are the new administration's Help Wanted pages. These plum jobs include all the senior policymaking positions in the departments, from cabinet members down to the third or fourth level of assistant secretaries, who may number a dozen or more in the larger departments.

Foreign governments marvel at this permanent revolution in the corridors of power, otherwise known as the transition. They must wait for several months after the outgoing staff members at the National Security Council have cleared out their files from the large, high-ceilinged offices on the third floor of the old War Department building, leaving only the furniture and the ornate fireplaces, until the incoming team has begun to "formulate policy" with its own National Security Staff Memoranda, Presidential Review Memoranda, or whatever new name is chosen for its foreign policy papers.

Just below the top level in the departments and agencies is a twilight area where rules governing who stays and goes are murky. Presidents, more and more, are moving out the old and putting in their own hands. Nixon, it is said, got rid of half of those who had worked for Johnson, Carter three-quarters of those brought in under Nixon and Ford, Reagan everybody given a job by Carter. The turnover ensures a chronic absence of institutional memory. "It's a business every four years of teaching new dogs old tricks," grumble the few top civil servants who survive.

For a good reason, change is swiftest and most brutal in the Executive Office of the President, to which the NSC belongs, and which has some 1,700 people scattered in more than fifteen other bureaus. The Executive Office is the White House's direct extension into what incoming Presidents normally view as enemy territory. New Presidents tend to view transitions as races to control a hostile and sluggish middle-level bureaucracy before it smothers yet another would-be master. Republicans in particular are prone, even today, to think of Washington as a Democratic town, its bureaucracy staffed by descendants of the New Deal who will stop at nothing to sabotage Republicanism.

So determined was Eisenhower to wrest the machinery from two decades of Democratic control that he extended presidential patronage, despite objections from Congress and the Civil Service, to give himself more jobs to fill with loyal Republicans. To Eisenhower, accordingly, thanks are owed by many bright young men and women—Democrats, Republicans, or neither—working as "special assistants" to the great men of government. These are political secretaries—although they would hate to be taken for typists—drafters of policy, speechwriters, bag carriers too, and copious leakers, but above all, protégés. Special assistants are political eyes and ears for those at the top, who must work in their departments with career civil servants who will be there after the great man has moved on and whose wholeheartedness the great man naturally suspects. There is no formal requirement for being a special assistant, although having the right connection helps a little and having the right résumé—Harvard, Rhodes Scholar, law review, clerk on the Supreme Court, that sort of thing—helps a lot. They often rise, like Joseph Califano, who was special assistant to Cyrus Vance at the Pentagon, to positions in which they need special assistants of their own, although their detractors say that however brilliant, special assistants are, by temperament, number twos. Special assistants are prime examples of those client-patron relationships and old boy–bright young man networks which are seldom adverted to since they seem vaguely elitist and undemocratic, but without which bureaucratic Washington could not be operated or understood.

Candidates for President commonly promise to reduce the scope of political appointments, especially in the foreign service, though here again, virtue and need are at war. The tradition of making political creditors ambassadors continues as vigorously as when Ambrose Bierce defined "consul" as "a person who having failed to secure an office from the people is given one by the Administration on condition that he leave the country." The Midwestern governor who got an Asian embassy as a plum for helping in the 1976 presidential campaign knew the names of none of the Chinese leadership, had never heard of Giscard d'Estaing, and—all according to a disgruntled foreign service officer who had served under him at the embassy—was astonished to learn that Korea was divided, with governments in both North and South. The Italian newspapers caught the spirit when they reported, believably but mistakenly, that Reagan was about to appoint Frank Sinatra as ambassador to Rome. As did Dick Tuck, the political humorist who worked on Bobby Kennedy's 1968 presidential campaign. One of his duties was walking the senator's dog, Freckles. Reporters gibed at the indignity, but Tuck would reply: "To you it may be just a dog, but to me it's an ambassadorship."

In putting together and running an administration, those who will help the President most directly—his White House advisers—tend to be close, trusted, long known, from the President's own state, and, lately, more and more the men who ran his election campaign. Each group gives the White House its distinctive tone. Kennedy, favoring an air of savvy cultivation, mixed South Boston with Cambridge, Irish-American friends like Ken O'Donnell and Larry O'Brien with academics such as McGeorge Bundy and Arthur Schlesinger. Lyndon Johnson had Texans—Bill Moyers, George Christian, and Harry McPherson—but also Abe Fortas, a well-known Washington lawyer and a tenacious hawk about Vietnam, as well as Joe Califano, who worked on the Great Society social programs. Nixon's team consisted of devoted men from the West Coast who idolized organization and method, most notably H. R. Haldeman, an advertising man, and John Ehrlichman, a lawyer–campaign adviser, both jailed after Watergate. Ford's team, like Ford, was ordinary, but had holdovers from the Nixon administration who had kept their feet dry, such as Alexander Haig and Donald Rumsfeld. From Georgia, Carter brought in Ham Jordan and Jody Powell, who let Annie Leibovitz photograph them as Butch Cassidy and the Sundance Kid for the cover of *Rolling Stone* and who exuded a general feel of guileful unstuffiness. They were tactically brilliant in the series of set pieces that make up a presidential primary campaign, but unable to cope with many-front war in political Washington.

Reagan's triumvirate of Ed Meese, Jim Baker, and Mike Deaver made him, in his early months, the most smoothly managed President of recent times. Meese, an ex-prosecutor from Oakland who worked for Reagan in California, quickly became known as "Prime Minister Meese." No slave to method—his desk, under a portrait of an enormous bull elephant, in the coveted northwest office of the White House west wing, looked to a visitor early in the new administration like a mess of open drawers and loose-leaf briefing books—Meese had long before become comfortable as Reagan's alter ego. Jim Baker, a rich Houston lawyer who had worked not for Reagan but for Ford in the 1976 election, was asked to run the White House staff, providing the method that Meese lacked, and by 1982 was emerging as first among equals. Deaver, who balanced the two, was another old Reagan retainer.

The men around the President are the ones who count, for good or ill, in an administration, much more than the cabinet, now only a worthy totem. Almost every new President, including Reagan, makes a display of his cabinet. Nixon put a full cabinet on parade at the Pierre Hotel in New York as a show of unity and readiness before he took office. At a safe distance from power, this was his cabinet's high point. The Nixon White House in practice worked deliberately around the cabinet secretaries. Reagan—or rather Meese and his colleagues—also set out to run a strong White House. Shortly after taking over, Meese could be found in his office taking phone calls from cabinet secretaries who were clearing fairly junior appointments with him. Carter made the mistake of giving his cabinet members too free a hand in picking their deputies, and discovered too late that the departments were left short as a result of men and women loyal not to the cabinet secretary at the top but to the White House.

The cabinet, not mentioned in the Constitution, has by tradition included the department secretaries, positions laid down by law and subject to Senate confirmation. Cabinet meetings of Presidents today are, or quickly become, formalities. These are not meetings to decide policy. There is no collective responsibility. Members have a say in their own area of responsibility, but the White House usually cuts them down quickly if they stray beyond this or criticize out of turn.

Cabinet secretaries serve two other masters besides the White House. Much of their time is spent on Capitol Hill, justifying themselves and administration policy to congressional committees, where they are treated courteously but without undue respect. They are also expected to lobby for the interests their department represents. The AFL-CIO expects the Labor Department to support a fair deal for working men and women and to defend union interests. Exporters look to the Commerce Department to resist boycotts and embargoes against foreign miscreants, dreamed up as punishment by geopolitical planners at the State Department or NSC, which threaten to damage American interests in international trade. Farmers count on the Department of Agriculture to make sure that anti-inflationary policies aimed at lowering food prices do not interfere with their subsidy programs. Environmentalists wage a generally losing fight with developers and mineral exploiters for influence at the Interior Department, which manages two-fifths of the national land.

The defense industry expects the civilian boss at the Pentagon to agree that each service—Army, Navy, Air Force, and Marines—is woefully underequipped and in need of a new arsenal all its own. The less the chief knows, from the point of view of the military-industrial lobby, the better. Harold Brown of the California Institute of Technology, who was Secretary of the Air Force during the long bombing war over Vietnam, knew the military well and was able to argue down the generals when they asked for new weapons they did not need. Brown was not popular on this score. Caspar Weinberger, an innocent in the world of missile throw weights and strategic bathtubs, was welcomed at the Pentagon. "A fiscal Puritan" is how he described himself early in 1981 as he set before Congress a stupendous five-year military rearmament plan costing $1.5 trillion. To the generals, it must have seemed like Thanksgiving.

No lobby is as strong or as independent as the defense lobby. In his farewell address more than twenty years ago, Eisenhower warned his successors to "guard against the acquisition of unwarranted influence, whether sought or unsought, by the military-industrial complex." Asked to explain himself a bit at his last presidential press conference a few days later, the General said he was objecting to the notion that "the only thing this country is engaged in is weapons and missiles—and I'll tell you, we can't afford that." Eisenhower was all for national security but not for defense policy dictated by the needs of the aerospace sector or treated as if the defense budget were itself a weapon.

Defense planners in Washington—and Moscow—did not hear. The nuclear arms race hurtled on. Technical advantage enabled the Americans to make each innovation first. In the late 1950s, the Russians were briefly claimed to be ahead with long-range missiles, and in the early 1960s, they put sixty-four antiballistic missiles around Moscow, only to dismantle them later, under treaty. As of 1981, the Americans had roughly 7,500 nuclear warheads, loaded on 1,628 ICBMs and 376 long-range bombers. The Russians had 6,800, on 2,330 ICBMs and 150 bombers. This does not include short- and medium-range weapons. Arms control talks have aimed less at disarmament than at agreement to increase these terrifying arsenals at about the same speed. Some strategic theologians in the West say the Russians will shortly have a brief period of nuclear "superiority," which should end abruptly in 1989 or so as new, supposedly superaccurate American missiles are put in place. Others think that, at these levels of destructive potential, the small-gauge comparisons on which such theories depend are largely meaningless. Nuclear strategies continue to be spun ever finer, nevertheless, in an effort to rationalize the appetites of gluttonous defense sectors neither side is able or willing to tame. Attempts to limit the export of conventional weapons also look fruitless. In 1982, the Americans were expected to sell $16–$17 billion worth of arms abroad.

Ten companies, in 1979, supplied the Pentagon with 31 percent of its military purchases. These were General Dynamics ($3.5 billion), McDonnell Douglas ($3.3 billion), United Technologies, whose chief, Alexander Haig, became Reagan's first secretary of state ($2.6 billion), General Electric ($2 billion), Lockheed ($1.8 billion), Hughes Aircraft ($1.6 billion), Boeing ($1.5 billion), Grumman ($1.4 billion), Raytheon ($1.2 billion), and Tenneco ($1.1 billion). The top fifty contractors accounted for almost three-fifths of all sales. General Dynamics and McDonnell Douglas depend heavily on military sales. Others, like GE, are far more diversified. Some, like Boeing outside Seattle, bulk large in local economies. Henry Jackson, the defense hawk from Washington State, became known for his views as "the senator from Boeing." By the opposite token, two dovish politicians, William Proxmire and Les Aspin, from the dairy state of Wisconsin, which has a relatively small defense economy, riled Rockwell International with their opposition to the B-1 bomber, for which Rockwell was the prime contractor. "If only," grumbled a Rockwell lobbyist, "we could have built the damn thing to run on milk."

Southern and Western states still produce an undue share of hawkish politicians. The South has a military tradition. Aerospace industry set up in the fair-weather West during World War II. The spread of defense subcontracting has altered this tidy picture today. Defense dollars flow into most congressional districts in quantities that representatives must reckon with. So the defense lobby is not just independent and strong, but wide.

Defense spending used to be thought of as a way the government could revive a flagging economy without conservative opposition. Joseph Alsop, the retired columnist of hawkish views, was heard to say during the Carter years: "What this economy needs is a good arms race." While defense dollars may stimulate a bit of growth, they also provoke a lot of inflation, or so many argue. The Pentagon is a weak taskmaster with contracts. Costs soar. Aerospace is a high-wage, capital-intensive sector. Defense dollars create few jobs. Defense suppliers have to import extra quantities of scarce materials in which America is not self-sufficient. Less than a year after Weinberger proposed the $1.5 trillion rearmament program, it was trimmed once and the budget director, David Stockman, was saying it had to be cut again.

There is, by comparison, a weak lobby for the ordinary soldier, who is easy to overlook in the nuclear geodrama. The United States had roughly two million people under arms, including 170,000 women, as of September 1981. The Army had 775,000; the Navy, 540,000; the Marines, 191,000; and the Air Force, 569,000. Since 1973, when a thirty-three-year experiment with conscription was brought to an end, the All Volunteer Force has been tested more harshly by domestic critics than by any foreign enemy. Could it attract enough of the right recruits? At the start, there were three big advantages. Thanks to the 1950s baby boom, there was a large pool of young men. Several years of high unemployment made a military career relatively appealing. Force requirements were falling. Even so, the AVF was barely able to supply the active forces, let alone the reserves. The aging of the population is now working against it. Much is made of drug addiction, although the Army's figures of 7 percent on drugs, while startling, hardly suggest the epidemic of caricature. The Army's ranks, it is often remarked, are a third black. What is less noticed is that only 7.5 percent of Army officers are black and that among the enlisted men, two-thirds of the blacks are high school graduates, while only half the whites are. Few of the AVF's critics are ready to propose a return to the draft, with exceptions like Senator Sam Nunn of Georgia, and the political outcry would be enormous if they did.

The military-industrial turbine purrs with fierce energy in the background, yet among ordinary Americans there is little spontaneous expression of the martial spirit, which has seldom been strong in peacetime. Patriotic observances are made at veterans' halls. Honor guards present flags at state occasions and political conventions. Yet except for such marginal ceremonies and save for those living on the edge of military bases, the armed forces are almost totally out of sight. The Fourth of July is a day of town pageants, not military parades. On television, war is muffled in comedy by reruns of *Hogan's Heroes* and the very popular *M*A*S*H*, about a couple of field surgeons in Korea who break the rules and profess to hate the Army.

The shrewder hawks have long worried about the disconnection between men and machines in the modern forces, about the overconcentration on nuclear weaponry, and about the Pentagon's weakness for fancy planes and weapons that spend half their useful life in the repair shop. To attempts to improve the conventional forces, however, let alone restore the draft, there is a formidable obstacle. In a nuclear age, Americans remain to be convinced what a large standing army is for. Support for keeping American troops overseas is seldom unquestioned, and few Americans have good memories of two land wars in Asia.

Administrations that leave other important interests unrepresented quickly find themselves in trouble. Wall Street frets unless there is a latter-day financier sitting at the secretary's desk under the portrait of Alexander Hamilton in the large corner office on the Treasury's third floor. Carter could have saved himself a lot of trouble by acknowledging this. Instead, he appointed as secretaries of the treasury two men who did not come from the department's banking and finance constituency. Michael Blumenthal was head of Bendix, a home-appliance giant, and William Miller was chief of Textron, a military-industrial multiglomerate. Either could have made better than average commerce secretaries. As treasury secretaries they were flops, digging a moat between the White House and the Money Power instead of building a bridge. This was not entirely their fault. Like others in industry, they were too prone to believe that the opinions of financiers on Wall Street mesh with what the bosses of Smokestack America are thinking. They don't. Businessmen making money selling goods want from the federal government policies that expand trade, keep business good, and help their industries when they get into trouble. Businessmen making money out of money want prudent monetary policies, balanced budgets over the course of the business cycle, and a sound dollar. Carter would have saved himself trouble by persuading some mighty banker, broker, or insurance business leader to head the Treasury. Instead, it seemed, he listened to the advice of one innocent in the White House, who told him: "We don't have to bother about the dollar. International trade is only 10 percent of GNP."

In picking Donald Regan, Reagan was guided by the desire to avoid Carter's mistake. A tough, streetwise boss of Wall Street's largest brokerage and financial supermarket, Merrill Lynch, Pierce, Fenner & Smith, Regan pleased financiers at first. He faced an immediate dilemma, though: either keep in with Wall Street by opposing plans within the administration for a large income tax cut the big money managers thought inflationary, thereby jeopardizing his standing with the Reagan White House, or accept the tax cuts at the risk of opposition from Wall Street. Regan chose the second course. After big tax cuts were enacted, the financial markets tumbled, and Regan found out that being a cabinet officer can be almost as difficult as being President.

For running their administrations, Presidents may not have a permanent cadre of senior civil servants to rely on—or to frustrate their plans. There is, all the same, a pool in Washington of gentlemen-in-waiting ready to serve. There are plenty, though still not enough, women-in-waiting now, too. Those in waiting are usually Democratic or Republican in the limited sense of tending to serve administrations of one stripe or the other. This partisanship is more by convenience than from conviction. These men and women are products of the great universities and law schools. By training and outlook they tend to think that certain matters—relations with the Soviet Union or management of the dollar—would be best left to them, not the politicians.

There are some—like James Schlesinger, an economist turned defense hawk who served and was fired by Ford and Carter in turn—who do join Republican or Democratic administrations. There are apparatchiki who move from administration to administration, like Frank Carlucci, the number-two man in Reagan's Pentagon, who has been in government posts since Kennedy, or the genial international economist Bob Hormats, who bounced from the Nixon-Ford NSC, through Carter's Treasury to Reagan's State Department. Professional diplomats may change jobs, but they need not lose rank when new Presidents move in, and at the top of the State Department or the diplomatic corps certain faces, like Philip Habib's, Harold Saunders's, or Roy Atherton's, become familiar to several Presidents.

Washington provides plenty of waiting rooms—the Brookings Institution or the Carnegie Endowment for International Peace (Democratic, though the association would be denied), and the American Enterprise Institute, the Georgetown Center for Strategic and International Studies, or the Heritage Foundation (Republican), as well as the big law firms, like Covington & Burling, or Wilmer, Cutler & Pickering —where the Outs can mark time, write books, recover for another round, and make dollars.

One hallmark of this Washington policy establishment is how compartmentalized it has become. For the foreign policy clerisy and the economic technocrats are only two of dozens of armies of experts. As the organism has grown, its cells have divided, ever more elaborately. In this process of splitting, according to Hugh Heclo of Brookings, the professionals have bunched into a growing number of "issue networks," also known as "iron triangles" or "policy whirlpools." Its members are professional staff members in Congress, lobbyists for large institutions, and bureaucrats in one of the departments. In background, training, and outlook they have their expertise and professionalism in common. In their jobs, in a sense, they are interchangeable and they often do change. Taking only the area of health, this is split into several clans, including those concerned with hospital associations, insurance companies, health planning groups, medical schools, hospital equipment makers, or preventive medicine advocates. Making policy, in short, has become subject to an ever increasing division of labor, and generalists —except perhaps as press officers, speech writers, or cartoonists—are in decreasing demand. The rise of narrower experts has gone hand in hand with the coming of the hired political consultant and "single-issue politics."

Neither the political neutrality nor the expertise of the policy professionals has gone untarnished. The days when John Kennedy could say at a White House economic conference that most of the problems faced in politics were no longer matters of party program or philosophy but "technical" and "administrative" questions seem innocent and far away. Gone is that confidence—some would have called it overconfidence—shown when Kennedy, on another occasion, said: "Give me the facts and figures on things we still have to do. For example, what about the poverty problem in the United States?" The experts and the technocrats are more modest than they were, less agreed among themselves, and readier to acknowledge when they have no answers. The record of economic advice and prediction is particularly poor and the better economists are ready to admit this. Charles Schultze, who worked for Johnson at the Budget Bureau—helping conceal, claimed the Republicans, the true costs of the Vietnam War —and later as chairman of the Council of Economic Advisers under Carter, said, when presenting the 1981 federal budget: "I am paid to make economic forecasts and I get paid even when I make the wrong ones." David Stockman, Reagan's budget director, acknowledged that in making his first budget, he had simply thrown out old assumptions in favor of an economic model that better fitted the Reaganite supply-side theory, which in turn, according to Stockman, rested on little more than "faith." The Vietnam War left the reputation of defense and foreign policy intellectuals in ruins, although this was not necessarily an end to future government employment. Cyrus Vance, Harold Brown, and Robert "Blowtorch" Komer, who ran the pacification program in Vietnam, all got senior posts under Carter.

The defense and foreign policy intellectuals—the New Mandarins, as Noam Chomsky called them—came under attack from the left in the 1960s for their supposedly scientific and value-free arguments in support of the Vietnam War. By contrast today, it is government social policy experts who find themselves set upon, by conservatives who claim these experts have entrenched themselves in the Washington policy establishment and acquired a vested interest in the welfare, regulatory, and environmental programs they promote. The left was, on the whole, more evenhanded in its suspicion of the Washington policy establishment, since it doubted the depth and effectiveness of liberal social reform just as much as it questioned the wisdom and good intentions of interventionist foreign policy. Today's conservatives tend to save their scorn for government intellectuals working on programs businessmen dislike, and spare those working, for example, on defense.

At its fullest, conservative criticism of the Washington policy establishment suggests that it has become peopled by members of a "new class" of unimagined number and influence, spawned by the postwar expansion of universities, hostile to business, magnetized to government, devoted more to marketing their expertise as social engineers than to helping cure the ills they complain of. Washington teems with lobbies for clean air, industrial safety, consumer rights, welfare recipients, or the handicapped, true. So it does with lobbies—and much more fatly endowed ones—that oppose them. Politically, there may be much to choose from between the young men and women who work, for example, at Ralph Nader's Public Citizen lobby, the Friends of the Earth, or the Children's Defense Fund and those who toil at the American Petroleum Institute, the United States Chamber of Commerce, or the American Medical Association, but in education and background there are few differences, both being professional, middle-class products of the postwar college boom, as are the university-trained young men and women who gravitate not to Washington but to business.

The term "intellectual" to describe anybody working in Washington may cause surprise, but it is meant, in this context, merely to cover those working with their heads, not their hands, while trafficking in policy and government. The Washington political style disconcerts true intellectuals—social critics—since it is oblivious of political and economic ideas, even as it is haunted by them. It is intensely practical, untidy, compromising, impatient with what might be done and always cutting through to what can be done, by making deals, bargaining, or subterfuge.

Just as Washington has no great university, so it has no true commercial life, and businessmen find it as alien a place as intellectuals do. The cost in misunderstanding is the price paid for having the capital in a federal district, not in a city like New York or Chicago, with a commercial and an intellectual life of its own.

Washington and bureaucracy, to most Americans, are virtually synonymous terms. Congress, the lobbies, and the White House have all grown bureaucratic, paper-filled and staff-heavy. Political Washington, for all that, is not hierarchical. Status conscious, yes, and intensely so, but too fluid and disorganized, at least in its upper reaches, to be hierarchical. There is no office plan saying who counts and who does not count. That has to be learned with every change of administration and frequently in between.

There are many badges of influence. Titles alone are a treacherous guide. The third-ranking under secretary for policy may underrank but outinfluence the second-ranking deputy secretary. The number of reporters at an official's press conference can be a sign. So can the number of appearances on the Sunday network public affairs talk shows, *Meet the Press, Face the Nation,* and *Issues and Answers.* Television exposure, while essential, is not enough. Opinions must be circulated, leaked in background briefings or over dinner, to appear in the *Washington Post.* The seeker of influence must be quotable. "I had lunch the other day with Don, and he thinks . . ." or "I gather from Paul Volcker that . . ." or "Jim Baker says that . . ." It does not matter that the name-dropper exaggerates. The Donald Regan lunch may have been a fund-raiser with three hundred guests. The remarks of Paul Volcker, the chairman of the Federal Reserve Board, may have come from published testimony before a congressional subcommittee. Jim Baker's words may be fourth-hand and garbled. To the power whose name is dropped this hardly matters at all. Counterfeit or not, being quoted is the coinage of influence.

As political Washington is a town of transients, like other exclusively capital cities—Canberra, Brasilia, or Bonn—a need is felt by some for social gatekeepers. There is a social register, known as the Green Book. This includes senators, the more respectable members of Congress, some diplomats, and others with power or money. Those divorced are excluded, as are all but two journalists, although Washington gives reporters a high status unknown anywhere else in the world. Not appearing in the Green Book, however, is no mark of permanent failure at the social game of out-of-office politics which counts for so much in political Washington. For as the journalist Tom Bethell, a conservative eye, observes, this Washington is utterly open and democratic. Almost everybody is given a chance. There is no membership list or table fee. A player may never get asked back, but everybody is asked once and gets a start in the game.

These are some of the reasons the best books about Washington— political Washington, that is—are novels, and none better than Henry

Adams's *Democracy*, a story of power and corruption set in Washington after the Civil War. The wealthy heroine, Mrs. Lightfoot Lee, visits the city in search of "Power," sets up a salon with her sister, and becomes attracted to the dour Senator Ratcliffe of Illinois, his party's king-maker and the manipulator of a weak President, "Old Granite," modeled on Rutherford Hayes. After much incidental business, Mrs. Lee rejects Senator Ratcliffe, having learned that his great influence in the city involves a readiness to lie, cheat, and break others more scrupulous than himself. The book has worn well. Whatever Adams may have intended, Senator Ratcliffe, although an ungodly bore, emerges as a much more solid and vital character than the overrefined and prudish Mrs. Lee, who leaves Washington at the end of the book for a tour of Europe.

If power has flowed back again down Pennsylvania Avenue from the White House to Congress, once there it has tended to vanish. This has made a President's third job—dealing with Congress—all the harder. "The discipline has gone," says Senator Robert Byrd, the Democratic majority leader, upended and made minority leader when the Republicans, in 1980, won control of the Senate for the first time in more than twenty-five years. "It went with the breakup of the Southern bloc," he explains. His office is a tall, narrow room with pale-yellow walls and large windows, sparsely furnished with elegant early-nineteenth-century mahogany chairs. Byrd is talking about the difficulties of managing the Senate majority, troubles amply inherited by his Republican successor, Senator Howard Baker of Tennessee. Byrd's regret is neutral, technical almost. Dominated as it was by reactionary Southerners, the old Senate was easier to manage. Now nobody knows who is in charge.

Bobby Byrd of West Virginia is a remarkable example of that common American phenomenon of political rebirth. Byrd was butcher, welder, blue-grass fiddler, and dabbler in the Ku Klux Klan before his election to the Senate. Once there, he sided with the segregationists. In 1964, he filibustered against the civil rights bill. As Byrd moved up, however, the old order was breaking down. Southern Democrats were losing their grip, Northern Democrats were drifting rightward, and Bobby Byrd was drifting centerward to meet them. By 1977, he was deep enough in the mainstream to become majority leader.

In alliance with conservative Republicans, Southerners could defeat

liberal senators on roll-call votes at almost any period in the quarter of
a century between 1938, when the Southern Democrats deserted
Roosevelt, and the early 1960s. Southerners monopolized the committee chairmanships. These were then positions of great power. Giving
out committee assignments according to length of uninterrupted service—"seniority"—helped perpetuate the Southerners' grip. Seniority
was not to be given up lightly in either Senate or House, where Southerners, even smaller in relative number, were also disproportionately
strong. When Truman asked Carl Vinson of Georgia, the vulpine
chairman of the House Armed Services Committee before whom generals and admirals would quake, if his name could be put forward for
secretary of defense, the old Swamp Fox from Milledgeville replied:
"Aw, shucks, I'd rather run the Pentagon from up here."

Southerners were a rock on which voting coalitions in Congress
could be built or wrecked. As the Democratic majority swelled, however, with Democrats from the North, Southern influence slowly
waned. Desegregation in the early 1960s was their undoing. Filibuster-
ing against the 1964 civil rights bill split them from their Republican
allies. After this futile act of obstructionism, they lost their confidence.
Age and reform took care of the rest. In an extraordinarily brief period
of time, the power of the Southern chairmen was gone. In 1969,
Southern conservatives held ten of the Senate's sixteen standing committee chairs. At the start of the Ninety-sixth Congress, in 1979, they
held only three.

Liberal Democrats waited long for little. Only Foreign Relations,
chaired by Frank Church of Idaho, and Judiciary, chaired by Ted
Kennedy of Massachusetts, fell into liberal hands, properly speaking.
The other committee chairmen were as mixed a bunch as the Democrats themselves, including instinctive centrists such as Alan Cranston,
a workaday alliance-builder from California, which, in keeping with its
Geminid nature, normally sends to the Senate one serious politician
and one clown; cold war New Dealers, such as Henry "Scoop" Jackson
of Washington; and senators not to be pigeonholed, like William
Proxmire of Wisconsin, dispenser of the "Golden Fleece Award" for
creative waste of public funds.

When these chairmen were all swept out again two years later, the
Republicans who took their places showed no more common pattern.

The more senior Republicans, such as Charles Percy, Charles Mathias, Bob Packwood, and Mark Hatfield, share a muffled, live-and-let-live fiscal conservatism very different from the radicalism of the angry young men supported by the New Right and the Moral Majority. A large share of the chairmanships fell into moderate conservative hands, although these were balanced by Rocky Mountain senators and conservatives of the far right, such as Orrin Hatch and Jake Garn of Utah, as well as by Jesse Helms, protecting North Carolina's tobacco subsidies as chairman of the Agriculture Committee.

Even if they were united by outlook, the chairmen would not be the powers they once were. Nothing has replaced the old order uprooted by reform Democrats in the 1970s. More power was given to subcommittee chairmen and in 1974 the number of chairmanships allowed any one representative was limited. The upshot was that almost one representative in three became chairman of some subcommittee or other. Too many chefs and not enough pot washers? Yes, thinks the owlish Representative David Obey of Wisconsin, a reformer himself who believes the dispersal of power has gone too far. Besides this proliferation of subcommittees, the growth in congressional staff, now numbering about twenty thousand, has made every representative an expert on something and, claim conservatives, encouraged unnecessary legislation. Aides speak through their senators, of course, as well as the other way around. An influential group of liberal staffers did put a distinct stamp on social, environmental, and foreign policy legislation in the early 1970s. By the same institutional token, but with opposite political results, a group of conservative staffers, known as the Madison Group, became influential in the 1980s.

The weakening of committee chairmen ought, in theory, to make possible a return to stronger guidance from the party leaders, if not to the cattle-herding methods of Speaker "Uncle Joe" Cannon of Illinois, also known as "Foulmouth," who ruled the House for six famous years until he was deposed by progressives in 1909. Stronger leadership might be more possible if knowing who was Democrat and who was Republican were easier. Even when the Democrats kept their majority in the House in 1980, there were enough neatly coiffed and polyester-suited conservative Democrats to team up with Republicans to support the new president. The problem of these "Boll Weevils," mostly but not entirely from the South, was not new for the shaggy, beleaguered Speaker Tip O'Neill. In the Watergate election of 1974, forty-three Democrats got in from previously safe Republican seats. A new liberal age? Not at all. Most of these young men and women were no more progressive than the Republicans they replaced, which should have surprised nobody, coming as they did from Republican districts. Throughout the next few years, the lopsided majority apparently enjoyed by the Democrats behaved in ever less predictable ways, leading Frank Moore, Carter's congressional lobbyist, to complain that a new Democratic alliance had to be stitched together in Congress for every separate bill.

The pressures leaders can bring to bear on errant party members are few. Representatives are still expected to be just that, emissaries in Washington who represent the needs and interests of their constituents. Failing to do this is punished at the polls more swiftly and certainly than not toeing some indistinct and shifting party line. When Al Ullman, chairman of the House Ways and Means Committee, and John Brademas, Democratic whip, lost their seats in 1980 to obscure Republican upstarts, this was not chiefly because their mainstream Democratic outlook was out of touch with the times—the overwhelming majority of like-minded Democrats were safely returned. Rather, as powers in Congress, they had come to be seen at home as having lost touch with their districts, neither of which—eastern Oregon and South Bend, Indiana—is easy to reach from Washington.

Sitting congressmen all the same have clear advantages over their challengers at election time, such as free mailing privileges and well-staffed offices in their home districts. Congress has refused to accept public financing of congressional elections, which would at least start incumbents and challengers out with the same amount of money, and in so refusing has kept the advantage incumbents usually enjoy in raising campaign funds. Since contributions from party funds to congressional races account for so small a part of the total spending, amply supplied by the lobbying interests, parties have little financial leverage over representatives.

Senators, by contrast, have grown vulnerable, perhaps since their baronies are usually so much bigger than the half-million-odd congressional district, their voting record more exposed, the interests they must represent so much more diverse. Senators, it is often said, are the "pointmen" of American politics. The percentage of senators seeking reelection who were reelected was 64 percent in 1976, 60 percent in 1978, and 55 percent in 1980, all elections with different national outcomes, suggesting that senators of either party cannot afford to be complacent. More and more, senators are having to stand up and be counted.

Far from being statesmen of an upper chamber loftily balancing the popular excesses of the lower house, as antiquated theory and their elaborately formal style on the Senate floor might suggest, senators are harassed creatures chairing committees and making up their minds on how to vote on the floor on several different bills on the same day. When Scoop Jackson came to the Senate in 1952, sessions lasted about nine months. Now they last eleven or more. Although the number of bills has not risen much, a mere 3,800 or so a session, the number of recorded votes has soared, from under three hundred then to more than a thousand today. Party discipline in the Senate is even laxer than in the House, and senators pay little penalty for not voting with their party. Policy groups and lobbyists, however, acting as unofficial whips, batten upon senators, watch how they vote in committee and on the floor, give them scores, and publish regular performance ratings. Ratings are recorded by such groups as the National Association of Businessmen, the American Conservative Union, the Committee on Political Education—the political arm of the AFL-CIO—and Americans for Democratic Action. Liberal Democrats like Senator Ted Kennedy or Paul Tsongas of Massachusetts get, for example, high scores from ADA and low ones from ACU. It is the other way around for Senate leaders of the New Right, like Jesse Helms. To dismiss congressional scores as another American fixation with grades, ratings, averages, and statistics of all kinds is easy, but mistaken. Campaign contributors want to know how the politicians they have helped elect are voting. Otherwise, how would they know whether or not their investment was worthwhile?

To the extent that parties in Congress are weak, lobbies on Capitol Hill are strong. Lobbyists have never had very good reputations. Walt Whitman thought they belonged with "the lousy combings and born freedom sellers of the earth." McKinley begged off a request from his rich backer Mark Hanna for the appointment of a friend, saying he would do anything for Hanna but could not have a known lobbyist in his cabinet. The very word conjures up a disreputable presence lurking in a Thomas Nast cartoon. Claud Wild, Gulf Oil's Washington representative in the 1960s, recycled, on his own account, hundreds of thousands of petrodollars among the town's politicians. More than a dozen leading industrialists were fined in 1973 for illegal campaign contributions. Koreagate and Abscam kept reputations sullied. No wonder most Washington lobbyists call themselves "legislative counsels" or "advisers for congressional relations."

The scandalous reputation is not so much undeserved as beside the point. Lobbies make the system work. Theirs is the double coinage of facts, arguments, and expertise, on the one hand, and legal campaign contributions on the other. The first helps hard-pressed senators and congressmen make up their minds. Never threaten, never beg, and never think you're always right, was George Meany's advice to labor lobbyists. Charls Walker, a banking lobbyist from Texas who worked for Nixon, has a rule of never trying to lobby a politician on a subject he or she knows more about. Campaign donations are not only reelection lifeblood; dangled in front of potential opponents, they keep senators and congressmen in line.

Americans can be refreshingly frank and unhypocritical about money and politics. They can laugh indulgently at the distinction drawn by Boss Plunkitt of Tammany Hall between "honest graft" and "dishonest graft." When it was said of Boss Plunkitt that "he saw his opportunities and he took 'em," he treated this as a great compliment. Politics, to Boss Plunkitt, was a trade, like the grocery business. Politicians were middlemen who took a cut. This tradition persists, although it is under constant attack from good-government reformers. Chronic scandal does surround the huge sums of money routinely exchanged in the business of politics, sometimes over and sometimes under the counter. Congress does from time to time undertake to clean out its stables, but rather in the spirit of the police chief Captain Renault, who tells Rick, the proprietor, in the film *Casablanca*, "I am shocked, shocked, to discover gambling in this club," as the croupier deftly hands him his winnings. Elaborate limits were placed on presidential —but not congressional—campaign spending in 1974. These were quickly and ingeniously circumvented by "independent" committees, permitted to spend money for a candidate's election so long as they did not pay the candidate directly. Reform efforts today are usually directed at trying to neutralize the advantage of business donors. Republicans habitually outspend but do not necessarily defeat Democrats. Though poorer, Democrats may be more cost-effective.

Mencken was once asked why he continued so keenly to follow politics and he replied that this was like asking why people enjoyed going to zoos. The best way of looking at a politician, wrote E. E. Cummings, was "down." The most gifted politicians can have trouble obeying the simple rule, attributed to the Texas millionaire and Democratic lawyer-fixer Robert Strauss, "If you can't eat it, drink it, or sleep with it within twenty-four hours, then get rid of it."

Considering the frequency of the Sudden Political Downfall, it might be thought it would cause less attention than it does when the mighty are indicted, tried, and sent to jail. Yet Americans can also be affronted by corruption. The mixture of worldliness and moralism with which Americans regard their politicians is a puzzle. It seems so wasteful of talent, to wink at the crime and then punish the miscreant if he is caught. Do Americans look down on politicians because politics is corrupt? No, it is the other way around. They look down on them for deeper reasons. If they held the profession in higher regard, they might not banish its members so readily for what almost anywhere else would be treated as peccadilloes.

Bryce called Americans "unreverential" toward politicians. Tocqueville made much of their lack of deference to elected officials. Americans have scant natural respect for appointed leaders or ingrained habits of obedience to authority. Despite huge differences of wealth, the egalitarian streak is strong: Each person is as good as the next and nobody, by education or background, can claim allegiance from others. Elected officials, being ordinary men and women, bring no prior authority to the job. Office is not privilege and politics is not a club. Every politician is replaceable, as Nixon learned, if he did not know it already.

All this might seem to make a fourth difficulty to add to the three Presidents face today: a skeptical public, a balkanized administration, and a fractured Congress. Yet what suspicion of authority ought to add is perspective. For there is a deep, conservative distrust of government in America. Government is not currently designed to operate with spontaneous efficiency. Quite the opposite. Politicians are told to govern and denied the means. Distrust of politicians comes from distrust of power. This is a fundamentally conservative system of government. It only acts decisively when many different forces unite to push it in one direction. Without that, the President's job is not meant to be workable. Of course, not all Americans have the same interest in weak government. This dispute is the stuff of party politics.

5

LIMPING DONKEYS
AND LUMBERING ELEPHANTS
Democrats and Republicans

To REPORTS of the breaking down of the two political parties, it is tempting to repeat what was said of Coolidge's death: "How could they tell?" Never strong or intricate structures, the Democratic and Republican parties come together every four years for a noisy, exuberant nominating convention. For thirty years or more these have been little more than anointment ceremonies. The Ford-Reagan struggle in 1976 was really over before the two got to the Republican convention in Kansas City. In between presidential campaigns, national parties have for some time now led a ghostlike existence. To be national at all, the parties must be very broad churches. How else could Ted Kennedy, Shirley Chisholm, George Wallace, Jerry Brown, and Henry Jackson call themselves Democrats? Ronald Reagan, Bob Packwood, Jack Kemp, Mac Mathias, and Strom Thurmond Republicans?

It is tempting, too, to agree that between Democrats and Republicans, once in office and off the hustings, there are few important differences. Lord Bryce was told that the two parties were like bottles with the same label and nothing in them. Many since have accepted this. Every four years, Gore Vidal has said, Americans have a chance to choose between the Democratic and Republican wings of the Property party. In his third-party phase, George Wallace used to say: "Democrats, Republicans, put 'em in a sack, shake 'em up, and it don't make a dime's worth of difference which comes out because they're all the same."

With the New Deal, the Democrats became the party of government, both as the majority party—holding the White House or both houses of Congress between 1932 and 1980 for all but four years—and as the party that set out to use government, whether to steer the economy, provide for welfare, or act as "countervailing power" for the have-nots against the haves. With World War II, the Democrats became internationalists, and in 1948, Dixiecrats aside, the party of civil rights. Modern Republicans were the opposition, the party of fiscal caution, isolationism, and free enterprise, unfettered but not necessarily unaided by government.

Skepticism about party differences gets support because political labels and reputations have often meant little in office, especially for Presidents. Franklin Roosevelt campaigned to cut spending and balance the budget. Truman of Missouri was not expected to take any interest in foreign affairs. Eisenhower, a military man and an adopted Republican, kept the defense budget steady and raised domestic spending. Johnson, a Southern Democrat suspected by liberals, pushed through the Civil Rights Act. Nixon, the free enterprise conservative and "Who lost China?" cold warrior, imposed wage and price controls and went to Peking. Carter, a conservative Southern populist campaigning under Democratic colors, who promised lower defense spending and national health insurance, raised the first and never got around to the second. What is striking in this list is that until Carter, every President governed less conservatively than he campaigned. Each President, regardless of party, very broadly accepted what could be called the Democratic Idea of strong, activist government, both at home and in foreign affairs.

Try as it may, American politics cannot do entirely without ideas. The Democratic Idea is what provided a thread through the labyrinth for the better part of forty years. Under other names, the Democratic Idea is Welfare Capitalism or the Liberal Consensus.

From Franklin Roosevelt's time, modern conservatives have defined themselves as opponents of the Democratic Idea. Reconciled to being unable to capture the government for any length of time, let alone control it, modern conservatives concentrated instead on trying to limit its scope. To the extent that conservatives saw themselves as the political voice of business, they had another opponent in organized labor. After successful struggles with business in the 1930s and 1940s, industrial unionism reached a plateau in its influence. The federal

subsidies. This was Johnson's own high point, and a high point for the Democratic Idea.

Republicans in this period got modern religion, too, helped by the defeat of Goldwater, which seemed to silence their conservative wing. In 1968, Nixon knew he could not get nominated without the support of the Republican right, and he correctly sensed he could best get elected by running for "law and order" against the politico-cultural revolution of blacks, the young, and antiwar protesters. In office, though, Nixon's break with the Democratic Idea was far from clean. In January 1971, he let on that he, too, was now a Keynesian in economics. His "New Federalism," designed to return spending initiative from Washington, led to large increases in federal spending as money was raised to return to the states. Partly because he faced a Democratic Congress, his years saw much environmental legislation, affirmative action, and regulation of business. Nixon also was preoccupied first with foreign affairs, and then with Watergate. His presidency brought only some of the changes at home his conservative supporters had once hoped for. Early on in his administration, the Buckley Republicans had issued a conditional "withdrawal of support."

All the while the Democratic Idea was losing its hold. Slow growth and high inflation—"stagflation"—left economists at a loss. In the 1970s, a new breed of young Democratic politicians began preaching an economic gospel of limits and retrenchment as inflation pushed wage earners into higher and higher tax brackets. "Bracket creep" might not have been heard of outside economic departments, but almost every taxpayer felt its effect, and Democratic governors like Michael Dukakis of Massachusetts and Jerry Brown of California knew what a rightward pull it was having on Democratic voters. In 1978, exasperated California property-tax payers voted themselves a huge tax cut, a revolt imitated widely elsewhere.

Vietnam, Watergate, and OPEC opened American eyes and narrowed American horizons. Conservative politicians and conservative ideas benefited most. Monetarism in economics, which had once, like spontaneous generation or geocentrism, been thought safely dead, became fashionable again. Bright young lawyers in Washington, who since the New Deal had written the regulations, turned instead to unwriting them, as deregulation became the smart game in town. Interest shifted from old Democratic remedies for long-term unemployment, like pub-lic-sector jobs, to tax breaks for industry to encourage new capital investment. Resentment among some whites at the extension of black rights—by school busing and affirmative action—festered. Attitudes toward crime and punishment hardened. The death penalty, after a brief holiday, returned. Religion reappeared in public life. Parents disappointed by progressive experiment in the schools began asking for a return to basics. Matters thought closed, like abortion, were bitterly reopened.

Jimmy Carter fought the 1976 presidential election under Demo-cratic colors, but the party's slogans sounded hollow in his mouth. Carter was a party outsider, a Southerner, a fiscal conservative. "Tight as a tick," Carter's spokesman, Jody Powell, called him. He was un-known and distrusted both by McGovernite Democrats—who were nevertheless unable to unite to "Stop Carter"—and by traditional Democrats, who backed in turn the soporific Henry Jackson and the ailing Hubert Humphrey. Carter's and the Democrats' was a marriage of convenience. Speeches at the Democratic convention rang with New Deal slogans, Truman promises, Great Society vision, and even Nader reformism. Almost nobody was taken in. Carter did not cam-paign at the head of the old Democratic coalition. It had broken up. Rather, he separately assembled each of its parts. The resulting whole lacked any governing idea, a fact which quickly became apparent once Carter took office and allowed his administration to be peopled with Democrats at war with themselves. The Ninety-fifth Congress, 1977–1979, unpredictable as it was, showed how weak the Democrats had become, as labor law reform was defeated, national health schemes postponed, and oil price controls lifted.

Agreement had broken down among Democrats about foreign pol-icy. Two months after Johnson's "Great Society" address, two batta-lions of Marines had gone ashore at Da Nang. The war split the Democrats so deeply that by 1976 they no longer had a single recogniz-ably internationalist point of view. On the one hand were defense-minded Democrats such as Senators Jackson and Moynihan, fixated still on the historical memory of Munich, attracted to strategic theories of geopolitics, and prone to organize every foreign policy argument around the rivalry between the United States and the Soviet Union. The second group, fixated on the Vietnam War, was typified by the liberal senators swept out in 1978 and 1980—McGovern, Church, Clark—and by many of the younger advisers in Carter's administration, men like Anthony Lake and Richard Moose, who were against Nixon's war policy. Their concerns were as much conflicts between the world's poor and rich as competition between Russians and Americans; they wished to restrain American military adventures abroad, took an optimistic view of international organizations, and thought that foreign aid helps the United States. The division was partly a matter of generations, although the "doves" had elder statesmen like George Ball, and the "hawks" young lieutenants like Jackson's Senate aide, Richard Perle, who worked cleverly and tirelessly against the SALT treaty and was rewarded with a senior job in Reagan's Pentagon.

The Vietnam generation won several skirmishes, but continually lost ground, and was routed by the coincidence of the Iranian revolution and the Soviet military action in Afghanistan. Within Carter's administration, the dogged, lawyerly Cyrus Vance, a moderate "dove," was no match for the hawkish, self-assertive, and publicity-wise Zbigniew Brzezinski.

Agreement had also broken down among Democrats about welfare and social spending. Neoconservative Democrats joined Republicans in arguing that where Johnson's Great Society programs had failed they should be cut and where they had succeeded they could no longer be fully afforded. Every voice in the argument had its own favorite report by a team of social scientists, showing that schooling made little difference to poverty or black advancement, or that schools mattered most; that housing was really the key, or that housing would do little unless accompanied by jobs. Programs were attacked from the left, too, on the grounds that expectations of what these programs could do were inflated and that liberal reform could never do enough. Few social scientists who studied actual programs—such as food stamps, begun in 1961 but greatly expanded in 1967, or the Follow Through and Head Start school programs—could find support for the view that they were failures. Quite the opposite: they were in their own terms noble successes.

Politically, for the Democrats, this was all beside the point. Support among voters was too narrow for going further, particularly since it was widely if wrongly thought that while New Deal social programs helped all, Great Society ones unduly helped blacks. After 1972, Democrats badly needed to win back the "Wallace vote"—a loose code for working-class Democrats, red-necks in the South, modern Copperheads in the North, who were resentful at having to make, as they saw it, the main sacrifices for a multiracial society at the behest of the "pointy-headed liberals" whom Wallace loved to mock and who, they felt, did not represent their class interests. Appalled by McGovern in 1972, they had voted heavily for Nixon. Carter, particularly in the South, won back the Wallace vote for the Democrats, if only briefly, but to do so Carter himself had to sing an anti-Washington tune. Once in office, he began to reduce increases in social spending in favor of rearmament. In this, Carter was warmly opposed by Ted Kennedy, who picked up the old Democratic standard. The faithful loved him, but the faithful were a minority even in their own party, as Kennedy's faltering 1980 campaign showed.

Agreement had broken down, too, about civil rights. Affirmative action split black and Jewish Democrats, who had marched together in the early 1960s. Joe Rauh, a veteran Washington civil rights lawyer, recalled a debate at Temple Sinai in Washington about the "reverse discrimination" suit brought by Alan P. Bakke, a white would-be medical student, against the University of California Medical School at Davis. Rauh defended the school's preferential admissions scheme to help minorities. Afterward, a stocky woman went up to him, "with blood in her eye," Rauh recounted, and said: "We've done enough for them. They don't appreciate what we've done for them already."

Economic change aggravated these difficulties for the Democrats. Rather slower growth and much rapider inflation in the 1970s made it harder and harder for the Democrats to evade the question of who within their broad constituency—business, labor, rich, poor, or middle class—should make the bigger sacrifices of present income for future prosperity.

For forty years, the Democrats were the party that reached out and gathered people in, while the Republicans were the party that turned inward and kept people out. Democrats had in Roosevelts or Biddles old wealth, as well as new money in Harrimans and Kennedys, not to mention raw political talent in Johnsons or Humphreys, who started out with next to nothing at all. Considering the party's ambition to reconcile irreconcilables, it is astonishing it showed such vigor for so long. Democratic strength among working-class voters did not make it a working-class party. In fact, it makes almost more sense to view the party from the top down than from the bottom up.

At its height, the party was an elite coalition of financiers, lawyers, and industrialists, linked particularly with corporations on government contract or doing business abroad; it included university-trained specialists and administrators, purged of Marxists or socialists; it rallied a reformist, anti-Communist union leadership; it worked, in parallel, with Eastern or "moderate" Republicans who accepted the Liberal Consensus. Neat as all this sounds, the Democrats also depended for voting strength until the 1960s on the segregationist wing of the party in the South, a reminder of the doctrinal untidiness of American parties.

Astronomers report that there are certain very distant stars that pulsate in quickening rhythm and then explode with bursts of extraordinarily condensed energy, only to collapse upon themselves, virtually disappearing altogether, before repeating the whole cycle again. Such is the modern Republican party. There have been as many premature reports of its death as of enduring Republican majorities. Instability is its second name. Look simply at the past decade. At the beginning, many Republicans thought they were poised to become the new governing party that would put the Democrats into the position of a near-permanent minority the Republicans had occupied since Roosevelt. There followed the Watergate landslide for the Democrats in 1974 and the defeat of Ford in 1976, which left the Democrats with a comfortable majority in the Senate, a huge majority in the House, and all but thirteen of the state governorships. Kevin Phillips, a Republican commentator, who had written, in 1971, *The Emerging Republican Majority*, decided that the Republican party was nearing a state of "critical non-mass." In 1980, the dense, disappearing Republican star exploded in a shower of light once more and the political talk was, again, of party realignment and new Republican majorities, although this did not last out Mr. Reagan's first year.

There is a sense in which 1980 was the election that Watergate postponed. Feeling a conservative wind ten years before, Republicans were correct to think they would be its natural beneficiaries. Though Watergate produced Democratic victories, it did not bring in liberal or traditional Democrats, but rather Republicans under a safer name. Certainly, in Carter, Watergate hardly brought in a recognizable Democrat at all. Republicans were correct to think of themselves as the natural party of conservatism. However right-wing Democrats were becoming, conservatism was not and could not be the party's heart. Besides, McGovern or Kennedy Democrats were still too strong within the party to let it become undividedly conservative, even if they were too weak to capture the party nomination.

Yet the Republicans have in modern times been chronically prone to self-destructiveness and adept at the missed opportunity. In 1912, they split and let the Democrats steal the Progressive mantle, a source of much subsequent trouble. In the 1920s, the Republicans, comfortably ensconced in power, stood pat and let go the farmers and the craft unions, as they later did the blacks. Almost every four years since 1940, Republicans have fought a grinding war between right and center, between Main Street and Wall Street, between the insurance salesman or country banker from Nebraska or Utah and the international money manager from New York. Taft versus Dewey, Taft versus Eisenhower, Goldwater versus Rockefeller, Reagan versus Ford, were all bitter struggles between the primitives—as Rockefeller, echoing Dean Acheson, called them—and the establishment moderates.

To call the last two struggles is perhaps to overstate things. Bitter, yes, but hardly struggles, for a struggle takes two. The passion, the will for victory, the certainty of the righteousness of their cause, all lay with the primitives. So, increasingly, did control of the nominating process. The establishment moderates—Rockefeller, William Scranton, Clifford Case, and Jacob Javits—thought of themselves as the best, but more and more they came to lack conviction. In 1964, at the San Francisco Cow Palace, Rockefeller was booed and shrieked at for half an hour by Goldwater delegates. Reporters for the *New York Times*, the very symbol of the Eastern establishment, were hissed. Rockefeller hardly deserved this, since he had already, in 1960, fatally weakened the moderates' hand by agreeing not to press his campaign against Nixon.

In 1976, the moderates haunted the Republican convention at Kansas City as strangers in their own house. The primitives just missed nominating Ronald Reagan, largely because Ford was in the White House and even Republicans were able to stop themselves from ditch-ing a sitting President. Ford fell somewhere in the middle of the Republican spectrum. Moderates could accept him; he had just enough conservative support. That much was clear even before Kansas City. Yet Ford had to pay a price for the nomination. Early in the year, at conservative insistence, he allowed delays in SALT talks with the Russians which were to help cripple them later. At Kansas City itself, Ford had to watch the Republicans formally disown Nixon-Kissinger diplomacy.

Four years later, the Republican establishment, or such of it as remained, was unable to agree on a candidate to "Stop Reagan," commonly, but incorrectly, thought too extreme to be electable. As Alan Greenspan, the Wall Street economist who had worked for Ford, said, John Connally, a former Democrat, had three-quarters of the chief executive officers of the Fortune 500 behind him and this accounted for precisely 50 percent of his total support. For the rest the establishment had to bank on George Bush, the stiff, none too bright son of a Connecticut senator, packed off to run an oil business in Texas, where he had yet to win a statewide election, and on Gerald Ford, who interrupted his play at the Jackie Gleason Golf Classic in Fort Lauderdale to hint he might be available for the nomination, but then dithered until it was too late.

By the 1980 Republican convention in Detroit, the primitives were in triumph, although Reagan's circle were still so unaware of the scope of their conquest as to seek Ford's help in uniting the party. Henry Kissinger, Rockefeller's protégé and the Republican establishment's prize exhibit in the world at large, gave a speech to the delegates that amounted to an admission of past mistakes, a speech to which the distracted delegates barely bothered to listen. Robert Scheer, of the *Los Angeles Times,* who did listen, commented that it was like hearing a confession at a purge trial.

Mr. and Mrs. Republican Primitive, to meet, are not enraged or frothing with resentment. Far from it. They are friendly, warmly so; flushed, not with drink, but with the excitement of the occasion. They would, one is certain, take in a stranger and smother him with hospitality. They are flattered by a questioner's interest in their hometown and proud of their children and grandchildren. They like Reagan, not for his winning smile or because he performs so well on television, but because he says what they think and has been saying it for the better part of twenty years. This is important to understand, for they are deeply serious about their politics, which for them is a natural extension of their morals or religion, and quite as starkly black and white. Politics, to them, is less the art of the possible than a sequence of moral imperatives. They are crusaders—against abortion, against equal rights for women, against pornography. As uncurious about the wider world as the old Taft Republicans, they are no longer isolationists, but interventionists who want America to restore the world to a simpler, less menancing condition. Great believers in conspiracies, they are prone to think of the Council on Foreign Relations or the Trilateral Commission as spiders at the center of a web that stretches across the national life. Unimpressed by the great universities of the East, suspicious of modern thinking, they may no longer believe Harvard and Yale are staffed by subversives, but they think they are crowded with snobs. Important in their own towns, they have for years felt neglected, mocked even, on the national stage, in the big newspapers, and on television, although now they are coming more into their own. They are comfortable with modern machines such as the drive-in church or the New Right's direct-mail, computerized political action committee, but they are profoundly antimodern and they dislike big cities, especially New York. They are not racist in any obvious way and would have found nothing strange in Reagan's remark during his television debate with Jimmy Carter that when he was a boy growing up—in the small Midwestern town of Dixon, Illinois—racial prejudice was not a problem. Like the poor, black Americans, for the primitives, are invisible, not really there. Reagan took time off during the Detroit convention to talk to a group of the city's black businessmen, on the importance of helping establish black businesses in the inner cities. The trouble today, Reagan told them, is that with so few black-owned businesses, dollars come into the black community, and circulate only once or twice, creating little work before "going out into society again."

If Reagan is their messiah, a chief apostle is Jesse Helms, the Senate leader of the New Right, ultraconservative in economics, foreign affairs, and above all "social issues," such as abortion, school prayer, capital punishment, and sex education. The positions Jesse Helms adopts are the sort that Goldwater Republicans used to take in Democratic districts with majorities of 70 percent or more, where Republicans had no chance of being elected and where there was no cost to campaigning as a right-wing gargoyle.

Helms is a tall, affable man with round glasses and a pale, lugubrious face. A devout Baptist, born in Monroe, North Carolina, in 1921, Helms is one of the first and the least compromising of the modern Southern Republicans. His polite, somewhat starchy manner hides a political determination and a talent for raising money that friends and enemies have learned to respect.

His first brush with politics was a racist campaign in 1950 against Frank Graham, former head of the University of North Carolina. A Democrat then, Helms helped Graham's opponent, who ran handbills saying: "White People Wake Up!" After a brief stint in Washington, Helms went back to Raleigh as a television commentator, and railed for the next twelve years against integration and moral laxity—which included, for Helms, the assignment by a state university teacher of Marvell's "Ode to His Coy Mistress" to his English class. Switching to the Republican party, Helms in 1972 ran for the Senate and won. There, for eight years, he remained a curiosity, introducing doomed resolutions on matters of import to the New Right but to almost nobody else until the 1980 tide floated him off. The eight years were not wasted. Helms built up a record of doctrinal purity with the New Right and mastered the new money-raising technology, pulling in $6 million for his own reelection campaign in 1978 and nearly $8 million to help favored candidates of the New Right in 1980.

Two separate, older strains of modern Republican conservatism—the anti-Communist traditionalism of the Catholic right, typified by William Buckley, editor of the *National Review,* and the free-market Libertarians—keep their distance from the New Right, which is more a climate of resentment and a money-raising system than a body of ideas. Buckley, a gifted controversialist, founded the *National Review* in 1955, quickly to see it become the voice of the Republican ultras. The son of an Irish-American businessman who got his money in Latin American oil leases, Buckley made a splash soon out of college with *God and Man at Yale.* This championed Christianity and the individual against secularism and collectivism, recommending, by the way, a purge of Yale's "socialist" faculty, which included at the time such notorious subversives as Paul Samuelson, whose best-selling textbook was to teach several generations of college students their elementary Keynesianism. Unlike the Libertarians, who espoused an extreme individualism and laissez-faire capitalism, Buckley conservatives defended traditions of family and church threatened by the modern marketplace.

This internal strain—between tradition and free enterprise—is strong, too, among the neoconservatives, a prolific but loose association of intellectuals concentrated in New York, who have given the modern Republican revival most of its argumentative zest. Angered by preferential treatment given women and racial minorities, disillusioned by the Great Society, appalled by what they took to be American passivity in the face of Russian opportunism, this once left, once liberal group of writers and social critics has devoted a considerable gift for polemic to trying to strip liberal Democrats of their last remnants of decent intellectual clothing.

Critics more than program drafters, social thinkers more than economists, the neoconservatives are ambivalent about bluff defenses of the free market. Irving Kristol, the Godfather of the movement, one of its few Republicans and the only one to accept the label "neoconservative" without resistance, raises only two cheers for capitalism. Daniel Bell, the Harvard sociologist, with whom Kristol founded *The Public Interest* magazine, explored the "cultural contradictions" of modern capitalism, which by its very success threatens to undermine the virtues of hard work, family loyalty, and respect for authority on which it depends. *Commentary*, published by the American Jewish Committee and edited by Norman Podhoretz, by his own account an escapee from the New Left, is the most widely read neoconservative journal. Over the years, it has published well-known attacks on Democratic ideas and programs—"Limits of Social Policy," "Is Busing Necessary?," "Liberty and Liberals," "Growth and Its Enemies," and "Liberalism vs. Liberal Education"—which set out neoconservative themes of hostility to radical feminism, belief in the work ethic and the meritocracy, the importance of family, and a loss of confidence in government intellectuals. Neoconservatives insist that they have not moved right but that liberals, especially liberal democrats, have moved left. The neoconservatives are odd bedfellows for the Republicans. Intellectuals without apology, they have, to use a Republican yardstick, never met a payroll. They are all the same very pro-business, or at least against business's critics, and they have provided Republicans with a fund of ideas the Republicans would have found hard to produce on their own.

Reagan himself, an ex-Democrat and once head of the Screen Actors Guild, seems comfortable with all these strains of modern conservatism, but then there is so much his affability makes him comfortable with. One message of his election, nonetheless, was quite clear. The great majority of voters were not interested in the bill of fare circulated by the New Right for the moral improvement of the nation—not, at least, according to Martin Anderson, the President's first domestic policy adviser. Anderson, a Libertarian follower of Ayn Rand, is an academic from Stanford, who under Nixon was one of the principal architects of the all-volunteer army. He occupied a neat upstairs office in the White House west wing. In a three-piece tweed suit under a large crop of graying hair, Anderson looks like a genial, bemused teddybear. Anderson had poll findings by Dick Wirthlin, the White House pollster, to show that the overriding domestic issue in voters' minds for the election was the state of the economy.

Reagan's "extremism" was plainly his greatest liability in the 1980 election. It showed his great political skill that he could campaign both as the standard-bearer of the Republican right and as a candidate appealing to the "alienated middle," the large, independent mass of voters John Anderson, the Republican-turned-Independent, hoped would go for him. These voters, broadly middle class, are conservative in economic outlook, in favor of a strong foreign policy, so long as this does not mean ruinously high defense spending or sending young Americans off to fight—reservations notably stronger among women voters than among men—and tolerant on moral questions that have intruded into politics. Anderson did well among them, considering the disadvantages under which any third-party or independent candidate labors. He got 7 percent of the vote, ensuring him federal campaign funds in the next election. Until then, Anderson could contemplate his future, give lectures, and update his mailing list, which is said to be three times as long as the Democrats'. The hallmark of these voters, however, is their independence. Typically, they vote on "issues," personality, and party, in that order. They split tickets and vote differently from election to election. Thirty years ago, such voters were rarer. Today they may make up a third or more of the electorate. Plainly, they are an important group for any emergent Republican majority to hold on to, but almost by definition, they are not kept voters.

What Reagan should do about the economy, the 1980 election results did not make clear. The message was "Do something!" Reagan's own outlook on business was heavily colored by the California friends who set him up in politics in the first place. These were men like Justin Dart, the drugstore chain magnate, Henry Salvatori, an independent oilman, and Holmes Tuttle, a Los Angeles car dealer. None of them had much contact with the federal government, the big unions, or foreign markets. To that extent, they were shielded from the conditions of trade faced by most American companies today, so that their outlook was sheltered and parochial. They were not even typical of California. This huge state is often crudely linked with the newer states of the so-called Sunbelt as if it did not include a tenth of the nation's population, account for a slightly larger share of the national income, and contain extraordinary economic variety. Bechtel, the San Francisco-based engineering multinational, which provided Reagan with two top advisers later—Caspar Weinberger and George Shultz—or the Bank of America whose boss, A. W. Clausen, Carter picked, and Reagan confirmed, as head of the World Bank, are representative of the California economy, if any businesses are. Untypical as Mr. Reagan's original business backers might be, they voiced a demand, echoed in thousands of Reagan speeches over the years, of "Get government off our backs"—a demand shared by businessmen everywhere, large and small, local and national. The new administration promptly set about hobbling the agencies businessmen complained loudest about, particularly the Environmental Protection Agency and the Occupational Safety and Health Administration.

Economies, however, do not live by deregulation alone. If it is true that the United States is investing $150–$200 billion a year too little, then a remedy is needed. The Democrats failed to answer the question of how to fill this gap. The Republicans were elected largely by attacking the Democrats: They had let the federal budget grow too large; they had paid too much attention to social equality and too little to industrial efficiency; they had let inflation grow, pushing up interest rates and discouraging investment even further. None of this could help the Republicans answer the question of how to fill the investment gap for themselves.

From the outset, it was not difficult to see where Reagan's difficulties would lie. Even as he took office his economics was at cross-purposes with his politics and his most loyal conservative followers were at odds with the broader coalition of voters that had elected him. Reagan had one audience to please in Wall Street, which wanted, as it usually does, tight money and smaller budget deficits. Wall Street wanted the Kemp-Roth tax cut delayed. Reagan had another audience to please among his conservative followers. Most of these favored his economic program but were concerned, too, with a burdensome "social agenda." Reagan had yet a third audience, among defecting Democrats. Some 43 percent of union households had gone for Reagan. Though some of these might have responded to the New Right social agenda, most of them swung to Reagan for his promise of economic recovery. He had campaigned for their votes as a New Deal Democrat. At the Detroit convention, Reagan had spoken with feeling about Franklin Roosevelt and reminded listeners that he, too, was once a Democrat. His message was not of limits and hard choices, but of abundance and growth.

With close to 9 percent unemployment at the end of his first year in office, predicted budget deficits of $100–$150 billion, and inflation that had fallen but might shoot ahead again with economic recovery, it was plain that the going would not be easy. The strains within the Reagan coalition tempted the Democrats to sit back and say: "Well, let the Republicans screw it up for a while." One Democrat on Capitol Hill said only half jokingly: "What the Democrats need now is a really deep depression." The Democrats needed more of a strategy than this, unless they deserved defeat. Bad as their future may have looked, Democrats were able to tell themselves that, like the Republicans, the party had shown remarkable powers of recuperation before. The Democrats, in 1980, lost many of their most dependable supporters—among blue-collar workers, Catholics, white ethnics, and Jews—without winning in return traditionally Republican voters among the middle-class, white Protestants, professionals, and the richer suburbanites. Since 1968, the Republicans have in fact averaged 51 percent of the vote, against 43 percent for the Democrats.

Democrats were divided among themselves. Their left was split into so many lobbies with some overlapping interests but by no means common aims. Naderites, women's groups, black groups, the small

Socialist party, and the leadership of the more socially minded unions, like William Winpisinger of the machinists. This has always tended to be the fate of left-wing Democrats. They face an unenviable choice. This is either to try to win the party, as the McGovernites did in 1972, or to strike out on their own. Even if these groups had a common economic strategy, which they do not, the political air in the United States has never been kind to parties of the left.

"Why is there no socialism in the United States?" foreigners have often asked, even if the question strikes Americans who have not thought about it much as rather like wanting to know why a rhinoceros has no trunk. The absence of a socialist tradition with any enduring strength is a puzzle, nevertheless. Industrialization was as brutally disruptive for Americans as it was for Europeans. The resistance to union organizers, from the courts and in the streets, was just as fierce. Yet no genuine working-class party really ever took root. At its peak, in 1912, the Socialist party had some 117,000 members and had, in the eleven years since its birth, managed to get 1,200 office holders elected across the country. Yet its presidential candidate in 1912, Eugene Debs, won a mere 6 percent of the popular vote, a high point not reached before or since.

Werner Sombart, the German sociologist, who had visited the United States a few years earlier and who was, at the time, a social democrat, thought the answer to why there was no socialism was that "all Socialist utopias turned to nothing in America on roast beef and apple pie." In looking for an answer, others have noticed the divisions between native Protestants and Catholic immigrants, predictably exploited by employers; the fact that it was often Democratic ward bosses, not unions, that provided many early social services; the lack of entrenched landowners, of standing armies, or of an established church, against which the nineteenth-century banner of science and socialism might have been raised; the early enfranchisement of working-class voters as well as the institutional handicaps facing any third party; and perhaps strongest of all, the reflexive muscular reaction of businessmen and politicians when native socialist movements did stir.

If a socialist left, in a European sense, has not been a strong political force in America, there is nonetheless a recognizable progressive tradition, with the hallmarks of local initiative, self-rule, and direct action. There are several reform groups scattered across the country today that belong in this line: the New Orleans–based Association of Community Organizations for Reform (Acorn), Tom Hayden's Campaign for Economic Democracy in California, or the Ohio Public Interest Campaign in Cleveland. Many of those working in these groups are veterans of the New Left and the antiwar or civil rights campaigns of the 1960s. Their bill of fare, which tends to concentrate on economic issues such as promoting—or at least limiting cuts in—social services, resisting plant closures, and advocating worker participation in industry, sounds modest enough to European socialists but, in American terms, counts as radical. Doctrine plays little part in their lives. "Socialism is rheumatism," in the words of Dennis Kucinich, the former mayor of Cleveland, a progressive Democrat, who stood up to the city's bankers and businessmen and was soundly defeated for his pains when he ran for reelection. "Don't give me your 'ism,' " he liked to say. "Tell me what you're going to do." These groups can play a role as a leftward anchor for the Democratic party, preventing it from drifting too far toward the right. Their members can also be counted on to do invaluable backroom work in political crusades, to which Democratic politicians may or may not lend their support. Otherwise, at a national level, the American left is an uncertain presence. Where it goes depends to a large extent on where the Democrats go. After their defeat in 1980, the Democrats faced the three choices usually confronted by a beaten party: It could do what the Republican moderates did during the long years of Democratic ascendancy and adopt the policies of its rivals; it could wait to benefit from Republican mistakes; or it could try to patch up the leaking vessel of the Liberal Consensus and see if welfare capitalism could be refloated in new economic waters. As to retaining the party's identity, this last was the most promising, but also the most difficult. There were adventurous steps the Democrats could, but probably would not, take. In the 1970s, the party made only token efforts to mobilize the half of the electorate that does not vote. At a guess—and only a guess—more of these would vote Democratic than Republican. Yet party advantage aside, it cannot be a sign of health in an electoral democracy when half the electorate—and probably the less well-off and less well-educated half—is allowed to become, in effect, disfranchised.

6

LOOKING BEFORE THEY LEAP

Finance

SUPERFICIALLY, but only superficially, people's capitalism in the United States is alive and well. On the reckoning of the New York Stock Exchange (NYSE), the number of individual owners of corporate stock and shares of mutual funds increased by an impressive 4,570,000 between 1975 and 1980, from 25,270,000, or 11.9 percent of the total population, to 29,840,000, or 13.6 percent. The median age of the stockholders was 45.5, which means half were younger than 45.5 years old and half older. Over one million more of them were male than female: 15,479,000 to 14,361,000. This sexual imbalance is mainly because American boys are more likely than American girls to receive gifts of stock from relatives and godparents. Exclude the 1,452,000 boy stockholders and the 828,000 girl stockholders, and the number of adult stockholders is just about equally split between the sexes: 50.9 percent are men and 49.1 percent women. California is the state with most stockholders, 3,718,000, followed by New York, 2,698,000, and Illinois, 1,859,000. Wyoming, with 41,000, and Vermont, with 40,000, have the fewest.

A census of the number of stockholders skates over the crucial fact that while the number of them has been going up, the value of their stockholdings has been coming down. Throughout the 1970s, individual Americans sold more stock each year than they bought, and those who did so had good reason to congratulate themselves on their foresight. In the twelve years between President Nixon's first inauguration and President Reagan's, the Standard & Poor's 500, a better guide to the overall performance of stocks than the more closely watched Dow Jones industrial average, showed an average annual return of 8 percent. This average annual return, which takes in both dividends and share price movements, exactly equaled inflation—but that was before taxes or the commissions charged by brokers on share trades. Take taxes and commissions into account and the average stockholder lost money, after an adjustment is made for inflation, during the 1970s.

One glum statistic in the otherwise ebullient NYSE census tells the sad story. The median portfolio (half of all adult share owners above and half below) was $10,100 in 1975 but only $4,000 in 1980. At the end of these five years, only one adult stockholder in six had a portfolio worth $25,000 or more. The increase in the number of stockholders, it turns out, is due, in part, to more people buying stocks on the over-the-counter market and on the American Stock Exchange. Both are smaller, less solid markets than the NYSE and quote some highly speculative stocks that Wall Street professionals call "cats and dogs." Many of the individuals buying small quantities of these stocks are taking a flier, and are gamblers rather than investors. A second, bigger reason for an increase in the number of stockholders coinciding with a big drop in the median value of their portfolios is the tremendous growth in stock purchase plans offered by companies to their employees. Participation in many of these plans is only quasi-voluntary. The employee who exercises the right to decline to buy on a regular basis a small quantity of the company's stock runs the risk of being seen as someone lacking confidence in the company's future and, by inference, the quality of its management. This is untactful and is no way to go about winning a pay raise or a promotion.

Overall, it is hard to escape the conclusion that the drastic decline in the median portfolio from $10,100 to $4,000, which is more like a drop to $2,500 when account is taken of inflation, indicates that Americans are becoming more risk-averse; that they are less willing than they were to invest in corporate stocks, which have a notorious habit of going down as well as up in value; that they are concentrating their investment in relatively safe things, like bricks and mortar and other tangible assets and also, recently, in money market funds, which, by investing in short-term government securities, are as safe as houses and offer a good return.

This change in investment patterns has helped push house prices through the roof while stock prices, after allowance for inflation, are not within sight of the levels they reached in the bull markets of 1966 and 1968. This has caused an extraordinary shift in the wealth of American families. One household in five in the United States has at least one stockholder, but stocks are no longer the dominant form of personal assets. Whereas in 1970 the value of stocks owned by American households exceeded, slightly, the value of their real estate holdings, by 1980 their real estate holdings were more than twice as valuable as their stocks.

Not all Americans have lost interest in comparatively risky investments. The excitement of the Chicago commodity markets attests to that. So does the size of the New York Stock Exchange, which lists 1,570 companies with 33.7 billion common shares outstanding, worth, at the start of 1981, $1.2 trillion. Beside it, the stock markets of Italy, France, and West Germany are almost invisible. The citizens of these European countries are inclined to regard stocks as something for the Rothschilds, the Flicks, the Agnellis, and other rich families to interest themselves in. Though Americans are still less cautious investors than Europeans, and still generously swap stock tips at cocktail parties and barbecues, they are far less interested in the market than they were fifteen or twenty years ago.

Of course they are less interested, brokers retort. The market went wild in the go-go years of the 1960s, when stock prices discounted everything but the Second Coming. When the inevitable hangover set in, stockholders vowed themselves to more sober investment behavior in future. Their determination to stay clear of stocks was reinforced as the country's economic self-confidence was shaken, successively, by the landmark devaluation of the dollar on August 15, 1971, by the OPEC cartel's greedy, effective price fixing, by the movement of the trade balance into chronic deficit, and by an inflation rate more usually associated with South than North America.

Sanguine Wall Streeters, crossing fingers, are inclined to say all this will change for the better, and Americans will come flocking back, when a sustained bull market gets going again and the greed of investors overwhelms their fear of loss. Their spirits were raised by the election of President Reagan together with a more conservative Congress committed to reducing taxes, including taxes on capital gains, which had been already cut from a maximum of 49 percent to a maximum of 28 percent during the Carter administration. These Wall Streeters, for reassurance, cite the growth years of the 1950s, when, after the gloomy predictions of a post–World War II depression were confounded, investors gradually suppressed their memories of the great crash of 1929 and with increasing confidence started buying corporate stocks. The buying was encouraged by the brilliant "Own Your Share of American Business" campaign masterminded by Kenneth Funston, the 75-inch-tall president of the New York Stock Exchange, every inch of him a salesman. When he took this job in 1951, fewer than 6.5 million Americans were stockholders. By the time he left, in 1967, it was more like 25 million, and capital gains on stocks were by then as pervasive a subject of conversation at the dinner parties of the ambitious middle class as increases in house prices were to be a few years later. The buying power of these individual investors helped power a market advance that drove the Dow Jones industrial average, the index based on thirty blue-chip industrial NYSE stocks that is quoted nightly on the television news, up from 239.92 to 905.11 during the Funston years. The subsequent 1960s high of close to 1,000 is, after adjustment for inflation, equivalent to about 2,800 in 1983.

Will history repeat itself? While the market has confounded the skeptics before, and the Reagan administration is keen to encourage capital formation, it is by no means certain that stocks will again become the central form of savings and investments for individual Americans, or that Americans will raise their savings rate from around 5 percent of their income to around the 20 percent of the envied Japanese, who are now so often reeled out by bankers and brokers as a role model for Americans to emulate. Harry Keefe, founder of the Wall Street firm of Keefe Bruyette & Woods, in shrewdly explaining the disinclination of Americans to save more, told a congressional hearing as long ago as 1974: "I don't need to save for my retirement. I don't—unlike my father. I don't need to save for sickness and I don't need to save for my education. We have developed a social philosophy in this. So much of the incentive for the individual to participate in the stock market has been removed, which is why I started a firm to deal exclusively with institutions, because I felt that is where the action was going to be. I submit that the individual investor no longer has the incentives he had twenty years ago to participate in the market. He no longer has the incentive to save for retirement. His company is doing that for him."

Though Keefe did not say so, and the securities industry is disconcerted by the thought, Americans may have acted rationally in veering away from stocks, and not just because investors in real estate, Chinese ceramics, stamps, farmland, and gold have done far better in recent years than investors in the stock market. The proportion of private-sector employees in corporate pension plans has climbed from a quarter in the 1950s to half of a much larger labor force today. These pension funds provide duller but much safer protection against poverty in old age than reliance on personal savings or the charity of the family. And these pension funds concentrate their investments in stocks and bonds. This gives the members of the pension plans a large indirect interest in the market. Those who add to this exposure by buying stocks on their own are, in effect, spreading risk too thin. Instead, the prudent, risk-averse investor that the average American family has become is sensibly reducing exposure to stock market fluctuations by putting more of its savings into money market funds, houses, even gold. And so diversifying its risk.

As America has developed a mature capitalist economy, the money managers of the big financial institutions like the bank trust departments, the pension funds, and the insurance companies have come to dominate the stock market, as they have always dominated the bond market where fixed-interest securities are traded. These managers of other people's money by now account for around three-quarters of the daily volume of trading in stocks on the New York Stock Exchange, and the average size of a share trade has, as a result, more than doubled during the past decade. The change has made profits for the Wall Street firms much harder to come by, both for the retail brokerage houses, which buy and sell shares mainly for the general public, and for the investment banks, which perform the same function for the institutional investors.

These difficulties came about, first, because the big institutions demanded and, after a bloody struggle, got the abolition of fixed commission rates on share trades and have used their buying muscle to push down rates on large stock trades to levels that are barely profitable for those who handle their stock market business; and second, because though individual Americans lack the power to exploit their theoretical freedom to negotiate commission rates, they, too, have put pressure on

Wall Street profit margins, having become relatively less interested in stocks. To retain their customers, the big retail brokerage houses, led by Merrill Lynch, have tried to evolve into financial supermarkets, offering a whole slew of services from money market funds to insurance to credit cards to tax shelters. The high cost of overhead has forced many smaller firms out of business or into shotgun mergers. Wall Street has changed from a place ruled by partnerships headed by rich, clubby men into an area where ever larger, ever fewer firms do battle to survive and where the demarcation lines between a brokerage house, an investment bank, and a commercial bank gets more wavy and less distinct every year.

Yet to outward appearances the financial district at the tip of Manhattan that is known as Wall Street, and is now more than ever the capital of world capitalism, is unaltered. The tall buildings built for men with big egos are strong, bold, and eccentric. The thoroughfares have agreeable country names: Beaver, Market, Water, Cedar, and Pine streets, where at lunchtime the dead-end kids who do the menial jobs on the New York Stock Exchange floor and work as back-office clerks at the brokerage houses smoke marijuana. The executive offices of most brokerage houses and investment banks in the area give stunning views of New York harbor and their furnishings seem intended to excite the cupidity of a set designer for the British *Masterpiece Theatre* programs on public television: prints of polo players and of huntsmen in pink beside a handsome old clock with a loud tick at Paine Webber; an impressive collection of leather-bound copies of *Punch* on the bookshelf of Richard Jenrette of Donaldson, Lufkin & Jenrette; murals of nineteenth-century scenes in downtown Manhattan around the expansive partners' dining room at Salomon Brothers; a green eye shield on the desk of Alan Greenberg, senior executive at Bear, Stearns, and on the wall a picture of him lying atop a kudu shot on safari in Africa.

Many brokers dealing with individual investors are as old-fashioned as these surroundings. They cultivate the investment adviser's equivalent of the doctor's bedside manner. They will inquire solicitously about how a customer's golf game or bad back is coming along before trying to persuade him that an over-the-counter stock in a Silicon Valley biotechnology company is a must, even though the company has never paid a dividend and reported an after-tax loss of $4 million in the past quarter. Not until the visitor enters the trading rooms of the big investment banks does the iron fist concealed within this velvet glove come into view.

The men and women working in these rooms feel no need to be personable. They are not dealing with private investors, whom they call, with a blend of scorn and affection, either "little guys" or "Aunt Minnies," but with hardheaded professionals responsible for investing mountains of money for pension funds, endowments, foundations, and universities. At the other end of the telephone are the money managers of Prudential Insurance, Metropolitan Life, Morgan Guaranty Trust, Citibank, and other money weight champions, which have billions rather than millions to invest.

When business is slow, the people in these trading rooms are listless and bored. When the markets are active, moving fast either upward or downward, they are like clockwork toys that come to life. Then the men and the increasing number of women employed in these trading rooms talk about money matters, and only about money matters, into the telephone. Every so often they glance nervously to catch up, with the aid of video displays, on the latest price movements on the bond, stock, options, commercial paper, and other markets. Conversation with the customers is abrupt: "We've got a big chunk of Telephone [AT&T]. Do you want us to cut you in?" Talk among the traders themselves is brisk and harsh.

"We really screwed Goldie," brays one at Salomon Brothers after besting archrival investment bank Goldman, Sachs on a deal. "Salomon and Merrill are up to their necks in shit," gloats another at Morgan Stanley, as co-managers Salomon Brothers and Merrill Lynch try desperately to sell in a collapsing market a $1 billion debenture and note offering by IBM. These are people who if they are not from New York came to New York to make it. They take pride in viewing themselves as aggressive competitors and are just as combative playing tennis or golf or bridge as they are at the office. If they have an attribute in common, it is respect for people who have achieved material success. Obversely, Wall Streeters, more than any other group of Americans, have no time for losers. Once-famous people can become forgotten overnight.

While it is easy to think of many victims of Wall Street's amnesia, James Needham is perhaps the most spectacular of the recent casualties. Until 1972, he was a commissioner at the Securities and Exchange Commission (SEC), the Washington regulatory agency responsible for supervising the securities markets. He was then offered, and accepted with alacrity, a five-year contract at an annual salary of $200,000 plus $100,000 in expenses, dollars worth much more then than they are now, to become chairman of the New York Stock Exchange, which is sometimes known as the Big Board. Though the title was different, the job he was hired to fill was essentially the same as that held by Robert Haack, then president of the Exchange.

Members of Wall Street's establishment had determined that Haack's contract would not be renewed when, two years earlier, in a speech to the Economic Club of New York, he spoke approvingly about the possibility of the brokerage houses abandoning fixed commission rates on share transactions. The establishment was livid. This was heresy. Fixed rates had been sacrosanct ever since twenty-four brokers meeting at Corre's Hotel in lower Manhattan had signed the agreement in 1792 that is usually taken to represent the founding of the NYSE. It stated: "We, the Subscribers, brokers for the Purchase and Sale of Public Stocks, do hereby solemnly promise and pledge ourselves to each other that we will not buy or sell from this date, for any person whatsoever, any kind of Public Stocks at a less rate than one-quarter of one per-cent Commission on the Specie Value, and that we will give preference to each other in our Negotiations."

Haack had acted as a Trojan horse for critics of this profitable restrictive practice of fixed commission rates. Worse still, he had behaved as if he were the real leader of the NYSE. He had apparently not understood, or willfully disregarded, the fact that he was supposed to be the Exchange's chief performer on the public stage and to stick faithfully to a script drafted by the big men of Wall Street: By Bernard Lasker of Lasker Stone & Stern, an exceedingly reactionary though able conservative, fervent in his support for Richard Nixon. By John Loeb, the regal head of Loeb Rhoades. By Gustave Levy, then the equally imperious senior partner of Goldman, Sachs. By Robert Baldwin of Morgan Stanley, by John Phelan of Phelan, Silver, & Co., and by others of their ilk. Some of them were in a mood to sack Haack immediately. Their hand was stayed by the calculation that the Exchange could not afford a public row while the Vietnam/ Cambodia war was disturbing both domestic tranquillity and the stock markets and at a time when the advertisement of deep disagreements at its highest levels would weaken the securities industry's lobbying muscle with Congress.

Nevertheless, it was clearly understood by all involved that Haack would certainly not be invited to stay on when his term expired in mid-1972. Needham showed promise of proving a more effective, and obedient, spokesman for the industry. A former accountant, with Washington regulatory experience, he was rated both ambitious and deferential enough to campaign dutifully against fully negotiated commission rates and other reforms that threatened to make profits harder to earn in the brokerage business. But Needham, an intelligent man, quickly realized the task he was set was impossible, and confessed as much in private meetings with Exchange members.

He and several brokerage firms, with Merrill Lynch in the van, had come around to accepting that neither Congress nor the SEC would for much longer tolerate the perverse spectacle of NYSE members preaching the joys of unfettered competition to the rest of the citizenry while they continued to enforce and to benefit from restrictions on competition on commission rates. But Needham was unable to persuade a sufficient number of his own constituents to accept the inevitable. Against his own better judgment, he permitted himself to be pushed into battle. When the SEC in August 1974 asked the NYSE to amend its rules to allow fully negotiated commission rates from May 1, 1975, the following year, Needham boldly rejected the request. Asked what the Exchange would do if the SEC converted the request into a command, he snorted: "You can tell the SEC that Needham said if we don't get what we want, he'll see them on the steps of the courthouse in Foley Square." This is the federal district court in New York.

When early in 1975 the SEC did exactly what the questioner foresaw and ordered the NYSE to stop fixing commission rates from May 1, 1975, Needham turned around to rally the troops, only to discover that his army had melted away. Leaving their general exposed in the field, the chiefs of staff had settled for an unconditional surrender. When Gustave Levy was reminded he had once warned that Goldman, Sachs might resign from the NYSE if fixed commission rates were abolished, he said loftily: "That's all passé now. We're flexible."

John Loeb, an even fiercer old warhorse in defense of the status quo, caused an advertisement to be placed in the *Wall Street Journal* to announce: "Loeb Rhoades Is Negotiating."

Needham was by now an embarrassment to the NYSE. In fighting the good fight he had been defeated. The Exchange could not allow itself to be represented by a loser. What it needed, it decided, was a less combative elder statesman to restore détente between downtown Manhattan and Washington. The putsch was suave and swift. At a meeting of eighteen of the twenty directors of the NYSE in April 1976 in the Exchange's rococo boardroom, it was unanimously agreed that Needham would "resign" as chairman and be replaced by William Batten, a former chief executive of J.C. Penney brought out of retirement to head the world's largest stock exchange.

In the securities business, as in politics, there is little compunction about kicking a man when he is down. The managing partner of one large firm, after requesting anonymity, told *Business Week:* "Needham just hasn't provided any leadership." Another said, also anonymously: "He antagonized people everywhere he went, especially in Washington. The Secretary of the Treasury [William Simon] called me this morning and said it's the best trade that's been done on Wall Street in years." The unfairness of the verdict was breathtaking. Needham had been asked to do what just could not be done and had tried manfully. All knew it—but losers on Wall Street are without friends. James Needham, four years chairman of the Colosseum of capitalism, is all but forgotten. He became a director of, among other companies, Caesars World, the owner and operator of gambling casinos in Las Vegas and Atlantic City.

By eliminating easy profits, the abolition of fixed commission rates has sharpened the cutthroat phase on Wall Street. On precedent, this will lead eventually, through attrition, to the emergence of a consolidated industry. For just as in the car business Studebaker, Nash, and Packard have failed to survive as independent entities, so in the securities business the less robust, less well-capitalized firms are being faced with the choice of either going out of business or allowing stronger firms to acquire them.

Faced with this dilemma, most have settled for a merger, the Wall

Street euphemism for what is, in fact, often the takeover by a stronger firm of a weaker one. The corporate genealogy of Shearson Loeb Rhoades makes the point. More than thirty previously independent firms went into its making and several of its recent accretions were once famous, proudly independent names in the business: Spencer Trask & Co.; Hornblower & Weeks; Hemphill Noyes & Co.; Faulkner Dawkins & Sullivan; Shearson Hayden Stone; and duPont Walston. In 1981, Shearson Loeb Rhoades itself was, in effect, acquired by a much larger firm, American Express, which was diversifying its traveler's check and traveler's card business into the securities industry.

For those employed as brokers and investment bankers, the upheaval is often more frightening than challenging. They work in what is still, comparatively, a cottage industry. Firms that are members of the New York Stock Exchange, a definition that takes in most of the securities firms that matter, employ altogether fewer than 200,000 people, or fewer than one-quarter as many as AT&T. The profits of all member firms doing business with the public, a definition that excludes the floor brokers, total less in a year than General Motors or Exxon earns in a good quarter. But although the securities industry is small, it was until the late 1960s a good, steady line of work for its employees. All firms, efficient and inefficient alike, until then made money. Brokerage houses found it hard to go broke unless they got caught up in the backwash of a debacle in the commodity markets, as Ira Haupt & Co. did when a larger customer, Allied Crude Vegetable Oil Refining Company, engaged in scandalous speculation in salad oil.

Even in the great crash of 1929, firms on Wall Street, contrary to popular belief, did not go broke. Their customers did. The NYSE had 665 member organizations in 1929, only 16 fewer in 1930, and still had 591 member organizations in 1940, after the worst decade for the American economy since the founding of the Republic. Nor in the great crash did scores of brokers, or indeed ruined speculators, put revolvers to their temples or hurl themselves to their deaths from the windows of tall buildings, though this myth remains firmly embedded in the country's folk memory. Quite why this fiction passes as truth is a mystery. Perhaps it is because, as economist John Kenneth Galbraith suggests, broken speculators, like gamblers and alcoholics, are supposed to have a penchant for self-destruction and because the collapse of the stock market provided an explanation for suicides that were otherwise hard to explain: "Poor fellow, lost every penny he had in the crash." But whatever the reasons for the myth, the fact is that suicide statistics disinterred by Galbraith show that 17 New Yorkers in every 100,000 took their own lives in 1928, a year when a booming economy seemed the birthright of Americans, compared to 18.7 in 1929 and 19.7 in 1930. An increase, sure enough, but hardly one large enough to sustain stories about New York pedestrians carefully threading their way along sidewalks littered with the corpses of dead financiers.

Even so, it is true that securities firms survived rather than prospered from the autumn of 1929 until the end of World War II and did not really start making bumper profits again until the 1950s, dubbed the "Euphoric Decade" in Robert Sobel's history of the NYSE. With Korea quickly behind it, the nation was at peace, General Eisenhower was in the White House, minorities were tranquil, inflation was low. Everything seemed right with the world, at least as seen from Wall Street, a redoubt of male chumminess and clubbiness. Men had a monopoly on all the top jobs. The first woman member of the NYSE, Muriel Siebert, later the superintendent of banking for the state of New York, was not admitted until 1967, when blackballing her would have been impossible to justify. She was so qualified, as an economics and accountancy major and a senior analyst with Shields & Co., the Exchange could not in good conscience refuse to sell her a seat, for $445,000.

Good-natured clubbiness was easy to sustain while the profits rolled in during the Eisenhower, the Kennedy, and then the Johnson years. Almost every investor, it seems, could boast a substantial rise in the value of her or his stock portfolio. Robert Stovall of the brokerage house Dean Witter, a knowledgeable commentator on the market and a frequent panelist for PBS's *Wall Street Week*, recalls that the "lounge lizard" was often then the most envied broker in the smaller firms. Such a broker came to work late and left early, yet even when he spent most of his working day away from his desk he was immune to criticism from the partners. His family owned a bank or an electric light company or a chain of stores, and his parents, brothers, sisters, cousins, and aunts, and their rich friends and acquaintances, would automatically funnel all their orders to buy or sell stocks through him. Since these scions were a source of a good flow of business in good times as well as bad, brokerage houses were naturally eager to hire them. Securities executives who achieved their success the hard way still find it hard to hide their bitterness over the way such privileged men impeded their advancement. For a while, says one, it looked as if "the future belonged to Scott Fitzgerald's languid young men coming down from Princeton."

This nepotism has receded fast in the securities industry during the past fifteen years. Though still not completely extinct, the lounge lizards are on the endangered species list. The popular explanation for their demise is that the rich people they depend upon for their sustenance have become relatively much less a factor than bank trust departments, insurance companies, investment companies, foundations, endowments, and other institutional investors. Institutional and foreign investors still hold a minority of all the outstanding market value of U.S. stocks, but their proportion has expanded steadily from 9 percent in 1949 to 12 percent in 1959 to 18 percent in 1969 to going on 40 percent today. But, so it is said, brokerage houses depend for their profits on active investors, and these are the institutions. They accounted for only about a fifth of stock exchange trading in 1960, but for around three-quarters of it twenty years later.

As an explanation for the demise of the lounge lizard, this is, at best, a half truth. While it is true that few private investors—except perhaps for Saudi princes if they had a mind to—have the power to move the market that Arthur Cutten, Jesse Livermore, Joseph Kennedy, and other speculators were supposed to possess in the bull market that preceded the Great Depression, America still has numerous families with substantial private fortunes. Witness the Hunts, the Rockefellers, the duPonts, the Mellons, the Hesses, the Fords, the Pritzkers, the Gettys, and the Uihleins.

They and other private investors are disproportionately important to brokerage house profits, not least because they pay higher commission rates on share trades than giant institutions like Citibank and the Prudential. If they can no longer be relied upon to channel their orders through lazy but affable relatives employed by brokerage houses, it is mainly because profits have become harder for investors as well as brokers to earn. Private investors, especially those with substantial fortunes, need financial advisers who can guide them on tax shelters, bonds, options, commodities, money market funds, interest rate futures, foreign currencies, and overseas stock as well as a list of recommended stocks on the New York Stock Exchange.

The lounge lizards have just not measured up to this task. Nor have languidly run family businesses. F. I. duPont, a brokerage house involved in a desperate series of mergers that ended finally in its liquidation in 1974, is one example. It was presided over by Edmund duPont, a direct descendant of the founder of the early-nineteenth-century explosives business that evolved into the twentieth-century chemicals multinational.

Firms whose prosperity depended on whom not on what they knew have also vanished. The epitome was McDonnell & Co., which went into liquidation in 1970. At its head was James McDonnell, the grandson of an Irish immigrant whose close relatives had a remarkable talent for making good marriages. One of his sisters married Henry Ford II, then chief executive of the Ford Motor Company; another of his sisters married Richard Cooley, then head of Wells Fargo Bank; a third sister married a senior executive of United States Lines. McDonnell himself in 1950 married Peggy Flanigan, a blueblood and the sister of Peter Flanigan, later a senior aide in the Nixon White House, who was uncontaminated by the Watergate scandals. Peggy's mother was a member of the Busch family, with the biggest brewing business in the country, Anheuser-Busch of Saint Louis. Her father was president of Manufacturers Hanover Trust Company of New York, one of the half dozen largest banks in the country.

McDonnell's associates were not shy about drawing the attention of customers and creditors to their boss's relatives, particularly brother-in-law Ford, whose family and company continued to do business with the brokerage house after his marriage to McDonnell's sister ended in divorce in 1964. As Chris Welles comments in his book *The Last Days of the Club*, when McDonnell executives were challenged over their firm's increasingly shaky capital position, they could always reply: "Well, how much money do you think Henry Ford has?"

The brokerage house was known in the industry as a "Catholic house" at a time when religious affiliations had more meaning on Wall Street than they do today. Young Catholics from good families and Ivy League universities were taken on as stockbrokers. Lawrence O'Brien, a Kennedy Democrat at a loose end, was brought in for a while as chairman. James McDonnell's more prominent friends included

Jacqueline Kennedy and Cardinal Spellman, and he was chosen to advise the Archdiocese of New York on financial matters. But good breeding and good connections proved in the end no substitute for good management. The amateurish executives at McDonnell succeeded in losing enough money to put the firm out of business. They just could not discover an efficiently profitable way of integrating into the brokerage house's back office the management controls and new technology essential to handle the increased volume of share trading. The business failed, unusually, because it had more business than it could properly handle.

Such histories, and the discrimination so long suffered by those who did not have the triple advantages of being white, male, and Christian, have given many on Wall Street a peculiarly strong aversion to anything that smacks of nepotism. The family concern remains a proud enterprise to work or do business for in Middle America and the Southern states. In California and New York, most especially in finance, it is suspect. On the West Coast, the most common explanation for this is the one that makes most sense: People go to California to start afresh; to put behind them the stifling constraints of their family circumstances in Whitefish, Montana, Sleepy Hollow, Virginia, or Rolling Prairie, Indiana. In New York, an ambition to forget or overcome modest beginnings is a factor, too. Despite its travails, the city continues to act as a magnet for some of the most ambitious and talented, and assertive, people from the hinterland. They are determined over and above everything to achieve material success and they resent the fact that inherited wealth or privilege gives others a head start. Their drive makes for the hyperactive adults in the trading rooms of Salomon Brothers; Goldman, Sachs; and First Boston. The adrenaline they pump into the veins of the city is felt by visitors as soon as they begin jostling for their luggage at La Guardia or Kennedy airport and lies behind the cliché: "New York is a nice place to visit, but I wouldn't want to live there."

On Wall Street the jealous disdain for the family business has a further dimension. In the prevailing meritocracy, these businesses are seen as an anachronism almost bound to fail in competition against firms headed by professional managers who have made their own way to the top. Men like Peter Loeb at Shearson Loeb Rhoades and Robert Salomon, Jr., at Salomon Brothers are under pressure to work harder and smarter than their contemporaries to protect their reputations against charges of nepotism. Indeed, some firms are so sensitive to the risk of family favoritism creeping in that they have taken steps to avoid it.

At Bear, Stearns, one of the biggest New York investment banks, it was decided in 1970 that from then on no relative of a partner could work for the firm. The definition goes as far as first cousin and the rule is so strictly enforced that the children of Alan Greenberg, the chief executive, are disqualified from being considered even for summer jobs. Though in most other parts of the world successful fathers are peacock proud when their children follow in their footsteps, on Wall Street "like father, like son" is a tradition that firms are trying to live down. The failures of F. I. duPont, McDonnell & Co., and others have given the family business a bad name.

To European financiers, this extreme sensitivity of American financiers to charges of nepotism is quaint. Given the choice, they would prefer and be flattered to deal with a competent descendant of J. P. Morgan or another financial blueblood than with a career banker. This European prejudice has helped to sustain the most famous bank in the world in family hands ever since Mayer Amschel Rothschild started to amass his fortune as the son of a money changer in the Jewish ghetto of Frankfurt in the eighteenth century. In the twentieth, family members still preside over the two main financial branches of the Rothschild family, French and English. Of course, the Rothschilds have always thrown up competent managers, although in 1981 the bank of the French Rothschilds found itself on the nationalization list of the Mitterand government.

Anyone on Wall Street accosted by a small green visitor from outer space asking to be taken "to your leader" would be flummoxed. The financial district is not, as it was only a few years ago, the fiefdom of men of broad confidence renowned more for their good judgment than for their narrow expertise—investment bankers, like Gustave Levy of Goldman, Sachs, Robert Lehman of Lehman Brothers, and the still active Robert Baldwin. Nor is it any longer a place where investment banks are reckoned to be a cut above mere retail brokerage houses because they deal with the corporate and institutional elite while brokerage houses sell shares to the general public. The retail brokerage houses have poached shamelessly in investment banking territory and the investment banks have countered by introducing and expanding retail brokerage operations, aimed mainly at the wealthiest families and individuals.

If the green inquirer was willing to be directed not to an individual leader but to the leading firm, most passers-by would unhesitatingly send him along to the Merrill Lynch headquarters at the bottom of Broadway, only a short walk away from the floor of the New York Stock Exchange at the corner of Wall and Broad. Long known in the business as the "thundering herd," a name echoed in advertisements, filmed in Mexico, that feature running bulls, Merrill Lynch is by now a financial conglomerate rather than a brokerage house. Some of its activities are closely related to its historical strengths in securities transactions and financing: government securities, commodities, stock options and financial instruments, stock and bond underwriting. Others are shirttail cousins: international banking, economic research, life insurance, real estate.

Though Ph.D. theses have been written about the corporate strategy that underlies this diversification, for Merrill Lynch the explanation is straightforward. Perhaps because it was founded—in 1940—by Charles Merrill, cofounder of Safeway Stores, the brokerage house sees parallels between retail food sales, or what used to be known as "grocery shopping," and the sales of financial services. An Irish-American who has the gift of the gab, Donald Regan, chief executive of Merrill Lynch from 1971 until he went to Washington, likes to point out that it was not too long ago that a housewife, shopping list in hand, made the morning rounds of the corner grocery store, the fruit and vegetable store, the butcher shop, the baker, and all the other small neighborhood purveyors of food and household items. As she went from place to place, she squeezed the fruit, sniffed the fresh-baked bread, and let the grocer or butcher help her.

Regan traces the end of this way of shopping to the post–World War II population explosion, though historian Daniel Boorstin and others would put an earlier date on it. As Regan sees it, once cities like Los Angeles and Houston sprawled outward as tens of thousands of families settled in new suburbs, the shopper did not have the patience or inclination to traipse from store to store to buy what she needed.

arket in the eyes of the investing public into a
table place, they have even discouraged floor
as they used to on red-letter days, their unofficial
the Sun Shines, Nellie."

s the customers, for trading in the big-name stocks
ock Exchange is dominated by a group of increas-
estors—the professional money managers acting for
dowments, foundations, and universities. "Profes-
re in the loose sense of some upper-income people
vice for others. It decidedly does not imply good
getting rich in handling other people's money for a
al" money managers have shown extraordinary in-
ar in, year out, they have failed to match the market
e five years to 1980, only a third of the equity managers
nsurance companies succeeded in beating the Standard
in the ten years to 1980, less than a quarter did. In other
ajority of the clients would have done far better if they
neir pension money away from the "professionals" and

' not so
tennis court,
is sounds

She wanted to get in her car and drive to one place, and as more women went out to work, neither they nor their husbands had time for leisurely shopping. Simultaneously, great strides were being made in frozen foods, refrigeration, modern packaging, and faster distribution, combining to make possible the spread of a wondrous American institution: the supermarket. It was, says Regan, exactly what consumers wanted. It caught on in the West and quickly spread east. In only a few years, supermarkets were everywhere and proved so efficient they kept adding items: proprietary drugs, hardware, even clothing and lawn furniture.

Regan thinks the development of the supermarket, with its stress on convenience, quality, and competitive prices, with its dependence on modern technology, is not too dissimilar to what has happened in the securities industry. Forty years ago, individuals and organizations had to take care of their financial needs at several places. In effect, they went with their shopping lists to mortgage brokers, real estate brokers, and other specialists. These people were on friendly terms because they did not compete. Most of their activities were local or regional. But then the financial needs of individuals and business grew and became more complex. Better ways of handling them were called for. Technology, which had compressed the time needed for many financial transactions, was ready with the means. The supermarket concept of expansion and diversification was adopted by many financial firms, Merrill Lynch prominent among them. A dull stock market served as the stick, growth in other sectors of the money business as the carrot.

This Regan vision puts into focus a view of tomorrow's securities markets that makes Adam Smith's *The Money Game* seem romantically nostalgic. Just as the recent remake of *The Front Page*, starring Walter Matthau and Jack Lemmon, invoked an earlier, more racy period in journalism, so Jerry Goodman, the Wall Street watcher who writes under the nom de plume Adam Smith, is really writing about an earlier age. His financial gargoyles and reckless speculators and strong-willed individualists exist, just as green-eyeshielded reporters drunk by midday are still to be found in the recesses of small city newspapers, but they are all but gone.

Wall Street investment banks and brokerage houses today are led by professionals. They hire sober, ambitious, unsentimental men and women with MBA and CPA after their names, to deal with the equally unsentimental professionals hired by corporate America as financial officers. Loyalty is regarded almost as a weakness. Richard Jenrette of Donaldson, Lufkin & Jenrette, an executive in his fifties, recalls that until fairly recently it was considered unseemly for one investment bank to approach another's clients—for a Morgan Stanley or a Goldman, Sachs to call on a client of, say, First Boston. If a corporation was unhappy with the service provided by its investment bank, it was the one to make the first move in seeking a replacement. Most corporations were then loath to do this. Investment banking–client relations were founded on loyalty and trust. For better or worse, this age of chivalry is past. Investment bankers hustle for business as hard as anybody else and an increasing number of corporations are ready to lend the would-be interlopers a hearing ear.

George Ball of Lehman Brothers Kuhn Loeb, a Wall Street lawyer and a courtly gentleman who did a six-year stint at the State Department in the Kennedy and Johnson administrations, has a longer memory than Jenrette and confirms a "fundamental change" in the way investment bankers and their clients work together. The chief financial officers of corporations are "ten times as sophisticated as they once were." No longer do they rely on investment bankers to hold their hands: to tell them, for instance, when, how, and where to go to the market to raise capital by selling shares and bonds. The corporations have in-house experts who know the answers to some of these questions or know how to ask the right questions about the advice they are given to judge whether it is sound. The corporations, too, are willing to deal with several investment banks so that they get the benefit of each's reputed expertise: Lazard Frères in masterminding takeovers, Goldman, Sachs in handling commercial paper, Salomon Brothers in leasing, and so on.

According to Ball, the entrepreneurial company much too absorbed in making and selling things to bother itself with studying the pros and cons of the advice it gets from its investment bankers is a vanishing breed. So is the self-made corporate executive, the brilliant salesman or clerk who rose to the top with a blend of horse sense, flair, and hard work. Most senior executives, particularly those in charge of corporate finance, are well-educated corporate careermen. George Ball is not alone when he rates them "pretty cold-blooded." They are trained and

employed to
professional e
ers of yesterye

In consequei
teams of experts
management of Sa
rather than a one-
Phibro Corporation i
not the chief executi
firm's German-born gu
trageurs, the wheeler-de
chases of the volatile stock
Salomon Brothers is Richar
self-made men on Wall Str
Higgins.

The Salomon ethic is that
freund, a smooth diamond, says
they can enjoy a limited amount
much they become preoccupied

to elevate the stock m
more solemn, respec
brokers from singing,
anthem, "Wait Till
The sobriety suit
on the New York S
ingly risk-averse inv
pension funds, er
sional" is used he
performing a se
judgment. Whil
fee, "profession
competence. Y
averages. In th
at banks and i
& Poor's 500;
words, the m
had taken t
instead sele
Man

or yacht, because then they are not worth much to me.' This is harsh and it is, though paradoxically, outside his business life Gut freund is regarded by some of his more reactionary colleagues as a bleeding-heart liberal, as a soft touch for charities. He and his equally dedicated partners, however, succeeded in converting a modest bond-trading house into a full-line investment bank that has high standing internationally as well as in the United States. Rivals under the management of less hardheaded professionals failed to prosper and several have been absorbed by retail brokerage houses seeking to poach more effectively in the traditional preserves of the investment banks. White Weld has gone into Merrill Lynch, Blyth Eastman Dillon into Paine Webber, and, in a merger of investment banks, Kuhn Loeb has become a component of Lehman Brothers Kuhn Loeb.

Officials of the New York Stock Exchange are pleased by the sober, professional ethic that has gradually come to prevail in the securities industry. They have for many years deplored any suggestion that investing in stocks is akin to speculation, let alone to gambling. In seeking stocks with a pin or a Ouija board.

otherwise intelligent Americans are making the mistake of playing the man rather than the ball when they hold Wall Street investors to blame both for low stock prices and for the high interest rates that have hurt bond prices. Such questions as: "Will the long-term bond market survive?" "Will municipalities be able to afford to raise the money they need?" and "Are equities dead?" ought not to be directed at Wall Street at all. The securities industry merely provides a marketplace; stock and bond prices are merely a measure of value. The real strength or weakness of the country rests on the soundness of the businesses and the national economy these stocks and bonds represent. If America continues to spend more and invest less of its national income than other countries, its mature economy will inevitably become more arthritic and its bond and stock markets will perform more slothfully than those of capitalist competitors.

While Wall Street is of secondary importance in the national economy, it is far from peripheral. With all its faults, it is still the world's leading securities market, with no serious contender in sight. True, in recent years business corporations have raised in the securities markets only a tiny share of the funds they need to keep going and to expand.

In 1979, to take an extreme example, retained profits and capital consumption allowances provided them with about $200 billion of the more than $300 billion they needed. Net new corporate bond issues totaled only $21 billion; net new corporate stock issues only $3 billion. Such comparisons are misleading. While solid, established corporations can afford to dismiss the securities markets, and particularly the stock markets, as a sideshow that represents a store of value rather than a source of new capital, small businesses with ambitions to grow must be more respectful. Risk capital is still essential for their well-being. Such companies, though, find it ever harder to attract the attention of professional money managers. Most of the professionals are risk-averse sorts anyway. Those who were not were brought into line by the Employee Retirement Income Securities Act of 1974, which is known in the securities business by the acronym ERISA.

The act passed into law after the bear markets of the 1970s which succeeded the bull markets of the 1960s revealed scandalous mismanagement of pension fund assets, not mainly by crooks but by overcocky young handlers of other people's money. Called gunslingers by their detractors, they won clients by, for a while, successfully operating on the greater-fool theory. This holds that someone will always pay more for a glamour stock than you paid for it. ERISA compelled companies to start to fund pension rights and retroactively to make up any unfunded portion of the funds' liabilities. More important, it required, under its so-called prudent man rule, that pension fund managers should be made personally liable for imprudent investments.

The leeriness of the money managers toward entrepreneurial companies that are learning to crawl is matched by Wall Street's still important constituency of rich individual customers, more anxious to preserve their capital than to risk it in hope of making an old-fashioned killing. The majority of small investors, the two-thirds of investors who have portfolios worth less than $10,000, really do not count for much. Their trading activities are more a nuisance than a profit earner for the brokerage business. It is the 17 percent of investors with stock holdings worth $25,000 and more who are really cherished and these are, mostly, people who prefer the safety of blue-chip stocks to the excitement offered by the American Stock Exchange and the over-the-counter markets.

Chicago is the place for investors who want thrills. The high rollers still move the commodity markets and give the La Salle Street financial district a far rougher, more speculative feel than Wall Street—a difference dramatized at the opening, at the Chicago Mercantile Exchange, of a market to deal in currencies for future delivery. Dignitaries invited to the opening were served breakfast by scantily dressed models who represented the currencies to be traded. Miss Sterling wore a miniskirted Beefeater outfit; Miss Yen was in a geisha costume; Miss Mexican Peso wore a sombrero and not much else. To begin trading, a slightly appalled William Dale, then the United States executive director at the International Monetary Fund in Washington, an East Coast type with a fondness for preppy suits and bow ties, was asked to cut a ribbon comprising a chain of seven currencies. When his scissors, to his horror, almost snipped through a dollar bill, he hastily veered them away and sliced through the Queen's head on a British pound note instead.

As the cut currency ribbon fell to the ground, the traders watching the ceremony turned into dervishes, screaming to make their bids for currencies heard above the din from an adjoining pit, where eggs for July delivery were being traded. People still make old-fashioned financial killings, and are ruined, in the Chicago commodity markets, but most give them a wide berth. Only one American investor in ten is prepared to dabble in commodities or in financial futures.

The town and country banks of America are condemned, eventually, to disappear in acquisitions and mergers, just as many Wall Street firms and partnerships have. The nation is starting to forget the way so many banks went bankrupt in the 1930s, closing their doors on their unfortunate depositors, and the constituency for laws defended as necessary to prevent the repetition of such a crisis of confidence in banking is disappearing. Youngsters scoff at their grandparents' warnings about how irresponsible, even downright crooked, wheeler dealing by bankers contributed mightily to the crash. Their savings are today protected by government-backed insurance schemes, and shotgun marriages are arranged by government regulators to keep savings and loans and banks from failing. The old tradition of populism, which included a strong strain of resentment, particularly in rural areas, against the big Eastern city bankers, is also on the wane, and with it another source of resistance to concentration in banking.

Though the *Wall Street Journal* has concluded: "Except perhaps for federal bureaucrats and top executives of the Fortune 500, most Americans tend to regard huge organizations with suspicion and unease," it is a suspicion that is less strongly held than it was. Bankers are given a much easier time in appearances before the House Banking Committee than they were a few years ago, when the committee had a goodly smattering of populists, including its chairman, the redoubtable Wright Patman of Texas. As a young congressman, Patman had tried to impeach Andrew Mellon, President Hoover's secretary of the treasury. As an old one during the Kennedy, Johnson, and Nixon administrations, he continued fervently to believe that big-city bankers were parasitic usurers. When William McChesney Martin, for a long time the chairman of the Federal Reserve Board, was summoned periodically to appear before Patman's committee, the hearing room was packed with expectant spectators. An irreverent hum of approval would go through the chamber as Patman glared through thick spectacles at the head of the central bank and scolded him for letting interest rates for the working people of America trying to buy a farm or a house rise to what Patman regarded as the prohibitive level of 7 or 8 percent.

This populism, and the determination never again to repeat the mistakes of the Great Depression, helped to sustain the three great defenses against concentration in banking: ceilings on the interest rate banks could offer to attract deposits, a prohibition against banks opening branches in more than one state, and a demarcation line between the risky investment of merchant banks and the commercial banks which serve as the place where people maintain checking, deposit, and savings accounts. The really powerful constituency for these restrictions, however, was provided by bankers themselves, not at the 100-odd big money center banks concentrated in New York, Chicago, and California, but at the 14,600 smaller banks that remain independently in business in the United States.

Their influence in Washington is on a par with the American Petroleum Institute and the American Medical Association, and their best lobbyists are unpaid. They are the bank directors who have a quiet word with their congressman or congresswoman when the legislator returns to the home district. Often even this is not necessary. The representative was often an attorney for or remains a director of a bank and needs no persuading. As each bank has an average of fifteen highly motivated supporters, who are either directors or top shareholders or both, and most of these supporters are respected businessmen and businesswomen in the American heartland, the smaller banks can collectively field a team of more than 200,000 to lobby against any legislative initiative they dislike. High on the list of bills to be defeated have been those that have threatened to introduce into banking the sort of rough and tumble that has broken out on Wall Street since fixed commission rates were abolished.

The inconvenience of the 14,600-bank system these discreet lobbyists have helped preserve is realized by Americans only when they go to countries where the big banks have a nationwide branching system similar in its geographical spread to that of the gasoline companies and the supermarkets in the United States. In South Africa, almost every hamlet has at least two bank branches: one for Standard Bank and the other for Barclays. In Britain, the big four London clearing banks—Barclays, Lloyds, Midland, and National Westminister—have a national presence. A Londoner has no need to carry a wallet stuffed with credit cards in going to Cumberland or Dorset. A single bank card can be used to cash a check at a local branch of the bank he uses in London. If he is unlucky enough to lose his wallet, or have it stolen, the manager of the nearest branch of his bank can usually be counted upon to provide enough cash to help out.

When an American is as unlucky, the results can be embarrassing, even frightening, as Hella Junz found in New York when she was having coffee one evening in a fashionable Central Park South Hotel. When the time came to pay the bill, she reached down and discovered that her handbag had been snatched from beneath her chair, her credit rating along with it. The fact that she was formerly a senior economist with the Federal Reserve Bank and the United States Treasury and was at the time employed at a similarly elevated level at the First National Bank of Chicago, one of the largest banks in the nation, suddenly counted for nothing. The hotel was unsympathetic. It had heard her sort of hard luck story before. The cashier chided her for calling to cancel her stolen American Express card before the hotel had a chance to collect the money due on the signed copy made of the card when she booked into the hotel. Fortunately, Mrs. Junz had just enough cash on her person to take a taxi to the apartment of a friend on the upper

East Side. He lent her $150 to manage until her secretary in Chicago could arrange a rescue.

Still more exasperating was the experience of Evan Richardson, a British writer working in the United States, when on a sweaty day in August in Grenada, Mississippi, he left his jacket on the back seat of his rented car while he had a snack and a drink in a coffee shop adjoining a gas station. He came back to find a thief had stolen the wallet from the inside pocket of the jacket. Banks were unwilling to cash his traveler's checks—which were kept in the car's glove compartment and were overlooked by the thief—without proof of identify. This proof was in the stolen wallet. He could not, as he had planned, return the rental car at Memphis, Tennessee, and then fly on to his next destination, Amarillo, Texas, because he did not have the driver's license and credit cards necessary to hire another car when he arrived in Amarillo. Instead, he drove from Mississippi across Arkansas and Oklahoma to the Texas panhandle, stopping along the way at a motel whose management agreed to accept his traveler's checks without identification. He felt almost like a criminal on the run.

This anarchic system of banking has great compensations to offset its inconveniences. The owners and managers of the smaller banks know their customers personally rather than by computer printout, in a way that, say, the top officers of the Bank of America in San Francisco cannot possibly hope to know depositors and borrowers even in nearby Oakland, let alone in Los Angeles, San Diego, or Sacramento. They advance money as much on a person's character as anything else.

Most of the banks in America want to keep it that way. In arguing for the reinforcement of restrictions that helped to keep the big money market banks from invading their turf—notably the limits on interest rates on deposits and the prohibition on interstate branching—the representatives of the smaller banks have shown a truly remarkable ability to say one thing and do another. They are accustomed in their business, political, and even social lives to touting the advantages of uninhibited competition and to praising such capitalist fundamentalists as Milton Friedman and Irving Kristol. Yet they have for years lobbied legislators and regulators to retain interest rate limitations and not to allow the money center banks to establish a national presence.

They have lost the battle not in Congress but in the marketplace.

When inflation went into double figures, and interest rates on fixed-interest securities sold to institutional investors and wealthy individuals went into the teens, middle-income Americans began to realize that interest rates on bank passbook savings accounts pegged by law at a maximum of 5.25 percent were a swindle. Such low rates in inflationary times guaranteed that their savings would rapidly lose purchasing power. Real estate prices took off as people started to see houses and land as a hedge against inflation. They also determinedly began to search around for new forms of savings that offered a fair return. Several brokerage houses in 1978 and 1979 introduced as the answer money market funds, which gave their middle-income customers a chance to earn the high interest rates formerly available only to the wealthy, by pooling their savings and investing them in short-term, high-yielding, fixed-interest securities. A trickle of savings quickly became a flood as many pulled money out of banks and savings and loan associations. As the total diverted into money market funds lapped over $100 billion, even the smaller banks realized that the interest-rate dike was broken beyond repair. They needed the right to offer competitive interest rates to hold their own with money market funds and other high-yielding forms of savings, and Congress accepted the inevitable when it legislated the phase-out of interest-rate ceilings on passbook savings accounts—ceilings that dated back to the New Deal.

The other legislated inhibitions on commercial banks—the ban on interstate branching and the demarcation line drawn between commercial and investment banking—are rapidly, and inexorably, being either overwhelmed or circumvented by financial and technological innovation. On the lending side, the regional restrictions were made redundant when money center banks started to open loan production offices around the country and then to comply with the letter of the law by booking a loan made in, say, Houston at a New York headquarters office so that, technically, it was not an out-of-state loan. On the deposit side, the remaining restraints are being challenged by out-of-state cash dispensers and are threatened with total subversion by the prospect of depositors' carrying out retail banking from the home via a terminal and a telephone. The Glass-Steagall Act of 1933, which purported to build a "Chinese wall" between commercial banks and the securities industry, is being breached daily as brokerage houses swarm into activities that blur the distinction between brokering and banking—corporate advice services, cash management accounts, margin lending, credit cards, and money market funds, to cite a few.

The winners in the interest-rate revolution are savers. At last they are offered the prospect of a return that is within spitting distance of the prevailing inflation rate. The losers are the borrowers. Money is the raw material of the banks and these raw material costs were kept cheap by the interest-rate ceilings on passbook savings accounts and laws that, to the glee of the banks, prevented them from paying interest on checking accounts. With raw material costs so cheap, the banks were able to keep the cost of what they produced, their loans, relatively cheap as well and borrowers benefited. Those days are over. The revolution threatens to keep the cost of money tied much more closely to the anticipated inflation rate than in the past, as savers demand and can get a fair return. Americans are going to have to accustom themselves to the idea of paying permanently higher interest rates, relative to inflation, than in the past on mortgage and other loans.

Many small- and medium-sized banks are feeling the squeeze. Just as fixed commission rates on share transactions helped to keep relatively inefficient partnerships and family firms profitable by pushing up their revenues, so legal limitations on interest rates have kept relatively inefficient banks profitable by pushing down their costs. The legislated phase-out of interest-rate ceilings puts smaller banks at a disadvantage against the larger banks that can afford to invest heavily in new labor-saving technology and to exploit economies of scale. As their profits come under pressure, small banks are beginning to huddle together for comfort, as they have in Texas, where banks have merged within holding companies. Others will find takeover approaches from big banks ever more enticing and will begin to lobby Congress and state banking superintendents to relax restrictions on interstate branching so that they can accept a fancy bid from a mighty Chicago, New York, or California bank. High interest rates have already forced shotgun mergers among the "thrifts"—savings and loan and mutual savings banks—where regulators have taken a relaxed view of the restrictions against takeovers across state lines.

The restrictions on interstate branching helped to persuade Citibank, Manufacturers Hanover, Chase Manhattan, First National of Chicago, Continental Illinois, Bank of America, and other American money center banks to expand their operations far more rapidly abroad than they did at home. So did the faster growth of foreign countries relative to the United States, particularly East Asia and continental Western Europe as they made a phoenix-like recovery from World War II. In going abroad, the banks were following the lead of their big American customers, the industrial corporations that with the aid of an overvalued dollar evolved into mighty multinational corporations.

At home, these corporations occupy the heights of the American economy, and their payrolls, including domestic and overseas employees, are bigger than those of large government departments in Washington. General Motors, for example, with annual sales exceeding the gross national product of Denmark, employs nearly three times as many people as the Department of Transportation; Mobil, with sales higher than Denmark's gross domestic product, employs nearly ten times as many as the Department of State. They needed the help of their bankers abroad, in dealing with the complexities of raising foreign currency loans and protecting themselves against foreign exchange risks, but are increasingly independent of their banks in the United States itself.

American banks must plead with the corporate treasurers of Mobil, General Foods, and other businesses that possess impeccable credit ratings to borrow more. They offer interest rates below the prime rate, though this rate is publicly touted as the absolute minimum rate they will charge a customer. They are commonly rewarded with nothing more than a cup of coffee in a styrofoam cup for their sales pitch, and have to leave without making their loan. Do-it-yourself banking made such industrial corporations all but self-reliant for the money they needed at home. Like financial corporations before them, they discovered that they could raise money at a cheaper rate than the banks offered by selling unsecured short-term IOUs, known in the money markets as commercial paper.

In effect, they are cutting out the middleman. Instead of allowing the banks to borrow money at one rate from customers flush with cash and then to lend it out at a higher rate to customers short of cash, these corporations borrow the money by selling commercial paper to those who have money to spare. The lenders get slightly higher interest rates on the commercial paper than they would by investing in large certificates of deposit with Chase Manhattan or Security Pacific; the borrowers obtain the cash they need at a slightly lower interest rate than they would get from the banks.

It is not a new idea. Goldman, Sachs started helping corporations to market commercial paper in 1869. General Motors fifty years later became the first corporation to sell these IOUs without the aid of an investment bank. However, though the idea has been around for a long time, the takeoff of the commercial paper is more recent. The value of these IOUs oustanding increased from $8 billion in 1964 to well over $100 billion in 1980.

The commercial paper market is elitist. The main rating agencies are Moody's Investors Services, Standard & Poor's, and Fitch Investors Services. A company that does not merit their highest ratings might just as well borrow from the banks, since it will have to offer a high premium on the paper to attract buyers and even then might get a cold shoulder. Those who buy the commercial paper—corporate treasurers taking in others' washing, insurance companies, bank trust departments, pension funds—are not willing to risk a moment's sleep over it. They aim to get a slightly higher return on their cash than they would by putting it into short-term government paper or bank certificates of deposit, without assuming any more risk. So industrial concentration in America is helped along by the big fry being able directly to raise the working capital needed at a cheaper rate than the small- and medium-sized fry can get from their banks.

Overseas, these multinational corporations are less self-reliant because the special expertise of the banks is harder to duplicate; and the names of the biggest American banks have often become more familiar abroad than they are at home as, through overseas branches and offices, they have gained a leading role in the several-hundred-billion-Eurodollar market. Their overseas presence has also made it easier for them to win a profitable stake in lending money to government and quasi-government borrowers who find themselves stripped of foreign exchange as OPEC oil prices push their balance of payments into deeper deficit. In the repayment crises of Zaire, Turkey, Poland, Jamaica, Argentina, and even Iran, the banks have so far emerged unscathed. Indeed, they usually profit from such credit crunches. The client country agrees to higher interest payments in return for a postponement on the repayment of principal.

American politicians and newspapers continually fret about this,

While the bank manager was eager to help, he had to explain regretfully that he had no way of telling whether the German notes were genuine or not. He eventually thought of a solution. A teller at another branch of the bank had recently gone to Bavaria to attend a wedding. The tourist was sent around to the branch, the teller said the notes looked genuine enough to him, and dollars were then handed over in exchange for them after a telephone call to the bank manager who had sent the tourist around and after a search for the currency conversion rate in the pages of the *Wall Street Journal.*

Stock analysts for the big retail brokerage houses, people of generally high intelligence who take rightful pride in their financial sophistication, are commonly as parochial as the American public. Brokers with access to these analysts' research reports are able to offer knowledgeable advice when a customer asks whether he should purchase the shares of, say, ITT. When the customer wants to know whether Siemens of West Germany or Ericsson of Sweden might be a better investment, there is a long silence at the end of the telephone. The broker has not the slightest idea and does not know whom to turn to for guidance.

This is changing, slowly. Morgan Guaranty, the trust account manager of well over $20 billion of other people's money, startled pension funds by sending them letters stating that 5 percent of their assets would be invested in foreign securities unless they objected. The letters were accompanied by a stack of statistical materials showing that foreign stocks had, on average, performed better than American ones over several years, and Morgan Guaranty's pension fund clients were for the first time in their lives forced to ponder the pros and cons of American workers depending indirectly for part of their retirement income on dividends from such exotic entities as Broken Hill Proprietary in Australia and Kao Soap in Japan. Merrill Lynch, the biggest brokerage house, is another pioneer. In 1979, it began publishing a regular series of analysts' reports on foreign stocks. A blue band replaced the usual green band at the top of these Merrill Lynch reports, to alert customers that they were out of the ordinary.

Seemingly perversely, this new American interest in overseas stock markets coincides with an unprecedented stampede by foreign companies into the United States. This is not, though, as perverse as it appears. American investors putting their money abroad and foreign companies setting up shop in the United States are responding to the same stimuli. After years in which a floating dollar was a euphemism for a sinking dollar, American stock and bond buyers began to question the wisdom of having all their nest eggs denominated in dollars. They invested overseas to get some of their dividends and interest payments denominated in foreign currencies as a hedge against further dollar depreciation.

Meantime, a cheaper dollar had given foreign companies both the means and the incentive to come to America. Volkswagen is an outstanding example. So long as its factories, tools, and workers in Wolfsburg, Germany—chosen in 1938 as the site for the manufacture of Hitler's "people's car"—cost less than those of its Detroit-headquartered rivals, it could build cars in West Germany, pay to ship them across the Atlantic, meet American import duties, and still sell them at competitive prices in the American market. When the West German mark more than doubled in value against the dollar, and West German labor and capital costs surged, Volkswagen's German-made cars started being priced out of the American market. The solution was obvious. Volkswagen moved into a factory in New Stanton, Pennsylvania, built for but never occupied by Chrysler, and employed American workers to build Volkswagens for sale in the United States.

So many others have made the same calculation that foreigners came to control such household names as Brylcreem hair oil and Pepsodent toothpaste, French's mustard, Alpo dog food and Peter Paul candy bars, Libby's string beans and Chesterfield cigarettes, SOS soap pads and Clorox bleach. Australia's Rupert Murdoch bought the *Village Voice*, the *New York Post*, and *New York* magazine. Britain's Imperial Group acquired Howard Johnson, while Hongkong and Shanghai Bank acquired Marine Midland Bank and Britain's Midland Bank acquired Crocker National Bank. British interests purchased Gimbels and Saks, French interests Korvettes, German interests A & P. One Shell Plaza, Houston's tallest building, and Pennzoil Place, Houston's biggest, are in German hands. British Petroleum, through its subsidiary the Standard Oil Company of Ohio, has the largest stake in the North Slope oil field in Alaska. Union Bancorp in California and several of New York's largest banks, Bankers Trust and European-American Bank (formerly Franklin National), are controlled by foreign banks.

The change is profound. In the late 1960s, Europeans were reading a chilling best-seller called *Le Défi Américain*, titled *The American Challenge* in English. The author, Jean-Jacques Servan-Schreiber, a French journalist and political hopeful, informed trembling readers that American multinationals were buying up Europe and that Europe's industries, most especially those involved in high technology, were going to be tentacles of an American octopus. This meant, Servan-Schreiber warned, that decisions affecting Europeans as workers, consumers, and researchers were increasingly going to be taken not by their fellow Europeans but by American managers and boards of directors. At the time the prospect did not seem fanciful. The United States earned a surplus on its foreign trade in every year between 1889 and 1970. With the demise of sterling, the dollar was without doubt the world's preeminent reserve currency. This special status gave the United States a freedom denied to all others: in effect, to print bank notes to finance investments abroad. Theoretically, foreign central banks could then convert these bank notes into gold at the United States Treasury, but as American gold reserves dwindled, this became an empty promise which was withdrawn altogether at that White House press conference in August 1971.

What has happened since is that the economies of advanced industrial countries, most particularly the United States, Canada, and Western Europe, have become far more interdependent and integrated. Decisions on jobs, pricing, and investment taken in boardrooms in Detroit, New York, Houston, and Los Angeles influence the lives of all Europeans. They tend to resent it far more than the Americans whose lives are now influenced by boardroom decisions taken in London, Paris, Brussels, and Wolfsburg. The main reason for American tolerance may be that the foreign companies active in the United States have succeeded in passing themselves off as natives. Two of the biggest, Shell and BP, are past masters at this.

While their investment behavior has been strikingly similar to that of the American multinationals, who were busy buying up Europe when *Le Défi Américain* made its appearance in the bookshops, the motives of European business investing in the United States have been subtly different. When American companies invested heavily in Europe after World War II, they assumed—rightly, as it turned out —that economies recovering from wartime devastation would grow more rapidly than a maturing American economy which had come through the war unscathed. The mass of European multinationals investing in the United States do not assume the tide has turned and that the American economy will in the foreseeable future experience faster growth than the European market. They are coming to the United States as much in search of security as in pursuit of profits.

Their motives are hard for Americans fully to understand, and this lack of comprehension reveals as much about Americans as it does about Europeans. The pat explanation for European business people's insecurity, "fear of socialism," is misleading, even though it is true that Europeans have disagreed fundamentally among themselves since the early nineteenth century on the best way to organize their industrial economies. Economic collectivism has vied against economic individualism in a way that is foreign to the American experience. Unlike Americans who regard the superiority of capitalism as a revealed truth, Europeans do not link a belief in any particular economic system to patriotism. European businessmen naturally find this agnosticism of their countrymen disconcerting. They are reassured when they put their money into America by the way socialism is stigmatized as un-American.

European business investors in the United States have another motive, however, which is easier to sense and to smell than to give substance to. With the outstanding exception of the British, who have not been successfully invaded for nine hundred years, they do not in their bones feel that investment in foreign parts is necessarily more risky than investment at home. Americans, in contrast, are sure their country is more stable than any other. When big New York banks, like Citibank, Bankers Trust, and Morgan Guaranty, began reporting that they earned more than half of their profits overseas, American legislators worried aloud that banks were altogether too dependent on foreigners for their prosperity. Not even the banks offered the riposte Europeans regard as self-evident—that it is prudent for businesses to spread their risk and to reduce their exposure in any single market, including the home one. Lucky Americans are spared this sense of insecurity. They are confident that a political system that has remained, for all its faults, unshaken in its essentials for two hundred years has decisively proved its sturdiness.

Europeans lack this confidence in themselves and their countrymen, even when they are as rich as Friedrich Flick of West Germany, whose industrial holdings approach a value of $5 billion. In the back of his mind there is always the memory of how his industrialist father, the founder of the Flick empire, prospered in a German Reich that was supposed to last for a thousand years and then suddenly lost much of his fortune and all his freedom. The Red Army overran three-quarters of the Flick enterprise. The Allies sent Flick senior to jail for exploiting slave labor in his mines, foundries, and factories. His son was seeking to spread his risk when he became the predominant shareholder in W. R. Grace, the fifth-largest American chemical producer, and in United States Filter Corporation, a high-technology engineering company.

Hoffmann–La Roche, the Swiss-based pharmaceutical multinational that brought Librium and Valium onto the market and has large American operations at Nutley, New Jersey, also has dark memories. During the First World War it got clobbered from both sides. The Germans suspected it of supplying French customers from its German factories, while in France its products were boycotted by doctors who thought it was pro-German. In Britain it was blacklisted after rumors circulated that it was producing poison gas for the German army. Then the Russian Revolution wiped out Roche's entire Russian market, which before 1914 had accounted for up to a fifth of sales. When Hitler annexed Austria, the company transferred all its interests outside the Nazi reach to Sapac, a Canadian holding company first based in Panama and then in Montevideo. The company's New Jersey operations remain defensively under this Sapac umbrella. As a senior Roche executive put it: "What happens if Europe goes Communist? You never know, you know."

Americans have no such real fears about the future of their country. Except for a few paranoid people in the John Birch Society, the Ku Klux Klan, and similar fringe groups of the far right, they are confident the White House will continue to be occupied by a believer in the American economic system. This century, the country has been spared the upheavals that, in Russia, Germany, and Japan, have turned society upside down, destroying an old establishment and the fortunes of old moneyed families. American society, in contrast, has remained astonishingly stable. In no other leading industrial country, other perhaps than Britain, have concentrations of family wealth been less shaken by war, revolution, and such economic upheavals as hyperinflation. Families that were rich and prominent at the turn of the century are scarcely less so today, and if their influence within the economy is not what it was, this is less because their fortunes are scattered—they are not, they have grown—than because the economy as a whole has outgrown them.

7

YOUR TOWN
Cities and Architecture

FOR MOST AMERICANS with enough money, the biggest investment of their lives will not be on Wall Street but on Walnut, Chestnut,
or Elm Street, in the house they live in. Owning a house in the
American suburbs or in an urban renewal section downtown is not just
a matter of finding a comfortable area where it is easy to bring up
children or a part of town close to work, shops, films, and music.
Owning a house represents an effort to find financial security. Housing
has become less a nest than a nest egg.

Doubters ought to listen to conversations among middle-class
Americans at mealtimes in almost any city outside Manhattan, where
well-off renters are still common and where those with money talk
about their houses in the country or their co-ops. Talk of houses brings
the shyest or most wooden dinner guests alive. House prices arouse
interest, passion. Talk that is desultory about politics or books becomes
animated when the subject turns to second mortgages, venal appraisers,
or coming areas. In Washington, a dinner guest will be told about a
shrewd couple who bought for under $30,000 a house on Ashmead
Place or some other part of the northwest section of the city that was
singed in the riots of the 1960s: a house that could be sold tomorrow
for $200,000. In the ranch-house suburbs of Los Angeles it is joked that
any politician with the gumption to form a "Higher House Price Party"
would be elected by a landslide.

Urbanologists have a term for it: They call it the post-shelter society. According to George Sternlieb, the director of the Center for

Urban Policy Research at Rutgers University, an outspoken academic who looks like a very large Telly Savalas:

> Housing in America is much more important as a form of investment and of forced savings (and tax savings), and as a refuge from inflation, than as a refuge from the elements. This is by no means to imply that all Americans are well housed—all too many of them are not. It does indicate, however, that the "safe, sound, sanitary" provisions of a generation ago no longer have relevance to the house search by middle America—the bulk of the voters—of today. Long-term, chronic inflation of the duration and extent which we are undergoing alters behavior with equivalent vigor. The first question asked by the home buyer in a good many areas is not: "Do I like the house?" That was a question of a previous era. But rather: "If I buy it, will I be able to sell it? And if I am able to sell it, will I be able to keep pace with inflation? Because if I fall off the train and make the wrong housing buy—or, God help me, buy on the wrong side of town, or worse yet, buy in the wrong town—it may be a good shelter but I'll never be able to get out from under it. I'd be immobilized forever."

A house, in other words, is no longer only or even mainly to keep out the weather. It is instead for middle-class Americans what gold napoleons under the bed are for French peasants and comely daughters that will bring bride prices of many cows are for rural African fathers. This is not to be sneered at. Americans are, on the whole, the best, most comfortably housed people on earth. In 1900, only the most affluent of families had two bathrooms in their houses: one for the servants, the other for the family. Now two- and three-bathroom houses are commonplace. So are such conveniences—still considered luxuries in Europe—as dishwashers, smoke detectors with alarms of their own to sound when the batteries are running out, humidifiers, built-in garages, garbage-disposal units, copper wiring, a separate bedroom for every child, a den, and a bar.

Though not all houses are as handsome as those in the television sitcoms, the benefits of home ownership have been widely shared. Before World War II, more than half the population lived in rented homes. Now two-thirds of Americans live in a home of their own. Nearly four out of five labor union members are house owners, a statistic that goes a long way to explaining why organized labor in America, by the socialist standards of Western Europe, is relatively unradical, unmilitant, a grouping of capitalist fellow travelers. Most of the houses are modern: three-fifths of the housing stock is less than forty years old. Houses have become steadily and expensively larger. The houses built at Levittown after World War II were 800 feet square. By the mid-1950s, the median size of newly built houses was 1,100 square feet. Currently it is over 1,600 square feet, although building costs are now rising so fast that limits may well have been reached in the size of affordable houses.

Like all benefits, housing so many Americans so well has a cost. The tax system that underwrote the long postwar boom in house building and house prices has caused more American capital to flow into mortgages than into any other single use—including business investment or state and local government financing. Most economists agree that this is one reason, and not a trivial one, why business investment in America has failed to grow as it should. Too much has been invested in accommodation and too little in new factories and new machines and in research and development to better the country's recently abysmal lack of success in raising its productivity or efficiency.

For any officeholder to state this obvious fact, still less to try to do something about it, would be to commit instant electoral suicide. A huge and powerful middle-class constituency of householders has successfully ensured that housing enjoys strong tax advantages over all other forms of investment, such as corporate stocks, bonds, or direct investments in small businesses, even though it is these alternative investments, especially those in small businesses, that contribute to innovation and create new jobs in the American economy.

Because when they buy a house Americans are able to subtract the interest payments on the mortgage from their taxable income, the higher the income of the house buyer and the higher the tax bracket, the bigger the tax break. The combination of inflation, tougher zoning and building codes, and a projected increase of thirteen million between 1978 and 1985 in the number of Americans in the twenty-five to forty-four-year age bracket virtually guarantees that house prices will continue to rise. The federal government is, in effect, allowing house buyers to depreciate an appreciating asset. A person can sell a house without paying capital gains taxes on the profit, so long as another house is purchased with the proceeds, and can take out $125,000 in capital gains after the age of fifty-five without paying any taxes whatsoever. Anthony Downs, an economist of the Brookings Institution, has looked at how this tax regime distorts investment: Take someone who bought a house with 20 percent down in California in 1976. The median price of existing houses in California rose 20.9 percent a year compounded from 1976 to 1980, so this lucky house buyer, if he or she did no better than average, achieved a 100 percent increase on the initial investment on the typical home *every year*.

With all its faults, this tax system has achieved its aim of housing a majority of the population. However you slice it, this is a huge achievement in a country where almost everyone wants to own his own home. The losers, a distinct minority, are those who have not got an equity stake in housing and are therefore at a great disadvantage in trying to break into a market where the other participants are able, in effect, to trade in one house for another. In housing, more perhaps than in anything else, class distinctions come into view that elsewhere Americans are successful at repressing. Americans who have bought houses are loath to see their values jeopardized by neighbors who let crabgrass spread, use the front yard to work on a rusty Oldsmobile, or collect junk in the back yard.

Black Americans are especially handicapped, and not just because they earn, on average, less than whites and have the odds stacked against them in a mortgage tax credit system that favors the better-off. They make up 12 percent of the population yet occupy seven out of ten public housing units in the country, and only 44 percent of black households own their own homes versus nearly 70 percent of whites. As landowners in rural areas, their position has actually grown worse. Blaming blacks themselves for missing out so heavily on the American dream will not wash. When the federal government first entered housing in a big way, during the Great Depression, the racism of the Federal Housing Administration was uncloseted. An official FHA manual stated: "If a neighborhood is to retain stability, it is necessary that properties shall continue to be occupied by the very same social and racial classes." The manual even encouraged developers and house owners to adopt a model covenant which said, in part, "no person of any race other than ——— [race to be inserted] shall use or occupy any building or any lot, except that this covenant shall not prevent occupancy by domestic servants of a different race domiciled with any owner or tenant." Louis Heren, then the Washington bureau chief of the London *Times*, remembers that when he bought a large house on the District of Columbia side of the Maryland border, where he was a close neighbor of Lyndon Johnson, then Vice-President, he was asked to sign a covenant which precluded sale to Jews and people of Eastern European origin as well as to blacks. When he refused, the covenant was deleted. Until then, other residents had gone along.

Since then formal barriers against black entry to the suburbs have been dismantled. Informal barriers that discriminate against them and others trying to break into the home ownership market remain intact. Zoning laws that effectively exclude low-income housing, by keeping large tracts out of development and by requiring low density on development land, serve to price out the first-time buyer. So do building codes that mandate standards urbanologists describe as "nice but not necessary," rules insisting, for example, on smoke detectors, water softeners, wide sidewalks, storm sewers large enough to cope with downpours of flood-like proportions, a ban on clearing land by burning, a fire wall between garage and living area, ground fault interrupters. All add dollars to the price of a house. This is tolerable, even welcome, for the haves, but a raised drawbridge for the have-nots.

Among those stymied by the "drawbridge mentality" in housing is William Levitt. Like many successful entrepreneurs, he is big-headed, high-handed, and so hard to get along with that other builders are surprised he has had only three wives. It was, though, this obduracy, this orneriness, that allowed him, against the odds, to do for housing what Henry Ford did for cars and McDonald's did for hamburgers— to mass-produce and to mass-merchandise them. Inspired by his wartime experience building houses under contract for the military, and then as a member of the Navy's construction unit, the Seabees, he decided to adapt the techniques of mass building to put up for profit houses for returned servicemen when peace broke out.

There was no worry about demand. For the men and women who had married and had babies after the war, anything was preferable to the in-laws' basement or a railroad flat. The simple Cape Codders that Levitt built, at a rate as fast as one every sixteen minutes on former potato fields near Hicksville, Long Island, covered only 800 square feet. They all looked much alike and had unfinished attics. But they had the overwhelming advantage of being inexpensive. Levitt, again like Henry

Ford, had introduced assembly-line techniques into an industry dominated until then by custom-built products. His assembly line, however, was different from Detroit's. Instead of the product moving along the line, the workers did. When the whistle blew in the morning to signal the start of work on a new street at this, the first, Levittown, the concrete men would pour twenty-five slabs as quickly as possible. Levitt did not like basements; they cost too much. As soon as the concrete dried, the carpenters arrived to put in the studs. Then separate relay teams came in to lay bricks, to nail laths, to paint and shingle the new house. Levitt broke down building a house into twenty-six simple steps. Altogether, 17,445 Cape Codders were built on these 6,200 Long Island acres thirty miles from Times Square. Although the houses were mass produced, they did not look all that different, at least externally, from those built in Massachusetts when it was still a colony. They were small but neat, unpretentious and, above all, cheap. Selling from $7,990 upward and costing $60 a month to carry, they were affordable for just about anybody who had a job. William Levitt was later to recall, in a conversation with Martin Mayer, the author of *The Builders:* "We started to sell in March, 1949. We advertised that beginning the next Monday we would accept deposits. It was bitterly cold; we set up a canteen. One of the women on the line was pregnant; we had to take her to the hospital to have her baby. That Monday night we closed, from seven-thirty to eleven o'clock, fourteen hundred contracts."

While the vets found the houses a dream, others thought them a nightmare. Architectural critics, Ada Louise Huxtable and Lewis Mumford prominent among them, predicted that the Levittowns would quickly become slums. A satirical song about little boxes made of ticky-tacky that all looked the same became popular. *The New Yorker* carried cartoons showing inebriated commuters stumbling into the wrong house. There was something unduly regimented about a suburb that looked from the air like an army barracks and where instructions from friends on how to find their houses would say: "You can't miss Daffodil Lane—it's in the D section." It is still a handy reference. The neighboring streets are Duckpond Drive North, Duckpond Drive East, and Duckpond Drive South (though nobody can remember a duck pond in the vicinity), plus Downhill Lane, Duck Lane, Dell Lane, Deep Lane, Dahlia Lane, Disc Lane, Dome Lane, and Deer Lane. There are no fewer than eighty-two lanes and streets beginning with the letter

S, from Saddle Lane to Sycamore Lane. As a New York cabdriver helpfully explained this system: "The streets are numbered alphabetical." Rules and regulations for Levittowners sounded military: Fences were forbidden, grass had to be cut weekly, clothes could not be hung from an ordinary clothesline but had to be hung on removable racks which could be used only on weekdays.

What the architectural or social critics overlooked or underrated was the American enthusiasm for home improvement. The original Long Island Levittown has become vastly better with age. Drive down its Azalea, Crabtree, and Primrose lanes today and you will be hard pressed to find an original Cape Codder. Almost every house has been changed. There are flagstones for walks, gaslights, hitching posts, freshly painted shutters, dormers, garages, bay windows, and swimming pools. And, inevitably, concrete and wooden ducks, deer, and jockeys in the gardens. Some of the houses now look like cottages in a Derbyshire village; others like California ranch houses or New England saltboxes. The same is true of the 17,311 houses at Levittown in Pennsylvania, which claims to be the first entirely preplanned city built in the United States since Pierre L'Enfant's Washington.

By 1977, the company Levitt founded had built more than 130,000 houses, in France, Spain, and Puerto Rico as well as the United States. Levitt was honored by the National Academy of Sciences, as one of the "outstanding contributors to building progress over the past quarter of a century," along with Frank Lloyd Wright, Mies van der Rohe, Eero Saarinen, and Walter Gropius. Tactfully forgotten was a history of segregation in his housing projects, which, for example, excluded blacks from the Pennsylvania Levittown until 1960.

Levittowns could not succeed today as they did then. About ninety million Americans now live in the suburbs, compared to sixty million in the central cities. Too many of those who have houses in good suburbs want to prevent others from doing the same. The exclusionists have fought hard and with much success for tougher environmental and zoning laws, for costlier building standards, and for other barricades against low-cost housing. Levitt himself declared, in 1977:

> The age of volume building in the U.S. is over. First there's a lack of sizable tracts suitable for building within reasonable commuting range of any major metropolitan center in this country. I personally don't know any.

Second, environmentalism and local land-use restrictions are here to stay and that reduces the amount of land and the places available for building. Third, the cost of labor and materials has priced mass housing out of the market. The median-priced new home in this country now sells for $48,800 [that was in 1977—in 1981, it was $68,900] and only 16 percent of the population can afford it.

Levitt had seen what was coming when in 1968 he sold out the Levitt Corporation to the International Telephone and Telegraph conglomerate in exchange for stock. ITT, in turn, sold it in 1978 to the Starrett Housing Corporation. William Levitt busied himself with building an "adult community," a euphemism for an old people's retirement park, in Florida. Levitt called it Williamsburg, using his first name, after the courts forbade him to associate it in any way with the Levittown trademark which he had sold along with his company.

For good or ill, architect extraordinary Philip Cortelyou Johnson has done even more than Levitt during the past fifty years to change the way America looks. The modernist taste he helped promote started out as controversial and has since become conventional. He is not necessarily recognizable as the influence he is, though, when one first meets him in his offices on the thirty-seventh floor of the Seagram Building. This is an expensive architectural masterpiece sheathed in bronze-tinted glass which he helped his mentor, Ludwig Mies van der Rohe, design for the Bronfmans, the Canadian whiskey family. The walls of Johnson's offices are buff, the carpets gray. The plastic molded chairs, with decorative holes in them, are green and hospital white. The Spartan furnishings and the emptiness of the rooms provide an austere welcome.

On first meeting, Philip Johnson is as disconcerting as his offices. Thin and elegant, he is in his mid-seventies, yet his nervous gestures and speech are those of a bright, quick, cheeky arts graduate who enjoys tweaking the establishment. Johnson called Frank Lloyd Wright "the greatest architect of the nineteenth century," denounced the GM skyscraper opposite the southeast corner of Central Park in New York as a "money making cheapie," explained that late in life he turned his back on modern architecture because it was "boring," and said that anyone who commissioned a building from him bought him. "I'm for sale. I'm a whore. I'm an artist."

Far from being a kept man, Johnson is in fact one of those rare people with both an original mind and a large enough private income to avoid the compromises that are a usual part of a successful professional career. His father, Homer Johnson, in dividing his estate among his children, gave his only son so much stock in Alcoa in 1926 that Philip had no need in his formative years to fret about money. Johnson has remained a spontaneous architect with few fixed ideas and a readiness to work with very different kinds of clients. In the 1950s and 1960s, he earned so many commissions he became almost the official American designer of museums. In 1975, the Reverend Robert Schuller, a television evangelist, decided to hire him to design a glass cathedral at Anaheim near Disneyland on the outskirts of Los Angeles. Schuller explained: "I think Phillip has the same quality that Walt Disney had—the enthusiasm of a boy who's never grown up."

This often naive enthusiasm has got Johnson into trouble. In 1934, he disgraced himself and appalled his friends by helping to form the neo-Nazi party in the United States, complete with a gray-shirt uniform. Subsequently he went to Germany and then to Poland, from where, after war broke out in 1939, he filed articles for Father Coughlin's *Social Justice*, which angered the British and pleased National Socialist Germany. Johnson later recanted and served as a private in the Army. When this flirtation with Nazism jeopardized Johnson's election as a trustee of the Museum of Modern Art in 1957, Mrs. John D. Rockefeller III said: "Every young man should be allowed to make one large mistake."

Johnson's exuberance and naiveté are apparent in his many buildings. "Philip, should I take my hat off or leave it on? Am I indoors or am I out?" was Frank Lloyd Wright's comment on seeing the glass house Johnson designed for himself in New Canaan, Connecticut. Equally controversial achievements followed: the pre-Columbian wing of the Dumbarton Oaks Museum at Georgetown in Washington; the Investors Diversified Services Center he designed with his partner, John Burgee, in Minneapolis, a vast structure described by Paul Goldberger of the *New York Times* as "a great glass circus tent pitched in the center of the city"; the black, asymmetrical twin-towered Pennzoil Place in Houston, which sticks up over the swampy Gulf plain like two sails; a headquarters building for AT&T in New York, topped off to look like an antique chest of drawers, which was brushed aside by Ada

Louise Huxtable, the magisterial architectural critic, as a "stand-up joke."

Within the profession Johnson has as many detractors as admirers. While Gordon Bunshaft of Skidmore, Owings & Merrill, the designer of the Lever Building in Manhattan and the Hirschhorn Museum in Washington, is to all outward appearances a courtly gentleman of the old school, with the face of a kindly basset hound, when the name Philip Johnson comes up he goes for the jugular. "He is a celebrity rather than an architect. There are great architects who are also celebrities, but he is not one of them. He says the sort of things that make clever remarks in print. In my bitter moments I think he is not working for his clients but for the press he will get."

Nevertheless, American architects, the pros zestfully, the antis reluctantly, agree that Johnson helped to alter radically the face of American building, when in 1932 he arranged with Henry-Russell Hitchcock a show of contemporary European architecture at the Museum of Modern Art. Called the International Style, it was infused with idealism and preached that the flat roof, the smooth glass wall, the unadorned facade, would be universal and that people would live better, cheaper, purer lives surrounded by such abstract, functional, simple shapes. It caused an immediate sensation. According to the architectural historian James Marston Fitch: "Together with its catalogue and the book which subsequently grew out of it, this show triggered the blast that lifted American architecture out of the parochialism into which it had slipped."

The swiftness with which the revolution took hold was astonishing. Architecture is the most expensive and most obtrusive form of art. Big buildings are commissioned and paid for by corporate and government clients usually leery about anything that smacks of the new. Yet within a few years, architects who designed the derivative neo-Georgian, neo-Classical, neo-Romanesque, neo-almost-anything buildings that enriched and confused the American cityscape between the late nineteenth century and the first thirty years of this century were treated as fossils. Steel-ribbed and glass-skinned buildings, called "upended cigar boxes" by those who did not like them, were the way ahead. How did it happen so fast?

One large reason was the long breakdown in communications between American architects and the European avant garde. American painters were enthused by modern European art before the Kaiser's war. American writers flocked to the Left Bank in Paris after Prohibition. American architects by contrast kept their distance from the revolutionary changes under way in their art form. They had already turned their backs on the great works of the pioneering modern architects of Chicago: Henry Hobson Richardson, Louis Sullivan, and Frank Lloyd Wright. According to Fitch, a large part of the explanation may have been the unchallenged prestige of the École des Beaux Arts in Paris, which seemed to be as completely untouched by these new winds as if it had been on Madagascar, and which had the American architectural schools "firmly chained to its eclectic chariot." American architects, says Fitch, seem to have gone blindfold through the grand tour. If they saw anything of the new works in Vienna, Berlin, or Amsterdam, it was not apparent in their own designs. Those who stayed at home were ill-served by their architectural journals. Between 1919 and 1929, these carried scant news from Europe and "grossly misjudged the significance of what they did report."

Having been left behind, the more intrepid American architects were, after the 1932 exhibition at the Museum of Modern Art, determined first to catch up and then to race past their European counterparts. They succeeded in both ambitions, with the aid of the influx into the United States of a brigade of great European architects, practitioners and teachers who, among them, had made up Europe's architectural avant garde. Prominent in their number were Alvar Aalto, Marcel Breuer, Serge Chermayeff, Walter Gropius, Erich Mendelsohn, László Moholy-Nagy, Ludwig Mies van der Rohe, José Sert, and Konrad Wachsmann.

That the architects of the International Style found it so easy to win acceptance and corporate clients is not, in retrospect, all that surprising. Steel and precision work were perfect for the United States, where excellent engineers were numerous and ornamental craftsmen rare, and where most buildings were by then being commissioned by corporate careermen who had no substantial ownership stake in the companies they worked for but had made their way up a salaried ladder. The outlook of these new managers was radically different from that of the old-school owner-occupiers they had gradually eclipsed. Their predecessors were the nineteenth- and early-twentieth-century captains of industry and banking, with outsize egos. Those men had owned as well as run their corporate fiefdoms and sought reassurance, permanence, and prestige in classicalizing designs for their "cottages" at Newport, for latter-day palaces like San Simeon or Biltmore, and for their company headquarters, Florentine or Venetian merchants' palaces transplanted to Rockefeller's Cleveland and Mellon's Pittsburgh. The corporate careermen lacked monumental, grandiose ambitions. The buildings they wanted would give their companies an impersonally modern image. The glass-and-steel structures of the International Style looked clean, neat, efficient, and up-to-the-minute. Best of all, they were less expensive to commission than any alternative.

By the 1950s and still more so in the 1960s, the United States was where architectural students from Europe and everywhere else came to look, to admire, and to learn. Unadorned structures of glass, steel, and concrete became the established style. Ornament and historical reference were taboo, at least in theory. The best in the Modern Style was very good and sometimes great, though the best also often broke the rules. The Seagram Building, commonly used as the standard by which unfavorably to compare the die-stamp blocks that line Sixth Avenue in Manhattan, broke the rules. It was expensively decorated with special glass and with bronze girders, run up the length of the walls not to hold them in place—that was done by unseen supports inside—but to relieve the walls of their flatness. "Less is more" was Mies van der Rohe's slogan. Samuel Bronfman, persuaded by his daughter to finance a modern classic, was prepared to pay for and get more.

Not every corporate patron was ready to be so bold. Across the country, American cities acquired new profiles, as banks and companies put up tall boxes that varied, to the untrained eye, only in the color of their glass. Above New Orleans, Houston, Denver, Des Moines, Phoenix, Philadelphia, and Baltimore rose these isolated towers, dwarfing the clutter of their surroundings, some often visible from the freeway at twenty miles or more, gangling only children.

A reaction was predictable. In small commissions, at first on their own or friends' or patrons' houses, then in even bigger and bolder buildings, American architects broke out of their box. In Columbus, Indiana, a showcase of contemporary building, thanks to the imagination of the boss of Cummins Diesel—the town's big employer—who told the town he would pay design fees for new buildings if he could choose the architects, Hugh Hardy and his firm put up an Occupational

Health Center with interior colored pipes and exposed girders, a building machine not unlike the Beaubourg in Paris. Standing out among the boulevards and palms of West Hollywood is an exhibition hall designed by Cesar Pelli of Yale. Known as "The Blue Whale," this is a vast, irregular, modern crystal palace, sheeted in glass with the look of washable blue ink. Historical references, irony, and jokes abound. Beside Denver's traditional red-stone state capitol stands a concrete parody of a medieval castle keep, pitted with odd-shaped lancets, guarding the city's not invaluable art collection. James Wines's firm, SITE, in several commissions for the Best retailing company, has produced works of architectural trompe l'oeil. Freeway drivers in Houston gape at least on first sighting the Best showroom whose broken white-brick storefront looks as if it is cascading into the parking lot. The Best store in Sacramento has no door, but at opening time a ragged wedge of bricks in one corner slides out on rails to let shoppers in.

Even the "corporate look" has grown mannered. Hugh Stubbins's Citicorp Building in Manhattan has a shiny metal skin and is sliced off on top at a sharp angle to accommodate solar panels, say the designers, but New Yorkers say it is so the city's leading bank would look like a giant figure "1." For the home office of the Pittsburgh Plate Glass Company, Philip Johnson designed an English Gothic cathedral tower, not so odd, perhaps, on recalling the many early skyscrapers encrusted with Gothic themes, but striking, indeed, when it was realized that the whole building, including the pinnacles, was to be covered in glass.

These new departures, lumped together, for all their differences, as "postmodernist," celebrated by some, deplored by others, have put the old avant garde on the defensive. Especially when not designing buildings, for whatever reason (usually a construction slump), architects elaborately explain what they are trying to do. In today's war of the architectural schools, "postmodernism" has taken on not only heavy artistic but also bulky social and political freight. Postmodernism, as summed up by Tom Wolfe, a leading chronicler of contemporary manners, was a reaction against the reigning American architectural style, which "in this very Babylon of Capitalism" had been reduced to "worker housing."

Philip Johnson, once the modernist revolutionary, has become the postmodernist counterrevolutionary. In accepting, in June 1978, the American Institute of Architects gold medal, he read out the charges against the old style he had helped promote: "It seems to me," he said, "that our sensibilities have changed in three basic respects. 'Modern' hated history, we love it. 'Modern' hated symbols, we love them. 'Modern' built the same look in any location; we search out the spirit of the place—the genius loci—for inspiration and variation." Johnson had no qualms about interpreting this postmodernist reaction as part of a much broader change in American thinking—a narrowing of goals, a recognition of limits, and a search for tradition—although he put a characteristically optimistic reading on all this:

> Now just why all this change should happen now, I don't know; maybe we got bored with glass boxes. Maybe we felt the new preoccupation with energy saving. Actually, it's much deeper than that; it's a big shift in the whole ideology of people in America and the Western world. We used to believe that we were going to create utopia in our lifetime. It was an American habit. We went to war to save the world for democracy—twice now—and we believed in ideals, we believed in certitude, and we were very moral, very Calvinist, about it. We Americans were very sure of ourselves. But are we today? I doubt it. How is it possible that a governor of the most progressive state in the United States, the governor of California, should be talking in terms of thinking small, the prophet being E. F. Schumacher? Why the new interest in Eastern religion and in all religions? Maybe reason itself isn't the only solution. Maybe tradition, maybe things of the heart count. Maybe progress isn't the only way. The whole world ideology is making a subtle shift. We are entering an era that I don't know the name of and even those that say they know the name of don't know the name of. But it's a great, adventurous pluralistic future.

It has to be said that "pluralism" in America, at least of visual style, has never been in great danger. The tall glass box, indifferent to its site, is far from being all there is to modern American building. A traveler who has seen only New York or Chicago may think of the skyscraper as the characteristic American building. Frank Lloyd Wright, the greatest early-twentieth-century American architect, hated heights, at least in architecture. The low, overhanging roofs of his flat, horizontal houses were perfectly adapted to what he like to call the "quiet level" of the Midwestern prairie. Inside, the open, often rambling plans of his houses, without rigid divisions, reflected how a democratic people wished to think of itself.

Yet all architects, imitators of Wright as well as modernists and post-modernists alike, have to share often minor billing for how man-made America looks with developers, city planners, zoning boards, freeway engineers, bridge-builders, commercial artists, small shopkeepers, home owners, signmakers, and franchise operators. The designer's urge to plan or to tidy up is permanently at war with commercial exhibitionism or personal fantasy. Americans have a boisterous way of defeating city plans more complicated than the grid. Consider what Dickens had to say, in his *American Notes*, about the nation's capital less than half a century after L'Enfant had drawn up his elaborate network of diagonal avenues:

> Burn the whole down; build it up again in wood and plaster; widen it a little; throw in part of St. John's Wood; put green blinds outside all the private houses, with a red curtain and a white one in every window; plough up all the roads; plant a great deal of coarse turf in every place where it ought not to be; erect three handsome buildings in stone and marble, anywhere, but the more entirely out of everybody's way the better; call one the Post Office, and one the Patent Office and one the Treasury; . . . leave a brick field without the bricks in all central places where a street may naturally be expected: and that's Washington.

Today the products of architectural design, modernist boxes or postmodernist nonboxes, compete with other forces that shape the American cityscape. The visitor may readily forget Exxon's oil company tower in Houston, Del Monte's fruit and vegetable business headquarters in downtown San Francisco, or General Dynamics' aerospace main office in Saint Louis, but surely not the gas station on East Marginal Way, Seattle, built as an outsize set of cowboy hat and boots, nor the vegetable stand in Castroville in the Salinas valley in the shape of a gigantic green artichoke, nor the filling station in Ashtabula, Ohio, with a flying saucer perched on its roof.

A few pop-minded postmodernists take inspiration from this style —American Zany, it should be called—but most planners and designers would not mind at all seeing it swept away, like the vanished Los Angeles real estate office in the form of a sphinx's head, or confined to Disneyland and its imitators. By professional need, planners and designers tend to believe that left to their own devices, nonprofessionals will make ugly surroundings. Commercial interests were not trusted to refrain from embellishing the often monotonous countryside on either side of the freeways with advertisements. Standards were imposed preventing unchecked commercialism, and Americans accordingly have these landscapers and Lady Bird Johnson to thank for forty thousand miles of almost billboardless interstate highway. When drivers, though, take freeway exists marked "E-Z Off, E-Z On," they can still descend to roadside strips with an uninhibited visual riot of red, white, and blue used-car-lot pennants, plastic signs for Wendy's, Hardee's, Big Boy's, Del Taco, and Taco Bell, advertising and art murals, two-story cinder-block shops with signs like "Here It's a Pleasure to Shop Not a Chore," and storefront evangelical churches. This freedom to look ugly in one's own way is in turn being challenged, however, as suburban shopping malls clear away, rationalize, and gather under one huge roof this commercial babel.

Respect for the past, however, does extend now to buildings considered to be of architectural merit. A body of opinion has grown up that Americans have an architectural inheritance that must not be razed, and this is a small but extremely telling change for a maturing people less sure about the future, more concerned than before about their past, and no longer convinced that the new is always preferable to the old.

Preservation is not anymore merely a matter of applauding the Rockefellers when they fork out millions to rebuild, brick by brick, the colonial town of Williamsburg; nor of uniting to save a single fine building, like the Arabesque Fox Theater in Atlanta, which was built originally as a Shriners temple, or the fairyland Abram Hatch House in Heber, Utah. Americans, long the world's perhaps most unhistorical people, are developing a sense of their past. They are not content anymore to see it walled off from everyday life and labeled, in Old English script, "Our Heritage."

Whole areas, sometimes whole towns, have been restored and declared off limits to the jackhammer and the wrecker's ball. Georgetown in Washington, Beacon Hill in Boston, what remains of Society Hill in Philadelphia, and the old towns of Charleston and Savannah stand out. Excesses are unavoidable and have not been avoided. In Georgetown, a port where pigs snuffled into the garbage in the eighteenth century, householders are scolded by the Georgetown Preservation Society for planting tomatoes rather than flowers in their front gardens. The poorer, mainly black, people who once made this part of Washington their home have been squeezed out by affluent whites and return only on Sundays to attend houses of worship, like the old Ebenezer Church on O Street, that continue to have black congregations. Similarly, the 260-acre French Quarter of New Orleans has moved upmarket since George Lewis blew his horn in sleazy night places on Beale and Bourbon streets. An article in *Smithsonian Magazine* lamented this change for the richer as not necessarily for the better: "Most appalling to those who love the old Quarter, local and outside real estate speculators have found that picturesqueness is a saleable commodity, and if the seedy old buildings are not picturesque enough they can be made so by a generous frosting of cast-iron railings, made, if necessary, of genuine plastic. And there is a general tendency to 'clean things up' for the tourists."

Gordon Bunshaft, one of the best of the architects in the narrowing modernist mainstream, grumbled when preservation groups in 1980 lobbied to save the art deco bas-relief sculptures on the face of the Bonwit Teller store in New York which was being ripped down to make way for a sixty-eight-story commercial-residential tower. When Americans take something on, he said, they always overdo it. After demolishing fine old buildings without a second thought during the nineteenth century and for most of this century, they have completely reversed tack and are saving "every damn thing" that is old, whether good, bad, or indifferent. George Sternlieb, who is not bothered about being labeled a philistine, is far more scornful. Only in their degenerate period, he asserts, were the Romans interested in history, and "nobody has ever called us Greeks. Our business is not charm, not small-scale, not preservation. Our tradition is biggest and best."

A visitor can sympathize with Sternlieb and still recognize that he is referring to an older America, for the continent he is talking about is already built. Huge construction companies like Brown & Root, which put up the American bases in Vietnam, or Bechtel, which is building modern Saudi Arabia, must go abroad to find proper outlets for their Roman energies. In America, the land is already paved, the rivers and sounds bridged, although plenty of repairs are needed. And what bridges: David Steinman's cantilever across the Carquinez Strait north of San Francisco, Gustav Lindenthal's lens-shaped trusses over the Monongahela at Pittsburgh, Othmar Ammann's George Washington Bridge across the Hudson, Joseph Strauss's ornate Golden Gate, C.

H. Purcell's double suspension bridge across San Francisco Bay to Oakland, James Buchanan Eads's bridge across the Mississippi at Saint Louis, Conde McCullough's concrete arches in Oregon, and of course The Bridge by J. A. Roebling across the East River between Manhattan and Brooklyn. To cross any of these is to comprehend what Sternlieb means, and his impatience with the fussier preservationism is understandable. Yet these bridges themselves—some of them more than a century old—"biggest and best" as they are, belong now to a past Americans think worth preserving.

The restoration of run-down parts of cities and towns—Capitol Hill in Washington, the upper West Side in New York, Chicago's Old Town, Kansas City's Westport, San Francisco's North Beach, Boston's North End—has become known as gentrification, an imported term from England to connote middle-class people moving into an area, pushing up house prices, and displacing working-class residents.

Among opponents and supporters there is a tendency to overstate the case for and against gentrification. The middle-class people that are coming in to restore neglected houses or, more commonly, to hire others to do this job for them, regard their activity as representing new hope for the city. As seen through their eyes, the prodigal well-to-do will resist and ultimately reverse urban decay as they restore rickety houses and bolster a depleted tax base.

"We shall not be moved" is the common, usually futile, rallying cry of the poor as they lose their homes to their economic superiors. For them, gentrification is a disaster. The prospect of being forced to apply for a billet in a public housing project, infested by cockroaches and criminals, is terrible to contemplate and the invading middle class, as seen through their eyes, are a breed apart. As a high proportion of the newcomers either have no children or have enough money to buy private education for their children, they have no direct interest in the quality of inner-city public schools. Similarly, enrollment in private medical schemes keeps them out of municipal hospitals and they are confident they will never need to apply for food stamps or welfare. Their return to the city threatens, therefore, to weaken the lobby for an improvement of the city services that the poor depend on most in adversity.

If it is desirable for middle-class and rich people to return in large

A.A.-K

numbers to live in the cities, this obviously means people already living there will be displaced. For not many people who can choose to live either in the suburbs or downtown are going voluntarily, whatever the color of their skin, to move into abandoned accommodations in the most benighted sections of a city: Harlem in New York, the Hough area of Cleveland, or the West End section of Saint Louis. They will opt for areas that are dilapidated rather than destroyed. Equally obviously, if the displaced poor are to be decently rehoused, this will require the construction or reconstruction of housing units too expensive for them to buy or to keep in good repair without the help of subsidies, and these subsidies can only come out of tax revenues. Because city governments that want the middle class to return are generally so short of money, they are unwilling to cope with the consequences and instead obfuscate.

The result is a tale of two cities. A few redoubts of the middle and upper classes in the cities, including the gentrified bits, get exaggerated attention from the boosters. Only 0.5 percent of the twenty million housing units in American cities were restored between 1968 and 1979, according to a survey by the Department of Housing and Urban Development. Vast areas that continue to deteriorate are all but ignored. Take New York. For the casual visitor—the businessman there for a convention or a vacationing family taking in the Statue of Liberty and a Broadway musical—the city appears to have made an impressive recovery from its perils-of-Pauline adventures with bankruptcy. Midtown Manhattan has experienced such a construction boom that by 1980 the ears of every worker and resident there were pounded all day, and often half the night, by the sounds of builders hard at work. Out of eyesight and earshot, much of the city is broken down, if not in ruins.

Across the Hudson River in New Jersey, the city of Newark is, as a whole, in far worse shape than New York. Detailmen, the salesmen and saleswomen employed by the pharmaceutical companies to market new drugs, can measure Newark's decline through the medical practitioners they see. In 1940, Newark had 753 doctors. By the late 1970s, there were fewer than 350 doctors in the city, and they fell into three broad categories: elderly doctors too old to move out to start new practices elsewhere; doctors who divided their time between an office in the city and an office in the suburbs and who were gradually cutting the number of days they spent downtown from three to two or less as their practice in the suburbs expanded; doctors caring for Medicaid and Medicare patients.

Other old cities are dilapidated, too. Look out the window on an Amtrak journey from Penn Station in Manhattan to Union Station in Washington, or drive from Buffalo on the east shore of Lake Erie to Cleveland on the south shore and on to Detroit on the west shore. Urban and industrial decay seems pervasive. Visit the center of Saint Louis and the cityscape is as rotten, and especially sad. Saint Louis's old houses are built of the country's sturdiest bricks, almost impervious to bad weather. As the houses are bulldozed down, the bricks are bought up by or sometimes stolen for builders putting up luxury houses for the rich in more prosperous parts of the country.

The damaged cities would be in less trouble if their city halls had anticipated and planned for a decline in population. Certainly this is a claim heard often in Cincinnati, an old city of hills and neighborhoods on the Ohio. Planners there early in the 1970s decided to reduce the public labor force through attrition and not to fritter away money on building new public facilities, but to concentrate instead on the upkeep of existing public services. They also, sensibly, designated deteriorating neighborhoods for redevelopment before they became slums. If most city managers have been less farsighted than those in Cincinnati, it may be because they, like most Americans, are much better equipped, psychologically, to deal with the opportunities of growth than to cope with the problems of maturity and decline. In a country with a strong tradition of hometown boosterism, it is difficult to accept that a city's population can fall at all, and almost unthinkable to anticipate a decline by a fifth or a calamitous 140,000, as it did in Saint Louis between 1960 and 1970. The instinct instead is to insist that a city's budget problems are temporary, to dismiss skeptics as cynics, and to campaign hard for revival by trying to lure in more business investors and more dollars from the federal government. For to be realistic rather than optimistic about a city's prospects, and to plan accordingly, is to slay what Robert Stern, a professor at Columbia University's School of Architecture, calls an American holy cow: "the notion that the history of cities is and always has been one of increasing population and therefore population density."

The reluctance to accept shrinkage has caused cities grossly to exaggerate the significance of the gentrification, or rehabilitation, of a few smallish areas. City managers rarely admit, without prompting, that recovering SoHo in New York is a pocket handkerchief when measured against the South Bronx, or that Society Hill in Philadelphia could be lost in those northern areas of the city that house poor blacks. Similarly, it takes persistence to get them to concede that in the late 1970s, three middle-income people emigrated beyond the boundaries of cities for every middle-income person who moved the other way, and that their city has not bucked this trend. In itself, this determination to keep eyes fixed on the doughnut and to avert them from the hole might be harmless. Indeed, Robert Embry, who was involved in city planning in Baltimore before joining the Carter administration's Department of Housing and Urban Development, may have a point when he reports that the wide publicity given to a "sweat equity" homesteading plan in Baltimore, which permitted people to acquire houses for almost nothing in return for agreeing to do them up, helped greatly to restore hope in the city's future, even though the number of houses restored in this way was minuscule beside the city's total housing stock.

The harm really begins when cities allow the rehabilitation of a few areas to blind them to the deterioration of the rest or, more serious still, when emphasis is put on reviving downtown to the neglect of the inner city. This distinction is not a fine semantic point. "Downtown" has come to mean the section of the city where the offices are and where people shop. The "inner city," a term that has acquired a pejorative ring, is where the poor and often dangerous classes live. Detroit starkly dramatizes the distinction. In 1967, after riots left forty-three people dead, Henry Ford II, then chief executive of the Ford Motor Company, was excoriated for having concentrated investment outside the city in the suburb of Dearborn. He reacted positively and rounded up fifty business leaders to come in as partners on a plan to bring the city back to life. Borrowing from the Allegheny Council's Golden Triangle redevelopment in Pittsburgh, they envisaged a cluster of office towers that would squat around a seventy-odd-story Detroit Plaza Hotel on thirty-three acres of land in the central business district. Known as the Renaissance Center, this development was to replace run-down warehouses, docks, and railway yards along the Detroit River. The posse of businessmen hired the man who seemed the best gun for the job: John Portman of Atlanta. As an architect-developer, a combination generally frowned on at the American Institute of Architects, Portman created the Peachtree Center, which helped enliven a drab, dispirited Atlanta and has now been imitated in many cities across the country. Portman's argument was that architects today have to give office workers and shopkeepers a reason to stay downtown, and so he designed block-sized buildings, with large insides providing some of the attractions of the city street without the disadvantages of bad weather, cars, and crime. The sniffier critics found his neo-Babylonian constructions childish or vulgar, but they have been a great commercial success. The original hotel in Atlanta is an inside-out ziggurat, loosely modeled on the fine old Brown Palace Hotel in Denver. The Detroit complex looks from the outside like a glass fortress. Inside, it is a three-dimensional maze of walkways, known as "people scoops," overhanging balconies for drinks, known as "cocktail pods," as well as small lakes, fountains, dozens of freestanding escalators, and several warrens of shops. Frenetic indeed, but judged narrowly by the standards of such developments, the Renaissance Center is a success. It has not done much, however, for inner Detroit, or for the city as a whole.

Nearby, a few blocks beyond Greektown, are pitted streets flanked by large, vandalized redbrick houses and vacant lots scattered with junk. Nearly two-thirds of the tenants of the Renaissance Center moved into it from older buildings in Detroit and this commercially brave urban development project has as yet done little to stop, let alone to reverse, a deterioration in the city's economic life. For thirty years Detroit's population has shrunk, and in the 1970s the shrinkage became more pronounced. By 1980, one in four of Detroit's families was receiving public assistance. Manufacturing, which accounted for 48 percent of the jobs in the city twenty years earlier, by then provided only 30 percent of them.

The impression has been allowed to get around that the expanding cities in Southern states are the opposite of Detroit, Newark, Buffalo, Cleveland, New York, and other victims of urban decay in the North. Listen to the boosters in Atlanta, for example, say that a humming central business beehive has put life back into the downtown and that this prosperity is gradually spreading into the inner city. While the boast is not baseless, it is exaggerated. The big and costly developments in Atlanta—Colony Square, the Omni, Peachtree Center, 101 Marietta, the Summit, Tower Place, the Hilton—are spread higgledy-piggledy around town. After dark, the large spaces in between are high-crime areas. By the late 1970s the city, like Houston, had close to the highest urban murder rate. Much of the blame was due to the city's newspapers, the *Constitution* and the *Journal*, otherwise fine, in their own terms. Together they spurred on feckless development by being uncritical cheerleaders for the property men. Somehow they had allowed themselves to be conscripted into the ranks of hometown boosters who, in Atlanta and elsewhere, have caused too little heed to be paid to the two forces that have come together to make so many American cities so ill equipped to cope with the late twentieth century: first, the failure of cities to foresee, and thus properly to adjust to, changes in their economic function; second, and not unrelated, the great success of the suburbs, a success achieved on the back of tax breaks, mortgage, and other government subsidies, including large highway spending.

If any broad statement about American cities holds true, and not many do, it is that they can be divided very roughly into two categories: the mature cities shaped before the car and the younger cities shaped afterward. San Francisco, New York, and Boston are examples of precar cities, where it is still quicker and more convenient, though not necessarily more comfortable, to get around downtown by foot or public transportation by day than by private car. At the other extreme are the likes of Phoenix and Los Angeles, where pedestrians walking more than a few blocks are either tramps or eccentrics, and where the city center —a courtesy term at least in Los Angeles, which has many centers or none—is hard for the out-of-towner to find without a map.

The older cities were quick in their day to install modern conveniences. Philadelphia tackled its sanitation problems before 1820 by installing a system of reservoirs, a steam pumping plant, and wooden mains. New York brought Croton water to its residents by 1842. By the time Philadelphia brought gas lighting into operation in 1835, it had been beaten by New York and Baltimore. Being modern a century and a half ago has become a handicap today. Legislators vote money much more readily for glamorous new projects than for humdrum maintenance and repairs. As a result, the decay in the infrastructure of the old, mature cities continues, no longer unseen but still undealt with. It is easy to be dazzled by Baltimore's redone waterfront and splendid aquarium, by Boston's Market Street development, by Manhattan's apartment building boom, even by the revival of downtown Cleveland. All these cities, though, are wearing out inside, as pipes, mains, tunnels, or bridges go without repairs.

Some old cities are in a better position to cope than others. Boston has gained liveliness from its undisputed position as the regional capital of New England, and from its many universities. Most precar cities have been rocked in muddling through a transition from their original function as centers of production to their new function as centers, mainly, of services and consumption. Since American academics tend to think in terms of problems and solutions, this is often labeled a problem, when in fact it is not so much a problem as an event.

Before the internal combustion engine supplanted steam and horse-power, industrialists in the United States had no alternative but to set up their factories in cities. They needed access to good transport, reliable services, and supplies, and above all, to cheap, abundant labor. All these only cities could provide and they had the additional advantage of offering conveniences of modern life that were, well into the twentieth century, still exceptional in nonmetropolitan areas and all but unknown in rural ones: gas and then electricity, waterborne sewage, and a wide choice of foods brought in year round by refrigerated railway cars. Urban housing had to be densely concentrated. Workers had to walk to work and the close concentration of factories suited the manufacturer and the distributor, the wholesaler and the retailer.

Streetcars began to upset residential patterns. By 1890, electric trolley lines, conveying two billion passengers a year, were overtaking horsecar lines. Middle-class city dwellers were able to afford this new transport and to move outside the pedestrian city to houses in suburbs. By 1900, only 44 percent of the metropolitan population of Boston, for example, lived within a two-mile radius of the city center, compared to 67 percent in 1850. While better public transport allowed a city like Boston to spread, it also strengthened the city as a manufacturing base and as a commercial and communications center. For middle-class employees with money to spend continued to commute back toward the center to work, and commercial establishments sprouted where trolley lines crossed. A woman was expected to walk only three or four blocks to do her shopping and at these strategic places it was customary to find a grocer, a dairy, a hardware store, a shoe shop, and in Catholic areas, a fish shop.

Public transport, most importantly, changed where people lived. As the middle class moved away from the working class, the wealthy moved still farther, into the countryside. Costly trolley and railway fares, limiting commuter travel to those who had the money to pay for it, acted as a kind of filter on class movement out of the cities. By the late nineteenth century, the large cities were roughly but clearly stratified by class. The rich lived in rich neighborhoods, comfortably separated from the poor. As people moved out, many cities annexed those areas where the middle class had gravitated. New York added more than 250 square miles near the turn of the century; Boston in 1914 doubled its area. Some states introduced automatic annexation procedures. By the 1920s, however, political opposition to the absorption of fringe districts had grown fierce. Large cities that had been increasingly populated by immigrants, and then later by blacks pushed out of farm work by mechanization, found themselves unable to keep pace through annexation or consolidation with suburban migration. This change was one of the modern suburb's parents. The other was the private car.

For by then the automobile had ushered in the start of a second revolution in American living patterns, one far more radical than the first. In the wonderfully lucid imagery of James Marston Fitch, the wealthy and the middle classes, like cream in a separator, were flung ever more distant from the center; and the rest of the population, in strict accordance with American housing tradition, moved into the backwash of the discarded homes. The cities lost their most powerful constituency. Civic pride among the better-off, and thus, in a capitalist society, the more influential, people waned as the car freed them from dependence on centralized public and commercial services. Suburbanites could now drive twenty minutes in one direction to take the children to school, thirty minutes in another direction to the office, or twenty minutes in still another to shop. The car was a centrifugal force. The middle class became independent of public transport.

The car was helped by an orgy of public works. The man who typified more than any other the energy and single-mindedness with which bridges were thrown up and new roads laid down was Robert Moses, a driving, brilliant megalomaniac who liked to say: "If the end doesn't justify the means, what does?" Moses' success in transforming New York and its surroundings for the private car was imitated across the country as federal, state, and local governments opened their treasuries to provide for the automobile. The social changes that followed brought huge pluses but also minuses.

Politically, the road-builders used to have everything going for them, including public opinion. As Lewis Mumford, the combative social critic, wrote in 1946: "Highways are an impressive, flashy thing to build. No one is against highways." Laying down a four-lane interstate is more glamorous than repairing a train line or removing the graffiti from subway cars. It has also won more votes than it has lost in statewide elections for politicians who have been able to grab the credit for getting the project going. The suburban middle classes who count on their cars to travel to work are increasingly more likely to take the trouble to go to the polling booth on election day than the inner-city poor who rely on public transport. And the "illegals," the immigrants who steal across a frontier into the United States, and are heavily concentrated in cities, have no vote at all. Most politicians, in consequence, have had a bias for cars over buses and trains, for roads over railway and streetcar lines.

Even so, it is above all money that has talked, or rather shouted. The repair and maintenance of public transport is labor-intensive. Most of the cash goes to unskilled and semiskilled workers. Putting down a new road or putting up a new bridge is far more capital-intensive. The makers of cement and steel and aluminum and construction equipment all profit from it. So does the American auto industry. More than thirteen million Americans make their living producing, distributing, selling, maintaining, repairing, fueling, cleaning, junking, driving, and creating parts for motor vehicles. Seven of the ten largest manufacturing companies in the Fortune 500 are engaged in either making vehicles or supplying them with fuel: General Motors, Exxon, Gulf, Ford, Mobil, Texaco, and the Standard Oil Company of California.

What their corporate lobbyists want from statehouses and from Capitol Hill they usually get. Measured against them, the public transport lobby is a puny vested interest that has been made even feebler by the success their opponents have achieved in convincing the public and politicians that money raised by roads should be spent on roads. Nobody seriously argues that the proceeds of taxes on cigarettes should be earmarked for the victims of diseases caused by smoking or that sales taxes should be spent only on the creation of shops and shopping centers. Yet efforts to siphon money raised on toll roads into general revenues where they can be used to finance other public services, including buses and trains, have always aroused fierce, obdurate resistance.

In New York, Robert Moses fought a determined and largely victorious rearguard battle to prevent the riches of first the Triborough Bridge and Tunnel Authority and then of his ally, the Port Authority of New York and New Jersey, being used to aid mass transport. The odds were weighted consistently in his favor. As his biographer, Robert Caro, noted: "In the background behind Moses marched a mighty division: the giant automobile manufacturers out of Detroit, the giant aluminum combines, the steel producers, the rubber producers, fifty oil companies, trucking firms in the hundreds, highway contractors in the thousands, consulting engineers, labor union leaders, auto dealers, tire dealers, petroleum dealers, rank upon rank of state highway department officials, Bureau of Public Roads bureaucrats, congressmen, senators . . ." Probably the greatest, and tallest, symbol of the triumph of the "highwaymen" over public transport advocates is the twin-towered World Trade Center, sponsored by Nelson Rockefeller, which looms over the skyscape of lower Manhattan. On the New York subways the passengers were the shock absorbers, crammed nostril to eyebrow in dirty carriages of great antiquity, while the Port Authority had money coming out of its ears. Together with Robert Moses, it had dreamed up project after project to stop any of the cash from being plucked by mass transport and so to avoid setting a precedent that would permit the profits of a public authority to be diverted into areas beyond the authority's competence and control. Stumped for new projects, it chose to invest its spare millions in these enormous buildings rather than to allow them to improve the subways. When the Deutsche Bank of West Germany came along in 1979 and offered to buy the twin towers, a move that would have brought in billions of marks for the American balance of payments, and a money transfusion for the anemic New York economy, it was rudely rebuffed. The Port Authority was not prepared to relinquish any part of its empire, no matter how lucrative the price.

Although poor public transport has made city living vexing for those who depend on it to get around, as a horror story it pales beside public housing. Architects and town planners must take the bulk of the blame for the tragic mistakes made in slum clearance, and to be fair, they do not duck the charges. Most now concede that their profession was tardy in recognizing the antisocial nature of modernist designs, even after the evils were pointed out, stridently, by such outspoken critics as Jane Jacobs, Herbert Gans, and Oscar Newman. Hypnotized by the modernist version of "towers in the park"—a vision that moved so smoothly into focus with the 150-year-old American tradition of zoning, which held that diversity of land use was bad for neighborhood stability—architects and planners designed model housing projects that looked wonderful on paper but in which nobody who could afford not to wanted to live. The bleak Pruitt-Igoe buildings in Saint Louis serve as a notorious example. Designed as a mass housing project by Skidmore, Owings & Merrill, a central pillar of the architectural establishment, Pruitt-Igoe was in 1951 given an honor award by the American Institute of Architects. Prospective tenants were not impressed. The Saint Louis Housing Authority practically had to rustle people to find occupants. Some 55 percent of the families were headed by women. Pruitt-Igoe, to the AIA's great, and deserved, embarrassment, quickly turned into a slum and was only put out of its misery when it was dynamited. The Cedar Riverside housing scheme in Minneapolis has shown disturbing signs of repeating the story. Chosen as a Gold Medal winner by the AIA in 1975, this model housing project was declared only a few months later to be "socially destructive" by a federal judge, who ordered the government to put no more funds into it.

Such errors, and they are numerous, were compounded by mass destruction in the name of urban renewal. Between 1949 and 1968, about 425,000 housing units, nearly all of them the homes of poor people, were torn down. Somehow new mass housing units for the poor were nearly always seen as preferable to the alternative of rehabilitating existing housing, even when sociologists stressed the sense of betrayal and alienation felt by families torn out of neighborhoods where they had put down roots. It is a mistake repeated in large European cities and is often attributed to the idealistic we-can-rebuild-society spirit that came out of World War II. Well-financed lobbyists, as in the orgy of highway building, also played a big role. Maintenance and repair of old houses, like that of public transport, was labor-intensive; the construction of vast new housing projects, like highway and bridge building, was capital-intensive and promised to earn much fatter profits for those on the business end of housing. Blacks filled 70 percent of the public housing units and their wishes took a decided second place to those of the builders and developers and their suppliers.

Fortunately, the evils of concentrating poor people in vast anonymous buildings, where one dirty or dangerous family on a corridor can make life unbearable for all the rest, has at last become obvious. The bad result is that virtually no public housing has been built during the past decade. The good result is that town planners now think hard before they bulldoze a neighborhood. It is being realized that the challenge for a mature, no longer young society is to repair, to maintain, and to rebuild. Cities are not part of the throwaway society.

None of this, though, is much immediate comfort to the man holding arguably the second most impossible job in the United States —Edward T. Logue of the South Bronx Development Office. Bullet-headed, florid-faced, bull-necked, and pot-bellied, Logue may look like a caricature of a machine politician, but he is really a compassionate, intelligent public servant with a robust sense of humor and of public purpose—all qualities needed to escape abject failure.

The South Bronx used to be a shabby, genteel, lower-middle-class neighborhood. It was once inhabited mainly by Roman Catholics and Jews—a past still to be seen in the many synagogues and Catholic churches and the paucity of Protestant churches—and most of these people were well pleased to leave. They have been gradually replaced by blacks and Hispanics as poor as the Jews and ethnic Catholics who settled there more than half a century ago. Tenants outnumber home owners nine to one and the area's decay is an appalling monument to what badly conceived rent controls can do to a place. In Logue's words: "If you as an owner of a multifamily property cannot count on getting an adequate return on your property, something gives and what gives is not the return. You don't paint. You don't repair. Pretty soon something big breaks down. The security system at the front door starts to go or the roof starts to leak." Soon a once sturdy building becomes a slum. Yet everywhere in the South Bronx where there are owner-occupied houses, they tend to be in what Logue, with only a little hyperbole, calls "terrific shape," even when they are in the most wretched of locations: under a bridge or next to a busy highway crossing.

Abolishing rent controls will not now encourage landlords to restore these properties. Many people who live in the South Bronx have fallen off the train. They are what the news weeklies call the underclass: people for so long put out of sight and out of mind by the rest of society that they are too poor to pay an economic price for their accommodations. If their rents went up, they could not and would not pay them. Sending in the marshals would cause more social problems than it would solve. The answer may rather be to try to convert the tenants, or at least some of them, into owner-occupiers through the urban equivalent of the Homestead Act of 1862—an approach that worked, on an admittedly small scale, in Baltimore.

Instead of government subsidizing high-density multifamily developments in areas like the South Bronx, which are occupied by fewer and fewer people, it could offer remaining residents the urban answer to the suburban dream: a single-family town house with a small yard and perhaps a garden. To do this, neglected and abandoned houses would have to be acquired by government at their fair market value—which is, incidentally, often far below the value put on them by the courts—and then resold for a token sum to local people ready and willing to repair and maintain them. Subsidized financing would, of course, have to be proffered: perhaps mortgages with an interest rate as low as 4 percent.

Though all this would cost a lot, so does the neglect of slum areas. The four underused subway lines that go through the South Bronx are maintained, indirectly, at public expense. So are the plumbing mains, the electrical wiring, and the gas pipelines. Police patrols and fire stations and roads in run-down areas soak the taxpayer, too. The hidden costs are even larger. Children who could in less wretched circumstances grow up into useful adults are instead young hoodlums destined to become a burden to all. Then there are the sludge effects of slums as they slowly, yet inexorably, expand. Respectable people living on their fringes are put to flight by the spillover of noise, of cockroaches and rats, of vandalism, alcoholism, and drug-related crimes. And the whole city suffers as the ugliness of the slums, and as tales of their mayhem and degradation, provide a deterrent against business investment.

Robert Stern, a distinguished architect and a professor at Columbia University, is an exuberant advocate of the suburban approach to city problems, but even he agrees that this approach confronts large political obstacles. Though the infrastructure and the industrial bases of the great Eastern cities in the United States are not much younger than those in the large European conurbations that came out of the industrial revolution and are much older than the infrastructure and industry of the devastated cities of West Germany and Japan that were rebuilt after the Second World War—the Yokohamas, Essens, Nagasakis, and Colognes—there is an American reluctance to come to terms with this urban maturity. Because the country as a whole is still seen as comparatively young, as part of the New World, it is far easier to win public support, and public subsidies, for a project that has yet to be built than for something that already exists. As a result, the sheer wastefulness of putting up taxpayers' money for new infrastructures—sewage pipes, gas lines, electric wires, and so on—to attract a larger population to Staten Island, when these services are already in place and underused a few miles away in the South Bronx, is rarely noticed and still more rarely commented upon.

A large segment of the American middle class is loath to see governments, whether they be local, state, or federal, bring in at public expense a stepladder that permits the deserving poor to aspire to a middle-class style of life. Indeed, prejudice against public, as opposed to private, enterprise is so strong that until recently, public housing authorities felt obliged to kick tenants out when their family income rose above a specified low level. The fact that this provided an institutional disincentive against people striving to improve their circumstances by earning promotion and more money was disregarded. So, also, were the risks of confining public housing to the poorest and least successful inner-city dwellers. A more amorphous yet still formidable obstacle to an urban homesteading scheme for people is the position of a suburban family home as a cherished symbol of middle-class respectability. Many of those who have achieved this status want to put up barriers against those who are still on the outside looking, longingly, in.

America's great cities are suffering today, too, from the aftereffects of an old cultural prejudice against cities, rooted in Puritanism, utopian idealism, and an intellectual distaste for urban Europe. Jefferson, though he recanted somewhat in his old age, saw the city as a leprosy on the body politic, as the opposite of his honest republic peopled by self-reliant yeomen. Walt Whitman in 1871 peered through his "moral microscope" and detected "cities, crowded with petty grotesques, malformations, phantoms, playing meaningless antics." Thoreau's *Walden* celebrates the isolated individual, living in nature. James Fenimore Cooper praised the wholesomeness of country life, and Horace Greeley, the great nineteenth-century editor of the *New York Herald Tribune*, was a tireless preacher of rural virtues and city vices. "Secure to the family," Greeley wrote, "the inducements of a home, surrounded by fruits and flowers, rational village movements and sports, the means of education and independence. Get them out of the cities and would-be cities into scenes like those, and the work is done." The anti-urban prejudice was reinforced, unintentionally, by the writings of famous muckrakers. Frank Lloyd Wright was hostile to cities, and the anti-urban, anti-bigness tradition lives on in the back-to-the-landers and the whole-earthers, as well as in such contemporary small-is-beautiful advocates as E. F. Schumacher and Amory Loving.

For most of this century, the big city was where Americans came to make something of themselves, like Judy Holliday, the not-so-dumb blonde, new to Manhattan, in *It Should Happen to You*, who in order to get some attention, spends her last dollars to display her name for a few hours on a billboard at Columbus Circle. Today, go-ahead young men or women are just as likely to want to go and live in as escape from a small town. Between 1970 and 1978, over 2.7 million more people moved out of big metropolitan areas than moved in. According to the 1980 Census, there was heavy growth in the past decade in small towns with a population of 50,000 or less. The strong anti-city and pastoralist strain in American thinking has tended to interpret this movement as part of the "back to the land" vogue and a sign of a "return to the countryside." Actually, it is nothing of the kind. In the late 1960s, a few couples from Boston or New York did migrate to rural Vermont to start communal farms and a few people left San Francisco to build strange arks in the woods of Mendocino. These are not the people moving to small towns today. For what is happening is not a ruralization of city people, but the continued suburbanization of the countryside. This is a further revolution, following the suburbs and the private car, which is changing how America lives. Until recently, the countryside was attractive for the rich to visit on weekends. For most Americans to find work there, for companies to do business there, was not thinkable. This, slowly, is changing. Since World War II, pushing into the countryside and the small towns, came highways, the Bell system, power lines, cable television, national brand stores, and retail franchises. Small-town America, in other words, has finally been absorbed into the national market. Companies, especially technology-based companies, can afford to locate plants just about anywhere they can find this minimum of social infrastructure. New machinery is making it easier for such companies to "decentralize"—picture phones, telecopiers, two-way cable televisions, and computer information banks. The success of such a movement into America's small towns depends, of course, on the movement's remaining small. For if everyone were to follow the lead of the few people and fewer companies that have begun this half revolution of growth in the exurbs, as planners are again calling them, then the attractions of small-town America would quickly vanish.

8

THE FAT OF THE LAND
Farms and Farming

AMERICA is the world champion in agriculture, but it has won and retained the title by concentrating its agricultural land into ever fewer hands. A third as many people live on farms today as did thirty years ago, and the number of farms has been halved. Even so, a majority of the surviving farms are each too small in acreage to matter. Four-fifths of the country's farm production is grown and raised by only one-fifth of the farms—the farms the Agriculture Department describes as either "medium-sized" or "large." The efficiency of the farms is indisputable. When a bumper harvest is brought in, everybody benefits: Americans, because mighty and expanding agricultural exports help hold back inflation by propping the dollar, which needs all the help it can get; non-Americans, because without abundant and relatively cheap American feed for their cattle, pigs, and poultry they would pay more for their meat and eat less of it. The obverse is that American farmers rely more than ever before on the world market for their livelihood. About 110 million acres, one cultivated acre in three in the United States, are now planted for export and chances are that in any year about two-thirds of the national rice crop, three-fifths of the soybeans, half the wheat, two-fifths of the cotton, a third of the tobacco, and a quarter of the corn will go to foreigners.

The market was not won by super yields. American farmers grow less food grains (wheat, rye, and rice) per acre than farmers in either Western or Eastern Europe. Their yields of soybeans and feed grains (corn, barley, oats, and sorghum) are better but not wonderful. The world market has been won instead by American farmers being blessed with a profusion of good farmland. Where California is not desert or mountain it is a man-made garden, a grower of almost everything and the richest agricultural state in the Union. Go seven hundred miles, from east to west, through Indiana, Illinois, and Iowa, and corn and soybeans look ready to take over the world; go seven hundred miles, south to north, through Kansas, Nebraska, and the Dakotas, and wheat is poised to smother the globe. On average, each American farmer clothes and feeds seventy-five Americans and much of the world besides. The big customers are the affluent: Japan, Holland, West Germany, Canada, and Russia. In feed grains, American farmers are supreme. The United States provides about 60 percent of all feed grains moving into world trade. It was not always so.

Between the two World Wars the United States was a net importer of agricultural products. Hitler and Tojo by going to war and interfering with other people's harvests changed this for a while, but by 1950 the United States had again moved into deficit in its farm trade. America produced such large quantities of the temperate crops it grows best that it could not sell them commercially on the world market. These surpluses became so embarrassingly large that Congress during the Eisenhower administration passed Public Law 480, the so-called Food for Peace program, that got rid of the stuff to third world countries in exchange for funny money. Most economists now conclude that these exports often did the recipient countries more harm than good. The dumped food discouraged farmers in the third world from increasing production. This, though, is over.

Rising demand from countries that can pay their bills in hard currency has made the United States more choosy about who qualifies for food aid. It can afford to prod recipients to introduce agricultural reforms that will help make them eventually self-sufficient, or at least less dependent. In a good year, the agricultural sector can today be counted on to earn the United States a surplus of above $20 billion on its balance of payments. But though the gains for the American farmers and the American economy are large and obvious, they are not without a price. American agriculture depends for a high share of its income not on relatively stable domestic demand but on unstable foreign demand. This is not, of course, to suggest that foreigners are somehow less reliable than Americans: merely to make the obvious point that foreigners will continue to grow most of their food and only import enough from the United States to meet the gap between domestic production and domestic demand. The gap is America's agricultural export market. Its size is both unpredictable and volatile.

The agricultural policies of its foreign customers contribute to the instability. The ten-member-country European Common Market has opted in agriculture for a system which permits prices for European farmers, and to European consumers, to remain largely unaffected by the size of the European harvest. Import levies allow the quantity of imports to be adjusted upward or downward to close the shortfall.

Russian farmers and consumers, too, are insulated from fluctuations in the supply and price of agricultural commodities. Russia's farm production has actually expanded more since the early 1960s than the farm production of the European Common Market or the United States. Even so, the Russians have at long last decided to break with an ancient agricultural tradition of using farm animals as their food reserve. Under the old system, when the harvest failed, people ate first their animals and then the food the animals would have eaten. Now when their harvest disappoints, the Russians increase their imports of grains from the United States so that they can continue to feed their animals as well as their people. It is a rational decision. Much of Russia's cropland is marginal and on a latitude to the north of the United States, some of it as far north as Hudson Bay, and the Soviet harvest suffers yo-yo gyrations. Grain production of 240 million tons in one year can fall by 50 percent in the next.

Burgeoning foreign demand is accelerating the controversial move away from mixed farming and towards more specialization in American agriculture, and toward larger farms as more affluent grain farmers buy up their neighbors' land to secure economies of scale. Immense foreign demand for what America grows and raises has also created the paradox that the United States is a net exporter, at one extreme, of the most modern technology (aircraft, computers, weapons) and, at the other extreme, of the most basic commodities, raw unprocessed agriculture, while it remains a heavy net importer of raw materials and standardized manufactured products. But as Professor Gale Johnson of the University of Chicago rightly argues, this is not really strange at all. Agriculture as practiced in the United States has become a high-technology industry with a high ratio of capital to labor, rapid changes in methods of production, a great willingness to adopt new ideas, and a large flow of resources into research. The cost, in research, capital investment, and lives turned upside down, has been enormous. Only the most astute farmers have survived the changes. The others are now town and city folk; or mere "hobby farmers," who have another job and can farm only in their spare time.

The illusion that not much has changed is maintained at such events as the summer picnic held each year to raise money for the fire department at Brighton, a village in the southwest segment of Illinois, not far from the outer suburbs of Saint Louis. The Scheffels, the Schneiders, the Beuttels, the Huebeners, the Schroeders, and scores of other farm families of mostly German origin come together to talk and to drink Burgoo soup. The size of their appetite is advertised by the recipe for this stew-thick gruel: "200 lbs. potatoes, 200 lbs. navy beans, 60 fat hens, 120 lbs. beef brisket, 60 lbs. smoked pork jowl, 400 lbs. beef bones. Cook for about 24 hours. Water as needed; seasoning to taste." To look at, these farm families are very close to the comfortable stereotypes city people have of farmers. Their clothes make little concession to fashion. The women wear plain outfits. The men look like the cowboy in the Marlboro cigarette advertisements. The children are scrubbed clean and brushed hard—and far more respectful to their parents and more polite to strangers than is usual elsewhere in America.

All sense of having stepped into an earlier world passes, however, the moment the conversation begins. Both the men and the women fret that they are losing their figures, and talk about new exercises to get back into shape. A few years back, farmers would have quickly sweated out a couple of bowlfuls of Burgoo soup at work on their fields. Now, like sedentary city cousins, they feel they must jog, swim, or play handball to prevent their getting tubby. Another talking point is the new silo. Marty Huebener has irked and intrigued his neighbors by having had an oxygen-free cobalt-blue silo built on his farm, three miles outside town. He has done this under pressure from the only two of his six sons who will work the farm when he retires. The new blue silo, it is said, costs more than twice as much as the conventional silver type. Huebener's neighbors waver between scorn for his extravagance and desire for an equally handsome structure of their own. The argument comes out for Marty Huebener when somebody reminds the group that a large part of the cost of any silo would qualify for investment tax credit and can be depreciated for tax purposes against income.

The girth of American farmers and their heavy investment in machinery are closely linked. For theirs is a high-technology business that requires less sweat of the brow than high capital-labor ratio. The Harvard economist John Kenneth Galbraith grew up on a mixed farm in Canada. To anyone raised on a farm, he later said of the experience, nothing afterward could ever seem like real work. He was showing his age. Farming has changed out of recognition since then. To do the job, one need no longer be "the sort of man you could attach to a cornsheller as you would an engine" that Willa Cather described in her prairie novel *O Pioneers.*

Thanks to two revolutions in less than a century, American farming is no longer hard work. The drudgery has largely gone, though in the huge Western and Southwestern fields, stoop labor is still common. About the time of the Civil War, horsepower began replacing manpower. The second revolution was the move from horse to mechanical power. The number of tractors exceeded the number of horses and mules for the first time in 1955. This went with the introduction of better seeds, better breeding, the exact application of fertilizer, and the increasingly sophisticated use of chemicals as weed and insect killers.

At sowing time and again at harvest, farmers must still spend sixteen hours or more a day in the fields, but plowing, disking, harrowing, and cultivating are far less arduous than they were. Tractors are equipped with power steering, air conditioning, crush-proof cabs, stereophonic radios, as well as sensing devices that alert the driver if the flow of seed or herbicide is interrupted. Some of the machines are as large as brontosauruses, yet less tiring to drive than a New York City taxi. The controls are light enough to be worked easily by a wife or child.

The weight problems of the Brighton picnickers are only one sign of how different farm life is from the way it is commonly imagined. When their crop is brought in, farmers are free to take months off. They like to joke that in the 1980s, crop rotation means wheat/Hawaii/sorghum/Florida. Those who persist in keeping animals are far more closely tied to their farms. Finding vacation help to mind a dairy herd is not like asking one's apartment neighbor to take the cat for the weekend. Feeding farm animals takes time. They get lost, break fences, get sick, and generally make a damned nuisance of themselves. Jerome Sonka, who farms near Cedar Rapids, Iowa, has taken the escape route used by many farmers in the Midwest, where winters are cruel and long. He has sold his pigs and decided to stick to crops alone. This for him means less profit in return for a good deal more leisure. As his children are now all grown up, he can afford the trade-off. Young farmers ambitious to expand or to own more land (which costs up to $4,000 an acre in the Midwest) and lease less of other people's continue to raise livestock. But even for them, hard work, far from being necessary, is a strong sign that they are sticking to old-fashioned methods and equipment that cut down profits and efficiency.

The very idea that the farmer's own sweat brings more losses than rewards, that profits are earned by working less hard but smarter, cuts deeply against the grain. For if anyone best embodies the old American virtues of toil, independence, and thrift, it is the farmer, or at least so it is widely supposed. It is an illusion. Nothing, in fact, could be more misleading than the common use of the word "conservative" to describe the American farmer. For if this is meant to include an abiding respect for the traditional way of doing things, then the American farmer, to the contrary, is a vanguard progressive, even keener on buying new gadgetry than are affluent Texans.

American farmers had to take a modern outlook almost from the start. Otherwise, they would never have accomplished the extraordinary feat of settling a continent in the eighty years between the time the Western settlers began spilling in appreciable numbers over into the Allegheny plateau and 1890, when the census indicated the land frontier was closed. These early farmers had to clear land themselves. The very combination of abundant land and scarce labor required farmers to be ready to try new methods and to use new machines as soon as they became available. By 1812, nearly all the necessary parts for a successful reaping machine had been developed in England and Scotland. But it was not until almost twenty years later that Cyrus McCormick, an American, got them working together smoothly and saw how to make the result into a thriving business. Why not an earlier entrepreneur in another land? There may have been a slight cultural block in the country that started the industrial revolution; as Denis Brogan put it: "Americans love machines; the English love dogs." The strongest reason was surely that while most European countries had a surplus of farm labor, in America, with its vast expanses of fertile and available land, farm labor was in short supply.

After the Civil War, the Americans had the extraordinary historical good fortune to develop farming and industry almost in lockstep with one another. Agriculture, outside the defeated plantation South, was never the backward sector it usually has been at some stage or other in almost every other country's economic development. Forward-looking American farmers were a vital link in this chain.

American farmers are not even "conservative" when this word is taken to mean a sincere acceptance of free enterprise. They are as two-faced as everybody else about the virtues of the uninhibited competition of free markets. Farmers resist government interference when prices and demand are strong, but when markets weaken they clamor for price supports, acreage set-asides, cheap credit, and other forms of government intervention. Farmers, it is true, still like to see themselves as their own men or women, and most of those who own or run farms are not at anyone's beck and call. Any member of Congress from a rural district who took country talk about sturdy independence seriously would, however, quickly be out on his ear. Texas cattlemen want the government's help to keep Australian and Argentinian beef from stampeding onto the American market. Dairy farmers want subsidized milk prices that reflect the favorable cost/price ratios of sixty years ago and ignore modern productivity. Peanut and tobacco growers look to the government to manipulate production and prices. Sugar growers demand quotas to restrain imports from tropical countries with lower wage costs. On the farm, "big government" is no villain—not, at least, that semi-autonomous province within it known as the United States Department of Agriculture. Under the department's benign paternalism, farmers have prospered and become a sound credit risk for rural bankers.

Nor was this always so. Attitudes have changed with farm technology. At the Mid-American Dairy Farm in southern Illinois in the summer of 1979, four generations of Oertels could be found at work. Otto, aged ninety-two, was weeding honeydew melons. His son, Leland, fifty-seven, was cleaning the cowshed. Leland's son, Frank, thirty, was milking the cows. Frank's son, Jason, aged nine, was helping his mother, Bonnie, in the kitchen. The older men recall when milking took hours to finish. Frank has no trouble milking forty-five Holsteins in his antiseptic milking parlor within an hour. From lack of practice, he admits, he lacks the finger muscles for hand milking. The Oertel family makes no pretense at self-sufficiency. Milk churns rust in the basement of its nineteenth-century farmhouse, beside blacksmith's tools. The milk from the Mid-American Dairy Farm's Holsteins is now picked up daily at the farm for pasteurization, homogenization, vitamin D irradiation, to be packaged for delivery to a food store. The Oertel family buys its milk, and its butter and cheese as well, from the store. The contents of the family's refrigerator look little different from those of a household in Chicago, Minneapolis, or Detroit.

The big difference between Frank, on the one hand, and his father, Leland, and his grandfather, Otto, on the other, is over money. In the summer of 1979, Otto Oertel recalled as if it were yesterday the sufferings of the Great Depression. For farmers this began shortly after World War I, when falling agricultural prices made it almost impossible for them to earn enough to meet loan repayments. Ever since then, Otto has regarded going into debt as foolish, and even sinful. For Frank, profitable modern farming depends on the skillful exploitation of other people's money. That is doubly so when rapid inflation tilts the tax laws even further in favor of the borrower. They can, as Frank knows, deduct interest expenses from taxable income while the lender or saver is taxed on the income from interest even when the interest rate is left in the dust by the inflation rate. The argument for going deeply into debt is so compelling that Leland, less cautious than Otto but more cautious than Frank, eventually came around to accepting it. But still, from time to time, he warns his son that the cost of a new gadget may exceed its usefulness and advises him to let others pay for the pioneering work.

At the Oertels' farm nothing is better thumbed than the illustrated product booklets, known to farmers as "wish lists." These are put out by Massey-Ferguson, John Deere, Allis Chalmers, International Harvester, and other makers of farm machinery. According to Warren Puck, a John Deere dealer in Manning, Iowa, farmers can scarcely afford not to buy. Though he has a vested interest in saying this, his reasons make sense. On a new tractor the farmer gets an investment tax credit and he can subsequently depreciate the tractor against his taxable income. Inflation also helps Puck's sales pitch. If prices keep jogging along, the farmer can hope that when, say, ten years from now, he comes to sell the tractor, he will get the same price he paid for it —admittedly in depreciated dollars. This reasoning is hard to resist. Such calculations have helped to make American farming a capital-intensive business and, of course, to enrich the farm machinery industry, although high interest rates interfere with this, as International Harvester and Massey-Ferguson know to their cost. The Department of Agriculture, in a recent census of farm machines, counted 4.4 million tractors, 3 million trucks, 535,000 grain combines, 605,000 corn pickers and picker shellers, 615,000 pickup bailers, and 270,000 forage harvesters.

Politicians from farm states, like Senator Robert Dole of Kansas, must understand these apparent contradictions. Dole is a deceptively relaxed conservative Republican with a partisan, sometimes cutting, wit. He went along with President Nixon's failed attempt to put a right-wing mediocrity, Harrold Carswell, on the Supreme Court. He votes for a bigger defense budget and for arms sales to leprous governments like Chile's; he votes against tougher antipollution limits for car exhausts and opposes federal aid for abortion. During the Watergate scandals, the White House could count on his support until almost the end, when Senator Dole was in a tough reelection fight. Then when he was asked whether he wanted President Nixon to fly in to campaign for him, he replied: "I wouldn't mind if he flew over." His right-wing credentials won him the vice-presidential nomination at the 1976 Republican convention in Kansas City. President Ford needed a hard-liner to appease the Reaganite losers. Senator Dole was his man.

Yet this scourge of liberals, this preacher of self-reliance and the old-time fiscal religion of balanced budgets, routinely voted alongside Senator George McGovern on government help to farmers until the prairie liberal from South Dakota was defeated in the 1980 elections. He and McGovern could agree on higher subsidies for farmers, even though they could agree on almost nothing else.

Nobody, however, seriously regards Senator Dole as a hypocrite. Kansas is by far the biggest producer of wheat among the states. It is simply assumed that a senator from Kansas will vote for the interest of his constituents. This is so even on legislation that contradicts avowed doctrine. This disinclination to take ideology seriously, or indeed to expect anybody else to, when the principles become inconvenient, is typically American. Agriculture has probably received more govern-

A.A.-L

ment aid than any business other than defense, which is also a hugely successful earner of foreign exchange for the United States. Nor has this government help caused disabling inefficiencies. Farm families now make up less than 4 percent of the population of the United States, yet they produce most of the food and natural fiber for clothing worn by Americans, not to mention the feed grain moving into world trade. Farm exports exceed imports by a two-to-one margin. Together Iowa and Illinois grow one-sixth of all the corn in the world. Kansas and North Dakota grow more wheat than the whole of South America.

Such statistics alone are hard to grasp. Stalin would have been less impressed than Khrushchev was by the sheer scale of the Midwestern farmbelt. In the 1930s, American farmers were no more productive than farmers in the third world are today. American grain yields then averaged less than 1.5 tons per hectare (about 2½ acres). Now American yields are around 3.5 tons per hectare. The Agricultural Adjustment Act of 1933 in the Roosevelt New Deal and public intervention since then must take much of the credit. The AAA gave the secretary of agriculture authority to reduce acreage or production in agreement with farmers and to make marketing agreements with processors to support prices. The Roosevelt administration recognized that while consumers' demand for basic foods did not vary much with price, even a small surplus could cause a sharp collapse in the price of farm products and so in farmers' incomes. However successful for farmers, the first attempts by government to bring demand and supply into balance failed with the public at large. Critics of the New Deal made political hay with the government-supported slaughter of six million piglets, to make pork more expensive.

The policy since has grown subtler. The federal government has, through trial and error, come up with schemes to boost demand during the fat years, to put a floor under farm produce prices in lean years, to encourage farmers to stockpile grains when prices are low, and to subsidize farmers to reduce surpluses by paying them to let land lie fallow. Both conservatives from rural areas in the states of the Old Confederacy and liberals from the North supported passage in 1954 of Public Law 480, the Food for Peace program. The conservatives did so because they wanted to prop up farm income, the liberals to keep the world's hungry from turning in despair, as they saw it, to communism. To Americans, the program seemed an enlightened combination of self-interest and generosity. In a sense it was. Many takers, however, like India, found the help double-edged to the extent that it frustrated expanded output from their own farms.

More controversial is the food stamp program, in many ways the domestic equivalent of Food for Peace. Without doubt the vast expansion of food aid through this program has played an enormous part in overcoming lasting hunger in the United States, as more would admit if it were not now so unfashionable to put in a good word for any of President Johnson's war on poverty legislation. At a cost of around $10 billion a year, a tiny fraction of the defense budget, the food stamp program has in the Field Foundation's opinion done a lot of good, although it is demeaning to have to buy food with stamps, not cash, as this marks off the food stamp user from other shoppers. It was the Field Foundation that in 1967 sponsored an investigation by a group of physicians that revealed widespread hunger and malnutrition in the United States. A decade later, the foundation again supported a group of doctors, who returned to the same regions. It reported: "The doctors' latest findings suggest that food aid programs may represent one of the unsung, yet most effective, anti-poverty efforts of the past 15 years. Where in 1967 the physicians saw many children with swollen stomachs, dull eyes and open wounds, there were fewer visible signs of malnutrition and its related illnesses."

Few voters, it seems, are listening. Americans have a peculiarly strong aversion to other people getting something they do not earn, and candidate Reagan won more votes than he lost in the 1980 presidential election by promising to tackle abuses in this and other antipoverty programs. He, like everyone else, had heard stories about people driving up in flashy Cadillacs to use food stamps to buy crabs' legs, filet mignon, and smoked Nova Scotia salmon. The steps taken under the Carter administration to combat chiseling were made firmer by the Reagan administration. Few legislators were ready to question whether the red tape and bureaucratic busybodiness needed to enforce such controls would cost more than the abuses did.

On the supply side, Congress has given farmers a financial incentive to cut output during times of agricultural surplus by taking part of their land out of production. In his novel *Catch-22*, Joseph Heller pokes fun at this intervention. The father of a character called Major Major becomes rich by getting paid by the government not to grow alfalfa and then becomes richer still by using his money to buy more land so that he does not grow even more alfalfa. Visitors to California a couple of years ago were told of the Sacramento valley planter who got one water subsidy from the state authorities during the drought to irrigate his dry land and another from the federal government not to grow anything on it. Retailing such stories is a favorite parlor game for American free-market fundamentalists who attack government intervention in agriculture as unwarranted interference with the workings of a capitalist economy. If governments would only withdraw, they claim, world supply and demand in agriculture would find an equilibrium. Though it is difficult to prove them incorrect, the chances of their hypothesis being tested are small. Even if the United States were willing, which is itself doubtful, there is virtually no chance of the Russians, the Europeans, or the Japanese participating in such an experiment.

American farmers themselves would take some convincing. In poor years the "set asides" have subsidized their incomes. They have usually taken their poorer land out of production and earned more from the government for not planting on it than they would have by working the land. The federal government, too, has given them an insurance against falling prices due to surpluses. At the same time, farm productivity as measured by output per person-hour has increased since 1950 at a yearly rate of around 5 percent, against less than 2 percent for all other industries.

Farmers have successfully responded to the growth in demand and since the great Russian purchases of 1972–1973 have become far more sophisticated financially. The episode passed into the American political lexicon as the "great grain robbery" and radically changed the attitude of American farmers to marketing. As long ago as the 1920s, some farmers acquired radios to bring them information to help decide what to raise and when to sell. Until the big Russian purchases, however, it was still common for farmers to put aside some of their crop to feed their animals and then to sell off the surplus as they needed the cash. The Russian deals put an end to this casualness. Farmers wince to this day when they recall how they were suckered into selling their soybeans at three dollars a bushel to the great grain houses in 1972–1973, only to see the price soar to over twelve dollars. Since then American farmers have become avid, sometimes obsessive, market watchers. They still rely for farm news on such trade magazines as *Farm*

Journal and *Progressive Farmer*. They still read the patriotic country newspaper *Grit*, a unique mixture of Will Rogers humor, pious sentiment, and seasonal advice. Many also nowadays take the *Wall Street Journal*. While they milk their cows, slop their pigs, or disk their fields, they listen over their headphones to radio reports of the latest flutters on the commodities futures markets, where they have learned to make hedge sales and purchases.

As former Senator Herman Talmadge noted in a foreword to a 1979 report, "Status of the Family Farm," published by the Agriculture Committee: "Over the past 40 years, our agriculture policies have been directed primarily toward maintaining reasonable incomes for the nation's farmers and supplying American consumers with an abundant supply of high quality food and fiber at reasonable prices." The policies have succeeded, but with the result of hurrying the concentration of land ownership in the United States. This is exactly the reverse of what is usually meant by land reform.

The gains in productivity have come from large investments in big machines. Almost obsessively, farmers have striven to grow or raise more at less cost. Improved seeds have increased output. So have artificial insemination, embryo transplants, and other breeding methods that have begun to supersede sexual intercourse for livestock. Fertilizer is used so lavishly the soil is sometimes little more than an anchor for plants. Poisons enough to provide corpses for a shelf of whodunits are sprayed on the average-sized field, especially when it is planted with a crop like cotton, which could once be reduced to almost nothing by bollworms, boll weevils, and other insect pests.

While in purely productive terms the achievements are extraordinary, the social costs of the great forward leaps in American farming have been fierce. In the cottonbelt of the South, the cornbelt of the Midwest, and the wheatbelt of the Great Plains, the fields today are empty of people. The human toll of the movements of people was heavy.

In the Mississippi Delta, the virtual absence of animals and people on the plantations is almost eerie. It does not, after all, take a long memory to recall seeing fifty or sixty black cotton pickers working in a field or a multitude of small sharecropping farms where red-necked and black-necked growers eked out a living. Mechanical cotton harvesters, desiccants, and defoliants sent them all packing after the Second World War. Their dogtrot and shotgun houses were bulldozed away for the consolidation, first, of cotton fields, then of soybeans, which have since, as a crop, dethroned King Cotton in the Deep South. Some fields were flooded for dams where catfish could be farmed. These fish convert feed into flesh more efficiently even than battery chickens. They are mass-bred in the humid South much as trout are farmed elsewhere.

The fall in labor costs as one cotton-picking machine was able to replace many black cotton pickers has helped make already rich cotton growers even richer. William Falls is one such. On first acquaintance he is easily mistaken for someone of modest means. He dresses like a workaday farmer and drives a modest car around his farmland that lies between the Tallahatchie and Mississippi rivers. He complains that what he calls his "darkies" are earning more than three dollars an hour, as against three dollars a day in the 1950s.

His house displays his trophies. It could easily pass as a replica from the White Highlands of Kenya, where members of the British officer class settled after the First World War. The carpets are obviously valuable; knickknacks are made of gold and studded with precious stones. Two dozen hunting guns, together with five or six handguns, are displayed in glass cases in the parlor. The walls are festooned with the mounted heads of animals shot in Central and East Africa, such as impala, eland, waterbuck, and kudu. American big-game animals and bighorned wild sheep from the Gobi Desert stare out, too. Yet William Falls describes himself as an overtaxed member of the middle class. He wonders, gleefully, what will happen if the middle-income earners ever decided to gang up on the undeserving poor. It sometimes seems that nobody in the United States will ever admit to being well off, let alone rich. Wealthy farmers, like wealthy businessmen, assume that everyone in an income bracket stretching from five to seven figures is middle class.

Another member of this self-described, and immensely elastic, middle class is Big Daddy Warren, a large-boned, large-voiced fellow who retired after bringing in forty-three cotton crops. His political views veer even further to the right than those of William Falls. He eats often at Lusco's, a distinctive restaurant in Greenwood, Mississippi. He is hard to miss. He wears a bracelet with the words "Big Daddy" studded on it. He reckons welfare programs have made both whites and blacks, whom he calls "nigger boys," soft and have helped underwrite an inflation rate that means "a million dollars is not much money anymore."

These and other, less flamboyant cotton growers are among the most spectacular winners in the mechanical/chemical revolution in American agriculture. The losers are found in the ranks of people who took part in one of the greatest migrations in history. This exodus—which was all but forced—caused the most upheaval in the states of the cotton South, but has changed farming everywhere.

From 1940 to 1960, a net of 21.5 million people left farms, an average of more than 1 million a year. This far exceeded the excess of births over deaths among farm people. The drift has continued since, if slowly. The farm population has consequently declined from 30.5 million people in 1940 to fewer than a third as many. In 1950, there were 5.6 million farms, with an average size of 214 acres; in 1960, about 4 million farms, with an average size of 297 acres; in 1970, just under 3 million farms, with an average size of 374 acres; and in 1980, fewer than 2.7 million farms, with an average size of more than 400 acres. The revolution is not yet over. The farm labor force is sure to shrink further as bigger farms continue to gobble up small farms and as mechanical harvesting becomes as efficient in vegetable and fruit growing as it is already in grains, cotton, and soybeans. Tomato growing is a pointer. University researchers opened the way for mechanical harvesting by inventing a tomato plant on which most of the fruit ripens at about the same time and has a hard skin that resists bruising. Since it also, like broiler chickens and ITT's Wonder Bread, does not taste much like the real thing, the "hard tomato" has its critics. They criticize agricultural scientists for wasting further time and public money working on a seedless cucumber or on an all-green cauliflower got by crossing the white variety with broccoli. Scientists and farmers profiting from their research are not put off by the fuss. California grows four-fifths of the processed tomatoes grown in the United States. Nearly all of them are harvested by a machine that severs the vines and shakes the fruit loose. About three-quarters of these tomatoes are then sorted by a machine that rejects most of the rotten, green, or blemished tomatoes and gets rid of the dirt.

The labor savings are large. According to Robert Curley, an agricultural engineer at the University of California: "A typical harvester without electronic sorting requires a sorting crew of 16 to 22 people. With electronic sorters the hand sorting crew is reduced to three to five people per machine. A modern tomato harvester with electronic sorting and a crew of five people can harvest 25 tons to 35 tons per hour." Wine grapes are harvested by trunk shakers. A machine with grasping steel fingers that can tell ripe from raw fruit is being used as a picker of oranges. Research is under way for mechanical harvesting of broccoli, cauliflower, onions, and bell and chili peppers. One experimental machine being tested for lettuce picking uses a gamma-ray sensor to determine head density. Peering still further into the future, genetic engineers predict perennial corn; crops that can produce nitrogen and so supply their own fertilizer; potatoes and tomatoes on the same plant; plants that tolerate the high levels of salt in heavily irrigated soil.

This means vegetable pickers, too, many of them Mexican-Americans, will eventually be forced off the farms onto the unemployment and welfare rolls in the towns and cities. They will move off the land just as Tom Joad and the other Okies in *The Grapes of Wrath* did when their farms turned to red dust and the moneylenders foreclosed, and just as the blacks of the South did when mechanical cotton pickers lost them their homes and their livelihood. These displaced Mexican-American vegetable pickers will have skills not easily marketable in urban America and it will be remarkable if they are not typecast, just as the displaced Okies and blacks were, as shiftless, lazy, and good for nothing.

As the size of a profitable farm has grown larger, and as land costs have soared, a fundamental change has occurred in American farming. Besides being a land of opportunity, the United States until recently offered a great opportunity in land. People who wanted to own a farm of their own could do it by climbing the "farm ladder." This took sweat and courage. Luck helped. But it could be done. The first step was to learn how to farm. This could be as a student at a land grant college, but gaining practical experience working as a hired hand was always essential. The second step was to become a tenant farmer by leasing land from an absentee landlord and then using the tenant's share of the proceeds to buy nearby acres that could be farmed at the same time as the rented land. The third step was the accumulation of sufficient acreage so that one could be rated a farmer rather than just a tenant farmer. This ladder is no longer there. One is often told in rural America that unless a person inherits a farm or marries into one, she or he has little chance of owning a farm of a size that will provide a full-time living. If this is an exaggeration, it is only a slight one.

Land prices rose so steeply during the 1970s that the capital gains, usually unrealized, made by farmers on their land each year exceeded their net annual income from farming. Farmers who were mocked by their neighbors when they bought good land at $600 an acre ten or fifteen years ago acquired a belated reputation for shrewdness. The land doubled, tripled, and then quadrupled in value. Few investments, other than oil or gold, did better. Blacks, in particular, have sold out small plots to neighboring white farmers expanding their land. On the estimate of the Emergency Land Fund, a Southern-based nonprofit organization dedicated to halting the decline of land ownership by blacks, only 3.5 million acres of land in the United States are today owned by blacks. This figure is down from 6 million acres in 1969 and even farther down from 15 million acres owned by blacks nationally around the turn of the century. About 90 percent of the black-owned land in the United States is in the South.

Also losers are people of limited means, both black and white, who yearn to be farmers. According to the Department of Agriculture in "Status of the Family Farm": "The large capital requirements for getting started in farming mean that new entrants or their families tend to be wealthier than the average person or family. Thus, the market selection process for new entrants abets the trend to fewer and larger farms." Some buyers of farmland are doctors, dentists, and others who have substantial incomes or savings they want to shelter against taxes. Some are foreigners seeking insurance against wealth or income redistribution in their own country by siphoning some of their money, secretly, into farmland in the United States. Most commonly, though, it is established farmers who are buying up more land to add to existing farms. The prices they pay make sense only because they already own land—they are extortionate for anybody trying to break into farm ownership for the first time. A farmer in the Midwest who acquired, say, 800 acres at $600 each some years ago can justify the purchase of an additional 100 acres at $2,000 each with the calculation that the average cost of the land still works out at a mere $755 an acre, or still far below its average current value. Also, the debt servicing will not prove too burdensome. The interest charges on the money borrowed to purchase the extra 100 acres are deductible from income for tax purposes. The 800 acres will earn a return sufficient to repay the debt. A newcomer trying to break into farming is at a hopeless disadvantage. The land at today's inflated prices will often not produce a cash flow sufficient to meet the interest payments, let alone to pay back the principal.

Thomas Jefferson, who thought that "small landholders are the most precious part of the state," would be disappointed. The tax system and agricultural policy and market forces are combining to concentrate land ownership. About 6 percent of all farms already account for over half of total farm receipts, and it is hard to see how a small-is-beautiful counterrevolution could occur. Though the declared goal of public policy through most of the past half century has been to make the family farm prosperous, agricultural economists are not baffled for an answer when they are asked why that policy has failed. Farm families are smaller. Often none of the children want to continue farming, so the land is sold. A 160-acre tract of good land was just about as much as any family could cultivate when it relied on horses for power. Now 160 acres will hardly provide a subsistence outside places like New Jersey, where highly intensive market gardening is practiced.

A large impediment to efforts to reverse, or at least to slow, land consolidation and protect the smaller farm is the inability of Congress, or of farm organizations, to decide what exactly constitutes a "family farm." All recognize that farmland owned by an industrial corporation like Tenneco constitutes an agribusiness and politicians win easy applause when they deplore the buying of farmland by businesses and foreigners. But they are attacking a straw man. The idea that faceless corporations are taking over American agriculture is a myth. Slightly more than 1 percent of all farms in America are corporate farms, accounting for 15 percent of total cash receipts, and over 90 percent of them are owned by fewer than ten shareholders. This indicates that most so-called corporate farms are really incorporated family-owned farms and that the consolidation of American farms into cumbrous units is due not to giant corporations' investing in farmland but to the expansion in the acreage of family farms. In recent years, about three-fifths of the land changing ownership has been added to existing predominantly family farms, and it is clear that the greatest threat to the "family farm" is not a faceless corporation but other "family farms."

So far the country has gained mightily, in economic terms, from the consolidation. Small farms are usually inefficient. But this does not mean there is no end to the process—that consolidation will inevitably continue to bring further gains. In farming, biggest is not necessarily best. Indeed, the evidence suggests that while a medium-sized farm—the definition of which varies with geography and the crop—is usually more efficient than a small farm, large farms are less efficient than medium-sized farms. Why? The most likely explanation is that a farm family has a profit incentive to take the care that distinguishes the good from the indifferent farmer and to work the long hours still needed during crucial peak periods in farming, such as those seasons when the crops are put in and taken out. Efficiency declines when the farm gets so large that the family members have to hire less motivated, less careful employees to do much of the work.

Diagnosing the disease has proved easier than coming up with a cure. No constituency yet exists in the United States for curbing the acquisition or consolidation of farmland, let alone for redistributing it. When legislators rail against agribusiness and swear to preserve the "family farm," the definition of a "family farm" is commonly so loose as to be worthless. It has come to mean the landed gentry as well as the dirt farmer, a Minnesota mixed farm with a few dairy cows as well as such huge spreads as the Kleberg family's King Ranch in Texas. The four divisions of the King Ranch support 60,000 cattle and nearly 3,000 oil and gas wells and sprawl over 850,000 acres, an area larger than Rhode Island. The founder of the ranch, an ex-sea captain named Richard King, obeyed the succinct advice of a friend, General Robert E. Lee. "Buy land and never sell." Other farmers have concluded that this makes sound sense. Each year, fewer farmers and fewer farms account for a larger slice of America's farming. Each year, rural people have a sharper point when they joke that the only way for an outsider to get into farming is to marry a farmer's son or daughter.

9

TOMORROW'S AMERICANS

Schools

AMERICANS are screened for life in their schools. Not any-more into classes for bright, not-so-bright, and unbright children, but in schools for children of the rich, the not-so-rich, and the poor. For the child, even the dim child, born into the well-to-do home is more likely to go to college than the child, even the bright child, of the poor, and a college degree is today an all but essential entrance qualification for the race for jobs with high pay and status. Preferably a postgraduate degree, now that mere graduate ones have become devalued by overabundance. Such degrees offer their holders far more than a head start —more like a half-mile start over a mile course—in the career stakes. The probable losers can be spotted at an early age in a country where job entry is ever more structured. They are the children who go to public schools in relatively poor areas that send fewer of their pupils to college than public schools in better-off areas and far fewer than the close to 100 percent college enrollment reported by such excellent, and expensive, New England private schools as Andover, Exeter, and Groton.

At this other extreme from the enclaves for the rich is the bleak, almost treeless landscape in Todd County, South Dakota. At intervals across the miles of bare plains are Indian 400s, tract houses where members of the Sioux tribe live. There are eight thousand people on the Rosebud Reservation, one of the state's two largest. For the Sioux, life is hard. To the west, in the Black Hills, Crazy Horse annihilated Custer and his men. A doomed, frustrated resistance among the Indians continues. Violence, alcoholism, and traffic accidents are common on the reservations. For the men, there is little work. The big employer, which gives jobs mainly to the women, is the school district.

Scattered over Todd County are several public schools where Sioux children go to learn English and, reluctantly, to become Americans. At Mission, an old trading post on the Keya Paha River, North Elementary is a school of some size. Into the countryside, the schools get smaller. Electricity is a recent thing at Springcreek school. Okreek has a one-room schoolhouse. The children are gathered in by bus from miles around. When it rains, the unpaved roads turn to mud. Teachers have to know how to handle four-wheel drives.

On Rosebud, many of the older Indians speak only their native Lakota. Some of their grandchildren know only a few words of English when they go to school. Their very names show how they are both Sioux and American: John Makes-Room-for-One-More, Francis Never-Miss-a-Shot, Elvis Presley Running Horse.

The Sioux and the school officials carry on the old wars between Indians and whites. Almost all the school administrators are white. They live "up on the hill," as the better parts of American towns are called, even though Mission has no hills. When money was made available by the federal government in the late 1960s for remedial schooling, the Sioux, at first, chose not to accept. They quarreled with the Bureau of Indian Affairs, with the school board, and with instructors from the federal remedial programs. Then they decided to accept on condition Indian teachers had a say in running the program. The Sioux were understandably suspicious of white attempts to help them. The remedial program was to teach young Sioux English, reading, and basic arithmetic. For a time, it worked. The old quarrels never died, though, and in 1977 the school district threw the remedial program out. Still, one white teacher, who learned Lakota, recalls with pride sitting on the steps of a one-room schoolhouse listening to the Sioux children inside reading aloud in English.

Only slightly better off is a tiny township with a redbrick rural school on a hill near the Ozarks in northwest Arkansas. Once the schoolhouses were more scattered, but eventually they were consolidated into this one elementary school. Most of the children are used to long bus rides every day. The ride, through rolling hills, past lakes, is pleasant. Tourists come here from neighboring Oklahoma and Missouri to fish. This helps provide the district with an income, although it always used to be poor.

Cut-off, traditional, this corner of Arkansas was hardly affected by business booms and busts, not having had far itself to fall. With a Dogpatch reputation, the area, until a recent tourist and retirement-home boom, saw little change in decades. The first striking thing about the children, all of them white, is how healthy they look. They are thin, with prominent bones and pink cheeks. Thanks to a lean country diet, they are, by American standards, underweight. The second striking thing is how they speak. By some strange linguistic trick, these small children, who have never set foot in London, let alone the East End, all speak with distinct cockney accents.

Their teachers are reserved with outsiders, coldly polite but hardly friendly. They were creationists before creationism, as one would expect in the heart of the Bible Belt. They would not think it strange at all to hear that fellow teachers at an elementary school in neighboring Tennessee refused to use a textbook that described the evolution of the solar system, as this seemed to foreclose the possibility that it was created instantaneously in its present form. Nor would they laugh at the same teachers for refusing to read aloud, but always spelling out, letter by letter, the word "maggots" in a children's book called *Herman the Fly,* in the belief that "maggot" was the slang term for homosexual.

The children at Sapello School in Las Vegas, New Mexico, a town fifty miles east of Santa Fe, are poor, but they are neatly dressed, well turned out with pride. Las Vegas is a stable community, older, like so much of New Mexico, than the United States. The names on the parish gravestones remind one that the Spaniards were colonizing this beguiling land before the Puritans set foot in frigid Massachusetts. The Hispanos are proud of their background, and dislike being taken for Mexican-Americans. The older families that call themselves Hispanic, after all, go back well before Mexican-Americans began arriving in any numbers as aliens in the United States. Though they tend to be looked down on by the Anglos, they have a stable society, traditional habits and, where numerous enough, control of their towns. The school reflects this. The two-story brick building is nothing fancy. The school district has a tight budget, but the teachers want to teach, the children to learn. In the elementary grades, the children are as quiet and well behaved as any bunch of seven- or eight-year-olds can be. The school gets federal remedial funds. The children learn English as a second language. Their test scores suggest that for them this is a success. Not so long ago, Anglo teachers in nearby schools had a simple way of handling children who spoke Spanish in class. They beat them. In less benighted times, even as the national debate about bilingual education goes on, both teachers and charges speak Spanish in class.

Tupelo is a town of about twenty thousand people in the hills of northeastern Mississippi, with few distinctions save for being the birthplace of Elvis Presley. On the edge of town is a run-down black section. The local public school is "integrated," although almost no whites are to be found there. Discipline, as in most small-town or country schools, is good. The children are poorly dressed, in T-shirts and cutoffs. Unlike the children of Flippin, they do not look healthy. They have town diets. Their test scores, according to the teachers, are poor.

The school district was integrated after threats from Washington that money from Health, Education and Welfare, as the department was then known, would be discontinued if the district did not comply with court orders to break up segregated schools. The Tupelo school board was not convinced that it wanted the funds in the first place. But, as elsewhere in the South, compliance eventually came to look easier than resistance. Not that the board complied, except to the letter of the court order. Word went out that this school was where "dummies" could be sent. Among the few whites in the school could be found an unusually high proportion of backward children.

Iron River lies in an old mining and manufacturing district on Michigan's isolated upper peninsula, next door to northern Wisconsin. Like Flippin, Iron River is poor, but for different reasons. Business never touched Flippin. In Iron River, it came and went. The drive up from the nearest airport, at Iron Mountain, passes attractive countryside with maple trees and lakes, but shut-down mines as well. The people of Iron River are reserved, taciturn. When there is work, they are hard-working. The area has a union tradition and usually goes Democratic. Unlike that type of American, not uncommon in the South, for whom friendliness and effusive politeness with strangers can be shallow, these north Michigan people are "nice deep down," in the words of one who knows them well. By the late 1960s, the area's mines were just about all long since closed. Life in Iron River was hard. Schooling, still, went on.

The local elementary school is a traditional building. There is no wire-mesh fencing on the windows. That is only for big-city schools. The building is not fancily done up, like elementary schools in a prosperous suburb. There are no carpets on the floors. The library is scant. Many of the children at their desks are fair-haired, blue-eyed, and pale-skinned. Iron River has a large number of Polish families. There are also a few Italians. The restaurants provide solid country food. As the school's test scores show, it gets results. The school is the center of heavy politicking, as so often in smaller communities where school board politics may be the only game around. In depressed areas like this, schools also provide regular jobs. With politics, naturally, come scandals, not big enough ones, perhaps, to shock outsiders, but in Iron River they still tell of a school superintendent who diverted funds from Washington meant for kindergarten reading to buy an electronic scoreboard for the high school football team.

Dort School, in central Flint, by contrast, is in the thick of industrial Michigan. Josiah Dallas Dort was a carriagemaker who teamed up with William Durant to make Buick cars, before General Motors absorbed their enterprise. Flint has five GM plants making Buicks and Chevrolets. Workers, black and white, came up from the South in the two great auto booms, 1910–1930 and the 1940s. They live, black and white, in separate neighborhoods and send their children to separate schools. The children at Dort are black. Life in Flint is uncertain for everyone now that the car industry is in trouble. Families move a lot. Children come in and out of school, entering in midyear and leaving before the school term is finished. In mobile America, this is a common, little-noticed problem for the public schools, which have to depend on strong support from their communities if they are going to be any good. Despite the handicap, Dort School tries, and there are strong bonds between teachers and parents.

When the futurologists, today's soothsayers, rummage for portents, it is odd how they pay so much more attention to the invention of wonder machines or to statistical projections than to schools and universities. For the sixty million or so Americans at school—meaning just about anything from kindergarten to the top graduate departments of the best universities—are, in human terms, the next United States. True, these children of rural Arkansas and New Mexico, Rosebud and

Tupelo, Flint and Iron River, may not be typical, but then what schoolchild is?

Their schools are at the bottom of the stupendous pyramid of American education, out of sight, overlooked but holding up its enormous weight all the same. Few of the children at these schools are likely to go past high school. In any year, ten million or more Americans are at college. That is three or four times the share that the more elitist, and more frankly elitist, Western Europeans send to college. But that means three Americans in five end their education, all the same, with high school, and it is a far higher proportion at Rosebud, Iron River, and the rest.

The children at these schools are all "socially disadvantaged," to use the anesthetic language of social science. They are black, Hispanic, Indian, or poor white. These very groups account for a disproportionate and growing share of young Americans in the public schools, with the comparatively low, and declining, birthrate of middle- and upper-class white Americans.

The educational enterprise in the United States is dauntingly large, with around ten million students in colleges and universities, forty-five million in public schools, and another five million at private schools, many of them offering religion as their fourth R. In the public sector, the little red schoolhouse has passed into history. Today's public school buildings in the wealthier districts are often on a pharaonic scale. A new secondary and elementary school in the suburbs looks like a regional concert hall *cum* cultural center in a prosperous German town. High schools seem to be built around the indoor basketball court—with seating for several thousand in towns where the games are a big attraction—and the heated swimming pool, to which the classrooms are simply functional appendages. Universities are small, or not so small, cities with their own shops, fire departments, banks, and police.

The sheer numbers of consumers of education—more than a quarter of all Americans—is dazzling, too, until it is remembered what being at school means. The kindergarten toddler with his Superman lunchbox and the history student crossing Harvard Yard with the *Viking Portable Nietzsche* in her book bag are both at school. So are the woman in her thirties who decides to take an auto repair course at the regional campus of her state university and the Vietnam service-man who uses veterans benefits to get a machinist's apprenticeship at his local community college.

This open, unsnob use of the word "school" is a nice conceit. It puts —or pretends to put—everyone on the same footing. That the step from Groton to Harvard is nonetheless shorter than from Shelbyville High School, Shelbyville, Indiana; that a degree from Swarthmore or Wellesley will impress the dean of graduate admissions more than one from the University of Miami, a.k.a Suntan U; that an M.B.A. from Stanford draws a higher starting salary than the equivalent from Ball State University at Muncie, Indiana, are all instances of the general truth that some American schools are more equal than others.

Though this is recognized by all, a show of equality has been historically important for public schools among a people divided rich and poor, Catholic, Protestant, and Jew, native born and immigrant, black and white, city and farm. Submerging these divisions in the classroom and forcing the children into the native Protestant mold was felt to be the public school's first job. Book work took second place. It was with this guiding principle that America's public schools undertook to teach all comers, to offer secondary education to children whether or not they were going on to college, to avoid splitting children into "academic" and "vocational" streams, and after World War II, to attempt to keep all children in full-time schooling until the age of seventeen.

To Americanize and to equalize. That was, until recently, the public school's great mission, the standard by which it would be judged. The schools all the same had to teach, to fill the day. With what? When the National Education Association put out its Seven Cardinal Princi-ples of Secondary Education in 1918, the imposing list contained: Health, Command of Fundamental Processes, Worthy Home Mem-bership, Vocation, Citizenship, Worthy Use of Leisure, and Ethical Character. Besides "Fundamental Processes," which meant reading, writing, and arithmetic, there was nothing about learning subjects at all, not even as an afterthought. This tradition has never died, although educationalists have periodically thought up new names for it: e.g., Charles Prosser's "life adjustment" a generation ago, or "survival skills" today. It was this strong tradition that Denis Brogan described in his famous observation that for American pupils "their schools are doing far more than instruct them; they are letting them instruct each other in how to live in America."

Few people have been as ambitious for their schools as Americans. Certainly not, for instance, the British, who have traditionally run a caste-ridden education system, where rich children, dim and bright, are Brahmans and children unlucky enough to be born both poor and dim are Untouchables. When measured against the high American ideal, failure was predictable, even though the schools have often done better than their detractors predicted. Nevertheless, today's concern about the public school is well founded. The gap between ideal and achievement is widening. So is the gap between good and bad public schools, and between the public and private sectors in education. Schools were never equal, but there was a time when Americans wished them to seem equal. Now many do not even wish that.

That onetime rock of support for the public schools—taxpaying parents with children of school age—is slowly washing away. Only three adults in ten today have children at public school. The rejection rate in local voting on new bonds to finance schools of about 50 percent is double what it was in the 1950s. More important, the public schools are losing their most powerful constituents. Lawyers, journalists, bankers, the corporate elite, politicians, and doctors who can afford it, blacks as well as whites, are taking their children out of the public schools. In consequence, as school enrollments have fallen, private school attendance has remained stable at about 5 million pupils. Attendance at non-Catholic private schools has risen from 700,000 in 1960 to around 1.7 million.

Some of these parents opting to pay a premium for their children's education are unreconstructed racists seeking to maintain segregated schools. Others, sometimes an overlapping category, are the stricter sort of Christians and Jews who want religion brought into their children's education. A high and rising proportion of parents sending their children to private school are more interested in excellence than equality, in elitism than democracy. For them it is a plus that the private schools, unlike the public ones, are under no obligation to teach all comers. That they can keep out or expel the handicapped, the unmotivated, the slow learners, the misfits, and other hard-to-educate children. For education is a zero-sum game. Every hour a public school class devotes each week to activities intended to help the underachievers catch up is an hour wasted for the overachievers, who tend to come disproportionately from the better-off families, where learning is likelier to be encouraged. Also a plus for fee-paying parents is that the professionals, the teachers, in private schools—religious and secular—are not dictated to by democratically elected school boards dominated by well-meaning amateurs. Indeed, John C. Esty, president of the National Association of Independent Schools, in 1977, saw their resistance to new ideas and to outside pressures as a reason for the growing popularity of private schools. "Families are past caring about educational theories and experimentation. They ask only that their children be exposed to decent adults, unharried by excessive numbers and extravagant demands, who can help them individually. That seems to me to be the special attraction of the independent schools."

The chances are that the rise of the private schools will be matched, seesaw-like, by the decline of the public schools. With their smaller classes, and comparatively well-behaved, well-motivated pupils, the private schools have an advantage over the public ones in competing to recruit the best teachers. This competitive edge is sharpened as the defection of the best-off families from the public schools weakens the lobby for publicly financed education. Add to these advantages the exclusivity of the private schools, which permits them to confine backward and other difficult pupils to the public schools, and Paul Haupt, who is undertaking a national study of public schools for the Carnegie Foundation, is not being fanciful when he raises the specter of American public schools becoming "a dumping ground for rejects."

When ratings-happy Americans want a quick reading of the nation's educational health, they take a look at the national SAT scores. SAT stands for Scholastic Aptitude Test, the multiple-choice exam taken by 1 million to 1.5 million high school students in search of university places each fall. Most sought-after colleges with high admission requirements use SAT scores as a strong guide to who gets in. Each student gets a score, on the mathematics and verbal section, from 200 to 800. The national average, give or take a few arithmetical steps, is got by totaling the scores and dividing by the number taking the test.

The national SAT scores, in fact, are for schools and universities what the Dow Jones industrial average is for Wall Street. The SAT does not tell educators how Putnam Phelps and his friends at Choate are doing compared with Vince Savarese and his friends at Kennedy High in South Philadelphia, any more than the Dow tells investors what is happening in auto or electronic stocks. Like the Dow, the SAT averages are a rough-and-ready measure. Even if their flaws were tidied up, they would not tell educators what American children were learning, how much they knew, or how well educated they were. Nonetheless, for a brief answer to "How are American children doing in school?" the SAT scores are the numbers people watch. Up is good, down bad. And there's been just about no up in the SAT now for over a decade and a half.

Brokers look back to the 1960s as the go-go years for stocks. Educationalists remember the same post-Sputnik years as a golden time for the SAT. Scores peaked in the 1962–1963 school year with a national average of 478 in the verbal test and 502 in mathematics. From there they slid each year with gathering speed. In 1980, the corresponding figures were 424 and 466. Serious Americans take this slippage seriously. Daniel Greenberg, the science columnist, has asked: "After the greening of America and along with the graying of America, are we witnessing the dimming of America?" Before rushing to answer Yes, one needs a closer look, if only because of the Will Rogers caution: "The schools aren't as great as they used to be, but they never were."

One attractively simple explanation for the falling SAT averages is that the increase in the number of students taking the test was attributable to more pupils from large, poor families with few or no books aspiring to go to college—pupils of the sort who, lacking much support from home, generally do badly on tests. According to this reading of the scores, the average was dropping because the pool of students had been diluted. Although a disproportionate number of the pupils doing badly were black or Spanish-speaking, this explanation was neither racist nor cause for despair. Neither group had been properly schooled before. Once in college, they would catch up. The averages would revive.

It would be good were it that simple. The Carnegie Foundation for the Advancement of Education and the College Entrance Examination Board, which runs the SAT, set up a blue-ribbon panel in 1975 under Willard Wirtz, Kennedy's and Johnson's secretary of labor, to look into all this. The panel set out its findings in 1977. Yes, it reported, the decline in SAT scores in the late 1960s and early 1970s was due in part to a new pool of underprepared pupils taking the test. After that, all students, except those with the very highest scores, began doing worse. Wirtz's panel asked if, perhaps, the tests were getting harder. No, they were not. On the contrary, it decided, the scores had, if anything, lately become a bit inflated. The decline continued after the Wirtz study, although it may now have stopped. In 1980, only 29,000 students got more than 650 in SAT verbal tests, compared to 54,000 in 1972. For mathematics, 73,000 scored more than 650 in 1980, compared to 94,000 eight years earlier.

Nor are the SAT scores the only ones to retreat. The American College Test, the Iowa Testing Program, and the Minnesota SAT all show drops among students as a whole—black or white, suburban or city, well-to-do or poor. Only among the best students, as in the SAT tests, is there little sign of deterioration. Today's bright crop, in terms of sheer book work, may be marginally better than the bright kids of the 1960s, if less original and less adventurous. As for the rest, it is hard to resist the conclusion that they are more stupid, less attentive, or less well taught than children of their age were ten and twenty years ago.

Ask a parent why all this is happening and the odds are, according to the polls, that the first reason given will be "discipline." Parents mean there is not enough. Poor discipline can refer to just about anything, from open classrooms to the gradual disappearance of homework to assault with a deadly weapon. Outright violence rightly and naturally works parents up most. Press and television agree. For reporters, school stories are usually as unpromising as a third-grade outbreak of chicken pox, unless there is really bad news. Stabbings in the playground, doping in the lavatories, braining teachers with lead pipes—that happened to a substitute teacher the authors know at a Southside Chicago high school—make readers or viewers sit up. Or at least they did before they became routine. About 110,000 teachers report physical assaults every year. One in four reports something stolen. It is not kid stuff. The third-largest police force in the country is the full-time detail patrolling the Los Angeles schools.

Who cannot sympathize with the thirteen-year-old boy who begged his father to take him out of Chicago's Nicholas Senn High School, far from the city's worst, because it was so violent he couldn't learn anything? The boy had come in from basketball practice to find a teammate lying face down in the shower with a nine-inch knife in his back. He wanted to go to live with his uncle so he could transfer to the suburban, white, academically pushy Highland Park High. And who cannot understand, in turn, his father replying: "No; life's going to be rough and you better find out about it now." The son understood, up to a point. He became a reporter and obligingly reckons he would not have made as good a one if he had gone to a comfortable, middle-class school. He had learned, at Nicholas Senn, to get on easy terms with people with whom he had little or nothing in common.

High schools are not, though, notably more violent than American society at large. The ages of fifteen to twenty-four are the peak years for violent crime, and since teenagers are in school until seventeen and eighteen, and for much of the day, mayhem is all but inevitable. Shocking as the numbers and the stories are, the blood spilling is neither new nor pervasive. The schools have lived with it before, and they can live with it again. High fences around schoolyards were put up not to keep truants and softballs in but to keep, not very effectively, the delinquents out. Ask parents if the public schools in general have bad discipline trouble; they will say they have. Ask what complaints they have at their own children's school and, according to the polls, the complaints grow weak and vague. The violence that bothers them is unanchored, abstract, elsewhere. The discrepancy would be hard to fathom if classroom disorder were as bad as often painted. Stories of violence grow in the telling. During the bitter Ocean Hill–Brownsville school dispute in New York in 1968, a union teacher was thrown out by the insurgent local school board for allegedly letting her pupils toss their desks about the room. At her hearing, according to Diane Ravitch, a writer of educational history, the teacher was able to show that the desks, like furniture at sea, were firmly bolted to the floor.

What is depressing for the public high schools is that belief in their brutalism and disorder seems almost beyond refutation. When anecdotes go at it, one on one, the violent story usually wins. Whatever the truth of the matter, the myth now seems stronger than the facts. And for the schools, more damaging.

Of course, dissatisfaction with America's schools is nothing new. In the *New Republic* magazine in 1930, the educational writer Boyd Bode wrote: "To the casual observer, American education is a confusing and not altogether edifying spectacle. It is productive of endless fads and panaceas; it is pretentiously scientific and at the same time pathetically conventional; it is scornful of the past, yet painfully inarticulate when it speaks of the future." While American parents and teachers, like parents and teachers everywhere, have blamed the schools, usually coupled with the media, for society's ills, the American educational system has heaped up extraordinary successes.

In 1930, when Bode published that broadside, only half of the fourteen-to-seventeen-year-olds were in high school. Today high schools keep more than 95 percent of fourteen-to-seventeen-year-olds. America converts a far higher proportion of its young people into college graduates than Western European societies, which, more or less consciously, use their educational system as a social separator. The American educational system remains open, even welcoming middle-aged people who want to resume their studies in later life. In Europe, by contrast, it is almost taken for granted that formal education comes to an end when people leave schools in the midteens or, for those few that go on to higher education, when they leave the university. True, the elitism of the European educational system means that Europeans can say, with some justice, that it is not until the age of twenty-two or twenty-three that the well-educated American equals or surpasses the well-educated European: that at almost every age up to there the well-educated European will be ahead. What is equally true, though less obvious, is that American schools are a success when measured against their own democratic standard, in which educating the many is more important than cramming the bright.

Nonetheless, measured against their own past successes (witness the SAT scores), American schools are not only failing to make the progress taken for granted in a once forward-looking, optimistic land, but are actually losing ground. Dissatisfied parents hold the teachers primarily responsible for the slippage, along with their two chief representative bodies: the American Federation of Teachers (AFT), which is opposed to competency testing for experienced teachers, though not for entrants into the profession, and the National Education Association, which is opposed to any kind of competency testing because, it asserts, teacher competency cannot be measured by written tests.

The dissatisfied parents are not short of ammunition. During the

Chicago teachers' strike in the winter of 1979–1980, a striker told a television interviewer: "I teaches English." When teachers in Wales, Wisconsin, a suburb of Milwaukee, sent in written proposals for a curriculum, their spelling mistakes included "dabate," "woud," "seperate," and "documant." In a South Carolina court where Aniese Boyd, a fifth-grade teacher, challenged Batesburg-Leesville Middle School's refusal to renew her contract, she was given a ten-word vocabulary test. She defined the meaning of "suffrage" as "people suffering for some reason or another" and "ratify" as "to get rid of something." She could neither pronounce nor define the word "agrarian." Nevertheless, the judge ordered that she be rehired. He pointed out that her dismissal notice contained a spelling mistake and bad grammar, and that there were seventy-seven grammatical errors in the first eighty-two pages of the official school district policy manual.

Forced on the defensive, teachers are hard put to answer. For years they claimed that they would teach better if they had smaller classes, better salaries, and more time to prepare courses. As John Sawhill, the ex-president of New York University, has pointed out, teachers got all these things, and still teaching did not get better. Between 1950 and 1979, pupil-teacher ratios in the public schools improved from 30–1 to less than 20–1. Teachers' salaries rose briskly in real, inflation-adjusted, dollars from 1960 to 1970, though they slowed in the seventies. By the end of that decade, public school teachers were making $15,000 to $16,000 for nine months work, a modest salary for a job that, according to David Imig, executive director of the American Association of Colleges for Teacher Education, has come to combine the roles of "mother, father, priest or rabbi, peacekeeper, police officer, playground monitor and lunchroom patrol," but a big improvement all the same in a country that has always paid its teachers atrociously.

For those gains they have made, the teachers have in large part their unions to thank. Between 1970 and 1980, as school enrollments declined, budgets grew tighter, schools closed, and teachers faced a buyer's market, the membership of the National Education Association rose from 1 million to 1.7 million, while its rival, the American Federation of Teachers, led by the rumpled, dogged Albert Shanker, rose from 140,000 to over half a million.

The unions have helped make teachers more politically aware, and increased their clout. At the 1980 Democratic National Convention, one delegate in ten was an NEA teacher. The unions have also made it harder for school boards negotiating teachers' pay to exploit teaching as a vocation for dedicated, selfless, and idealistic people. But the critics of the unions and their members claim that teachers have at the same time forgotten how to teach, how to expect the best, how to make children think it important to learn.

Take a typical target of the traditionalists' criticism, Ralph Kane, a high school teacher from Pico Rivera in Los Angeles County. Kane came into teaching with the big increase in teachers during the early 1960s. One of his first discoveries was that he could not accept the mystique of testing and grading which saturated the schools. Grading children of unequal ability, he found, was "a little obscene." In his twenty-odd years as a teacher, Kane proudly admitted to giving "A"s and "B"s to dozens of students of less than average academic ability. True, inflated grades meant that many students simply would not have the knowledge and abilities usually associated with high grades. But in a credential-worshiping culture, he could not find it in himself to condemn his students at the outset by sending them into the world with low grades. Many of his colleagues felt the same way.

Describing the change in attitude in the 1960s, Kane says: "Work as an end in itself lost some of its sanctity, while the needs of individuals gained ascendance over the demands of institutions." Like-minded teachers are against the drive to test all students for "minimum competency" before giving them high school diplomas. Inflation of grades and diplomas has positive social and political value to them. Every teacher knows, these inflationists argue, that lots of children are going to fail. Splitting children at the end of high school into failures and successes, goats and sheep (those without a bit of paper and those with one), would not make much difference to how much they learn in school, but it would make a big difference when those who failed looked for work.

Besides, as Jerrold Coombs, an educationalist from the Pacific Northwest, asks, what is "minimum competency"? Can it be pinned down to a test? No, he thinks. Not all adults, he says, need to read and write well. "Many adults we would ordinarily judge to be successful," he thinks, "do little writing or computation." Nevertheless, they manage successfully.

The wish not to fail students by giving them low grades or denying them high school diplomas until they have shown they have a few elementary mental skills is understandable. A high school diploma is of such little scholastic value to begin with that being denied it is a truly crippling handicap. Nobody, it is tempting to say, should be kicked off the meritocratic ladder so early. Such egalitarian thinking is common in American schools, confused as it may strike the more traditionally minded. Teachers like Kane and Coombs are in that old, Dewey-eyed American tradition of education which sets greater store by equality and experiment than by efficiency and achievement.

Indeed, ask Americans who is their greatest educational thinker, and they will say, without hesitation, John Dewey, the believer in ungraded schools, "human growth," and discovery of the hidden potential in each individual child. Grasp this hopeful vision, and one has got the alter ego of American schooling. Dewey's Laboratory School at the University of Chicago, however, was considered far too impractical, or more particularly, expensive, to become the model of the American high school. Teachers, school boards, and parents like to believe that the spirit of Dewey blessed their enterprise, but to run their schools, a more practical, down-to-earth guide was needed. This was the psychologist Edward Thorndike, who promoted widespread use of IQ tests, first for the U.S. Army in World War I and then afterward for the nation's schoolchildren. Thorndike typifies the efficiency-minded outlook of the testers and regimentalists which dominates American schools.

Unfortunately, for kids who do badly in high school, college-entrance deans and would-be employers are Thorndikes, not Deweys. In a grade-worshiping society, inflating a high school student's grades is a cruel kind of help. "We've enlarged the circle of winners," says Kane. The circle is enlarged, but only for a short time. Giving everyone a high school diploma simply passes on to somebody else—the community college, the employer—the job of failing the unqualified. Gary Berrien of Florida found out the hard way what inflated high school grades can mean.

Gary, a black teenager from Jacksonville, had not had a job since leaving high school. Watching television one day, he saw the appealing U.S. Army advertisements promising recruits an apprenticeship if they joined up. At the recruiting office, Gary discovered he needed a high school diploma before he could sign on. Gary did not have one, even though throughout his high school years he had got more than passing grades. The year Gary left high school, a Florida law had come into effect requiring all high school students to take a "minimum competency" test before getting their diplomas. The test set a very low standard. Nevertheless, Gary had taken it and failed.

After being turned down for the Army traineeship, Gary, with legal help from opponents of the competency test, sued the school system. Gary's lawyers argued that his passing grades—evidently highly inflated —had given no warning of how little Gary was actually learning. The "minimum competency" test was unexpected, unfair. Gary had been cheated out of a diploma his teachers, by their grading, had led him to expect. The federal district judge, George Carr, agreed. Gary got his diploma. So did several hundred other Florida schoolchildren caught in the same trap. Judge Carr, all the same, upheld the idea of minimum competency testing so long as students were given fair warning and so long as it was not obviously discriminatory in its effects. On the first try, three-quarters of those failing were black, only a quarter white.

Disapproval of grade inflation is not a matter of class or color. The black economist Thomas Sowell has written angrily about "the shock of the first magnitude" for black children "to discover that your intellectual performance is miles below that of others around you." Sowell believes it deeply wrong for teachers to treat black children—or other low achievers—more softly than others. At Cornell University, he observed several habits practiced by university teachers on black students who failed to shape up academically: steering them away from tough courses, marking them "incomplete" but not failing them, postponing throwing them out. He quotes one professor who, disgusted with himself at giving in to students who badgered him for better grades, said: "I give them all 'A's and 'B's and to hell with them."

Apart from the three explanations for falling SAT scores already canvassed—indiscipline, inadequate teachers, and lax grading—the Wirtz panel also indicted television and too much choice in high school courses. The case against television looks plausible, but only until it is cross-examined. By the age of seventeen, most teenagers will have watched television for fifteen thousand hours or more, far longer than the eleven thousand hours they will have spent in the classroom. Television interferes with homework. But this is not new. Television watching was widespread in the 1950s. And before television, there were radios and comic books. To all but a few kids, homework will always be a bore.

The case against the wide range of courses offered to high school children has more substance. Gannett newspapers recently sent a team of reporters into two dozen high schools to find out what was going wrong. They found courses for credit given in "astrology, marriage simulation, cheerleading, student government, child care and mass media." As John Sawhill puts it, courses like these give high schools "a means of preventing students from failing when they cannot educate them." In consequence, colleges complain more and more about the lack of basic skills in the students the high schools are sending them, especially the dog-like way many of them write and spell. An economics teacher at the University of Southern California says that his students' grammar is bad and their spelling atrocious. Some of them do not know to capitalize "I" when referring to themselves. On entering City College in New York, two-thirds of the city's high school graduates need remedial classes—an astonishingly high figure even when account is taken of CCNY's highly democratic admission procedures.

Colleges may grumble, but they must take some of the blame. In the late 1960s, partly in response to pressure from counterculture students and to criticisms of hierarchical barriers between college teachers and students, universities began relaxing their entrance requirements. More courses became optional. Learning, save for the exceptionally bright, is always a sweat, so students opted for the easier subjects.

Foreign language skills, always a weakness in English-speakers, American and British alike, are as a result likely to decline further, and they are already abysmal. Shortly after Alexander Haig, who himself showed trouble enough speaking his native tongue, came in as President Reagan's first secretary of state, he was informed that only one foreign service officer in the American embassy in Nairobi could speak Swahili, the lingua franca in East Africa; that when a Soviet soldier sought political asylum in the American embassy in Kabul, Afghanistan, he could not find anyone who could speak Russian; that none of the more than seventy staff members of the European Division of the Office of the Secretary of Defense could speak German or French.

High schools have naturally responded to the new permissiveness in university entrance requirements. Why should they teach a hard subject like French or German if their pupils could get into a university without a foreign language? Why, similarly, teach them to write essays or learn algebra when there were softer options? As stricter requirements were dropped, performance fell. In Massachusetts, for example, when high schools between 1971 and 1975 increased the number of optional English courses, the SAT scores fell off, almost uniformly.

With the increase in "electives," the notion of a common education, some shared body of knowledge that an educated child should possess, began to weaken. Teachers spent less time on hard subjects, more on easy ones like the environment and the media. Worse, a new type of vague and cloudy subject was encouraged, such as consumer affairs, "values clarification," and death, to add to the already heavy extracurricular burden of learning to drive a car, not to take drugs, and how to pick an effective contraceptive. As Diane Ravitch wrote in the *New Republic* for April 18, 1981: "Uncertainty about what students should study reflected uncertainty about why they should study, and this self-doubt undermined the teachers' sense of purpose and authority. This confusion, quite understandable in a time of student unrest and societal permissiveness, made it increasingly difficult for teachers to impose demands on students, which in turn led to lower teacher expectations."

A difficulty for the traditionalists—those who would get back to basics—is the rigid, almost industrial system of quality control entailed by the standardized test and the standardized textbook. The deadening format of the multiple-choice question, so easy to prepare for, so simple for teachers, or machines, to correct, offers children almost no encouragement to puzzle problems out for themselves. It is surely responsible for the poor quality of writing that the colleges complain of. How strange that a country that puts such store by individual initiative should build its schools around a system of rote learning and exams that discourage thinking for oneself. This does reinforce certain typical American intellectual characteristics: determination to find answers to every question, a respect for individual facts, an impatience with ambiguities or shades of meaning. There is also a price to pay: a certain mental passivity, an unwillingness to question authority or ask why, a weakness at blending fact and opinion that comes out clearly in the poverty of students' writing.

That crutch of poor teaching, the textbook, is an equal villain. Since American schools are locally financed and controlled, the textbook is one of the few truly national elements in American schools. Without the textbook, indeed, it would be a mystery how this vast, diverse land produces five million high school graduates every year with broadly similar views of their country and the world. It is not exaggerating to say that the school textbook is an important instrument of national conformity and propaganda.

The term "textbook" does not do justice to the weight and range of standardized educational ordnance rained upon the schools by the publishing industry. Children in kindergarten learning to read do so with the help of "instructional material" put out by educational suppliers. Boys and girls learning to add or subtract fill in blanks on little sheets of printed sums purchased in bulk by their school board and copyrighted by Houghton Mifflin or Harcourt Brace. Their first efforts at written composition are done in printed booklets with photographs of "situations" on which the fledgling writer must comment. To spur the child on, there are questions, prompting written answers: "Why is the girl in the tree?" "What is the seal in the garage doing?" Once launched in its little coracle of "basic learning skills," the child voyages through an ever-thickening sea of educational material.

Textbooks and educational materials are a more than $1 billion industry. During the big school boom, the echo of the baby boom, they were the most dependable side of the book business. CBS, Raytheon, Litton, and Xerox entered the market, long dominated by a few well-known textbook publishers, such as Harcourt Brace, Houghton Mifflin, McGraw-Hill, and Ginn. More than twenty states, mainly in the South and West, adopt textbooks statewide. Marketing is a highly competitive business. "If you can sell your reading program to the city of Los Angeles," says a consultant for SRA, IBM's educational subsidiary, "you can make millions." In Prince Georges County, Maryland, the school district purchased an SRA English dictionary for every child in the school system. Considering the size of their markets, publishers tend to run for safety with a single bland product that will suit all trends, offend as few as possible. This is safer and more profitable than writing several lively textbooks. Committees write the texts and judge them before publication to make sure they have not offended some group or other. One result, complains a Houghton Mifflin editor, is textbooks quite as deadening and unchallenging as the upbeat, patriotic histories of the past. As Frances FitzGerald has shown, history textbooks supposedly written by distinguished historians continue to appear in new editions long after their deaths, in weak, ghosted prose, diluting their well-known views.

In concentrating on the uniformity of American schools, typified by the textbook and the standardized test, it is easy to miss the strong tradition of local control. American schools have never had a ministry of education to impose a single national pattern. They remain in important ways a patchwork. Local control is underpinned by the system of elected school boards and the financing of schools from local property taxes. This is manifestly unfair, although long tolerated in a country that thought it believed in equal schooling, since rich districts can afford good schools while poor districts cannot. It is also inefficient and against the broad national interest, since it means more is spent on the education of a dumb rich kid than on a bright poor one. Courts and legislatures, notably in California, have tried to reform the system, with only mixed results.

School districts, it is true, have had to give up some of their independence in exchange for money from their states or from the federal government. In the 1920s, more than four-fifths of the money for public schools was raised locally. Today less than half comes from local sources. Rather more than two-fifths comes from the states and just under 15 percent from the federal government. This has given the states—and to a lesser extent the federal government—more ways to nudge, cajole, or threaten recalcitrant school districts. In the Southern states, because of a traditional miserliness toward schools, especially black schools, modest amounts of federal aid quickly bulk large in total school spending. In many Southern districts, it is as high as 25 percent.

To the extent that anyone is in final charge—and in the United States, with its tradition of divided powers, that must always be doubtful—what control there is remains for all practical purposes with the locality. School boards, after all, can take the extreme step of closing their schools altogether. That happened in Prince Edward County, a tobacco-growing backwoods in the middle of southern Virginia, where men in white suits call one another "Judge." Rather than comply with orders to integrate its public schools, the county board, in 1959, simply shut them down. The courts only managed to get them open again five years later. White children went to hastily fixed-up private schools. The right-wing columnist James J. Kilpatrick sent several dozen books to help them out. Black children stayed at home. This was perhaps exceptional. Yet other school boards—North and South—find subtler ways of evading what to them is interference from Washington. Faced with unpopular school policies from afar, the locals will always cry "community control."

Schools in different parts go their own ways in less divisive matters than race. Spending per pupil varies considerably, from $1,300 a year in Mississippi or $1,500 a year in Alabama and Georgia to $2,400 a year in Oregon or Massachusetts. Teachers' salaries usually take up about three-fifths of a school budget and account for much of the difference. In Mississippi, teachers get about $11,500 a year, in Massachusetts, $17,000, although the gap is less than it was.

Bible Belt schools are still dimly persnickety about what children can't read. The public schools of Cambridge or Berkeley have a zest for experiment, by contrast, as one could expect from two liberal-minded university towns. New Mexico and Tennessee, neither of which have universities of the first rank, have two of the best high schools in the country, since the student body at the Los Alamos and Oak Ridge schools includes the children of scientists at the big government-run atomic plants.

Come who may is the nearly universal rule for American high schools, with some famous exceptions, such as the Bronx High School of Science and Stuyvesant High School in lower Manhattan. Both maintain strict entry requirements and for years have produced a stream of scientists, mathematicians, and doctors. The filmmaker Saul Landau remembers Stuyvesant: "There was a tough exam to get in. These were bright kids. They'd been told since the age of six months that they were going to be geniuses. They came to school with violin cases. By fourteen many of them knew more mathematics than the teachers. They'd give their own classes. The school had a 98 or 99 percent college yield. The kids were brilliant."

More striking than anything, though, are differences between rich and poor, black and white, within cities. Take Chicago, which has one of the most de facto segregated school systems in the country. Its high schools, strapped for money, are badly run, neglected, and violent. Yet just outside Chicago, in the prosperous lakeside suburb of Winnetka, is New Trier High School East, deservedly famous for its strong academic reputation. This excellence is not uncommon in the Midwest. Parkway West School in the suburbs of Saint Louis and Walnut Hills High School in Cincinnati have strong reputations. With less of a taste for private schools than Northeastern parents, the upper middle class in the Midwest have tended to spend more in property taxes for better public schools.

Perhaps all this is to say that lacking strong central direction, American schools tend to be unusually faithful mirrors of their immediate surroundings. From time to time, the Supreme Court tries to make them reflect broader views, although the Court is hardly the godless, unbelieving body one might suspect from its fundamentalist critics. In the rankling matters of religion and schools, the Court has usually trod with caution. The justices of 1925 came to the defense of parochial schools by agreeing with the Society of Sisters that children could not be obliged to attend public schools, but could go to church schools instead. The Court's ruling in 1963 banning prayer in public schools, prompted by the Baltimore nonbeliever Madalyn Murray O'Hair, whose children were mocked and who lost her job because of her campaign, aggrieved those who feel that the United States should declare itself to be a Christian country and prompted a campaign to have the ruling overturned by constitutional amendment.

The tradition of localism in American schools often means that teachers are under the thumb of the school board, the parents, and even the pupils. The Parent-Teacher Association—widely renamed the Home and School Association, as the older name seemed to exclude children—suggests the extraordinary degree to which consumer sovereignty prevails over the classroom. It follows that the producers, the teachers, are in an unusually weak position to do what teachers everywhere are supposed to do: stand up for a body of knowledge that they insist must be taught to each rising generation. Their lack of influence has caused Al Shanker of the American Federation of Teachers to complain: "Teachers are surrounded by parents who feel they could do as good a job teaching their children if they weren't too busy making more money." His irritation is understandable. Localism and democracy in the schools is closely bound up with a well-recognized strain of anti-intellectualism in American life; a refusal to defer, in education, to knowledge.

Just as outside the South there has never been much of an officer corps, and just as in a fiercely religious country there has never been much of a priesthood, so in a country that venerates schooling there has never been a caste of learned people whose word went unquestioned by outsiders. Along with a certain amount of mockery, teachers are, or rather were, loved, looked up to, idolized even, but not taken seriously or given professional respect. Until quite recently, grade school teaching was poorly paid even compared to white-collar clerical jobs, and widely denigrated as "women's work." The children are the losers. Intelligent young women once relegated to teaching are today going into the new higher-paying jobs that are opening up for them as accountants, lawyers, and doctors. This defection helps explain why only 6 percent of incoming university freshmen in 1979 planned to teach, compared to 25 percent in 1968. As enrollments decline, openings for teachers will diminish, too.

Even if schoolteachers were in a better position to tell parents what their children should be taught, they would still be faced with that strong American demand that what is taught be of obvious use. The requirement that knowledge be practical runs from top to bottom. Book learning is at a positive discount in public life. Take the last eight Presidents. Truman was hard to fool, Eisenhower a superior manager, Kennedy plausibly cultivated, Johnson preternaturally shrewd, Nixon capable of large as well as small thoughts, Ford genial, Carter a sponge for facts, and Reagan an uncanny public performer. Each of them had distinctive talents, but none of them is an example of a sound general education. Stevenson never got over being labeled an egghead. The general rule of thumb for politicians is to appear less bright than you are, a rule Kennedy broke. Sam Ervin, the chairman of the Senate's Watergate panel, was trained at Harvard Law School, but loved to pretend he was just a plain country lawyer. And for years one of Ronald Reagan's stock lines—he went to an obscure Midwestern college—was about the Yale Ph.D. who couldn't tie his shoes, which left lunches of

"Although often critical of the Church, [Erasmus] remained a faithful Catholic. Because Erasmus spread the new learning and sought a deeper and purer religious devotion he is regarded as a Christian humanist." The parents shot back: "How can a Christian be a humanist. . . . It is impossible to be a Christian humanist . . . if you embrace the humanist manifesto, you embrace that there is no God."

The Gablers are against history books that reveal the weaknesses in worthy historical figures. They want no books that fail to exalt family, patriotism, and work. Books dwelling on conflict between parents and children are out. Their list of "questionable writers" is frankly racist, including as it does the black writers Langston Hughes, Richard Wright, Dick Gregory, and Malcolm X. Lastly, books on pagan culture affront them, as do works "not on basic subjects."

Laughable as this is, it would be wrong to treat it as buffoonery that could easily be squelched. Local control remains a strong tradition and the Gablers are providing a service many school districts or state boards like. The courts are reluctant to interfere. In 1972, the Supreme Court refused to review an appeals court finding that the New York City school board was within its power in restricting student access to a disputed book, Piri Thomas's Down These Mean Streets. In 1979, a federal judge rejected the idea that there was a specially privileged "book tenure" for schoolbooks in public school libraries. "One of the principal functions of public education," he said, "is indoctrinative." And in the United States, the parents must have a say in what is indoctrinated. Academic freedom is usually thought of as protecting teachers from outside interference. For schools, many Americans subscribe to the upside-down definition offered by William F. Buckley, Jr., in God and Man at Yale: the freedom of men and women to supervise the educational activities and aims of the schools they oversee and support.

The lack of educational backbone in American schools, the bowing to consumer sovereignty, has broader consequences as well. The Gablers, after all, cater to a minority taste, although, like much of the New Right, they are quick to seize new techniques for spreading their gospel. Schools, though, quite generally are used to being pushed around for social purposes that have little directly to do with formal instruction. "Society has acquired," in Henry Steele Commager's words, "the habit of 'using' the schools to teach whatever society happens to be interested in"—whether this is citizenship, when immigrants come in; the dangers of communism, when the cold war calls; science, when the Russians are thought ahead; private enterprise, when the welfare state threatens; or Christianity, when the Supreme Court will not require that it be taught.

This vulnerability of the schools arises partly because, with good reason, Americans are not ready to give sharp answers to the question of what their schools are for. Should they be frankly elitist, the way many European school systems are, with different tracks for academic and vocational education? Or should they stick to the ideal of offering equal opportunity for all? Should they have a strong academic syllabus? Or should they teach children more directly to prepare for life in American society? Should they be aiming at producing the next generation of technicians and skilled white-collar workers, or should resources be spread more evenly, using schools to overcome many inequalities in American society?

Answers to such questions would be hard to find even if there were a ministry of education to give single answers fitting the whole American patchwork. For Americans do not really want to find answers to such questions. It would impose too many awkward choices. They prefer a compromise that enables them to cling to the ideal of opportunity in schools for all, while maintaining, in practice, to the most casual eye, a plainly elitist system; they prefer not to maintain separate academic and vocational schools, although the single, consolidated high school has a heavy load of nonacademic subjects to pad out the school day, including driver education and cheerleading; they prefer to mount bold crusades to integrate their schools, while tolerating, in actuality, a still stark division of black and white schools.

Schools were both the great liberal hope and its great disappointment in the 1960s. It seemed so right then to expect that greater equality and social peace could be had by changing the schools. The roots of poverty and racism, it was recognized, ran deep, and what better radical solution, to the individualist American mind, was there than to start with the human raw material, the children? The public schools had always had social and political jobs to do besides instructing children. They Americanized generations of immigrants. They were a ladder of social advancement. They were a safety valve, insurance against the formation of rigid class lines. If, in practice, they had been allowed to become divisive, black from white, city from suburb, country from town, then this could be corrected with imaginative use of federal money.

Lyndon Johnson knew the schools could be a social ladder. He had taught, if briefly, in the country and in Houston's high schools, and organized the teachers there. Without some schooling he would not have made it from the Pedernales to Washington, not been noticed by his rich Texas backers or by Roosevelt's circle. Johnson cared about the public schools, and the Elementary and Secondary Education Act of 1965 was the fruit. This was the first of the Great Society programs. It was, in many ways—the speed of its passage in Congress, the personal interest of the President—the purest of Johnson's social triumphs. The act was the first large federal support for education since an ex-Vermont storekeeper, Senator Justin Morrill, persuaded Congress to part with millions of acres of public lands for the founding of agricultural and technical colleges. It was the first big injection of federal money—$1.3 billion—into the public schools ever. The money was to go to remedial schooling for children from needy families.

There were problems. Could children at parochial schools benefit? Kennedy, a Catholic, had dodged that. Johnson, a member of the Disciples of Christ, had no inhibitions. What would the courts say, he asked his lawyers, if money went to Catholic pupils? Would that violate separation of church and state? So long as Catholic schools did not directly receive the money, the courts would approve. Catholic children, Johnson ruled, should benefit, too. Congress, to general surprise, agreed. That black bon vivant Congressman Adam Clayton Powell bottled up the bill in committee. He wanted the House leadership to vote his committee housekeeping expenses they were holding back on. Johnson was furious at the delay. Give Powell his expenses, he told the leadership, and get on with it. The bill was out of committee by the week's end. There were complaints. Too little money was being spent; the federal funds were tied to state spending, so that the worst areas, such as the South, would get least; still, it was a start, and liberal backers of Kennedy—John Kenneth Galbraith, John Gardner, Wilbur Cohen—thought it a triumph. Johnson insisted the signing be at the broken-down Texas schoolhouse where he had gone to school. His seventy-two-year-old teacher was hauled back from retirement in Rough and Ready, California, to be there.

Federal spending on education more than doubled between 1963 and 1967, from less than $6 billion to $12 billion. At the same time, school revenues climbed as property tax revenues rose in the economic boom. For a time, money seemed no obstacle to reform. Not that money was everything. When many of the gains made by youngsters helped by the 1965 Head Start program seemed to wash out as they grew to the age of nine or ten, more selective programs, such as Follow Through, were introduced. The tide of educational reform continued into the 1970s. In 1975, Congress allotted money to schools so that handicapped children could be taught in the same classrooms as ordinary children, the less to feel excluded. And bilingual teaching was required where children spoke Spanish, a drift toward biculturalism later to be resisted by the Reagan administration.

As for the stark division in American schools of black and white, the record was most mixed. In 1954, the year of the Supreme Court's *Brown* decision against segregated schools, all but one of the twenty largest cities had a white majority in the public schools. Today, seventeen of the top twenty have nonwhite majorities. It stood to reason in the 1950s and 1960s that, first in the South and then in the North, the public schools should be treated as future solvents of racial barriers. Southern schools, segregated in law, were at the time of *Brown* not only separate but unequal. Three times as much was spent per pupil in white schools in the South as in black schools. In the Deep South, it was five times as much. In the North, schools were segregated as well, although this fact, plain to anyone who looked, had to be demonstrated by researchers such as Kenneth Clark, who found that in the mid-1950s the New York City school system was not keeping an ethnic census of the public schools. What had worked, according to educational legend, for the European immigrants could be made to work again in the public schools for blacks. That schools alone could not bear the burden of the change required, and that there would be resistance from whites as well as from blacks, for whom integration would mean struggle, didn't then seem to be serious obstacles.

Nearly thirty years later, it appears that where integration has been tried, it has both worked and not worked. It has worked because the segregationist's darkest visions were shown to be baseless, not worked because the integrationist's greatest hopes of what could be done with the schools alone has not, could not, be realized. In many of the large cities, North and South, segregated schools continue to exist, by design or neglect. New York, Los Angeles, and Chicago have as divided school systems as any in the nation. Busing, the solution reluctantly arrived at by exasperated courts, has also worked and not worked. In cities like Charlotte or Wilmington, black and white agree the record is good. Elsewhere busing failed because of white obstruction and because black parents, in the words of Roy Innis, CORE's director, were "tired of being guinea pigs." In Atlanta by 1973, white flight to the suburbs to avoid school busing was so strong and the Nixon administration's support for busing so weak that black politicians and parents agreed with whites to reduce busing for desegregation in return for increasing the number of black officials in the school system, even though the national headquarters of the NAACP in New York strongly disapproved.

What does the record show? Black children now spend almost as much time in school as white children. Half the white children born between 1918 and 1922 were likely to reach twelfth grade, whereas half the blacks born in those years would only reach ninth grade. That gap all but closed for their children. For whites born between 1933 and 1937, the median grade completed was between twelve and thirteen, in other words, the first year of college. For blacks of the same ages, the median grade was twelve. For children since, the gap has continued to narrow. Are they learning as much as each other? No, but again the gap is narrowing, if more slowly. While 90 percent of white children born between 1948 and 1952 graduated from high school, only 80 percent of blacks of the same ages graduated. This is because black pupils tend to "repeat" grades—that is, fail promotion from one grade to the next as their age group moves up—more than white students. In 1976, for example, 11 percent of whites but 20 percent of black seventeen-year-olds were enrolled in the eleventh grade, a year behind most seventeen-year-olds. These apparently encouraging figures, though, mask the fact that graduation alone is no measure of how much pupils have learned at school. The fact remains that graduation rates aside, blacks remain, overall, woefully behind.

The large decline in the dropout rate among black high school students is progress, very encouraging progress, but it may be costly. Unexpectedly, perversely, increasing school attendance by black youngsters has coincided with a dramatic fall in their participation in the labor force and with growing rates of unemployment for young blacks leaving school and looking for work. The gap between these black youngsters and their white contemporaries has grown. This raises the question: Are poor black Americans losing in the job market what they have gained in extra years of schooling? And if so, what really have the extra years of school done for them? As schooling is prolonged, so black youths get less work experience. In the words of the social scientist Robert Mare: "When race differences in school attendance were wider, blacks suffered from poorer educational credentials, but were partly compensated by their earlier entry into the labor market." As Mare sees it, now that black and white enter the job market at roughly the same time, though not necessarily with equal credentials, the old advantage blacks used to have of an early start has been eliminated. If schooling is looked at chiefly as a preparation for work, then more education for young blacks may be by itself a delusion. And anyway, for the time being, blacks have gone just about as far as they can go in the schools.

Three decades after *Brown*, the question is not how much more progress can be made on race in the schools. Nothing stands still. A reaction has set in. The struggle, instead, is to prevent a sliding back. For despite efforts by black and white to get more integrated schools, despite the success, in some cities, of busing, despite advances for the black middle class, who more and more are turning to private, particularly parochial schools, despite all these things, American schools are still sharply divided by race. There are signs that as middle-class blacks move out of the central cities some of the suburban schools will become more integrated, but it is a small movement that conveys naught for the comfort of the city schools. As well as being overwhelmingly black, they stand to lose their leavening of black pupils from middle-class homes and to become overwhelmingly poor as well.

The losers are Democratic liberals of the Truman-Kennedy-Johnson-Humphrey-Mondale vein. The public schools, as much as Vietnam, were the rock on which the old Roosevelt coalition, which kept this political tradition strong after 1932 in Congress, foundered. So long as the push for integrated schools stayed in the South—which it pretty well did until a decade and a half ago—the fault lines dividing working Americans, black and white, in the North did not really matter. But there is another saying: "In the South, they don't care how close blacks get as long as they don't rise too high; in the North, they don't care how high the blacks rise, as long as they don't get too close." Once white Americans in the North were called on to end segregation, benevolence went, among those wearing white as well as blue collars.

In the autumn of 1968, a long-rankling dispute between black community leaders in Brooklyn and the New York teachers' union broke open. At immediate stake were jobs for seventy-nine teachers the insurgent local school board wanted suspended. The quarrel was much broader than that. Nine of ten New York teachers were white. Many were Jewish. The Ocean Hill–Brownsville school district, where the trouble centered, was heavily black. The issue was tinted "racial" from the start. Black politicians called the teachers racist; the teachers called the black leaders anti-Semitic. Before Ocean Hill–Brownsville was settled, Albert Shanker, the union leader, had taken his teachers out on strike three times. Long after the immediate quarrel was forgotten, Ocean Hill–Brownsville would be remembered as a poisoning of old alliances between blacks and Jews in heavily Democratic New York.

Pontiac, Michigan, is where the General Motors Truck and Coach plant makes most of the nation's yellow school buses. This workaday industrial suburb was the scene for the earliest and most virulent antibusing protests as courts began to order school busing for desegregation in the North. On August 30, 1971, a group of Pontiac incendiaries torched ten school buses. The full-chested, T-shirt-wearing Irene McCabe organized a Pontiac–Washington protest march. The following May, George Wallace won the Michigan Democratic primary outright, in a crowded field, with 51 percent of the vote.

White, working-class Boston resented the liberals of Cambridge and Beacon Hill who preached integration and sent their children to private schools. Boston's school war was another classic example of how in America race can still be made to divide more than class unites. Certainly, white Americans are unlikely to rally spontaneously soon for further attempts to bring poor black or Hispanic schoolchildren into the American mainstream. As Scott Thompson, the director of the National Association of Secondary School Principals, coldly put it: "The theme of the 1980s is quality, not equality." Whether he intends it or not, such comments are seen by many better-off whites as code words they can applaud. The country, too many think, cannot afford to bring the poor, black, inner-city schools up to the standards of suburban white schools and surely not up to those of the private schools. Busing for the purpose of integration is considered abominable. So they have concluded, implicitly, that the country may as well settle for the affordable status quo: good schools for those who can pay for them, not-so-good schools for those who cannot.

10

THE KNOWLEDGE-INDUSTRIAL COMPLEX
Universities and the Arts

AT THE PEAK of the educational and scientific pyramid, where research and development is carried on, the inability of the United States to afford to do everything is officially conceded. Not because the country has fallen behind. Rather, because other countries have caught up as the comparatively sedate pace of growth in its mature economy has halved America's share of the world's gross national product, during the past thirty years. Even so, the American scientific establishment gulped when it was told by George Keyworth, President Reagan's chief science adviser, that it would have to accept this truth. Keyworth, a no-nonsense nuclear weapons physicist and a friend of Edward Teller, father of the H-bomb, was speaking at a dinner in June 1981 sponsored by the American Association for the Advancement of Science (AAAS) before his confirmation hearings in the Senate. His audience confidently assumed he would play it safe with a tub-thumper of the America-is-number-one sort. Instead, he told them: "It is no longer within our economic capability, nor perhaps even desirable, to aspire for primacy across the spectrum of scientific disciplines. Undoubtedly, our country has relinquished its preeminence in some scientific fields, while others are strongly threatened through efforts in Europe, Japan, or the Soviet Union." Keyworth saw no alternative to more "stringent and fundamental criteria" in distributing the federal government's R & D largesse, with a stress on "excellence" and "pertinence to national requirements."

This illusion shatterer was immediately recognized as a U-turn in the nation's official science policy by Allan Bromley, the Yale physicist, a former teacher of Keyworth and the president of the AAAS. Whereas all previous administrations since World War II had, he said, taken the position that the United States ought to be "first in all the fields in which we are active," the Keyworth address represented "the first time it has been stated publicly that this goal is no longer within our economic capability." Lesser scientists were ready to scold the new boss of the White House's Office of Science and Technology Policy for letting the country down with a speech that officially limited America's scientific ambitions. Bromley had no patience with escapists or those who put public relations before candor. "Dr. Keyworth," he said, "is stating what is increasingly a fact."

The change the Keyworth doctrine requires in the outlook of American scientists is, nonetheless, considerable. In the first thirty years of this century, they were not taken seriously, as is seen in the hold Europeans had on Nobel Prizes for science. Between 1900 and 1930, only three Americans were among the 29 Nobel Prize winners for physiology and medicine. All three of them were foreign-born: Alexis Carrel in France, Otto Meyerhof in Germany, and Karl Landsteiner in Austria. During the same three decades at the start of this century, only one of the 28 winners of Nobel Prizes for chemistry was American and only one out of 36 for physics. In the thirty years 1950 to 1980, the roles were reversed. The United States provided the greatest share of Nobel Prize winners in the following disciplines: 45 out of 73 in physiology and medicine, 17 out of 47 in chemistry and 36 out of 64 in physics. Of this thirty-year total of 98 American winners of Nobel Prizes for scientific subjects, 72 were American-born. In 1981, American scientists carried off six Nobel Prizes, if economics is included. The triumph was double-edged. For it was not clear to many in the research community that America would in future be as ready to pay the costs of coming first in every field.

Nobel laureates are the star performers in the American university system. If scientific excellence at the top is one of its two hallmarks, breadth of access at the bottom for a very wide range of students is the other. This, too, has to be paid for by someone. A withering of support for imaginative schemes like the Pell grants for university study and the guaranteed student loans program was coldly summed up by David Stockman, Reagan's budget director, when he said that anybody who wanted to go to college strongly enough would always find the money to pay for courses. That attitude appalls the universities. Jack Peltason, the president of the American Council on Education, the university lobby in Washington, spoke for many when he warned that the expansion of the universities since the Second World War had been an effective social safety valve and that it would be folly now to choke it off.

The American university system finds room today for somewhere between eleven million and twelve million students, rather more than the entire population of, say, Hungary, and only slightly less than Australia's. Western Europe's universities—from which Americans grafted long ago to create a prodigious hybrid all their own—come nowhere near to matching this effort. The French, who like a quick brain, send to college less than half as many per head of population as the Americans. Cram their universities as they may, the Italians fit in less than a million. The West Germans and the British open the educational citadel an even smaller crack. Proportionally, a third as many of their youngsters get to college as do students from American high schools.

Looking from the top down, people ask if in America more means less. The too hasty answer is Yes. The American university average is low. But atop the educational pyramid are universities second to none. From the bottom up, of course, the view is different. So is the question. Is the American university, like the school, as open and permissive as it looks? Is the difference in numbers between Europe and America another example of a tired, class-divided continent and a fresh, equalitarian new land? Up to a point, yes, but more emphatically, no. As accessible as the system is, the best American universities are highly selective and competitive. The plums are no longer reserved for the privileged, it is true, but they are still available only for a few.

Americans take justified pride in the breadth of their higher education even if this means putting up with foreigners who sniff at its shallowness. Outsiders love to mock its obsessive extracurricularism. And who can blame them? There is so much good material. Americans, besides, do their own mocking, whether in *Horse Feathers* in the thirties or *Animal House* in the seventies. Marshall McLuhan wasn't thinking of a half century's fads that gripped colleges, but he might have been, when he said that "children go to school to interrupt their education."

As for the football college or the fraternities and sororities, even Europeans weary of the caricatures, for this is what they are, and one-sided, too. European students do not spend every hour in the library. For sheer lolling about, it is difficult to beat the Oxford undergraduate. As to goofing off, the big difference seems to be that Americans have more toys and energy to do it with. And when it comes to window breaking or harpsichord smashing, Waugh's Paul Pennyfeather, from *Decline and Fall*, would think John "Buffalo" Blutarsky of *Animal House* a pathetic amateur next to any member of the Oxford Bollinger Club.

If judging American universities out of the classroom is a cheap shot, scoring solid points off what goes on—or does not go on—in the class is not easy, either. Not that this is not widely tried. Among foreigners, the British in particular treat the elaborate, continual grading system as a crude form of industrial quality control. Why students slavishly accept their lecturers' words with copious notes is beyond these critics. The textbook, they tend to think, is its own education in how not to think for oneself. And they feel that the excessively competitive system of marking encourages the notion that what matters is less mastering a subject than knowing more about it than the next student, which may be not very much.

Just, all of this, but also wrong. Unlike Britain and the rest of Europe, where university teaching tends to favor the bright, in American universities, except at the top, teaching is geared to the average. Just as most bright children are held back by the slow pace of American high schools, so are smart undergraduates at the average college. The best are given their heads at graduate school. Miss this and one misunderstands the American college enterprise altogether.

Not grasping it leads one to compare unlike with like—Oxford, Mississippi, with Oxford, England, rather than the two Cambridges with each other. An English friend made this mistake during a year spent at the University of Iowa Writer's Workshop. Among his duties was a course for undergraduates in nineteenth-century English literature. As an assignment he asked his class to read the first few parts of Wordsworth's *The Prelude* and to recount the main incidents in their own words. The results, neither very good nor very bad, contained some gems of innocent misunderstanding. The crag that looms up and scares the young poet during his ride on the lake in a borrowed boat appeared in one of the student's reports as "a monster, like Loch Ness." Another had gathered that during his time at Cambridge, "Wordsworth went hiking in the Lake District with his buddy, Milton." These and others were cobbled together into a piece of not kind humor in the London *Sunday Times*, deriding the poor schooling of the students in Iowa. The author made the mistake of showing a clipping of this piece to friends in New York, who did not think it was funny at all. Why pick on the average, they felt, when the best was next door at Columbia, Princeton, or Harvard? And could not an American find just as much to tease about, if so inclined, with a bunch of average English nineteen-year-olds?

Among the 2,500 institutions of higher learning in the United States there is so much variety that even astute Americans find it difficult avoiding such traps. Labeling and pigeonholing them all would take the patience of a botanist, although the Carnegie Foundation has come up with its admittedly rough-and-ready *Classification*. At the peak is the "Research University, I." This is the archetype, today's cathedral of learning, an unequaled factory, bourse, bank, and distribution chain of knowledge. Carnegie lists twenty-nine public and twenty-two private. Those ranked among the best today—the University of California at Berkeley, Chicago, Harvard, Illinois, Michigan, Princeton, Stanford, Wisconsin, and Yale—were, barring Illinois and Stanford, among the best when ranking studies were done in 1925. Each typically has several thousand students, if not tens of thousands of them, graduate and undergraduate; produces at least fifty new Ph.D.s a year; receives several million tax dollars for scientific or medical research; boasts a library that puts most national collections to shame; subsidizes scholarly books on its own press; runs schools of law, medicine, engineering, and business for aspiring professionals; and plays stepparent to a small host of semi-independent research institutes.

By no means all universities Carnegie puts in the category "Research University, I" are equals of the top ten or fifteen, although some, like Ohio State at Columbus, with fifty thousand students, are larger and some, like the University of Texas at Austin, are richer. Many specialize, like Texas A & M, famous for agricultural research. Riches do not necessarily bring prestige. The Permian basin oil field which it owns makes the University of Texas richer than Harvard, but it has yet to get an academic reputation to match the endowment.

At this level, the differences between public and private are lessening fast. Harvard and Yale have their clubs and so does Princeton, but snobberies of class or caste are weakening. The poet Karl Shapiro probably would not have written of the university today: "To hurt the Negro and avoid the Jew/is the curriculum/within the precincts of this world/poise is a club." More tangibly, costs are beginning to squeeze here, as they are at the Nobel Prize–winning peaks of R & D. Even where they are supposedly free, most tax-supported public universities have resorted to fees which are thinly disguised tuition charges. Private universities, in turn, have come to depend much more than before on public funds; much less on foundation gifts and endowment income. After World War II, the scale of the university enterprise grew so fast, the foundations could not keep up, important as Carnegie, Ford, Peabody, Duke, and other funds were. University endowments took a beating from inflation and the generally poor performance of the economy in the 1970s, reflected in a go-nowhere stock market. Many of them regretted following McGeorge Bundy's lead during his tenure as head of the Ford Foundation and diversifying into growth stocks; although as the bond market fell, they may have felt their decision to move out of bonds not so bad after all. University endowments actually fell by more than a quarter between 1972, when they were $16.2 billion, and 1974. By 1979, they had recovered to $18.3 billion, a real drop over seven years, considering the weakening of the purchasing power of the dollar. Public support for private universities continues to come either directly as research money or indirectly from fee-paying students on government loans and grants. Harvard, for example, traces about a quarter of its revenue to public sources, Princeton a third.

Trustees of private universities and regents of public ones tend, predictably, to be solid men or women from business or the law, with "a general upper-middle-class allergy to trouble of whatever sort," as Christopher Jencks and David Riesman put it in their monumental study of the modern university, *The Academic Revolution*. Regents, pressed by state legislators, sometimes feel they must make a public show of interference. California and Texas during the McCarthy period come to mind. Private trustees can be more discreet. Stories of interference like that of the University of Texas regents in the appointment of a new law school dean are rare because meddling of this kind is seldom that blatant.

Being the best, both public and private universities of the top rank tend to be choosy about whom they admit. Many state university systems are required by law to take all comers. And they do, at least from within the state. But not everyone goes to the main campus. To contain the wave of students from the postwar baby boom generation, as California's planners saw their job, a master plan was devised in 1960. All but the top 12.5 percent of applicants were initially barred from the four-year universities, all but the top 33 percent from state colleges, and the bottom two-thirds were shunted off to two-year community colleges. California's master plan was widely copied by other state universities.

Private universities, by contrast, have had to give up some of their freedom to turn away students at will, now that a poor national economy has squeezed their income and inflation increased mightily their costs. Those getting federal funds—and almost all the large ones now do, in huge amounts—must not discriminate against women, blacks, or applicants from other, underrepresented racial minorities.

Working down the educational pyramid, Carnegie lists "Research Universities, II" and "Doctorate Granting Universities, I" and "Doctorate Granting Universities, II." All these have graduate programs, do some research, and get federal grants. They number, together, about 130 universities. This group includes state universities in less populous states, like Virginia, founded by Jefferson; the best regional campuses of large state universities; smaller research universities, like Carnegie-Mellon in Pittsburgh or Georgetown in Washington, with its well-known right-wing think tank. In this category, too, are some of the larger, better-known denominational universities, such as Notre Dame or Marquette, both Catholic, Southern Methodist University in Dallas, and Brigham Young in Mormon Utah.

Below this level, the higher-education pyramid broadens out quickly. There follow roughly six hundred institutions that offer some graduate programs and a broad range of courses, but do little research and have no professional schools of their own. Below these in size, but not necessarily in prestige, are the liberal arts colleges, another six hundred of them. These are the university stripped to what many still think ought to be its main job—teaching undergraduates. Among them are some of the best schools in the country: Amherst, Swarthmore, and the "Seven Sisters"—Radcliffe, Barnard, Bryn Mawr, Vassar, Smith, Wellesley, and Mount Holyoke. These "Seven Sisters" used to be strictly women's colleges, although the first three long shared classes with Harvard, Columbia, and Haverford, respectively. All but the last two are now coeducational at some level. Lastly, there are more than 1,100 two-year colleges, community colleges, or junior colleges, the lowest layer of the higher-educational pyramid.

This dazzling structure has just been compared with a pyramid. And in a lifeless way, this is right, although it can also mislead the observer, since big institutions at the top may not be as good as smaller ones further down. To the high school student wondering where to go to college, though, the system shows a different face. The student has many more places to apply to than his or her counterpart in Europe. Guidebooks to college choices can be thicker than the Houston yellow pages. Americans can, quite literally, shop around. More than a pyramid, perhaps, the system, in real life, is like a shopping center—with Neiman-Marcuses, Sears, Roebucks, and Woolworths offering a similar range of products, but cheaper and of lower quality at each step, while all about there are smaller specialty stores, again of different cost and quality.

At first glance, American universities do seem to offer as much diversity as the most ardent pluralist could want. Whenever proposals for a national university have come up—George Washington would have liked one—the established universities have knocked the idea promptly on the head. The largest universities are all now not only nondenominational, to all intents and purposes, but interfaith. Yet there are also religious colleges—Catholic, Protestant, and Jewish. Every region of the country has at least one large "multiversity," often several, though the best are still concentrated on either coast or around the Great Lakes. New England is almost as dense with private universities as it is with private prep schools. Perhaps for this reason it has not produced a public university of the first rank. Southerners, until quite recently, tended to stick to their own colleges, even though they had none to match those outside. When sons of wealthy Southerners were sent North, they tended to go to Presbyterian Princeton, whose most famous president, Woodrow Wilson, was himself a Southerner. This provincialism is perhaps the beginnings of an explanation why, novels aside, the South, excluding Texas, has contributed so little to the modern intellectual life—let alone the scientific life—of the country. There is a magnificent exception. Between 1933 and 1956, North Carolina did make a home for Black Mountain College, a center of modernism in writing and the arts whose influence under the poet Charles Olson and the painter Josef Albers was deep and wide. In the Midwest, a strong booster tradition, a lucky combination of interested farmers or professionals and enlightened businessmen, helped create support for public universities, like Wisconsin's at Madison or Michigan's at Ann Arbor, which tended to outshine the private ones, even after the arrival of Chicago, a relative latecomer, founded with Rockefeller money in 1890. The public universities were normally expected to do something useful in return for the support they got from the state, and so have tended to specialize in areas of commercial interest. Indiana University, for example, is strong on engineering, no surprise, perhaps, in the state that holds the Indianapolis 500 every Memorial Day weekend, and is the engineering hub of the country.

At the top, at least, though, regional flavors are being blended away. Teachers go where the jobs are. Theirs is a *patrie de métier*, a loyalty to their profession, or rather subspecialty. In academic jobs there is now a national market. Indeed, it is one of the less noticed features of this extraordinary, polycentric network of academic labor that its practitioners are fully dispersed at hundreds of universities across the land—and often on other continents in the English-speaking world as well—out of sight and daily contact with one another, yet tightly linked into a common whole by scholarly journals, professional ratings, and jobs listings. The Austin scholar working on a new edition of *Don Juan* can cuttingly review a book of Byron criticism by a co-worker several thousand miles away in Seattle, whom he has never met and whose resentful or avenging gaze he will not have to turn away from as they meet between lectures or in the faculty dining room. For such a scattered profession, the annual meetings of the various academic associations take on special importance. These have become glorified job fairs, known as slave marts, where the traffic is less in ideas than in hot graduate prospects. There is probably less difference now among regions than between different universities within regions. "Parachute me into any one of ninety law schools," says Paul Brest, a professor at Stanford Law School, "and I'd have a difficult time figuring out which one I was in." The University of Wisconsin at Madison is more like the University of North Carolina at Chapel Hill than either is like lesser universities in its own state. Localism, it is true, increases as one moves down the higher-education pyramid. The share of undergraduates who go to college in their own state did not change much between 1934 and 1968, according to Jencks and Riesman, but remained at 85–90 percent. Yet when it comes to graduate education—and a prestigious graduate degree is what every ambitious would-be professional needs to have—local loyalties fade away. By the late 1960s, the share of graduate students studying in their own states had already fallen to half. At the top, then, for the elite, there is a national university system whose parts grow more and more alike. Diversity, more and more, is for the second-best.

The most striking feature of the whole system is its flexibility, at least on the upswing. To meet extra demand, universities expand at astonishing speed, an advantage of space which is lacking in Europe. When the Italians, for example, increased their university population quickly in the 1960s, tens of thousands of new students were crammed into a few existing universities, with explosive results. Americans spread the new students thinner. That diffusion is one reason the student movement in the United States was so much weaker than elsewhere.

Rapid expansion would not be possible if older universities blocked the way. But they do not. Harvard, Yale, and the rest of the oldest colleges never seriously tried to keep a monopoly on sound higher education. In a growing country, it would never have worked. Almost anyone can found a university. No charters or congressional permissions are needed. The system was expansionist from early on. Congress granted each new Western state two townships for a university. Then came the land grant colleges. Today state universities have coped with extra demand by the imperial expedient of setting up regional campuses as little colonies.

For planners in government or business, the enormous merit of the system is that it absorbs new students so easily. And unlike Topsy, who just growed, the system was planned. At the end of World War II, there were less than 2 million Americans at college. Thanks largely to the GI Bill, this rose 20 percent in three years. The main purpose of the bill was to hold homecoming GI's off the labor market during a widely feared second depression. "The bill was conceived primarily as an unemployment program," according to Carol Frances, who works at the American Council on Education and is one of the leading experts on university economics.

The returning GI's were as nothing to the children they fathered in the postwar baby boom. In 1947, George Zook, a university planner, reported to President Truman that further growth would be needed to contain the baby boom, provide a social safety valve, and train a new generation of white-collar workers. States began preparing master plans. And by the 1960s, when the oldest of the baby boom children began reaching college age, the system was ready to take them in. The university population shot up from 3.5 million in 1960 to 8 million in 1970 and 11 million by 1975. In that second decade, economic growth slowed down. Jobs were harder to come by. University expansion helped keep youth unemployment lower than it might have been.

The big expansion was at the lower levels of the educational pyramid. In 1975, 4 million of the 11 million were in two-year colleges, and of these only 2.5 million were studying for degrees. Much of the increase, accordingly, was financed at the state level. But in 1972, Congress voted money for Basic Educational Opportunity Grants, providing money for students to pay tuition. This was, in a sense, a massive, imaginative, concealed public welfare program, all conducted with typical American indirection under the pretense that it was strictly for education. Imaginative as it was, this expansion of college places brought its own problems. If reaching college is for the young middle-class American an expectation, not an aspiration, so is a solid, middle-class job. But these are not as easily provided as a college education. And the expansion of university places risks breeding intense frustration. Colleges, to use Erving Goffman's term, have to "cool out" students who are not going to get jobs to match their hopes. The huge expansion of higher education in the last two decades has done much less than meets the eye to increase equality.

In a country where anti-intellectualism among businessmen and politicians is never far beneath the surface, there is a present danger that the humanities will lose most in the educational cost squeeze. That danger will be much increased if the "pertinence to national requirements" test that George Keyworth has advocated for science spreads to other disciplines. For such cost-benefit analyses are always biased against the humanities, since it is even harder to measure the importance, say, of a better understanding of history or philosophy to the well-being of the nation than the importance of the redwoods in California, wolves in Minnesota, or oxygen in the Rappahannock River. Universities barking for customers in today's buyers' market try to sell would-be students on the occupational not the educational value of the courses they offer. Take this full-page mid-1981 advertisement in the *New York Times:* in 72-point letters, it shrieked: "Why our students have an advantage over those at certain extremely expensive universities." It went on, in smaller print: "All great universities promise to make their students fluent in liberal arts. But the liberal arts graduate who doesn't know how to make a living in the real world is not a happy person. Neither are the parents who had to foot the bill ($25,000–$40,000). The mission at the University of Bridgeport is to prevent this kind of casualty." In a box below: "Some chilling facts you should know," including the calculation that between 1978 and 1990, some 13.5 million college graduates would be competing for 10.2 million suitable openings, the rest competing for whatever jobs they could get. The message is obvious: In this race, do not get caught with a degree in Byzantine history or Dutch literature. Defense of the humanities has been made more difficult by well-meaning exaggeration. Thus Irving Kristol in 1968, prematurely, wrote: "Liberal education . . . no longer survives on the American campus." A similar tendency for overstatement crops up in the studies that worthy bodies undertake into the subject in the United States every eight or ten years.

You cannot help sympathizing with the members of these blue-ribbon panels and their rapporteurs. The feeling they show to their subject recalls what Henry James had the governess tell Maisie in the museum: "It must do us good, it's all so hideous." There is an audible gritting of teeth, a sound of weary girding against the great philistine public, whether this is lurking as business-minded university trustees, profit-oriented textbook publishers, or yahoo state legislators. There is no zest for learning, pride in scholarship, or justified boasting of accomplishments, although there could and should be. The tone is anxious, apologetic, troubled. Take a recent sample, *The Rockefeller Report on the Humanities in American Life.* It is possible to plow through its 170 pages of thick prose without once learning what the humanities are.

The very term is made to suggest something recondite, even alien. Here is how the worthy commission summed up "humanities":

"The essence of the humanities is a spirit or an attitude [multiple-choice thinking, there] toward humanity. They show how the individual is autonomous and at the same time bound, in the ligatures of language and history, to humankind across time and throughout the world."

Since the men and women who produce this stuff are intelligent and cultivated people, it is a puzzle, unless one realizes that such reports are elaborate exercises in grantsmanship—that is, appeals for money. For apart from university professors, their assistants, their students, and a very small public, few Americans are presumed to care at all widely about the products of scholarship. There is not a wide audience for serious criticism of the arts. The moderately demanding *New York Review of Books* has a fortnightly circulation of some 125,000, the leading literary monthlies and quarterlies not much more put together. For all its airs, public television seldom rises above the level of breezily intelligent midcult.

Such observations are less snobbish and obnoxious than they sound. American middle-class culture is certainly no more philistine than its German or British equivalent. Considering only the prodigious scope of cultural consumption in the United States, with an orchestra and art gallery in almost every large city, it may arguably be less so. Yet in such a huge and diverse cultural market—with so many competing points of sale—the hawkers of scholarly wares have to shout the louder to be heard. Unlike France, and to a lesser extent Britain, the United States has no cultural capital that is also a university, government, and commercial center. The humanities lobby, in other words, is spread wide, but thin. Looking narrowly at the East Coast alone, there are the brains in Cambridge, the intellectuals, artists, and cultural entrepreneurs in New York, and interested officials and politicians in Washington.

So there is a constant problem of how to maintain public support for academic or cultural pursuits that are dimly understood and felt to be of doubtful use. In asking for money, then, the last thing academics should do is let on that they enjoy their subjects or think them valuable for their own sake. For why would businessmen and politicians cough up for a recreation?

Hence the need to show, as obscurely as possible, that the humanities matter, that they do you good, and that although they are by their nature international, they do good by America. Much has to be made of methods and mechanics of distributing the humanities, although this in turn may be a blind. Academic complaints about the poor state of learning among students need to be taken cautiously. They are rather like farmers, in reverse. Farmers complain that the subsidy for their own particular crop is too low at the same time as they praise free enterprise and attack government handouts for others. So good academics bemoan the supposedly poor level of liberal education and rededicate themselves to the mission of teaching, while complaining of their weekly teaching load, which leaves them no time for research.

There is less cause for alarm if what is looked at is not the process but the product. American history has come of age. For a young scholar, this must be one of the most exciting fields to enter. There is far less interest than there was in the "high-sounding dramas of kings and princes"—or in presidents and senators, their republican equivalents—and much more in the lives of ordinary Americans. A new generation of social historians is unearthing what can be known about the American family, about men and women, about work, the workplace, and unions, about attitudes to sex or death, about reading habits, and about Americans at play. Economic history flourishes as a subspecialty. "Cliometricians" put computers to work for historians. Revisionists and antirevisionists argue about the drift—aggressive or defensive —of modern American foreign policy. There is a strong new school of Marxist historians as well. American history is freeing itself from the patriotic, nation-building history of the past. Its practitioners, coming of age since Hiroshima and Vietnam, are more critical and detached, less convinced of the inevitable rightness of the American mission. Without such historians, it is impossible for a country to acquire a past.

In philosophy, it is necessary respectfully to disagree with George Steiner, who told a symposium at Skidmore College in the spring of 1980 that American philosophy had been "thin stuff." Had that been said in the 1920s, it might have got a small hearing. Today it is a grotesque misjudgment. Alonzo Church, W. v. O. Quine, and later Saul Kripke have helped restore logic to the center of the enterprise, aided by several émigré logicians from Europe, such as Kurt Gödel and Alfred Tarski. American philosophy, to be sure, is light on great "thinkers on being," as Steiner put it, yet this can hardly be a defect of national genius—even granting such a dubious notion—since the metaphysical style is at a discount even in the German- and French-speaking worlds. To fault American philosophers for shying off big questions like "the meaning of meaning" or the nature of thought seems particularly odd in current circumstances. For philosophy as practiced in the United States is in one of those fertile periods in which it is aided by and in turn aids the sciences. Linguistics, psychology, cybernetics, and philosophy are all helping shed light on the extent to which people differ on one side from lower animals and on the other from machines, not unuseful work when speculating about man.

At MIT, Noam Chomsky revolutionized linguistics, the proof of his importance coming as followers busied themselves refuting large parts of his theory even as the framework stood. Nor is philosophy in America today noticeably narrow. Three political thinkers have all tried recently to give modern liberalism better theoretical underpinnings. John Rawls in A Theory of Justice has attempted a philosophical defense of welfare capitalism. Robert Nozick has written Anarchy, State and Utopia, a striking defense of antigovernment conservatism, and Ronald Dworkin, with Taking Rights Seriously, a collection of essays, has tried to put rights back at the center of legal theory, something that always bulks large in American political thought. After eyeing each other warily for too long, Marxist thinkers and linguistic philosophers have also begun making connections.

Another sign of philosophy's maturity in the United States today is the very fact that in no interesting sense is it uniquely or even typically American. It is international, or rather non-national. This is not simply because philosophy is no longer having to be imported—as Hegelianism was to Saint Louis, or French phenomenology to Northwestern. It is that the nationality of its practitioners—within the English-speaking world at least, an important qualification—simply does not matter anymore, surely one gauge of intellectual health.

Mixed together as they now are, in what the French historian Emmanuel LeRoy Ladurie has called, without any obvious hint of disdain, "the enormous ghetto of the English-speaking university world," British and American philosophers have not smoothed away all national differences. J. L. Austin, the leading Oxford philosopher of his day, was once lecturing at Columbia. In his dry, precise voice, he remarked how it was a curious fact about the English language that a double negative construction such as "He did not say nothing" entails an affirmative statement, "He said something," while there is no counterpart construction in which a double affirmative yields a negative. Austin was famously difficult to get the better of, and what he had just said seemed obviously, boringly, true. But a Columbia professor, Sidney Morgenbesser, who knew the language of New York better than Austin, let out a skeptical, nasal, "Yeah, yeah!" the perfect refutation, the double affirmative meaning "Tell me another."

Austin made up a rhyme to express Oxford's irritation with the Harvard logician Quine, who visited Oxford in the early 1950s and found its interest in modern logic rather backward. "Everything done by Quine/is just fine/all we want is to be let alone/to fossick around on our own." Since then the insularity of the English has passed. Americans and British teach at each other's universities. Paul Grice, a well-known Oxford philosopher, became the chairman of the department at Berkeley. During a seminar there once, he was arguing with Donald Davidson, an equally well-known logician from Princeton. Both men had developed, over the years, much-discussed and to some extent competing answers to one of the hardest puzzles about language: How is it that simply by using sounds we can make our thoughts understood to one another? How is it that words mean things? Perhaps because he came from a comparatively close-knit culture where— among members of the same social group, at least—much can be communicated through gesture and anticipation, a lot expressed without opening one's mouth, Grice favored an answer which began with what speakers want to do with their words—namely, in the standard case, impart some belief or other. Davidson, by contrast, coming from a polyglot-turned-monoglot culture in which explicitness is always at a premium, preferred to explain the meaning of someone's words in terms of the publicly statable conditions that make them true or false. Words, to Grice, were the speaker's tools; to Davidson, rules to be obeyed. From different points, both, though, were headed in the same direction, as Grice, a rotund man with a red face and long white hair acknowledged. "Donald," he said, "you and I are like two mountain climbers trying to reach the same peak from different sides."

Its subject matter, if nothing else, makes the study of American history American. What is peculiarly American about American philosophy—philosophy, that is, that is practiced in the United States—is, on the other hand, much less clear. Muddier still, if only because broader, is what is American about American art. This question used to have more bite when Americans' feelings of cultural inferiority to Europe were strong and when the arts were treated far more than they are today as lofty expressions of national character. Americans have thrown off their envy of European art, and with it the urge to seek out and celebrate the "American grain" in their own works has diminished.

Americans are justly proud of their painters, but this was not always so. American nineteenth-century painting was largely derivative from European models. Painters and architects went to Paris to study. The early American painter Charles Willson Peale was hardly championing his new country's art when he named four of his seventeen children Titian, Rubens, Raphaelle, and Rembrandt. To treat nineteenth-century American painting as having little of its own and looking to a European past fails to take account of visionary landscapists like Frederick Edwin Church and Albert Bierstadt, who depicted a strange new continent, but even today this view has not entirely lost its currency. In this century, modernism came late to the United States, and, arguably, was imported by Europeans such as Josef Albers, Arshile Gorky and Hans Hofmann. Painters of openly American themes, like Grant Wood and Thomas Hart Benton, were, in formal terms, quite traditional.

There can, for all this, be little quarrel that by the end of the Second World War, painting in America had come of age. So successful, in fact, was American modernism at cutting out a recognizable identity for itself when it did arrive, with its diverse and vigorous schools, that the United States, or more particularly, the hub of the art market, New York, won a reputation as the setter of the artistic terms of trade and as a domineering arbiter of modern talent. Once American painting found its feet, it was but a short step from dependence to imperialism.

A second reason the question of the Americanness of American art is less interesting than it was is that toward the end of a century in which exile and dispersion have spared artists no more than other people, notions such as the German spirit, the French mind, the English sensibility, or the American grain have lost most of whatever persuasiveness they may once have had. In America, where the expatriate artist has played such a large role, this is particularly true. There are modernist paintings, of course, with recognizable American elements. Jackson Pollock, it was said, painted the American landscape. Richard Diebenkorn paints West Coast light. Roy Lichtenstein used the quintessentially American comic book and Jasper Johns painted American flags. But these elements were raw materials, which spoke only very indirectly about America.

It is no slight to American painters, works, or schools to say that what strikes today's observer of the art world in the United States with greatest force is the sheer scale, range, prestige, energy, and munificence of the cultural enterprise. In it, the individual painter, and his works, are easily lost sight of. This is most obvious in the American art museum. When the French art dealer René Gimpel visited Toledo, Ohio, in 1923, he marveled at the "devotion to the cause of art" that he found everywhere, particularly among supposedly philistine businessmen. Gimpel felt this had given him a sense of "the fervor of the Middle Ages when its churches were erected." New York, Washington, Los Angeles, Chicago, Philadelphia, Boston, Detroit, and Cleveland boast museums that not only have paintings of the first rank but aim to be comprehensive, showing something at least from every period of Western art as well as samples of Asian, African, Pre-Columbian, and Islamic art.

In terms of civic pride, competitiveness, and popularity, and of the priesthood of museum officials and rich donors, there is something in André Malraux's riposte, when told that America's cathedrals were her railway stations: "No, they are her art museums." The parallel goes further. There are even puritanically minded worshipers who fret at the busy sale of what they take as today's equivalent of religious icons and relics in museum shops. By the late 1970s, more than 60 percent of the operating budget of the Metropolitan Museum in New York was provided by its services, including the museum's burgeoning shops. At the rival National Gallery in Washington, there are no less than four museum shops, one of which occupies the whole of a basement wing in the old building, where postcards, posters, and artbooks offer reproducible keepsakes to compete with the paintings upstairs. There are hundreds of smaller collections in city, university, or private museums. Between 1950 and 1979, according to Karl Meyer in his book *The Art*

Museum, half a billion dollars was spent on new museum space, equal, as Meyer noted, to "fourteen Louvres."

In the older museums, European painting predominated, although American painters have begun to catch up. When Amon Carter, Sr., the Texas oilman, endowed his museum for Western art in Fort Worth, this was not to house Italian primitives, but painters of the American frontier. An earlier generation of moguls wanted European painting in the grand manner. Joseph Duveen noticed early in his career as a dealer, according to S. N. Behrman, that Americans had money and Europeans had paintings. Duveen's success lay in exploiting this potential. He and other dealers helped industrialists like J. Pierpont Morgan, Henry Frick (the villain of the Homestead strike), and Andrew Mellon to amass—and later house in museums—prodigious collections. Their motives were mixed, as was their taste, but it would be too simple to treat them as putty in their dealers' hands. Frick's interest began early. When he asked the Mellon bank for a loan, its credit report on him commented that he might be "a little too enthusiastic about pictures, but not enough to hurt." He seems, according to the art critic John Russell, to have known at least what he did not like. In the great Frick Collection on Fifth Avenue, there is little to be seen, in Russell's words, "of social upheaval, mysticism and unsubdued passion," but plenty of splendor and order.

Tastes in collecting changed. John Quinn, a New York lawyer who helped organize the famous Armory Show of modern European painting in 1913, saw to it that Congress altered the tariff to allow contemporary paintings in duty-free. In 1908, Pierpont Morgan had asked Senator Nelson Aldrich to dinner to explain to him that he wished to donate his collection—most of which was then in Europe—to the Metropolitan in New York, but that importing it would cost him $1.5 million in duties. When the Payne-Aldrich tariff was passed the following year, old masters were duly placed on the free list. Thanks to Quinn's foresight, Americans were encouraged to bring in modern European paintings as well. Fine collections were built up, by Alfred Barr for the Museum of Modern Art, by Walter Arensberg and the Barneses in Philadelphia, and by Duncan Phillips in Washington. Collectors' tastes, since then, have grown more eclectic. American painting long ago lost the stigma of the hand-me-down or second-rate. Museums proudly display not only modern American painters but nineteenth-century American painters as well, another sign of coming to live with the past.

Some of the larger art museums have begun to advertise exhibitions on television. The promotion of the visual arts is as yet slight, however, compared to the exposure long expected of would-be best-selling authors. Pushed by their agents and publishers, authors promoting their books struggle to join the ranks of celebrities, in historian-curator Daniel Boorstin's sense of that word: "The celebrity is a person who is well known for his well-knownness." And they are not just writers of potboilers. It is a safe bet that many more people know Gore Vidal, Truman Capote, and Norman Mailer as television showoffs than have ever read their books. All three at their (unfortunately spasmodic) best are in the first rank of contemporary American writing. Capote's *In Cold Blood* is a harrowing chronicle. Mailer, like Tom Wolfe, succeeds in turning what might otherwise be subjects of ephemeral journalism—Muhammad Ali's eighth-round knockout of George Foreman in Kinshasa, Zaire, the life and death of murderer Gary Gilmore—into events to excite the imagination of future generations. Vidal may be a second-rate novelist, but he is a first-class essayist. All of them, though, have a tendency when on public view to pander to and to exaggerate a Peter Pan side of their natures—Capote by being cute, Vidal by trying to shock the grownups with his cynical wit, Mailer by displaying the kind of combative maleness that made Ernest Hemingway such a joke in his aging bullfighter phase. Since the mass of television watchers are assumed to have slight interest in literature, these and other literate people have to establish a reputation as entertainers and performers rather than as writers if they want to get invited back. A number of other authors of the first rank have sensibly decided not to exploit this talent, if they have it, and give commercial television a miss—Saul Bellow, John Updike, Bernard Malamud, and Philip Roth among them.

Not that some of their publishers are all that far behind television and Hollywood publicists when it comes to brassiness. In plugging in 1978 Silvia Tennenbaum's *Rachel, the Rabbi's Wife,* Julia Knickerbocker, the director of publicity at William Morrow, sent advance copies of the book to rabbis, anticipating their denunciation of it. She was not disappointed. Worshipers left many synagogues determined to buy the book to discover what the fuss was about. Such tricks, and the tie-ins with movies, are quite tasteful hucksterism when compared with the excesses offered by, for example, Oh Dawn. This New York firm has extracts of books printed on novelty lavatory paper. Its clients have included the handlers of the reprint rights for *The Book of Lists* and *The People's Almanac*.

By now routine are tours by authors to promote books that are slated to be blockbusters. Judith Krantz, the author of *Scruples* and of *Princess Daisy*, has just the kind of attitude for this ordeal that book salespeople applaud. "I'm no Joan Didion. There are no intelligent, unhappy people in my books. I want to be known as a writer of good, entertaining narrative. I'm not trying to be taken seriously by the East Coast literary establishment. But I'm taken very seriously by the bankers."

The harder, and more sophisticated, sell in the book business is commonly attributed as much to the concentration of publishing houses, sometimes into conglomerates, as to the influence of television. Like Wall Street partnerships, many of the family firms in publishing have either become publicly quoted companies, as Harper & Row has done, or part of large groups, as Viking has done in merging into the Pearson Longman empire. The ten largest publishing companies by now account for around three-fifths of all sales of trade books—those intended for general readership—in the United States. Paperback publishing is concentrated in still fewer hands. The eight largest houses, none of them independently owned, account for more than four-fifths of all sales of mass-market paperbacks. Morton Janklow, a lawyer turned literary agent, puts his finger on the commercial code that motivates so many of the conglomerateurs of publishing when he says the Hanes Corporation, purveyor of L'Eggs panty hose, ought to buy a paperback house because the two businesses have essentially the same distribution system. As if to confirm this bloodless view of publishing, Lord Gibson, a Pearson Longman mogul, told Viking bosses when they asked him to invest more in their publishing house: "I have to decide whether to give it to you or to put it into pistachio nuts."

Many industry insiders fear that this intensified pressure on publishing houses to steadily increase sales and profits, and on senior editors to concentrate on "big books" that promise to achieve both corporate objectives, has stacked the odds higher than ever against new authors trying to win attention. Witness the experience of John Kennedy Toole's *A Confederacy of Dunces*. It was rejected by just about everybody, including Robert Gottlieb, one of New York's most astute editors. In despair Toole committed suicide in 1969 at the age of thirty-two. When the book was eventually published, by the Louisiana State University Press, it was praised, and it won the 1981 Pulitzer Prize for fiction. The book's champion was Toole's mother, who by determined pestering finally persuaded Walker Percy, the novelist, to take a look at the manuscript. As Percy explained afterward: "There was no getting out of it; only one hope remained—that I could read a few pages and that they would be bad enough for me, in good conscience, to read no farther. Usually I can do just that. Indeed the first paragraph often suffices. My only fear was that this one might not be bad enough, or might be just good enough, so that I would have to keep reading. In this case I read on. And on. First with the sinking feeling that it was not bad enough to quit, then with a prickle of interest, then a growing excitement, and finally an incredulity: surely it was not possible that it was so good."

The task of Toole's mother may indeed have been made harder by the way publishers in recent years have often preferred to put their money on surefire best sellers than to risk it on a dark horse. The jackpot gets larger every year. In 1968, Fawcett caused a stir when it paid Putnam $410,000 for the paperback rights to Mario Puzo's *The Godfather*. In 1971, Avon bought the paperback rights for Thomas Harris's *I'm O.K.—You're O.K.* for $1 million from Harper & Row. The record stood for a month. Avon then broke it by paying Macmillan $1.1 million for Richard Bach's *Jonathan Livingston Seagull*. Since then even $1 million has come to seem a small sum. Taylor Caldwell, the pen name of the English-born Janet Reback, who was discovered by the legendary editor Maxwell Perkins, got $3.9 million on signing a two-book contract with Putnam. Bantam, a subsidiary of Bertelsmann Verlag of West Germany, bought the paperback rights from Crown for Judith Krantz's *Princess Daisy* for $3.2 million. United Artists paid $2.5 million for the film rights to Gay Talese's *Thy Neighbor's Wife*, a guide for the voyeur into the sexual exploits of American extroverts. The impression given off by the hype that customarily accompanies such deals is that American publishing has edged much closer toward the world of Johnny Carson than that of Max Perkins.

That is, of course, a gross caricature of what is happening. In part because even the conglomerateurs are coming to learn, through dyed-in-red-ink experiences, that book publishing is not just another mass-merchandising drygoods business. As one editor told Thomas White-side of *The New Yorker:* "It's a business that even when it's well run still shows jagged peaks and valleys in its financial statements. It drives broker types, and business types, crazy. Because what they teach you in the Harvard Business School is that if you merge a company properly and plan it properly, with five-year plans and all the rest, your curve is going to go like that." With this, he pointed upward with an arm. More important, the caricature overlooks the fact that the demarcation line between serious literature and literature that sells was far more marked in the nineteenth century and the golden years of the Lost Generation and of the great editors than it is today.

Neither Walt Whitman nor Nathaniel Hawthorne made enough to live on from his writing. Henry David Thoreau had returned to him by his publisher 706 unsold copies of *A Week on the Concord and Merrimack Rivers* out of an edition of 1,000. Of the remaining 294 copies, 75 were given away, the rest sold. Herman Melville's reputation, and sales, declined after he made a splash with such early sea stories as *Omoo* and *Typee* and the *Boston Literary World* said of Melville in 1885, six years before his death: "Had he possessed as much literary skill as wild imagination his works might have secured for him a perma-nent place in American literature." Edith Wharton, independently wealthy and a writer of novels that sold well, made a secret arrange-ment with Scribner's to enable them to offer Henry James an advance of $8,000 for *The Ivory Tower.* The money, unbeknownst to James, came out of Wharton's own royalties from Scribner's. In the 1920s *Abie's Irish Rose,* with a New York run of 2,500 performances, was far more successful commercially than any of the plays of Eugene O'Neill. Scott Fitzgerald's *Tender Is the Night,* whose sales stuck obstinately at 15,000, was an also-ran in the bookstores to Hervey Allen's *Anthony Adverse,* which sold more than 1 million copies in 1933 and 1934. Throughout this period and since, the American reading public has expanded. While middle- and lowbrow fiction continues to hog the best-seller lists, novelists of a higher rank, like John Updike, Brian Moore, John Cheever and Walker Percy, can now make a comfortable living from their craft.

This growth in the American market for more serious novels has coincided with, and contributed to, the gradual disappearance of that American sense of inferiority toward British writers. In the nineteenth century this complex had a commercial as well as a cultural explanation. Until the Chace Act of 1891, foreign authors lacked copyright protection in the United States and profit-motivated American publishers naturally preferred to pirate the works of British authors than to pay good money to the native ones. Despite the odds, a few American novelists succeeded in winning international fame. Charles Dickens, with only slight hyperbole, told a New York audience in 1842 that Washington Irving, the author of *The Sketch Book of Geoffrey Crayon, Bracebridge Hall,* and *The Alhambra,* was a household name for the British middle class. James Fenimore Cooper's Natty Bumppo (or Leatherstocking) tales, with their romanticizing of the noble savage, were perhaps appreciated even more by Europeans than by Americans. Louisa May Alcott and Harriet Beecher Stowe, both journeyman writers, and Longfellow also won an international following. The ranks of the nonfamous were still more distinguished. Thoreau, Whitman, Emerson, Melville, the reclusive Emily Dickinson, and, until *The Scarlet Letter,* Hawthorne remained as unheralded abroad as they were unbought at home. And this neglect of the best American writers, and an unwillingness to give them their due, continued well into the twentieth century.

As the historian Marcus Cunliffe has noted, the writers of the post–World War I Lost Generation agreed that life in Paris or on the Riviera was more stimulating than life at home. The young Hemingway told Max Perkins that there had always been first-rate writing and, in another category, American writing. Being Hemingway, he then said he wanted to be the writer who reversed that order. Even Ring Lardner, despite his plain man pose and his preference for being known as a newspaperman rather than a writer, took offense when a collection of his short stories was published under the title *Round Up.* He preferred *Ensemble* to these Western words. And Max Perkins himself, in writing an obituary *cum* tribute to Thomas Wolfe for *The Carolina Magazine,* gave credence to the old canard that whereas English culture was well formed, American artists were still struggling to reveal America and Americans to Americans.

Perkins wrote this only forty-odd years ago yet it seems antiquity.

Since then American English has become standard English and New York has supplanted London as the headquarters of English-language literature and publishing, though not of English-language drama. Even so, like the British, the American book-reading public retains one strikingly insular characteristic. Both are ready to read authors who write in English, even difficult ones like the Australian Patrick White, the Trinidadian V. S. Naipaul, and the Mississippian William Faulkner, who wrote books probably only fully accessible to people brought up in a racist society where for the ruling class an aristocratic sense of honor, albeit in a distorted form, still prevailed over the middle-class obsession with reputation. But in neither the United States nor Britain are many people willing to read books that appeared originally in a foreign language. In both countries the works of even the best-selling contemporary authors of Continental Europe and Latin America remain, with few exceptions, almost unknown.

11

RULE OF LAWYERS
The Legal System

Law schools are gradually coming under some of the same pressure to justify their usefulness that liberal arts colleges have long felt. America has one lawyer for every 440 of its people—versus one lawyer for every 10,000 people in Japan. Chief Justice Warren Burger has fretted aloud: "We may well be on our way to a society overrun by hordes of lawyers, hungry as locusts, and brigades of judges in numbers never before contemplated." Laurence Silberman, a former deputy United States attorney general, has gone further, saying: "The legal process, because of its unbridled growth, has become a cancer which threatens the vitality of our forms of capitalism and democracy." While both men were doubtless whooping it up for effect, lawyers have clearly suffered a decline in prestige, though not influence, since Tocqueville saw the American legal profession as the closest thing the then new country had to a national elite. In his view, the law, particularly English common law, embodied tradition and respect for the past, and judges provided a check to the excesses of popularly elected legislatures. Even in the 1830s, Tocqueville's judgment was apt only for a minority of American lawyers. The profession was barely organized. Law schools were few and far between. State bars were weak or nonexistent. Country lawyers flourished, practicing as they pleased, untrained and unlicensed.

Today, to claim that America's lawyers constitute an elite would be still further from the mark. An elite with half a million members would, even by American standards, be a capacious body indeed. Obviously, it is necessary to make some distinctions. In 1979, there were in private practice about 360,000 lawyers. Of these, two-fifths worked alone, three-fifths in law firms. Another 125,000 worked outside private practice—some 45,000 of them for businesses, as "in-house" counsels, some 30,000 for the federal government, and 41,000 for state and local governments. The remaining 9,000 of the 125,000 lawyers working outside private practice taught law.

The annual salary of that imaginary animal the average lawyer was $32,500 in 1979, good pay by most standards, but less than half what the average lawyer's mythical cousin, the average doctor, was making. The median earnings for lawyers include, for example, the modest sums earned by a small-town or country lawyer. It also includes mountains of money, like the $550,000 Joseph Califano amassed at the Washington law firm of Williams, Connally & Califano in the year before he joined the Carter administration as Secretary of Health, Education and Welfare, and the $352,375 Lloyd Cutler earned as a partner in the firm Wilmer, Cutler & Pickering (plus the $56,000 he got from corporate directorships) in the nine months before he was hired by President Carter as White House counsel.

Diverse as the profession may be, at its top there is a clearly identifiable elite, membership in which is best guaranteed today less by background, though that helps, than by having gone to one of the top law schools and done well there. Lawyers, particularly establishment lawyers, tend to scoff at the notion that those from the best schools necessarily make the best lawyers. Clark Clifford, the model establishment lawyer who has advised almost every President since Truman but who himself did not go to a top Eastern law school, likes to tell the story of meeting two senior partners from a prominent New York firm. One was from a well-known law school and had all the proper connections. The other was from an obscure town in the Midwest. Clifford judged the second far the brighter of the two, confirming, in the language of a different era, his principle that nobody should rise to be senior partner in a top law firm unless he has "started out repossessing pianos from colored whorehouses."

The rags-to-riches myth dies hard in America. So does its modern variant that college learning is no substitute for street smarts. Poor kids with brains who come from obscure places and the wrong places do make it in America, but as exceptions. For the surest pointer to the most successful of tomorrow's lawyers, look at the top of the graduating class in the best American law schools.

At the head of almost everybody's list of the top law schools come the following six: Chicago, Columbia, Harvard, Michigan, Stanford, and Yale. Each law school "class" provides an informal network that lasts throughout a career. This has always been true. Take, for instance, Yale Law School in the late 1930s. Lloyd Cutler, one of Washington's most influential lawyers, was there with Jonathan Bingham, the New York congressman; Potter Stewart and Byron White, both future justices of the Supreme Court; Eugene Rostow, later dean of the Yale Law School and arms control negotiator for the Reagan administration; Richard McClaren, who was to head the Justice Department's antitrust division; William Scranton, scion of a coal and steel family who went on to become governor of Pennsylvania; Peter Dominick, a future senator; Frederick Beebe, *Newsweek*'s chairman-to-be; and Cyrus Vance, President Carter's secretary of state until he resigned over the decision to attempt a helicopter rescue of the hostages in Iran.

Of the top six, the most expensive school, and certainly the one with the pleasantest surroundings, is Stanford, near Palo Alto on the peninsula south of San Francisco. Protected from the ocean by the Santa Cruz Mountains and far enough from the valley to escape the desiccating heat, Stanford has a climate in which it is difficult to imagine any work getting done, and the university fields a good football team as well as an outstanding water polo squad. When the university was endowed, toward the end of the last century, by the railroad baron Leland Stanford, in memory of his son, no expense was spared. On a trip to the East, Stanford and his wife stopped at Harvard to ask its president, Charles Eliot, about founding a university. How much would it cost? they wanted to know. Perhaps to dissuade the parvenu, Eliot gave what he thought was the very high figure of $5 million. Stanford's wife blanched, but after the briefest pause, Stanford said: "But, Jane, *we* can manage that."

Frederick Law Olmsted, the creator of New York's Central Park and the greatest American landscaper of the day, designed the grounds. In keeping with Stanford's interest in spiritualism, the driveway forms a vast Egyptian ankh. Associates of the famous H. H. Richardson firm designed the low, red-tiled neo-Romanesque buildings, skirted with arcades. The air smells of eucalyptus. Tanned, long-legged young women in Levi's cutoffs roller-skate nowadays between classes. As pretty a picture as they make, their wheels are less for amusement than for speed. Once one is inside the lightly air-conditioned buildings, any impression of indulgence quickly vanishes. Like so much in California that masks itself with a relaxed, inviting exterior, Stanford Law School is tough, businesslike, and competitive.

The recent dean, until he defected to private practice, was Professor Charles Meyers, a rascally-looking Texan who specializes in resources law. His office there was lined with oil and gas law reports. Meyers describes himself as a conservative. Like the university, the law school has a reputation for a rightward tilt. The campus is dominated by the somber tower of the Hoover Institution on War, Revolution and Peace, a think tank that leans, figuratively speaking, to the conservative side. Tuition at the law school in 1980 was more than $6,000. Some $850,-000 is set aside each year for scholarships, but poor students, all the same, must come up with $3,000 of their own or borrow it from the law school. Plainly, this is not professional education for the underprivileged. Stanford gets almost no money from the federal government. In this, it is like most other leading law schools. The university departments that soak up public money are the science, engineering, and medical schools, which do much expensive research. Legal research —which is basically looking things up in books—is comparatively cheap.

Stanford Law School relies for its sustenance on a large endowment, which it periodically tops up by dunning old graduates. As the most successful of the law school's graduates are earning several hundred thousand dollars a year in such well-known West Coast firms as Pillsbury, Madison & Sutro in San Francisco or O'Melveny & Myers in Los Angeles, they can afford to make fat tithes. Stanford boasts that while Harvard Law School gets a wider response from its begging letters than Stanford, graduates from Stanford give more per head. This is a disguised way of saying that Stanford lawyers, undistracted by liberal causes or good works, devote themselves almost single-mindedly to making money.

Dependence on such sources of finance raises questions of academic freedom. This is a difficult matter. Every large university needs to protect its sources of funds, private, government, or business. Each type of source throws up its particular pressures. At Stanford Law School these pressures are belittled as a much exaggerated threat—but then it does little to disturb the comfort of its mainly rich, mainly right-wing patrons. At Harvard such pressures are a subsidiary reason for an exceedingly embarrassing skeleton in the closet of its law school, of which more later. In Texas the pressures on academic freedom are more openly exerted.

The law school at Austin, regarded by many lawyers as the best in the Southwest, has for years supplied the big law firms of Dallas and Houston with future partners and furnished the state with many of its leaders in public life. John Connally, Robert Strauss, and Lloyd Bentsen are all graduates. So is James Baker, President Reagan's chief of staff in the White House. While not in the very first rank, the law school of the University of Texas is certainly among the richest. The university has usually been harsh with those who challenge the business ethic. It staged notorious purges of leftish teachers before as well as during the McCarthy witch hunts. C. Wright Mills, the prominent sociologist, left in the mid-fifties in disgust.

As for the law school itself, there is an almost inexhaustible well of financial support from its old graduates. The alumni foundation maintains a fund for the law school which is used to pay such things as professors' salaries and is replenished every year by donations from wealthy graduates totaling several hundred thousand dollars. Even the most independent-minded professor would hesitate before openly flouting the wishes of the alumni foundation.

In 1978, the dean's job at the Austin law school fell vacant. An advisory committee of teachers and students proposed a short list of candidates to replace the outgoing dean. The formal choice was up to the president of the university, Professor Lorene Rogers. This is the practice in most universities. The names proposed by the advisory committee, however, included too many non-Texans for Texan taste. As the university's reputation has grown, it has attracted many good teachers from across the nation. Yet the university, like the state of Texas itself, still hovers between parochialism and self-confidence. A Texan dean was still required, or so many of the alumni foundation contributors thought. They also felt that at least one of the names suggested belonged to too liberal a professor. Others on the list had foreign-sounding names and were, mistakenly, thought to be Jewish.

At the behest of the alumni association, President Rogers asked the student-teacher advisory committee for a fresh list of names. This the student-teacher body refused. In the summer of 1979, the advisory committee members were summoned to a meeting in her office. Arrayed behind Lorene Rogers's desk were six representatives of the alumni association, among them the chief justice of the state supreme court, a senior partner in Vinson, Elkins, Houston's largest and most influential law firm, a former governor, and two previous chairmen of the Texas University Board of Regents. Feeling, understandably, outgunned, the committee capitulated. When a new candidate was proposed to it, the advisory committee agreed to forward his name. The professor was appointed and took the new job, but only after two-thirds of the students and teachers of the law school had voted a recommendation to him to refuse. One of the candidates on the original short list resigned. Another took a job elsewhere.

In the thick of the Austin dispute was Frank Erwin, lawyer extraordinary and a former chairman of the board of regents. Erwin, who died suddenly in 1980, was a legendary figure in Austin. For a dozen years, beginning in the early 1960s, he ruled the university like an emperor. He was friendly with Lyndon Johnson and close to John Connally, who, as governor, made him chairman. A stocky man, shorter than either of his friends, Erwin nevertheless had their physical presence and their Texan gift of the gab. His position gave him huge patronage and he dispensed professorships and building contracts in strict accordance with his motto: "I love my friends and hate my enemies." Erwin rode about town in a white-and-orange Cadillac, the colors of the Texas Longhorns, the UT football team ("Hook 'em, 'Horns, y'all"). Even in retirement, practicing law in Austin, he was still spoken of with some awe. The door to his office in the Brown Building, near the state capitol, was marked, in the style of an English lord, with the last name only, "Erwin."

The door was kept unlocked. Visitors could let themselves in to find Erwin working at his desk. What was a reporter in the autumn of 1979 there for? He had heard about the dispute over the new dean and knew that Erwin had a view. Silence from Erwin. The case had aroused plenty of national attention, the reporter went on. Grunts from behind the desk. Didn't the case raise important issues of academic freedom? it was suggested. Erwin finished up some small piece of writing he had busied himself with, looked up from the desk, and firmly, but politely, said, "Bullshit!"

The law school, Erwin pointed out, gets money from the state of Texas. Indeed, the state's oil tax goes in part to fund education. The law school, Erwin argued, was not obliged to take money from the alumni foundation. If the professors wanted their salaries paid, however, they should expect the foundation to take a close interest in who was appointed law school dean. And as far as Frank Erwin was concerned, that was the end of the matter. Money buys power in Texas, just as it does elsewhere, but in Texas it is new money, which its makers have yet to feel the need to conceal.

At more august law schools the money of the alumni is usually seen rather than heard and on the rare occasions when it speaks it does so discreetly. Partly as a result, it took Jonathan Lubell twenty-five years to have righted a wrong done him by the *Harvard Law Review*. As a Cornell undergraduate, Lubell had been active in radical student organizations and so was summoned to testify before Senator William Jenner's Subcommittee on Internal Security when it arrived in Boston in March 1953 to conduct a witch hunt into Communists in education. Lubell took the Fifth Amendment. This caused him to be treated like a leper at the Harvard Law School and it was with consternation that officers of the *Harvard Law Review* learned that his grades in the summer of 1953 qualified him for membership on the *Review*. The motives of his opponents were mixed, but high on the list were concern that his membership would persuade alumni to sit on their checkbooks and fear that students associated with him would jeopardize their careers. Three members of the *Review* met with Lubell in a brownstone in Greenwich Village in advance of the 1953–1954 academic year to seek to persuade him to write a toadying letter that would make it easier for the *Review* to stomach his election. Instead, he wrote a forthright statement of principles and on September 3, 1953, third-year members of the *Review* voted 16–8 to keep Lubell out. It represents the only time a qualified candidate has been blackballed by the *Review*, whose earlier members included Dean Acheson, Alger Hiss, Robert Taft, Archibald MacLeish, and David Riesman.

The affair, according to the *National Law Review*, gained the aura of a "dark family secret" at Gannett House, the headquarters of the

Review, until 1977, when a second-year member of the *Review,* Bruce Howard, began to investigate what had really happened. When he was not given the cold shoulder he was given the runaround. But Howard, a former reporter with the *Washington Post,* was nothing if not persistent. "When people aren't cooperative it's a sign there's something there to be known," he decided. Howard's report, based on interviews with those either directly involved or with firsthand knowledge of the affair, finally persuaded the *Harvard Law Review* to publish, prominently, an unprecedented, handsome, but also belated apology to Lubell. It concluded: "We the editors of Volume 91 of the *Harvard Law Review* deeply regret the injustice Mr. Lubell suffered at that time. Painfully aware that this wrong cannot be fully remedied, we nonetheless have resolved to accord Mr. Lubell the status of affiliate membership in the Harvard Law Review Association." They also introduced a new rule: "No person otherwise eligible to be elected an active member shall be denied membership on the basis of his or her political or social beliefs, or because he or she exercised rights under the Constitution or laws of the United States."

The mainly student audience in a cinema near the campus of the University of Illinois in Urbana cheered when a political candidate in the film *Nashville* pledged, if elected, to introduce legislation to make it illegal for lawyers to serve in the United States Congress. That audience's prejudice is widely shared. In opinion polls, lawyers rank in prestige near the bottom along with advertising executives, and critics of the legal profession worry aloud that the United States is moving away from the rule of law toward the rule of lawyers.

At recent count, Washington had one lawyer in private practice for every sixty-four residents. Routinely, close to half the members of the United States Congress are lawyers. So were eight of the thirteen members of Jimmy Carter's cabinet in 1980. When Mr. Carter's Democratic lawyers cleared out their desks in 1981, Mr. Reagan's Republican ones moved in. Among them were Caspar Weinberger, the general counsel for the construction multinational Bechtel, at the Pentagon; William French Smith, senior partner in the large Los Angeles firm of Gibson, Dunn & Crutcher, at the Justice Department; William Casey, a New York tax lawyer, at the CIA. At the White House, Mr. Reagan's two closest aides are also lawyers—Ed Meese, a former Oakland prosecutor who taught criminal law for a spell in San Diego, and the Texan Jim Baker. These lawyers-turned-politician are atypical, but then so are the careers of so many of the half million in this most varied of professions. While the occasional country lawyer finds his job dull, this is certainly not a complaint that will be heard from the following lawyers seen hard at work in the two places in America where lawyers are thickest on the ground: New York and Washington.

The New York City criminal courts are housed at Centre Street in a tall building from the 1930s decorated in the style of the Works Projects Administration. Engraved over the main entrance hall is a solemn inscription: "Equal and Exact Justice to All Men of Whatever State or Persuasion." To the left are the Tombs, the city jail shut down for renovation after Judge Morris Lasker ruled in 1975 that being locked up there amounted to "cruel and unusual" punishment, forbidden by the Constitution. Cells at this prison are, though, still used during the day to hold people bused in from other jails to stand trial. White and black prisoners are separated to avoid racial violence. Young addicts suffering cold-turkey withdrawal symptoms each have small cells to themselves. Gays and transvestites are segregated in a separate pen, known as the "sissy tank." The other prisoners are massed in cages.

In arraignment court on the ground floor, the judge presiding for the morning is Alain Bourgeois, a thin-faced man in his late thirties with the pallor of a film habitué. His expression suggests keen intelligence and in his black robes he looks more like a seventeenth-century French Jansenist at a disputation than a New York City criminal judge. As the name suggests, his background is French, but he is a thoroughgoing New Yorker. Bourgeois made his name as a special investigator in New York's nursing home scandal. When named a judge at thirty-six, he was the youngest member of the state bench.

In his robing room, at the back of the courtroom, he entertains a group of junior high school children during a break in the proceedings. The robing room is a bleak, tall-ceilinged place with a couple of faded "Spy" caricatures on the walls. One of the girls in the group giggles and says, "You look awful young to be a judge." A tall, gangling boy asks if it is true that prisoners are issued only plastic knives and forks so as not to be able to make weapons from metal ones.

Back on the bench, Bourgeois works fast. This is the court where trial dates are set, bail given or denied. It is the ground floor of the criminal justice system. Young attorneys come forward with the defendants. Bourgeois scans the docket before him. Felonies are on yellow paper, misdemeanors on pink. Most of the morning's cases involve three-card monte dealers on petty gambling charges or young men accused of beating up their wives or girl friends with baseball bats. Bourgeois moves each case firmly and quickly. How does Bourgeois judge? Before him, on the docket, is a computerized previous conviction record, a probation report, and information about the defendant's "community ties." This last bit of information is important. If the defendant is known in his neighborhood, there is some chance that he will come to trial if given bail. But only a chance. Many defendants skip trial. Rearrest when caught for the next crime is the only practical way of netting them again.

Bourgeois doubts whether it is worth the taxpayers' money to prosecute three-card monte dealers. This is the sidewalk con game in which the dupe tries to spot the odd color among three quickly shuffled cards. The battery cases cause problems, too. Women often decide before cases come to trial not to give evidence against their men. But to get the charges dropped, the victims have to come to court in person, which few do, clogging up the court calendar with cases that must be heard and immediately dismissed for lack of prosecution evidence. After each case is dealt with, Bourgeois tosses the docket with a practiced hand through a large, battered slot at the side of the bench. At this level, like it or not, administration is nine-tenths of justice. "This is a pipeline with an infinite supply," Bourgeois says. "We just keep pushing it out the other end."

It is a muggy summer day in Washington. At the corner of Seventeenth and L Streets, a tall, pudgy black man, bleeding from several cuts, lies strapped onto a stretcher beside a police ambulance. The man has tried to hold up a florist, found himself trapped when the manager called the police, and burst out onto the street through a plate-glass window. A crowd has gathered. The wounded man is bellowing and trying to shake loose his straps. A dozen policemen are at hand. Finally the man is put, protesting loudly through a gag, into the back of the ambulance, which sets off, back door ajar. A policeman is kneeling on the man's chest, attempting to subdue him with a short electrical prod. This is not 1968, when the downtown area of Washington was swept by rioting, but a late July day in 1980, and this violent incident seems to have intruded from another time. Washington's downtown has been transformed in the last few years. There are sidewalk restaurants, newer and more fashionable stores, but above all, new office buildings which house the city's rapidly multiplying law firms. Across the street from the florist are the offices of Verner, Liipfert, Bernhard, McPherson & Alexander.

The penultimate partner, Harry McPherson, is a thin, slightly stooped Washington attorney with curly hair and a look of comic irony on his face. McPherson is a Texan and has a Southerner's feel for politics. He worked for Lyndon Johnson in the Senate in the late 1950s, after deciding to pursue a career in law rather than writing. McPherson later joined Johnson in the White House and became one of his closest advisers. McPherson is a quintessential political lawyer who ducks in and out between government and private practice. A mainstream Democrat, leaning to the conservative side, McPherson is on the editorial committee of the neoconservative journal *The Public Interest.* Even as a lawyer, he continued to write. A couple of his plays have been staged. One of his clients is Washington's Kennedy Center.

Verner, Liipfert is one of the city's smaller firms, but it is nevertheless highly successful. On a late July day in 1980, the firm is busy with a Federal Aviation Administration certification case. Pan American is the client. Will a new McDonnell-Douglas airplane require three pilots (as the Air Line Pilots' Association, which wants the work, argues is the minimum for safety) or only two (as the airlines, which will have to pay them, want)? McPherson takes time off to talk about practicing law in Washington. He describes the complexity of administrative procedures, the number of different agencies, boards, and authorities, the choice of legal avenues, and the variety of remedies. The subject is dry and seems at first to bore him. But he warms to it, describing an intricate case the firm took for the *Journal of Commerce,* the business paper. The *Journal* wanted export documents the Treasury would not release. The case wound through the government labyrinth, stopping at rule hearings, courts, and Congress. This is what appealed to him most about practicing law in Washington—"the number of arenas."

In the first rank of Washington political lawyers is Lloyd Cutler, who was an adviser in the Carter White House from the summer of 1978 onward. His firm, Wilmer & Pickering (the name "Cutler" was dropped during his government service), has among its clients Kaiser

Industries, CBS, Norton Simon, Pan American, and IBM. Cutler represented the drug and auto industries in the 1960s when they came under pressure to improve the safety of their products. His advice, which earned him the opposition of Ralph Nader and the consumerists, was for these industries to accept a little regulation to avoid being truly sat upon.

Cutler, all the same, keeps a degree of faith with his Democratic past. His father was a law partner of New York's New Deal mayor, Fiorello La Guardia. A star at Yale, thought of as a liberal school in the thirties, he clerked for an appeals judge on the second federal circuit (New York). In the 1960s Cutler did a share of *pro bono* legal work (help that is gratis or at nominal rates). Cutler thinks of himself as a liberal. In Richard Nixon's day, he was on the White House "enemies list." Yet he is first of all a lawyer, settler, negotiator. These skills he brought to the Carter White House. Cutler organized the American boycott of the 1980 Olympic Games in Moscow. He got Sears, Roebuck to threaten the reluctant American Olympic Committee with a withdrawal of the company's important financial support unless the committee complied with the President's wishes. His lobbying for the second strategic arms limitation treaty (SALT II) in the Senate brought it within a whisker of victory. Cutler is a consummate tactician and technician. As Steven Brill, editor of *The American Lawyer*, says of him: "Cutler seems to have no gut issues, no cause that anyone can remember him pounding the table about." Washington is a city where party differences and policy differences matter less in the long run than getting along. Cutler is unusual, or unlucky, in that his one important political patron, Jimmy Carter, should have been sent packing after only one term in office. All the same, he exemplifies the characteristic which is at once the great virtue and limitation of the political lawyer in Washington—that is, the ability to put superlative arguments for his client, whoever the client might be.

Waiting to fill the shoes of this generation of superlawyers are younger ones like Joe Onek (Cutler's deputy in the White House), Tommy Boggs (partner in Patton, Boggs & Blow, well-known Washington lobbyist, and son of the late Hale Boggs, a congressman from Louisiana), Terry Lenzner (who made a television name for himself as assistant counsel during the Senate Watergate hearings), and Mitch Rogovin (a trial lawyer who defended muckraking reporters as well as the objects of their inquiries, such as William Colby, ex-director of the CIA, and the Lockheed aircraft company).

Up on the fifteenth floor of the Criminal Courts building in New York, Judge Harold Rothwax, acting justice of the New York Supreme Court, is setting trial dates. Despite the name, this is not an appeals court, but a lower court for felony jury trials. Rothwax's court is sprucer than some others at Centre Street. On the walls are faded paintings with draped figures depicting various allegories of justice. It is near lunchtime and the cavernous room is almost empty. The court is filled nevertheless with noise and action. Defendants and their lawyers come before the bench, make their pleas, and are sent away. Rothwax runs the court firmly, as if chaos will erupt if he relaxes. New York judges are used to being attacked in the press for being either too "hard" or too "soft" on crime. Rothwax is too harsh for some, too lenient for others. Yet he is credited on all sides with running an efficient court. And in the bedlam of the American criminal justice system, that is as close as one judge can come to being "fair."

Rothwax, some say, looks like John Garfield; others suggest Jack Palance. With shiny black hair and a stubbled face, the judge does look as if he might have escaped from a 1940s or 1950s "B" picture. He tries to keep order in his court with sarcastic good humor. At issue is the date for the trial of a cocaine seller. The prosecutor gives the judge a report describing the narcotics stakeout and arrest. This involved several cars, and agents with similar names. On television it would be intelligible at a glance. The written report goes on for pages. Rothwax drops it, in disgust, on the bench and says: "This is a draggy write-up, I tell you. I'd like to find out what happened. This is of enormous interest to you, I'm sure, but not to me. Can't you guys write anything that tells me what happened?"

Birdlike twitter from a frail old man at the clerk's table has begun to distract the proceedings. The source is a public defender waiting for a defendant to represent in order to collect his fee. Like a boxing referee giving the first warning, Rothwax tells him to be quiet. Another public defender, in dark glasses, with a newspaper lodged under his arm, wanders in, hoping for a case. "That lawyer always drifts in five minutes before lunch to see if his case has come up," says Rothwax. "He looks distracted, and is distracted." The cocaine case is finally dealt with.

Next, it is the elderly public defender's turn. His client is a young, athletic-looking black man who looks alert but does not say a word. Evidently, he and his lawyer have come face to face for the first time in court. The public defender is hopelessly at sea. After a few words from him, Rothwax has had enough. "I am relieving you from this case," he says fiercely. "You are not able to relate to your client. You are not familiar with the case." Unprotesting, the old man shuffles away. The defendant is sent back to a holding cell until another defender can be found to take his case. Rothwax breaks for lunch.

Martin Lipton belongs to a younger breed of New York lawyer. His firm, Wachtell, Lipton, Rosen & Katz, specializes in corporate takeovers. Its offices are on Park Avenue. Both the address and the work he does make Lipton a bit of an upstart. For years the big general-practice Wall Street firms disdained work on contested takeovers. It was regarded as ungentlemanly for one corporation to acquire another against its will. This inhibition disappeared after blue-chip corporations began making tender offers to shareholders when their takeover approach was spurned by the directors of a company they wanted to acquire. While other law firms have entered the field, it is still commanded by two men, Lipton and his archrival, Joseph Flom. Lipton compares takeover battles to feudal wars, with the lawyers as mercenaries. Flom, of Skadden, Arps, Slate, Meagher & Flom, was first in the field. At one time, Lipton jokes, takeover suits could be quickly decided by asking, "Who has Flom?" In 1978, Flom was reported to have earned $1.1 million, a stupendous sum for a legal income. In reputation, if not in earnings to the final cent, Lipton has indisputably caught up.

When American Express tried to buy McGraw-Hill, the publishing empire, for $880 million in 1979, it hired Flom to lead the charge. McGraw-Hill was onto Lipton at once, asking him to head the defense. Flom filed a libel suit against McGraw-Hill on behalf of American Express. Lipton replied with a $500 million countersuit, calling the American Express bid "illegal, improper, unsolicited and surprising" (in that order). Lipton won.

Lipton teaches a course in merger law at New York University, and he keeps in with a loose-knit group of bankers, politicians, and businessmen who meet over breakfast at the Regency Hotel on Park Avenue. Lipton takes an interest in the city. His firm was at the center of New York's last-minute financial rescue in late 1975. He is a large, amiable man with thick glasses that magnify his watchful eyes. Despite a doleful face, he leaves no doubt that like every good lawyer, he is listening carefully to every word. In his office high above the avenue, Lipton describes some of the changes that are overtaking the world of the big-business law firm. For one thing, work done by lawyers employed in the legal departments of large companies is beginning to cut into the work of the large, general-practice Wall Street firm. Smaller firms, like Lipton's, are discovering that it pays to specialize.

Bourgeois, McPherson, Cutler, Rothwax, and Lipton are five lawyers out of roughly half a million. Even at glancing acquaintance it is clear that each of the five has clear-cut and important work to do. Yet why does America have so many lawyers? This is a unique investment of intellectual capital. Ex-chairman of the Federal Reserve Board Arthur Burns, later ambassador in Bonn, has been heard to complain that if only more superbright Americans went into business instead of into law, the country's economy would not be in the mess it is in. No other advanced capitalist country comes even close to putting so many of its most intelligent people into the legal profession. The Japanese, with roughly half America's population, make do with twelve thousand lawyers, no small achievement when it is remembered that American lawyers drafted Japan's postwar constitution. Island Japan, to be sure, has habits of obedience and tradition for settling disputes outside the law which the United States lacks, and whose absence throws Americans readily into court.

The United States, too, is a federal system with a forest of parallel powers and overlapping jurisdictions. Sorting out the inevitable conflicts of law needs lawyers. Yet even in the law-drenched Federal Republic of Germany, with its hierarchy of local, *Länder,* and federal authority, there are only forty thousand lawyers, a few thousand more than practice in Washington alone. Nobody is quite sure how to measure the volume of litigation in America, but it is estimated that local, state, and federal courts are handling twelve million civil suits a year. A nation that genuflects before the shrine of the free market every morning spends a prodigious amount of time in court complaining that the rules have not been kept.

The obvious question is why? The pervasive legalism of American life is indeed a puzzle, particularly in a nation with such a history of violence. Quick to spot a commercial motive, many Americans readily assume that the volume of law in America is largely due to lawyers' making work for themselves and their profession. There is a simple, hard-nosed plausibility to this point of view, particularly considering the hourly billing rate of $300 or more charged by the most expensive law firms. Lawyers, in this respect, are not immune to the skepticism which afflicts those other givers of professional advice, psychiatrists. Customers pay large sums for their services without being fully certain what for and often with the suspicion that the service, whatever it really is, might equally have been done by themselves.

The sources of American legalism are deeper than this, however. Influential as they are, lawyers cannot create their own demand. Why, then, are there so many lawyers? Because Americans need them is the only persuasive answer. Americans, for one thing, make much of their "Americanism." They are given to patriotic displays that would embarrass Europeans, for whom the show of nationalist sentiment stirs dark memories. Americans, particularly if they are recently arrived, carry citizenship as a badge of honor. This pride in Americanism cannot hide the fact that the country is a nation of nations, with people who once spoke—and often still speak—different languages, who have different social traditions, different expectations of public duty, different notions of what is just. Law, lawyers, and courts have thus had to provide much of the missing social glue. This is one reason why so many questions of personal morals, such as abortion and children's rights, end up in the courts. Since their politicians habitually duck tough issues, Americans expect their courts to decide an extraordinarily wide range of political questions as well.

Then again, the law itself is almost as varied as the American people. In fact, there is no single codified law at all. There are fifty different state systems of civil and criminal law, not to mention federal statute law and constitutional law. This diversity alone contributes mightily to the numbers and income of the legal profession. Considering that the Americans are a highly mobile people in a continental market with several dozen different legal jurisdictions, it would be very strange if they were not litigious. Efforts have been made to unify American law, and there is now something resembling a uniform commercial code. The states continue, all the same, to offer, à la carte, a wide selection of laws. Proud of its otherness, Louisiana still uses the Code Napoléon.

Consider how differently the several states treat certain modern rites of passage. The ages for compulsory schooling are eight to seventeen in Pennsylvania, seven to sixteen in Alabama. In 1956, segregationist Mississippi abolished compulsory school attendance altogether. The minimum age for marriage with parental consent ranges from fourteen for a girl in Alabama, New York, Utah, and Texas to eighteen for a boy in several states; without parental consent it goes as high as twenty-one for both men and women in Mississippi and Puerto Rico. The maximum age for statutory rape also varies. In many states it is eighteen, in Georgia, Maine, and Iowa it is fourteen, in New Mexico thirteen.

All that is certain is death and taxes? Not in America. In 1980, there were seven states where residents were not obliged to pay state income taxes: Florida, Texas, Nevada, New Hampshire, South Dakota, Washington, and Wyoming. Among those states that do levy income taxes, not only do the rates vary widely, but in some states the rate is steeply progressive, while in others it favors the rich.

When Mrs. Jean Harris was found guilty in a New York court of second-degree murder for shooting dead in March 1980 Dr. Herman Tarnower, a cardiologist who won fame as the author of the best-selling *Scarsdale Diet* book, she faced a minimum mandatory sentence of fifteen years in a maximum-security prison. She had formerly been a headmistress of the Madeira School, a finishing school for young women outside Washington, and if she had had the guile to slay her lover within the District of Columbia, she would have faced no minimum sentence for second-degree murder and might, conceivably, have won probation. There is not even a national policy on the death penalty. Murder in Indiana and you may be put to death for it. Murder next door in Michigan and you do not take this risk.

Nor do the states agree on laws governing labor unions. In the industrial states, where unions are strong, the law gives them protection. In the South and in Western states, where, with exceptions, unions are weak, state law is hostile to labor. The federal Taft-Hartley Act, for example, forbids closed-shop agreements between a union and an employer doing business in more than one state. As the vast bulk of commerce is across state lines, the closed shop is effectively outlawed across the nation. Unions, nevertheless, can make, under federal law, "union shop" agreements. Under these, companies can hire nonunion workers, but within thirty days the new employee must join the union. Many Southern and Western states, twenty all told, forbid even this type of agreement with so-called right-to-work laws. Examples could be multiplied; Conflict of Laws is always a popular course in law schools.

Conflict of laws not only makes work for lawyers; it also fosters three distinctly American attitudes to the law. First, the freedom Americans feel to pick and choose among competing jurisdictions, as if in a supermarket. Second, an obedience that is never absolute. Third, the use of laws as a tool for redress by citizens.

Picking and choosing—called "judge-shopping" by lawyers on the lookout for a favorable court—is seen as natural in a market society. Lawyers in New York, for example, would rather go to federal than to state court when a civil case falls on the borderline. In California, until quite recently, the preference was the other way around. Special-interest groups, too, shop around. Up until a few years ago, the ninth circuit court of appeals (for California and the other Far Western states) had a reputation for being hostile to the claims of environmentalists. The District of Columbia appeals court was reckoned more sympathetic. So if there was a choice, environmentalist lawyers would rush to get appeals filed in the District. Even within states, different courts have different reputations. During the draft protests of the Vietnam War, defendants' lawyers would try to avoid Judge Hauk and his fellow hawks on the Los Angeles bench and get their cases tried instead in the then more dovish San Francisco courts. When it comes to the law, then, Americans are in the lucky position of not always having to dine table d'hôte. And if they have served up to them a law or a judge's ruling that they do not like, they will not hesitate to ask for it to be sent back on appeal.

This judge-shopping contributes to the second characteristic attitude of Americans to the law—an obedience that is never absolute. Knowledge that the laws in a neighboring state may be more favorable or less severe makes any unthinking respect for the law difficult to maintain. Americans have also always felt unusually free to break laws they think unjust or illegitimate. Colonial juries spent much of their time acquitting smugglers and merchants prosecuted under the Navigation Acts. This tradition of civil disobedience has continued to run deep, if not wide. Abolitionists refused to accept the fugitive slave law. A century later, Martin Luther King and others used civil disobedience as a weapon in the fight against racial segregation. Impressed by its success, draft evaders used it as well. Not only would they not enlist for an unjust war, but they took the argument a step further. In court, they claimed that civil disobedience, in cases of conscience, should be protected by the Constitution. The attractive, if seemingly self-contradictory, idea that breaking the law could be legal was rejected, but only after having been heard on appeal.

Only in America would the argument have got so far. Unlike most Europeans, Americans do not readily associate the law with the authority of the state. Americans expect the law to be used, when necessary, against the state. Was it not the Supreme Court's order to hand over the disputed Watergate tapes that precipitated Richard Nixon's resignation? Do not Americans regularly sue the government and challenge its laws for infringing their rights? Americans' first words always should be "Don't tread on me," for they are encouraged to believe that nobody is their master. Americans are descendants of men and women who escaped lord, bishop, and bailiff. A habit of defiance survives, even if the conditions that shaped it have passed.

This readiness to assert their rights colors the third characteristic attitude of Americans to the law. It can best be appreciated by a contrast. What is the commonest English symbol of the law? It is the figure of Justice above the Old Bailey, London's criminal courts. How do the French symbolize the law? With a gendarme. In each case, the law is felt to be something non-negotiable, final, and much better avoided. To positive-minded Americans, nothing could be further from the case. To them the law is an instrument, something to be put to their purposes. It is not a hostile and usually implacable force. Elsewhere the hand of the law may belong to a police constable saying, "All right then, you'll have to come along." In America, it is far likelier to belong to a client's lawyer who is on his feet shouting, "Your honor, I object."

In a nation with so many customers for legal services eager to put the law to their own uses, American lawyers have had to be open and available. They do not make a mystery of their craft. Such inwardness would have been self-defeating. It may not be true to say that every American has a lawyer, but virtually every American's union or employer has one. Tocqueville observed that the law in America was becoming a vulgar tongue. There are few countries where so many people treat the law as a part of their everyday lives. The issues at hand need not be matters of high principle or politics. Frustrated by daily life—an uncle and a will, a county official and a zoning ordinance, a dentist and a root canal—the first piece of advice an American gets from another is "See a lawyer."

The openness of the law is evident in its informality. Unlike their European counterparts, American lawyers do not wear fancy dress. "Like rats poking through bunches of oakum," was Jefferson's description of English judges in their wigs. Today American judges, and only judges, wear black gowns. This lack of pomp is apparent at once in an American courtroom. Step into the criminal courts at Centre Street in downtown Manhattan. The walls are unpainted, the benches worn. Attorneys, clerks, guards, and spectators come and go amid a continual low chatter. Judges try to control the proceedings, but these teeter between informality and disorder.

In an English criminal court, judge, lawyers, defendant, and spectators are all clearly separated from one another, by elaborate and imposing carpentry. In France, where the defendant must prove innocence, judges and prosecutors sit aloof at a long curved bench above the rest of the court. In an American criminal court, it is quite different, as even stay-at-home Europeans have learned from imported television courtroom dramas. The defendant sits at a table with the defense lawyers. Courtrooms are large, plain, and functional. Real trials lack theatrical elements. Take the state criminal courts in Sacramento, California. Unlike New York's, these are a model of low-keyed and rather bloodless efficiency. No one is hectic or excitable. The courtrooms are carpeted and almost soundless. The furnishings are blandly contemporary. The court's business goes smoothly. Defendants in blue prison overalls come and go like items on a dull day at an auction. Allow your attention to wander and it is easy to miss a case. There is neither disorder nor pomp. This is a procedure, not a ritual.

The freedom for reporters astounds Europeans, particularly from countries like Britain, where the press is only half free. Rules protecting defendants before trial are weak. News leaks from the police and prosecutors often lead to defendants' being tried in the newspapers before they ever reach the court. Americans believe that unless there is an overwhelming reason for privacy, everything should be made public, and television cameras are beginning to get the same access to the courts as the newspapers have had. In Florida, instead of Perry Mason reruns, late-night television viewers can watch actual trials, taped for television earlier in the day.

To be so widely usable in America, not only have lawyers and courts had to be open; the law itself has had to be flexible. Adaptability to new circumstances is another of the hallmarks of American law. The colonists inherited English common law, which was law made by judges and, at least in theory, guided by precedent. Early American lawyers read their law in Blackstone's *Commentaries.* Burke claimed that according to his bookseller, as many copies of Blackstone were sold in America as in England. Americans, it was said, traveled west with a Bible and a copy of Blackstone. In keeping with the notion that the Americans had inherited a law governed by the past, Tocqueville wrote that like the English, the Americans esteemed laws not because they were good but because they were old. Yet almost as soon as it arrived, English common law had to be adapted to fit novel circumstances. A new continent threw up new cases to which old judgments did not apply. As a result, the doctrine of precedent was inevitably weakened. Not long after Tocqueville's famous visit, Lemuel Shaw, the chief justice of Massachusetts, was already adapting American law with new legal ideas to cope with the demands of the railway age. From very early on, American courts put law at the service of an expanding national market, breaking down, where necessary, legal obstacles to economic growth.

As American judges are less bound by codes of law or by legal precedents than judges elsewhere, they have, over the years, accumulated considerable power. They are also expected to make rulings about an exceedingly wide range of subjects, including many that might be thought matters of policy rather than law, such as capital punishment, school busing for desegregation, electoral districting, and campaign financing. In Boston, Judge Arthur Garrity ordered the city to adopt a wide-scale busing plan to overcome racial segregation in the city's schools. Judge Virgil Pittman in Mobile, Alabama, ordered the city to hold city elections by districts, rather than on a citywide basis, to reflect the black share of the electorate. And on rare, but striking, occasions American judges find themselves not only making policy but administering it. One of the most famous examples was Judge Frank Johnson of Alabama, who took over the state's prisons and mental hospitals after ruling that the state authorities were unfit to continue running them.

Considering how much power Americans give their judges and how little they grant their elected politicians, it is remarkable what slight interest they show in the federal courts. In 1980, federal candidates spent $430 million on their campaigns. In the same year, the President appointed several dozen federal judges, yet few outside the legal profession seemed to know or care. Not that the legal profession would necessarily welcome closer attention. It had a difficult enough time in the last century rescuing the law from the people. Many of the populist traditions of that time survive today. State judges are elected in many states. In several they may be recalled by petition. Even the lay lawyer survives, disembodied, on the shelves of the law section of chain bookstores, under such titles as *Do Your Own Divorce* and *How to Avoid Probate*.

The lack of public interest in judges also arises because, to use a term from advertisements for medicines that purport to cure colds, their influence is "time-released." Federal judges are appointed for life, often when they are in their forties, and are generally forgotten about for several years. Time passes, political moods change, and politicians move on. The judges remain, rising in seniority and confidence. Suddenly, cutting across the conventional wisdom of the day, their decisions begin going off like small time bombs. Justice Robert H. Jackson, one of FDR's liberal appointments to the Supreme Court, appreciated this. Considering that federal judges are named for life and congressmen are only elected for two years at a time, it is not surprising, he said, that Congress and the courts are often a generation apart.

Appointment to the federal bench is largely a matter of political patronage. To get on the bench, a young lawyer is well advised to have gone to university with a future senator or, failing that, to become a close friend of a senator shortly after. It is striking how many United States attorneys, or federal prosecutors, move up to become judges on the federal bench. The reason is simple. The United States prosecutor's job is by tradition a senator's patronage appointment, too. Some of the federal judges, when appointed to a district bench, lack even the qualification of previous experience. New judges go for a ten-day crash course at the Federal Judicial Center, in a large, pleasant house looking out over Lafayette Square, beside the White House. That aside, they may get absolutely no judicial training at all.

Americans never feel comfortable about letting anyone have unchecked powers. Judges cannot exercise their authority at whim. Refereeing much, though not all, of the legal system is the Supreme Court, the final arbiter on the Constitution. Anyone can read this document. It is brief, clearly written, and highly open to interpretation. The Court has reserved to itself the final power of saying what the Constitution means. Politicians who pass laws are elected. Supreme Court justices are appointed, for life. It all seems so undemocratic. How have they got away with it?

Good political antennae have played the largest part. When these get blunted, the Supreme Court justices find themselves in trouble. Still, it is not difficult to see why the Court even today is widely thought of as a priestlike body of lawyers which matches disputed laws against the Constitution to see if they fit. When announcing a decision, the Court is often said to "find" that an act is unconstitutional, as if there were a book in which to look up this sort of thing. The Court's rulings avoid plain English. It usually rules long after the immediate cause of controversy is forgotten. Nonlawyers must separate, if they can, the political ore in the Court's judgment from its constitutional lode. That the Court overrides its own precedents, that its members often reach divergent conclusions, even when supposedly concurring, or that the Court may reverse itself on an important point of constitutional law when one of its members has a change of mind, retires, or dies, has done little to damage the aura of respect for a judicial body still thought to be above politics.

Veneration for the Supreme Court opens it to two lines of attack from debunkers. One is to seek to prove the political character of the Court by lifting up the robes of its nine justices for evidence of scandal or intrigue. In fact, the paneled conference room where the justices meet to discuss cases is probably one of the least fertile sources for either. Only one justice, Samuel Chase, has ever been impeached, a blatantly political affair motivated largely by a Republican desire to get even with Chief Justice John Marshall's Court. Tried before the Senate, Chase was in 1805 found not guilty.

The Court's record of secret deliberation is a challenge to the inquisitive, the greater for having been so rarely broken, although *Time* magazine, National Public Radio, and ABC News have all on occasion run stories giving news of Court decisions in advance. The national best-seller *The Brethren*, by Robert Woodward and Scott Armstrong, offered an inside look at the Court which offended the justices, yet its only factual accusation of wrongdoing was never conclusively established. This was the charge that Justice William Brennan changed his vote in one case (leaving a man, thereby, in prison) in order to win over another justice on a separate case. A spy in the Court chambers would surely quickly die from boredom. The obligation to present reasoned, public judgments sets an inevitable limit on the scope of the Court arguments. While the Court has made plenty of scandalous rulings in its time, the nature of the scandal lay in the poverty of the judicial reasoning or the degree of political misjudgment. These mistakes were plain for all who wanted to see. The Supreme Court publishes the arguments with which it supports its decisions.

The Supreme Court "follows th'illection returns," as Mr. Dooley put it, but only up to a point. It does not turn quickly. The tradition of dissenting opinions makes more intelligible and less abrupt the process by which a minority view on the Court becomes a majority view. Rarely is the change in judicial or political philosophy as abrupt as Justice Owen Roberts's "switch in time," said to have saved nine, in 1937 during the row over Roosevelt's Court-packing plan. No two cases coming before the Court are ever identical, so the Court can always disguise new definitions in law as the discovery of subtle differences between cases. The Court, furthermore, works under rules of restraint which it imposed on itself. It is meant to avoid cases involving party politics or the political process, though this rule is sometimes sensibly breached, as in *Baker* v. *Carr* (1964), which established the principle of "one man, one vote." The Court also rears away from cases deliberately cooked up as tests of the Constitution. When the Court broke this rule in *Dred Scott*, the notorious collusive case before the Civil War, it blundered badly.

All this is to say that the form in which the Court makes rulings matters as much to its retention of authority as does their substance. The authority does not, after all, come automatically. The Court cannot send troops or impose taxes to enforce its decisions. To be obeyed, the Court must remain believable. Its success in achieving this comes, in part, for want of an alternative. Constitutional rulings are now so organic a part of American law that they could no longer be cut out without killing the patient. Americans, too, are positively encouraged to believe in the Court. President Truman appreciated that in the mazelike American system of politics, the President's office was one place for the buck to stop. In the equally mazelike system of American law, the Supreme Court is another.

The Court is also a place where difficult issues, such as affirmative action programs, get argued out, even if the questions of political and moral principle are cloaked in constitutional language. Lastly, the Court performs a symbolic role as the reconciler of differences. When the Court divides 5–4, as it not uncommonly does, on an important, contentious matter, it is as if it were saying to the loser, Try again; who knows, next time you may win.

Despite the name, the Court is not always supreme, not even regarding the Constitution. There are rare constitutional cases where Congress or the states get the final word. When divisions are deep enough, the Court is overwhelmed. *Dred Scott* was reversed by the Thirteenth and Fourteenth Amendments, but only after the Civil War. When the Fuller Court struck down the peacetime income tax in 1895, Congress passed and the states ratified the Sixteenth Amendment, making the tax constitutional. When it is listening to political signals, the Court avoids such rebuffs.

Even so, it is seldom that some effort is not afoot to trim the Court's power. "Impeach Earl Warren" stickers flourished in the 1950s. Conservatives who disapproved of the Warren Court's historic civil rights rulings proposed a "court of the union," composed of the chief justices of the fifty states, to review the Court's decisions. Then there are congressional efforts to impeach individual judges. Gerald Ford led the mean-spirited campaign in the House of Representatives in 1970 to impeach Justice William Douglas. At the level of the federal district courts, it has been suggested that reconfirming judges every eight years might provide a popular check on their authority. And routinely there are schemes to reduce the work load, if not necessarily the influence, of the appellate courts by limiting the sort of cases that may go forward to them.

Such direct efforts to trim the power of the federal courts rarely come to much because judges usually astutely test the political winds and adjust their sails. In *Roe* v. *Wade* (1972), the Supreme Court ruled that states could not prohibit abortions. It was a historic decision and anti-abortionists organized a campaign for a constitutional amendment with the effect of overturning this ruling. While the Court held to its course in permitting abortions, it did try to mollify the anti-abortionists by upholding in 1977 and again in 1979 an act of Congress which cut off federal funds to pay for poor women's abortions. In 1982, it agreed to hear cases on states' powers to inhibit, if not disallow, elective abortions.

Similarly, in 1973, when the Court struck down the death penalty, it kept open the possibility that it would accept state capital punishment laws that met certain constitutional standards. Many states did change their laws. The Supreme Court, in 1976, upheld a new model statute. After a brief reprieve, the death penalty was back, at least in three-fifths of the states. So it was with affirmative action programs to correct past discrimination with job quotas. In the *Bakke* case (1978), the Court ruled that the University of California Medical School at Davis was wrong to turn away the white applicant Alan Bakke while admitting minority students with lower grades. Yet in a case a year later involving a Louisiana chemical worker, who was passed over for promotion in favor of black workers with equal seniority, the Court refused to grant relief. Why? Among several reasons, the law was clearer about quotas imposed by institutions getting federal money (as the University of California does) than it was about quota arrangements agreed between business and union. Yet while this was one of the salient legal differences between the two cases, the Court's hesitation also reflected the doubts of the public at large about affirmative action. Once again, the Court was awaiting a clearer signal before taking a more decisive stand.

Such conflicting and partially contradictory rulings scotched the schoolroom notion that the Supreme Court can ever really offer "strict" interpretations of a brief, elegantly drafted, eighteenth-century document. Or that it can, as Justice Roberts memorably put it, lay the legislative triangle ABC on the constitutional triangle DEF and see if they fit. The notion of constitutionalism is, all the same, a highly serviceable one, in which many positively want to believe. Certainly it is not one that judges would ever want to see debunked for good. To them the Constitution plays an essential role in cloaking their exercise of power and protecting them from the charge of arbitrariness. To keep the notion serviceable, they in turn must be careful not to push their power too hard or stray too far from the political mainstream of the day. American appeals judges in this respect are not unlike the Roman curia, bending doctrine, where necessary, with the prevailing wind without ever provoking believers into concluding that the doctrine does not matter.

At the other, sometime raffish, fringe of the law is an American readiness to rush into court, which has always astounded foreigners and has recently provoked such anxious books as Jethro K. Lieberman's *The Litigious Society* and Marlene Adler Marks's *The Suing of America*. Some of the actions seem, on the face of it, farfetched: Supporters of the Washington Redskins going to court to seek the overturn of a disputed call in a football game against the Saint Louis Cardinals. A grown-up son in Boulder, Colorado, suing his mother and father for $350,000 for "malpractice of parenting." The mother of a raped child suing NBC for $11 million on the grounds that a depiction of rape on television triggered the offense.

Other actions, more serious, have won the plaintiffs damages running into seven figures. An Alaskan jury awarded $2 million to a man who accidentally shot himself with a defective rifle. In 1978, the Remington Arms Company settled out of court for $6.8 million with a Houston attorney paralyzed when a rifle misfired. A California jury awarded $3 million to a nineteen-year-old boy who dived off a railway bridge into a shallow creek, paralyzing himself. The railway company was held liable for not posting a "No Diving" notice. In New York, in 1976, a jury awarded a plaintiff $1.1 million as compensation for "traumatic neurosis" that set in after wrongful arrest for shoplifting.

The lawyers presenting such cases have about as much in common with Martin Lipton, Harry McPherson, and Lloyd Cutler as a gossip columnist has with James Reston. Perhaps the most famous of them is Melvin Belli of San Francisco, a rambunctious attorney whom *Life* magazine once crowned "the King of Torts." He is a hugely rich trial lawyer who was among the first to persuade juries in civil actions to award heavy damages. At times it seemed as if Belli was defending the 1960s against the 1950s. He helped the Rolling Stones when they had trouble putting on their ill-fated concert at Altamont. He has in his time defended "topless waitresses," the Berkeley Free Speech movement, Lenny Bruce, black prisoners at Soledad jail, and Jack Ruby, the killer of Lee Harvey Oswald.

Yet it is as a plaintiff's lawyer more than as a defense attorney that Belli made his name, and his money. Belli usually charges a third of the recovery if his client wins the suit, nothing if the client loses. In 1940, Belli argued for a San Francisco woman who lost her leg in a cable-car accident. Belli had a near-full-size model of a cable car erected in the courtroom. He understood that the key to a successful damage action was not only to be dramatic but to be technically convincing. Persuaded by Belli's flair and by his mastery of the technical details, the jury awarded the woman $225,000, an almost unheard of sum in those days.

In 1955, Belli represented victims of defective polio vaccine. He went on to do a thriving business in medical malpractice, appearing for the victim of a bungled sex-change operation and for two black teenagers who were sterilized without their consent. Belli sued an insurance company for intimidating thirteen doctors who were to give evidence in a medical malpractice suit. Belli is comfortable with the huge settlements he wins and the big payments he gets. "Juries are beginning to realize," he has said, "there's no limit to the value of human life."

Americans do at times seem determined to have it both ways—to be utterly reckless, like the nineteen-year-old diver, and to be covered against every risk, even from defective revolvers. And Belli and his fellow plaintiff lawyers seem to prey on this curious national trait. A visitor to the United States could be forgiven for concluding that Americans think each other invincibly stupid. Highway officials post signs along freeways with such unnecessary admonitions as "Stay alert" and "Stay awake." Frying pans are sold with redundant labels that say: "Do not hold handle while hot." Staircases in public places often have signs saying: "Hold handrail." Who but a moron needs to be told such things? In America, almost nobody. If the signs are not posted, however, and the moron is injured, the moron's lawyer may sue.

It is, though, stretching a point to lambast damage lawyers for pressing unnecessary damage claims. Stuart Speiser, one of New York's most successful accident lawyers, makes sense when he argues that readiness to give heavy negligence awards is fully justified today by the high cost of medical care and by the size of a lifetime's lost earnings in inflationary times. Nobody after all complains much when compensation is paid for damage to property, and certainly not the businessmen who get so exercised over product liability suits.

Nevertheless, damage lawyers are still looked down upon and their business is treated as suspect. Is it they who encourage Americans to sue? Or is it something else? Like Belli, most plaintiff lawyers take a contingency fee, which amounts to a previously agreed cut of the award if they win but nothing if they lose. In Britain and in many other common-law countries, the contingency fee is forbidden. British courts go still further in discouraging damage claims by setting "costs" against the loser, including money to cover the lawyers' fees for the winning side. These costs are often almost as heavy as the damages claimed. In America, courts will award costs, but these usually cover only the court filing fees, a tiny part of the overall costs of the case.

The origins of contingency fees are not rooted in greed, as critics of this system so often allege. They have a far more respectable history. Working men and women could only go to court for damages if there were lawyers willing to work for a contingency fee against robber barons with almost bottomless purses. The railroads, for example, made a habit of employing the best lawyers they could find to resist industrial accident claims—lawyers like Abraham Lincoln, who worked as counsel for the Illinois Central Railroad before he became President. His office's work included defending the railway against suits brought by injured workmen.

All the same, contingency fee lawyers were at the bottom of the pile when lawyers as a profession became fully organized at the end of the last century. Thomas Cooley, the self-taught railway lawyer who wrote the standard American textbook on torts, considered contingency fee lawyers a contemptible lot. Most such lawyers were single practitioners whose sudden expansion threatened the cozy monopoly of the profession. Many were Jewish. So professional exclusionism and anti-Semitism played a large part in the feeling against them as well.

Speiser believes that "lawyer-entrepreneurs," as he calls them, are essential if the rights of workers and customers are to be protected against large corporations. A big company normally has a large legal department of its own, with several dozen lawyers. If sued, these companies can turn either to their own counsel or to nationally known firms. When Ralph Nader sued General Motors for setting detectives on him when he was investigating GM for marketing the unsafe Corvair, the car giant hired Simon Rifkind of Paul, Weiss in New York. Both GM and Paul, Weiss had the resources to carry the case indefinitely. Nader was comparatively poor. His lawyer, Speiser, took the case on a contingency basis, his pay dependent on his client's eventual victory, which did occur.

Cynicism about American plaintiff lawyers who look for a "deep pocket"—a defendant with the resources to cough up huge damages —is easy to come by. It is also misplaced. The contingency fee system makes sense in the American context, and the extravagant growth of negligence law cannot be put, first and foremost, at lawyers' doors at all. Americans have never been as ready as Europeans to push social insurance arrangements far. The United States still lacks national health insurance. Its medical costs, set by doctors and hospitals, are, astonishingly, equivalent to around 10 percent of the gross national product. The badly injured cannot be sure that their bills will be covered. Few people sue for the hell of it, or because they are lured into claiming damages by venal lawyers. That is a caricature. Americans, by and large, sue because they have to.

The inefficiencies of the American legal system are more obvious than its strengths. The courts are increasingly used as an arena by parties seeking not a ruling on the merits of a case but to get their way through a war of attrition. Environmentalists use every legal ruse their attorneys can dream up to block nuclear power and other projects they deplore. The techniques of legal delay overwhelmed the antitrust laws even before the Reagan administration moved to weaken their enforcement by the Justice Department and the Federal Trade Commission. A classic case in point is the long and ultimately successful defense mounted by Cravath, Swaine & Moore for IBM against the government.

Cravath is among the most famous of New York's law firms. So famous indeed that when Richard Nixon, resting as a politician, told the firm that he would become a partner only if his name appeared on the shingle, he was told, politely, to go elsewhere. The IBM case reached court in 1969, after several preparatory years. It was not resolved until 1982, when the Reagan administration dropped the case as being without merit. Years had been spent in the "discovery" of literally tons of documentary evidence said to be germane to the case. One of the participants was the famous Bruce Bromley, whose ability to stonewall is legendary. In an unguarded moment of candor, in a speech at Stanford Law School, Bromley once confessed or boasted: "I was born, I think, to be a procrastinator. . . . I could take the simplest antitrust case and protract it for the defense almost to infinity. . . . [One case] lasted fourteen years. . . . We won that case, and, as you know, my firm's meter was running all the time—every month for fourteen years."

The costs of protracted litigation are huge. The profession attracts America's brightest and they come expensive. In summer jobs at good legal firms, the most talented law students are now paid at an annual rate of $45,000, which measured beside the earnings of senior partners, is small change. To blame lawyers, however, for the huge role they play in America's economy and public life is rather like a fat man's blaming a waiter for his obesity. In America, the government neither owns key industries, as European governments do, nor controls them, as Japan does, by a high degree of central investment planning. It works instead by regulation, and as the Washington saying goes, a rule needs one lawyer to write it, another to interpret it, and a third to appeal it. While Americans pride themselves on their efficiency, they are wedded also to a tradition of right of reply. If somebody is going to say or do something that may damage him, then, says the American, he has a right to have his say before he is affected. This does not make for efficient government, but for interests that can afford the legal costs it makes for reasonably open government. Lawyers, inevitably, are at the heart of this process.

Nor is there reason to think that the prevailing fashion of "deregulation" will much change the influence of the lawyer-in-government. Washington, as an exclusive center of power, may well be in for an eclipse. Yet two facts should ensure that lawyers-in-government need not race to find other careers. One is simply that deregulating industries requires almost as much legal manpower as regulating them. The second is if Washington's influence wanes, that of great cities in the rest of the nation is likely to rise. With deregulation there may come decentralization, and with it more work for redeployed Washington lawyers in Chicago, Houston, Denver, or Los Angeles.

Against all the weaknesses, claimed and real, of the American legal system must be set its great strength of openness. Despite their reverence for the Constitution, Americans are probably less mystified about their laws and legal system than any other people. They are simply too familiar with the law and too ready to resort to court to believe that the law derives mysteriously from tradition or must be diluted from abstract principle. To the assertive and disputatious, the law is less a set of cramping prohibitions than a supple instrument. It blends naturally with politics, and court cases are commonly extensions of political struggle by other means. The law, to Americans, is first and foremost a means of satisfying their claims and vindicating their rights. Seen in this light, the contrast between the country's litigiousness and its lawlessness, so often remarked on, seems less puzzling. For the American readiness to resort to violence and to rush to court are really opposite faces of the same boisterous individualism.

If the law is what Americans make it, then one has to know which Americans one is talking about. For, while the law may be an instrument for all, not all Americans have an equal grasp at the controls. The law means very different things to different classes, as Max Lerner pointed out in *America as a Civilization* more than thirty years ago. To Americans of wealth, the law is a means of harnessing their capital, protecting it, and putting technology to work. Nobody summed this up better than J. P. Morgan, the greatest of the financial robber barons. Of Elihu Root, who among many other accomplishments was the old mogul's attorney, Morgan said: "I have had many lawyers tell me what I cannot do, but Mr. Root is the only lawyer who tells me how to do what I want to do."

To ordinary middle-class Americans, the law means chiefly two things. One is "law and order," policing the city streets and protecting the suburbs. The other is taxes. To the unionized working class, the law, all too often, used to mean the court injunction against strikes, backed up by the state militia, although recent labor laws have been more evenhanded. To the poor, the law tends too often to mean trouble, although it is one of the great strengths of the American system that the law can also mean redress, as the great advances in the 1950s and 1960s for civil rights and defendants' rights show. For if grievances can be brought to bear on the courts with enough weight, the courts will listen.

The legalism, nevertheless, of so much of the country's political debate imposes a theatricality that often makes it difficult to keep in mind what the blunt struggles going on behind stage are really about. Americans do not blush when they use the quaint term "founding fathers" in discussing contemporary political issues. It is not taken as a sign of anachronism to ask what Jefferson would have done. In rereading the eloquent and intricately argued constitutional debates that preceded the Civil War, one must make an effort of will to remember that this was a quarrel about slavery and about the political terms on which the nation would industrialize and expand.

The story of the organization of American labor unions often appears to follow two disconnected paths—one in the streets and on the shop floor, the other in court, as labor lawyers patiently wore down the resistance of reactionary judges to modern social legislation. The same story could be told for black Americans in the struggle for equal rights after the Second World War, which involved one march in the streets and another in the courts. And in the 1970s and 1980s, the great political issue was the power of the national security state and the limits of *raison d'état* in a democracy. Yet this debate was refracted through constitutional argument about the proper extent of presidential privilege and the limits of Fourth Amendment freedoms. Constitutional argument dampens the force of political collisions. It acts as a necessary muffler. That is its strength. The weakness is that it causes people to forget that victories won in court, even if etched into constitutional law, are nevertheless provisional.

12

SOFT SOAP AND HARD NEWS

Television and the Press

THE GREAT INFLUENCE of television has extended into the courts. Walter Lewis, a prosecutor in Los Angeles, recalled for the newspapers a rape case he pressed a few years ago. The evidence against the defendant was, in his opinion, so convincing that the jury, he was certain, would pronounce a guilty verdict. He was confounded when the jury found the man innocent. Why? A middle-aged woman on the jury explained to him afterward that she was unable in good conscience to vote to convict because the defendant had not confessed during the trial.

"I have never seen that happen," the perplexed Lewis replied.

"You must not be very experienced," she said.

"I have been a prosecutor for eleven years," Lewis told her. "Why would you expect a defendant to do that?"

"It happens all the time," the juror assured him.

Slowly, Lewis realized why they were talking at cross-purposes. The juror had never been in a courtroom before but had watched countless trial dramas on television, where Perry Mason or another brilliant lawyer had forced a witness to break down under cross-examination and to confess, often with tears, to the crime. Many lawyers, for both the defense and the prosecution, now warn jurors not to expect that real trials are anything like the fictional ones they are used to on television. Prosecutors are understandably anxious to make the point that while Perry Mason's clients are nearly all innocent, about 90 percent of all defendants in America plead guilty, often to a charge lessened by plea bargaining.

Jurors raised on television have also come to expect a lot of scientific evidence and tend to assume that if such evidence is not presented, the police case lacks substance. So Mark Vezzani, another Los Angeles prosecutor, lays on the pseudoscientific evidence with a trowel to make sure the jurors' expectations are not disappointed. Of prosecuting a case where the police arrested two men beating up another, he said: "I confiscated their blood-splattered shoes and had the blood analyzed, then matched to the victim's blood. I didn't do this for the law— remember the cops saw the beating—but because the jury would expect it." David Glickman, an attorney in Beverly Hills, has made a still deeper bow to the television-lawyer ethic. "Knowing the jurors have been influenced by TV, I try to make the trial dramatic. . . . I use charts and enlarged photos and try to inject a little suspense. I pace things out and try to have interesting stuff both in the morning and the afternoon."

Los Angeles—at least that large strip of the city running from Santa Monica to East Hollywood where so many people seem to be in the grip, if not directly in the pay, of television—is different from the rest of the country. Confusing legend and fact is what is to be expected in the City of Dreams, and should not be treated as typical. Or so it might be comforting to think, were it not that Americans everywhere bow to television. The figures, though well known, are important enough to bear repeating. All but 2 percent of American homes have a television. Four dwellings in five have color television and at least half have two sets or more. As of June 1979, there were 746 commercial television stations and 267 educational stations linked with the Public Broadcasting Service. Four out of five homes with television could receive at least six stations. Nearly 40 percent could get ten stations or more. Now that cable television is spreading—by the end of 1982, it was expected that 20–30 percent of all homes would have cable television—the prospect of Americans picking and choosing from dozens of different stations is in sight. From the time American toddlers are first distracted by old Max Fleischer cartoons, *Sesame Street, Mr. Rogers' Neighborhood, Captain Kangaroo,* or reruns of *The Honeymooners,* to the time they leave school, it has been calculated that they watch, on average, some

15,000–18,000 hours of television, as against spending 11,000 hours in school, and see no less than 350,000 television commercials.

The average American watches thirty hours of television a week. Women, as a rule, watch more than men, since only half of all women work, while most men do. Those over age fifty-five, women and men, watch the most television, about thirty-five hours. There is no doubt about television's reach. The adaptation of Alex Haley's saga of an American black family, *Roots*, reached 36 million households in 1977. Audiences for the yearly National Football League Super Bowl are comparably large. If access brings influence or power, then television provides both in abundance. Nobody is quite sure what Americans have done to themselves by allowing this electronic drenching, but almost everybody believes that television does deeply affect those who watch, and, in this instance, believing goes a long way to making it so. Certainly, politicians and businessmen believe in the power of television.

Walk into an election campaign manager's office in Tampa, Pittsburgh, or Des Moines. The political maps on the wall will, more likely than not, show not the ragged lines of ingeniously gerrymandered electoral districts or wards, as they used to, but tidy, platonic circles indicating the broadcast range of the local television stations. News, advice, tips on how to vote that used to come from a party worker now come from television. A professional party man, Tim Hagan, the Cuyahoga County chairman in Cleveland, Ohio, a Kennedy Democrat who, like so many Irish-Americans, learned his politics in childhood as one of a very large family—he had twelve brothers and sisters—acknowledges the changes brought by television. "I feel like a feudal baron at the end of the Middle Ages," he said wearily during the 1980 presidential campaign, "or like a horse when the car came in."

The phrase "media event"—meaning an event arranged primarily with an eye to the television attention it will get—has entered the language of political campaigning. Politicians routinely arrange schedules to ensure that big happenings get play on one of the three evening network news programs. These were being watched in the autumn of 1981 by an average of 45 million Americans, all told. Nixon's trip to China in 1972 was carefully scheduled to allow the networks to give it maximum play. The President's return was made in evening television prime time—he waited in Anchorage for several hours so as not to arrive too early. The *Manchester Guardian*'s American correspondent, Peter Jenkins, reported the whole trip, from Washington, as if Nixon were Walter Cronkite's chance traveling companion.

Lyndon Johnson was convinced that television had altered politics for the worse. In retirement, he told a CBS producer doing a documentary on his career that what had changed most since he had started out in politics in the early 1930s was "All you guys in the media. All of politics has changed because of you. You've broken the machines and ties between us in Congress and the city machines. You've given us a new kind of people. Teddy. Tunney. They're your creations, your puppets. No machine could ever create a Teddy Kennedy. Only you guys. They're all your people. Your products."

Johnson's contempt for television was distorted by his respect for its power, more perhaps than it warranted. Suburbs and social welfare crippled city machines quite as much as television did. By no means all politicians before television were machine-made. Wendell Willkie, a politically rootless party outsider, sprouted and wilted without the intervention of television. Teddy Kennedy was a product not of the networks but of the Kennedys. Johnson, like Nixon after him, was convinced he was a victim of television. Politicians, though, cannot seem to agree on any general rule about television's influence. John Kennedy thought—with much justice—that newspaper publishers, being conservative, would not support him and looked to television to compensate.

Commercial advertisers have, since television's earliest days, believed the medium could help sell their brand, distract attention from their rivals, or at least stimulate appetites for their product, no matter what the brand. Today a dozen corporations routinely spend more than $100 million a year in television advertising. In 1979, Procter & Gamble spent $460 million; General Foods, $300 million; American Home Products, $165 million; General Mills, $156 million; General Motors, $147 million; Bristol-Myers, $140 million; McDonald's, $137 million; PepsiCo, $130 million; Ford, $127 million; Lever Brothers, $112 million; Coca-Cola, $105 million; and Philip Morris, pushing beer, among other things, $103 million.

When advertisers, in television's earlier days, used to sponsor particular shows, the paying piper's say as to the tune was often direct. An early CBS program called *Man Against Crime* was sponsored by Camel cigarettes. In instructions to script writers, the company wrote: "Do not have the heavy or any disreputable person smoking a cigarette. Do not associate the smoking of cigarettes with undesirable scenes or situations plot-wise." Nobody was allowed to cough on *Man Against Crime* and all mention of fire was forbidden lest viewers connect it with falling asleep with a lighted cigarette and burning down the house. Principals were instructed to smoke gracefully, never, neurotically, to puff. Cigarettes were never to be given to "calm the nerves," as this might suggest cigarettes were narcotic. Doctors were always to be presented in "the most commendable light." Camel had heard of a medical report in the offing that linked lung damage with heavy smoking and was anxious to propitiate the medical profession.

The Ford Motor Company also tried to influence the programs it sponsored. Ford forbade the filming of the Manhattan skyline to avoid giving publicity to the Chrysler Building. General Motors had to be dissuaded from withdrawing advertising from an episode of *Bonanza* that introduced a black character. The American Gas Association demanded the deletion of all references to gas ovens in a *Playhouse 90* version of *Judgment at Nuremberg*.

These efforts today seem naive more than menacing, especially since Americans have been warned for years about the "hidden persuaders." Like the other tobacco companies, Camel lost the war of television advertising when cigarette commercials were banned from the air. Big corporations, today, are generally less heavy-handed than they used to be when it comes to commercials. For one thing, network advertisers often do not know exactly when the advertising they have paid for will appear, which makes it difficult directly to affect the content of programs. Commercials can be switched at the last moment, so that programmers would be hard put to suit the wishes of individual advertisers, even if they wished to.

The prevailing commercialism of television is still plain, even in public television, so heavily underwritten by the big oil companies—as prestige advertising—that it became known as "Petroleum Broadcasting Service." Mobil Corporation, a million-dollar-plus supporter of public television, showed that the corporate itch to use a blue pencil had not gone when it tried to prevent the showing of *Death of a Princess*. Filmed by Anthony Thomas, a South African filmmaker, and banned by the authoritarian government of his own country, this documentary film reconstructed how it was that on July 15, 1977, the nineteen-year-old Princess Misha'al and her twenty-year-old lover were publicly executed in Saudi Arabia for the crime of adultery—a capital offense under Islamic law. She was shot and he was clumsily put to death with a blunt sword. Mobil, hugely dependent on Saudi oil for its profits, beseeched PBS "to review the decision" and then bought space on the op ed page of the *New York Times*—a familiar berth for Mobil's advertising—to put pressure on PBS to "exercise responsible judgment of what is in the best interests of the United States." Despite this, PBS would not be bullied and almost all local public television stations that had originally intended to went ahead and aired the disputed program, a second-rate effort that was given much more attention by efforts to suppress it than it would otherwise have drawn.

While commercial advertisers are convinced of the power of television to mold public attitudes—toward their products—the makers of the programs themselves are reluctant to agree that the network fare has a comparable impact, especially when violent shows are in question. The networks are understandably shy about finding out what link there is, if any, between the amount of violence on television and the amount of violence in society.

For many social scientists the verdict is already in on this question. As long ago as 1972, the U.S. surgeon general, the nation's chief health officer, delivered a report to Congress which concluded: "the overwhelming consensus [is] that televised violence does have an adverse effect on certain members of society." In his opinion, the evidence was "sufficient to warrant appropriate and immediate remedial action" since the "conclusions are based on solid scientific data and not on the opinion of one or another scientist." During congressional hearings on the report, Ithiel de Sola Pool of MIT, a member of the Surgeon General's Advisory Committee, rammed the message home: "Twelve scientists of widely different views unanimously agreed that scientific evidence indicates that the viewing of violence by young people causes them to behave more aggressively." The report led to the introduction of "family viewing time," a sop based on the fiction that children watch television for two hours after supper and that anything goes—"gore as before," as insiders put it—after nine o'clock. Networks presented this compromise as evidence of their social responsibility, while television's critics treated it as the smallest of breaches in the network practice of showing what it thinks the largest public wants and ignoring do-good busybodies who interfere.

What is much more interesting, however, than which side in the cloudy and difficult debate about television violence is correct—there are good arguments on both sides—is the fact that American taste itself is changing. For one thing, there is now a growing lobby against television violence. Even more important, Americans in their television fantasies seem to be laughing more and swaggering less. Compare the top ten programs, as rated by A. C. Nielsen, in August 1959 with the top ten twenty years later. Then the favorite programs predominantly featured the earnest violence of the wild West—*Gunsmoke, Have Gun —Will Travel, The Rifleman, I've Got a Secret, Peter Gunn, The Best of Groucho, Alfred Hitchcock Presents, The Joseph Cotten Show, Wyatt Earp,* and *Frontier Justice.* In 1981–82 these shows were most popular: *Dallas, 60 Minutes, Dukes of Hazzard, Love Boat, Alice, One Day at a Time, The Jeffersons, Happy Days, Archie Bunker,* and *Three's Company.* The contrast is quite striking. Today there is a stronger taste for news and documentary, known in the business as "reality programming," for bedroom comedy, known as "jiggle shows," for prime-time soap opera, for the domesticated bigotry of Archie Bunker, and for the army comedy of *M*A*S*H,* which has sustained surprisingly long-lasting popularity. The violence on today's crime and police shows, it is true, is much noisier and more strainingly brutal than the formalized violence of the Western shoot-'em-ups with their dispensable Indians and high body counts, but only a rash person would claim to know what the difference in style signified. What does seem to be clear is that Americans, on the whole, have taken a renewed liking to comedy and news, while more and more they tune out violent shows. This is less surprising than it sounds when it is remembered that the big middle-income audiences at which the networks aim are in their habits more settled, more family-bound—in a word, more middle-aged.

To television's critics, this is small comfort. The taste for news and comedy has not prevented the high-minded from continuing to pan almost everything that commercial television serves up. The popular *60 Minutes,* a documentary feature program which specializes in the exposé, can be a thumbtack in the rump of the rich, the powerful, and the unscrupulous, but it is criticized, too, for its sensationalism, its "kick-the-door-down" style of interviewing, and its knack of turning interview subjects into suspects. The new television genre of "docudrama"—the loose, fictionalized reconstruction of recent history, such as the Mississippi murder of three civil rights workers in 1963, the Israeli raid on Entebbe, or the Watergate scandals—is carped at for blurring the line between legend and fact.

The network's daily diet is criticized for being both bland and banal as well as violent, criticisms high taste has always and will always make of mass taste. There is to be found, it is claimed, on American commercial television hardly anything about science, or the nation's history; almost no plays, no dance, no opera; few serious documentaries. Instead, there are Greed Shows, such as *Let's Make a Deal* or *Tic Tac Dough*, fostering the American national belief in the sudden windfall, or tasteless People Shows, such as the *The Newlywed Game* or *The Gong Show*, as well as teary soap operas and bosomy situation comedies.

Against what, it must be asked, is American television being compared? When Americans go abroad and see foreign television, they are often able to put the strengths and weaknesses of their own country's offerings into better perspective. American television, for a start, runs virtually twenty-four hours a day, so it spreads its product thinner. There are much worse ways to spend insomniac early mornings than watching a rerun of a Preston Sturges comedy, a Samuel Fuller war movie, or a Raoul Walsh Western, for all the commercial interruptions. In other countries, television tends to go off the air about midnight, usually at the insistence of authorities much readier than their American counterparts to interfere with broadcasting.

American television, secondly, is a moneymaking business. National broadcasters, at least until the advent of cable, believed they could not afford to cater to narrow markets. Government-run television like the French, or mixed systems, like the British, can more readily oblige programmers to make allowance for minority taste. Where viewers' choice of channels is very restricted, broadcasters are in a much stronger position to set standards or impose tastes. In the United States, there are so many channels to choose from, the networks are ever afraid of losing their viewers to the competition, be it network or independent. Americans are habitual channel-jumpers, although there are pockets of resistance. For years, mountainous Vermont relied for television on the dim, wavering reception from a single, out-of-state station. Developers wanted to bring in cable television to offer Vermont viewers more channels to watch. The traditionalists were unimpressed. "Why d'you need more channels?" they asked. "Don't like the one, you can always turn it off."

The sheer amount of programming and the near-pure commercialism of the networks may help explain the mediocrity of much American television. Among the three major networks, CBS has most and ABC has least been able to dodge the charge of pushing the worst that television has to offer. The somewhat higher reputation of CBS has rested largely on its news programs—which have, until recently at least, usually been a distinct cut above those of the other two—and on the very grand demeanor of its longtime chairman, William Paley. A man priding himself on his taste, Paley would press his executives for better shows, yet he had no lasting complaint against the commercial success of James Aubrey, his president during the 1960s, who favored "broads, boobs, and busts" and filled the CBS lineup with *The Beverly Hillbillies*, *The Munsters*, and *Hogan's Heroes*.

Deserved or not, the networks' reputations are caught in the nicknames of their Manhattan headquarters: for CBS's forbidding tower, "Black Rock"; for nondescript NBC, part of the straggling RCA empire, at 30 Rockefeller Plaza, "30 Rock"; and for the headquarters of ABC, the youngest and smallest of the networks but by no means the least successful, "Schlock Rock." Long the laggard in the ratings war, ABC overtook CBS in 1976 and remained close to the top even after losing its first place to CBS again in 1980. In its drive for the top, ABC, as an executive explained, put out "the same old garbage done a little better." Convinced that children decide what's watched in most households and that the most lucrative market was among young adults with lots of discretionary spending power, ABC put on amusingly cretinous shows like *Happy Days*, *Laverne and Shirley*, and *Mork and Mindy*, and titillation with comedy *(Three's Company)* or with crime *(Charlie's Angels)*.

Is it really all as bad as commonly described? Is television today any better than the "vast wasteland" described by Newton Minow, President Kennedy's chairman of the Federal Communications Commission twenty years ago? Sports coverage, led by ABC, for sheer technique, is far better. Johnny Carson, on *The Tonight Show*, conducts banal interviews, but his stand-up monologue beforehand, the television equivalent of Art Buchwald's newspaper column, often gives a sharper sense of what's happening in America than a fortnight's worth of evening news programs. Phil Donahue's talk show, with mainly women in the studio audience, introduces calm and frank prime-time discussion of personal and sexual matters that could not have been mentioned on the air fifteen years ago. Dick Cavett, banished by weak ratings from ABC to PBS, seeks a more cultivated audience by asking bland questions gracefully of writers, musicians, and scholars, although his talk show suffers from never being convincingly serious or convincingly pop.

It is not quite true that there are few serious documentaries. Few compared with what? In particular, CBS mounts prime-time inquiries into weighty issues of the day, including national defense and America's relations with Israel. The popularity of Carl Sagan's *Cosmos* on public television suggests that there is an unfilled appetite for scientific programs. History—in the form of televised historical novels—is growing in popularity, too, with geography sometimes thrown in, as for example the very successful *Shōgun* "miniseries" about Tokugawa Japan.

Nor does television take itself quite as seriously as it did, now confident enough to be laughed at. Skits on the sort of television series Americans grew up with in the 1950s and 1960s were a comic staple of *Saturday Night Live*, one of the most enthusiastically greeted new programs in the mid-1970s.

Outside the commercial networks is the Public Broadcasting Service, the umbrella for the educational stations, commonly attached to universities and financed by local fund raising, corporate donations, and government grants—although the Reagan administration proposed to cut funds for public broadcasting. PBS does not escape the rule that in America, if one wants quality, one must pay for it, and viewers are frequently dunned for contributions. There is no British Broadcasting Corporation or Office de Radiodiffusion–Télévision Française in America to insist that viewers put up with three-hour productions of Jonson or Racine. PBS imports a large number of British programs, including Shakespeare as well as Edwardian costume dramas, pandering to that suppressed American fascination with social class, but it also airs locally produced concerts, plays, films, versions of American classics, political discussion shows, and the extremely popular *Wall Street Week*, polished talk about the culture of money.

To give even a passably favorable account of American television involves an element of special pleading. The "boob tube" is such an obvious target of attack that it calls out for a defense. Though there are high points, it has to be admitted that the general level is low. The advertisers still have too much sway, even if it is less direct than it was. Advertisers once helped kill television drama and it will take a time recovering. For the advertisers came to believe that television plays were too convincing, the human predicaments too complicated, the resolutions too difficult, causing their commercials, by contrast, to seem shallow and fraudulent.

East Side, West Side, a somewhat earnest series about social workers in New York, starring George C. Scott and Cicely Tyson, a young black actress, was a famous casualty of the American demand for positive results. Praised by television critics, it was, predictably, a miss with the viewing public and with the advertisers. Quickly, it was taken off. The lesson was not lost on the industry. Quinn Martin, the producer of *Barnaby Jones* and *The FBI*, told *TV Guide:* "I've been in business for quite a few years. I know that the antiheroic shows like *East Side, West Side* have lost—because the protagonist never won. We're hitting the great heartland of America, and they want shows where the leading man does something positive, and has a positive result. Every time you go against that, you can almost automatically say you are going to fail." Lee Rich, the producer of *The Waltons* and *Eight Is Enough*, agreed. "I approach things from a realistic point of view," he told *TV Guide*, "but I don't mean the nitty-gritty of *East Side, West Side* realism, either. By realism, I mean full characterization in which the people have flaws as well as virtues, anchored in a specific time and place. There's no need for cardboard heroes. People are willing to see protagonists make mistakes. But they do want to see them correct those mistakes and solve their problems and progress."

The phrase to attend to is: "the great heartland of America." Nothing else, except radio, has the national reach of television when it comes to advertising, programs, or news. It is not hard to see why it has become a commonplace in the past twenty years or so to say that television networks were unifying the country in new ways. Why television should be doing this so much more than radio, organized into networks for at least half a century, was not clear. Nor was it explained why Americans reading the same syndicated columns, the same sports results, the same cartoons, or the same wire service news stories in their different local papers should be so much more closely joined by television. The homogenizing power of television nevertheless became part of the conventional wisdom.

Perhaps there is some truth in it. Television news, to be national, had to offer a view of America shorn of local prides and prejudices. Perhaps it is true that by plugging a middle-class, middle-American culture intended to appeal to the reasonably well-off viewers the advertisers especially coveted, television, more effectively than could film or radio, did help wear down regional differences and sectional peculiarities. And if all this really is so, it is easier to understand why the networks, run by executives in New York, where the national news editors also work, supplied by programs from Los Angeles, and regulated by agency officials in Washington, are so sensitive to the criticism that they are out of touch with the "great heartland of America," which, without much foundation, is usually assumed to be thinking differently from opinionmakers in these three great cities. But then it is never very clear if "the heartland," "middle America," or the earlier "great unwashed" are meant as social or geographic terms or as mixtures of both.

Great claims were made for the effects wrought on ordinary Americans' lives by network television. Equally much is being made today about the coming upheaval from cable television and the information revolution. Everybody knows that new machines change people's lives. Even long afterward, nobody is very good at saying how. Who owns and controls the machine matters as much as, if not more than, what the machine does.

Television news, in particular, was invested with semimagical powers that were believed to have helped it rid the nation of Senator Joe McCarthy, segregation, an unwanted war in Vietnam, and an openly criminal President. The suggestion was that by watching the Army-McCarthy hearings—put on in some desperation by a fledgling ABC, without access to more appealing daytime programming—too many Americans saw what a hectoring bully he was; by seeing Bull Connor and his police set dogs on the civil rights demonstrators in Birmingham, too many Americans saw the evils of racism; by watching battlefront reports from Vietnam, too many Americans sickened of the war; and by watching the evasions of Nixon's officials in the Watergate hearings, too many Americans turned against the President.

Television, of course, played a secondary part in all these dramas. Given the belief, common in America, in hidden forces—whether Eastern bankers, international Communists, the guiding hand of the free market, or the Council on Foreign Relations—it was easy to blame or credit television. *Newsweek* took a poll in 1967 that suggested television viewing had encouraged support for the Vietnam War, not the other way round. In 1972, another *Newsweek*-sponsored survey indicated that television, far from horrifying viewers with its close-up military coverage, may have inured people to the violence. Johnson's often-quoted and possibly apocryphal remark, on seeing a skeptical report by Walter Cronkite from Vietnam early in 1968: "If I've lost Cronkite, I've lost Mr. Average American," was surely a judgment less of television's power than of the care the network news programs evidently take not to stray too far in their subtle and inevitable editorializing from mainstream opinion.

If it is insisted that television did in fact play a large part in these dramas, then it is difficult not to accept that it played a large part, too, in the rise of McCarthyism—the networks did cravenly accept the blacklist which for years made it impossible for many television writers and reporters to get work—the toleration of racial segregation, the original embroilment in Vietnam, and the acceptance of Nixon.

Television amplifies, it does not make, news. It is much vivider and quicker than newspaper reporting, but it is not as full. The twenty-three minutes of news on the half-hour evening news programs—the rest is advertising or network promotion—would occupy, if written down, considerably less than the front page of the *New York Times*. "Like writing with a one-ton pencil," was Fred Friendly's famous description of reporting for television. Minicameras, satellites, smart graphics, and other innovations have changed this, but not much. Making television news faster has not made it less brief.

Too much can be made of the differences between print and television reporting. They are a lot alike. Newspapers are not directly subsidized and television is not government controlled, as it is elsewhere, although television is regulated. Neither is openly associated with political parties, although many newspapers used to be more obviously partisan than they are today. Both are proud of the distance they try to keep between themselves and the administration of the day. At gatherings of the American Society of Newspaper Editors, the Association of Newspaper Publishers, or the National Association of Broadcasters, the barons of the press, network moguls, and news division presidents are never so earnest as in defending the rights and privileges of the press, and by extension of television.

Their freedom, embodied as it is in the First Amendment, which says, in part, "congress shall make no law . . . abridging the freedom . . . of the press," has to be fought for. There is seldom a time when a court here or a high Justice Department official there is not trying to open a crack in the formidable defenses of press and television. The courts recently have begun to broaden somewhat the very narrow definition of libel set up in *Sullivan* v. *New York Times* (1964), which made it virtually impossible for a political figure to sue with any hope of collecting. Reporters' claims to have special privileges when it comes to revealing confidential sources in court are getting less of a hearing than before.

Editors and news division chiefs are used to ducking politicians' bricks. Spiro Agnew was turned loose to break windows by the Nixon administration. Press and television bosses he lumped in with the "effete corps of snobs" pilloried by the Republican right as the "Eastern Liberal Establishment." When a television commentator made some bland observations falling short of total endorsement after Nixon's Vietnam speech in November 1969, Agnew reprimanded the networks for their "instant analysis and querulous criticism." In the midterm elections a year later, Agnew went after what the then White House speech writer William Safire suggested he call the "nattering nabobs of negativism."

Agnew gave clownish expression to a friction that is always there between administrations on the one hand and reporters and commentators on the other. Kennedy pressed editors to "get on board" over the Vietnam War, and is supposed to have asked Arthur Ochs "Punch" Sulzberger, who had just inherited the title of publisher at the *New York Times*, why his "young man" in Saigon, David Halberstam, who was filing skeptical pieces about the war, could not be replaced. Partly because there is no formal political opposition, press and television are easily credited with an adversary role. There are moments when this reputation is earned. The *New York Times* defied the Nixon administration in publishing the Pentagon Papers. The *Washington Post* helped bring Richard Nixon down with its Watergate coverage. Yet neither feat could have been accomplished without the help of federal courts or the investigative powers of Congress. The adversary role of the American press depends to a large extent on the fact that the courts and Congress can often act as a virtual countergovernment to the administration of the day.

Proud as the press is of its independence, there is less to boast of on the score of variety. It has often been said that there is no national daily newspaper. Strictly, this is true. The two largest American dailies, taking spring 1981 figures, were the troubled *New York Daily News* (1.4 million) and the *Los Angeles Times* (1 million). Only a small fraction of this circulation is outside New York or Los Angeles. Next to the leading papers of Japan—a country half the size—which have circulations of 10 million or more, these are minnows. *Pravda* has a run of some 11 million. In Britain, a quarter the size of the United States in population, the *Sun* and the *Mirror* have circulations of more than 3 million. All these are read throughout their countries.

The lack of a national newspaper is deceptive. Almost every large city, and many a smaller one, has its own daily paper, true, and this should suggest great variety. In fact, there is less variety than it appears. All but the largest newspapers, such as the *New York Times* and the *Los Angeles Times*, which are 85–95 percent staff-written, rely heavily on wire copy and on news services, supplied, in turn, from the biggest dailies. Syndication of comics and columnists makes for even more of a common product.

Variety has been reduced in telling ways within particular cities. There was a time, in the 1950s, when people in Manhattan could read the *Times*, the *Herald Tribune*, the *Mirror*, and the *News* in the morning and the *Post*, the *World-Telegram and Sun*, and the *Journal-American* in the evening. Thirty years before that, there were seven morning and seven evening papers, not to mention several papers in Brooklyn and the Bronx. Today New York has two morning papers, the *Times* and the ailing *News*, and Rupert Murdoch's ever-earlier afternoon *Post*.

The pace of consolidation seems to be quickening. Only a few cities, such as New York, Chicago, and Dallas, support independent competing newspapers. Washington lost the *Star* when *Time* magazine closed it down in 1981, leaving only the *Post*, which owns *Time*'s rival, *Newsweek*. In Chicago, both the *Sun-Times* and the *Tribune* have been losing circulation. Less than a third of all daily circulation today is sold in cities where there is genuine competition. In 1953, it was 90 percent. In 1926, there were more than five hundred cities with competing papers. Today there are under forty, and the number is falling. Many papers, like San Francisco's *Examiner* and *Chronicle*, have taken to joint production and market sharing in efforts to keep alive.

The American press has changed a lot since the days of anti-union crusades by Otis Chandler's *Los Angeles Times* or the last-ditch isolationism of Colonel McCormick's *Chicago Tribune*. The old newspaper barons wanted newspapers as a political voice, not just as profitable acquisitions. But "the last specimens of the Giant Primordial Gobblers," as A. J. Liebling called the Hearsts, Pattersons, and McCormicks, have given way to a newer type. The new owners of the largest chains—Knight-Ridder, with some two dozen papers accounting for an average weekday circulation of 3.7 million; Gannett, with more than eighty smaller papers, adding up, all told, to 3.4 million; and Newhouse, with twenty-odd dailies, totaling in circulation 3.2 million—tend not to "meddle with the locals," in Liebling's words, "so long as they come up with the tithe." S. I. Newhouse, founder of the chain that bears his name, said in 1968: "My papers have different philosophies, and they're about as wide apart as they can get. Some are Democratic, some are Republican. I am not going to try to shape their thought."

Like businessmen everywhere, newspaper proprietors tend, with some notable exceptions, to lean Republican—at least they do outside the South, and even there party loyalties are rapidly changing. De Gaulle said that his opponents could keep the newspapers as far as he was concerned, since he had ORTF, the state-controlled national television service. Yet to talk of "philosophies" in this context, as Newhouse did, is putting it too strongly. This is plain when the bland newspapers of today are read. Even where newspapers do take a political line, it tends to be cool, centrist in aim and tone, and unshrill, rather like the conservatism of today's *Los Angeles Times*. The modern press strains, in fact, for objectivity and balance. Reporters are taught to separate fact from opinion and to keep them rigorously distinct. Opinion is segregated on an "op ed" page and columnists are given semi-oracular status, largely because they alone enjoy a near-monopoly on signed comment. The separation of reporting and commenting is useful to the extent that respect for facts, tireless attribution, and thoroughness are virtues of American reporting. Yet the scrupulous listing of all arguments in a controversy, the careful balancing of Tweedledee with Tweedledum, and the taboo against introducing the writer's opinions into a story all too easily drain the life from reporting and encourage a wearying fascination with personalities and political technique.

To the claim that there is no national press, there are four partial exceptions: the *New York Times*, the *Wall Street Journal*, and the news weeklies, *Time* and *Newsweek*. In terms of circulation, 865,000 daily copies, the *Times* is not a giant, and three-quarters of that goes to readers in the New York area. Yet the *Times* is read in all fifty states and in most foreign countries, too. The old saying is: "If it isn't in the *Times*, it hasn't happened." Other papers, and as importantly, the network television news programs, take a lead from the *Times* in deciding what is and what isn't a big story. During the *Times* lockout in 1978, when the paper ceased publication for several weeks, it was noticeable how the television news programs lost their news sense. The *Times* is also an exception to John Kennedy's rule about newspapers' political leanings. While the *Times* endorsed Republicans in the 1940s and 1950s, it has, for President, backed Democrats since then.

But for the fact that the Monday-to-Friday *Wall Street Journal* covers only business and politics—a large "but"—and is treated differently from general-circulation papers for the purpose of advertising audits, it would undoubtedly be counted as a national newspaper, since it is available on the day of publication virtually anywhere in the country. In June 1982, the *Journal* had a circulation of two million, making it easily the single most widely read paper. Its gray, pictureless expanse is relieved by catchy headlines and by the middle column on page one, reserved for wry, offbeat reporting. In covering politics and current affairs, the *Journal*'s policy is to win readers not by daily saturation but by well-written and timely summary. Reporters are given generous deadlines for completing articles. A nervous recruit told his bureau chief in Washington that he had been on the paper two months and had only got three pieces into the paper. "I'd been meaning to talk to you about that," his boss replied. "You may be trying to do too much." The *Journal*'s editorial policy is "pro–free enterprise," according to Robert Bartley, the editor, even if "the business community isn't." Indeed, in the *Journal*'s editorial zeal there may well be an exception to the claim made earlier that newspapers no longer mount crusades.

13

GAMES AMERICANS PLAY
Sports

TELEVISION does not live by news alone, or soaps, or sitcoms. Television lives as well by spectator sports, and the finances of the two are closely intertwined. Television's influence on the games it shows is deep and taken for granted. The Madison Avenue techniques applied on television are borrowed by today's team owners. When Sonny Werblin, then president of the New York Jets, signed up Joe Willie Namath for $427,000 in 1965, he had a marketing problem. Namath's value on the football field was gilt-edged. The quarterback from Beaver Falls, Pennsylvania, had demonstrated, as an outstanding "amateur" quarterback at the University of Alabama, that he had everything it took to be a superstar in professional football. Although coach Vince Lombardi of the Green Bay Packers had a catch in his voice when he described Namath as "an almost perfect passer," perfect passing was not all that Werblin wanted from his costly rookie. Namath was also a handsome young man and Werblin thought that if he was properly marketed he could do much to increase women's interest in the game.

This was easier said than done. Namath was shy—supremely self-confident about his football abilities but introverted, even withdrawn, off the field. How could he be sold to the public as a swashbuckling sex symbol, as football's pinup boy? Werblin, a former theatrical agent, had the answer. He bought a llama-skin rug to line the floor of Namath's Manhattan apartment. His calculation was that women seeing photographs of the player would assume, even if not consciously, that he was as much a sexual as a football athlete. Whether Werblin's notions of what attracted women to football were right or not, Namath greatly increased the interest of women as well as men in the New York Jets. After his retirement from the game, he was hired by the makers of Brut to peddle their scent for men in television commercials. The white llama-skin rug did not, though, belong to Joe. It was entered in the accounts of the Jets as a club asset.

The pat conclusion often drawn from such incidents is that the businessmen and bureaucrats of American sports are transforming games into commercial enterprises. Stated that baldly, it has a ring of falsehood. The interests of the buyers of sports franchises are more complex. Businessmen rarely purchase an established sports team to make money. They are usually rich men already, seeking fun—and sometimes a tax write-off—and fame, rather than fortune. Ray Kroc made his millions selling billions of hamburgers as the founder of the McDonald's hamburger chain before he started losing up to $3 million a year as owner of the San Diego Padres. The late Carroll Rosenbloom made his pile on Wall Street as the largest single shareholder in Universal Controls Corporation, in the entertainment conglomerate Warner Communications, and in other publicly quoted companies, not by owning the Baltimore Colts and then the Los Angeles Rams. Oilman Lamar Hunt paid for the Kansas City Chiefs out of a mountain of money amassed by his crotchety father, H. L. Hunt, who said when he was told the team had lost $1 million in a year: "Well, at that rate, Lamar can't last longer than 150 years." George Steinbrenner, the boss of the New York Yankees, owns a shipyard. As financial writer William Henry Paul said in his book *The Gray-Flannel Pigskin:* "You can close a deal worth $50 million for a new ball bearings plant in St. Joe, Missouri, and you'll be lucky to make page 46 of the *Wall Street Journal.* But win the Super Bowl and every paper in the country, including the *Wall Street Journal,* will probably mention the fact right there on page one."

Since businessmen-turned-sports-entrepreneurs are seeking mainly to bask in the reflected glory of their players, it is overly simple to treat events like the Namath llama rug affair as examples of a straightforward lust for profits. They indicate instead that those professionally involved in sports have absorbed the broader corporate ethos and that when these clash with the values of sports, it is business-think that tends to win out. The owners, understandably, call on their previous experience as company managers when they take up their new hobby. Sports, like other parts of American life, have as a result become institutionalized and it is as futile to sigh for a return to the simple competitiveness of Ivy League football as to hanker for a comeback by vaudeville or for family sing-alongs around the piano to take the place of television. The spontaneous aggression of amateur sports is the inevitable casualty as sports become more ordered, more organized, and more tame.

Would-be reformers of sports in America concentrate their ire on decisions that make commercial sense but threaten the well-being of the game or its players. A case in point is the use of artificial turf on football fields, which so angers John Underwood, the author of *The Death of an American Game*. A study commissioned by the National Football League from the Stanford Research Institute and delivered in 1974 concluded that in almost every respect, natural grass was safer to play on than artificial turf and that football injuries could be greatly reduced by encouraging a return to a natural playing surface. The report might as well never have been written. In ignoring the report, and the supporting opinions of doctors who agreed with its findings, the organizers of the sport decided, in effect, that though a return to real grass might save limbs, it did not make good business sense. AstroTurf always looks fresh. Nobody needs to be employed to manure or cut or water it. After a rainstorm it is comparatively easy to dry out and the television companies prefer it to real grass because players are hard to recognize on a small screen when they get mud on their uniforms. Grass was rejected as a playing surface by the first four professional teams to lay out fields after the Stanford report—in Detroit, New Orleans, New York, and Seattle. Colleges that, after the report, called in Monsanto to supply AstroTurf included Arkansas, Michigan State, West Point, Kansas State, and Iowa State.

Other sports owners and promoters have listened hard to the ringing of television's cash registers. Boxing supporters who have paid $100 and up for ringside seats have had to accustom themselves to the idea that their convenience takes second place to those who watch the fight free at home on their television sets. When a preliminary bout ends at, say, 9:40 P.M., and the main event is due to be televised at 10:00 P.M., members of the live audience are expected to amuse themselves during the twenty minutes the ring remains empty. The tradition of not scheduling a definite time for the main event and allowing it instead to be set by the length of the preliminary fights lives on now only in small fight halls not yet invaded by the television cameras. Boxing for the promoters is much more a business than a sport and these halls, too, will doubtless fall in line when cable television expands into the predominant force on the airwaves.

Golf, too, has compromised. Match play has been all but abandoned in major tournaments because of its difficult scoring. Sudden-death playoffs have been introduced when players are tied after seventy-two holes, to satisfy the convenience of the television companies. Baseball, preeminently a summer game, has also made its bow to the cameras. World Series games are played by shivering players on cold October nights so that the sellers of beer and male deodorants are guaranteed a larger audience for their advertisements.

The general attitude of the sports establishment was aptly summed up by football's Bear Bryant, the famous coach of the University of Alabama: "We think TV exposure is so important to our program and so important to this university that we will schedule ourselves to fit the medium. I'll play at midnight if that's what TV wants."

Most of the concessions to television are justified by those who make them on the basis of swings and roundabouts. They claim, with some conviction, that the medium has done much to promote sports, as well as to bring enjoyment to millions of Americans who would not otherwise be able to watch the best that professional sports have to offer. They have a point. The Atlanta Braves are the only major league baseball team in the states of the Old Confederacy to the east of the Mississippi. Not everyone can take the time off, or indeed afford to travel, to go to the Kentucky Derby, the Indianapolis 500, or the Super Bowl.

Bringing enjoyment to millions is not, though, the owners' and promoters' main motive. For those professionally involved in sports, commercialism becomes dangerous only when it threatens to alienate those who follow their game. They sit up and take notice when fewer people pay to come through the turnstiles or turn on their television sets to watch a sports broadcast and then buy products that are advertised in the course of it. This is not, it must be repeated, because they invested in a sports franchise primarily to make money, but because their thinking has been so influenced by their earlier business experience that they cannot contemplate engaging in their new hobby in an unbusinesslike way.

So far the resilience of American sports supporters has proved remarkable. The custom of selling players like so many sacks of potatoes was long commonplace, until modified, though not ended, by Curt Flood's long and eventually successful campaign against the major leagues for the sake of freer movement by players' own choice. Babe Ruth was sold by the Boston Red Sox to the New York Yankees for $125,000 in 1919. When Willie Kamm, the popular White Sox third baseman, was traded to Cleveland in 1931, Charles Comiskey, the White Sox owner, wrote Kamm a brief three-paragraph letter, which began: "My dear young man" and then apologized for not seeing him in person before his departure. Professionals can expect to be moved, however, especially if they are popular and highly paid. More unusual is the American practice of moving a whole team from one part of the country to another. For Europeans it is not yet thinkable that Arsenal's home ground could be anywhere other than in North London or that Real Madrid could become Real Majorca or the Moscow Dynamos the Vladivostok Victors. After decades of stability, in the United States this kind of transportation has become almost routine. Beginning in the 1950s, the Brooklyn Dodgers moved to Los Angeles and the New York Giants to San Francisco, the Boston Braves to Milwaukee and then to Atlanta, the Saint Louis Browns to Baltimore, the Philadelphia Athletics to Kansas City and then to Oakland. In this town-hopping, even the wishes of the President of the United States can be gainsaid. When in 1971 President Nixon heard of the plan to move the Washington Senators from Robert F. Kennedy Stadium in Washington to Arlington Stadium in Texas, he "deplored" it and said that if it was carried out he would switch his loyalty to the California Angels, the team that was closest to his home in San Clemente, the "Western White House." He might as well have saved his breath. The Senators moved to Dallas–Fort Worth, and became known as the Texas Rangers.

In its sports, the United States is an island, and opportunities for jingoistic display are correspondingly few. England successfully exported its most popular working-class team sport, soccer, to the non-

English-speaking world and its middle-class team sports to the countries of the British Empire. Cricket caught on in India, Pakistan, the West Indies, Australia, and South Africa. Rugby is a national obsession almost amounting to a secular religion for white South Africans, with their boycotted Springboks, and the New Zealanders, with their All Blacks. In all these sports the pupils have caught up with their English master, and in some instances surpassed him. England has won the World Cup in soccer, the most prized trophy in international sport, only once since the competition was started in 1930, and even then it entered the final against West Germany with many of its supporters braced for defeat. As one British newspaper wrote on the eve of the game in 1966: "If perchance on the morrow Germany should beat us at our national game, let us take consolation from the fact that twice we have beaten them at theirs."

Americans are patriotic flag-wavers when they want to be, but in sports they stay aloof from this sort of thing because they so rarely get the opportunity. When the young American ice hockey team beat the Soviet Union's skaters at the chaotically organized Winter Olympics at Lake Placid, in upstate New York, there was a heavy venting of patriotic steam even among Americans not especially interested in ice hockey. When the White House, searching for ways to reprove the Russians for their actions in Afghanistan, pressured the American Olympic Committee into not sending an American team to the Moscow Olympics, by contrast, there was little opposition at home, since the following for Olympic events, where the United States no longer dominates, though loyal, is relatively small.

The most popular American sports are, for the most part, either unknown outside the North American continent or minor pastimes or played at a level Americans, rightly or wrongly, do not take seriously: football, with shoulder pads and helmets, the All American Game; basketball, for the very tall, the Real American Game; and baseball, the National Game. Baseball is played seriously in the Caribbean, in Central America, and in East Asia, notably Japan, but access to the World Series is confined to slightly more than two dozen teams in cities in the United States and Canada. Japan's baseball is not overlooked entirely. During the 1981 baseball strike, Japanese games were shown on American television, the only difference, at quick glance, from the American game being that the pitching speed picked up by radar gun was given on the screen in kilometers, not miles, per hour. American teams play exhibition games in Japan during the off-season.

Perhaps one day soon Japan, which competes with the United States in so much else, will compete in baseball, too. If so, Sadaharu Oh, who retired from the Tokyo Giants at the close of the 1980 season with a lifetime record of 868 home runs—113 more than Hank Aaron and 154 more than Babe Ruth—was too diplomatic to mention the possibility when he talked to *The Sporting News* about the prospects of baseball in the year 2000. Oh, nevertheless, had given baseball's future some thought. "In the year 2000," he said, "society will be more civilized and developed than at the present time. Science will make the world more sedentary, too, so baseball spectators will want to see more of the spirit of the game, especially since everything else will be automatic. However, the world will be short of wood for baseball bats. So I believe we will use aluminum or metal bats and the game of baseball will be very, very offensive and exciting because there will be more hitting." Shortage of land in Japan, Oh thinks, may require a new type of stadium that takes up less room, deepening center field but bringing the foul lines closer together. "Team play," he added, "has come to its logical limit already. So I don't think there will be any great changes there."

Basketball star Kareem Abdul-Jabbar, formerly of the Milwaukee Bucks and now of the Los Angeles Lakers, discovered in person that his height—seven feet two inches—meant more abroad than the fact that for a decade he had been the game's most dominant player. "In the off-season I've traveled around the world," he has said. "Outside this country nobody knows I'm a basketball player, but they regard me as a giant. Like in Thailand, the people there are very short and, wow, they didn't say much, but they stared. One time in Pakistan I had three hundred people following me."

American football, lastly, is commonly treated abroad as a puzzling tribal rite involving beefy men in ballet tights, teams of pretty girls with an available look bobbing up and down on the sidelines under such names as the Forty-Niner Nuggets or the Embraceable Ewes, and gnarled, overweight coaches, weeping over victory or suffering mid-game coronaries.

Foreigners are poorer for the caricature just as they are deprived—apart from the Japanese and a few others—by American possessiveness about baseball. The game is an even mixture of individual tasks—the strike-out, the home run, the unassisted double play—and teamwork: the sacrifice bunt, the double steal, the triple play, rare as it is. Baseball is not slave to the clock. If neither team can win in nine innings, each has as many more as it needs to get a result, although the Braves and the Dodgers did play a twenty-six-inning game back in 1920, ended by darkness in a 1–1 tie. The year before, the Giants got through a nine-inning game with Philadelphia in fifty-one minutes. Bernard Shaw thought that baseball had the advantage over cricket of being sooner ended. The game can seem excessively dull, but even when nothing is happening—when, that is, the pitcher is retiring one batter after another—something is happening, for a shut-out, a rare no-hitter, or that even rarer, unique Americanism, a perfect game, is in the making. All of these pitching feats—in which luck counts for a lot, too—are likelier to be unmade, though, than made, by the unexpected home run, by the hit that comes when the pitcher's concentration lapses. For baseball is a game of sudden reversals, of small mistakes exploited, of whole seasons hanging on a single play, like Goose Gossage's last pitch to Carl Yastrzemski in the bottom of the ninth inning of the 1978 American League East special play-off, with two men on, two out, and Boston only one run behind, a pitch which could have won the game and the division title for either team. Gossage was understandably nervous. So were millions of fans watching. "The worst that can happen to me is that tomorrow I'll be back home fishing," Gossage thought to himself, so he wound up, threw, and Yastrzemski popped the ball up for the final out.

Baseball is a conservative, rule-governed game. Fielders have allotted jobs in their positions—which have not changed in a hundred years—and room to excel but not improvise at the task. Offense and defense take turns; unlike basketball or football, the defense—the fielders—cannot steal the ball, and each team starts out with a minimum of exactly twenty-seven chances to get on base. The game has been treated as a metaphor of small-town America, with its unspoken cooperation, and of Taylorian industrial life, with its separation of tasks and statistical rating of performance.

Baseball is a game in which weighing too much, being too old, or drinking too much are not the penalties they are in other sports. Willie Stargell, 220 pounds and pushing forty, led the Pirates to victory, hitting .400 in the 1979 World Series. In 1980, the pear-shaped Luis Tiant, claiming to be under forty—"Luis was a national hero in Cuba when I was a boy, and I'm thirty," Tony Oliva once said—was still striking out batters with slow balls so tricky they might have put their ears up and barked on the way to the plate. Of Jimmy Foxx, a great slugger and drinker for the Red Sox, it was said that nobody knew if he was sliding into a base or just falling over. At a time when pious sportsmen join the Fellowship of Christian Athletes and preach virtue, baseball—a few teams like the Los Angeles Dodgers aside—puts little premium on wholesomeness or clean living.

More than any other sport, except boxing, baseball provides mental snapshots that last: Willie Mays running down an impossible-looking catch in the outfield at Candlestick Park; Lou Brock barely glancing up as he races to steal a base; Rod Carew, eyebrows raised, lips pursed in concentration, reaching out to knock a bad pitch for a single; Johnny Bench, in his red armor, kneeling creakily behind the plate on tired knees; Pete Rose, stubbled chin under a wiglike mop of hair, charging up to rescue a pop fly that has just ricocheted out of the catcher's mitt; the straight-backed "Gentleman" Jim Palmer, squinting haughtily over his left shoulder to hold the runner at first; Reggie Jackson struggling to remain upright after an unsuccessful attempt to unhorse the Marlboro cowboy on the billboard deep in the stands at Yankee Stadium; Sparky Lyle, morosely working his chaw, as he comes in to save a one-run game with none out and two on; the hyperkinetic Billy Martin kicking dirt over the home-plate umpire's shoes; white-haired Earl Weaver on the mound, holding out his hand to take the ball from a hangdog pitcher who has just allowed three runs.

On the face of it, foreigners have less reason to feel deprived by the American possessiveness about professional football. It is a relatively new sport. Baseball, rowing, and pedestrianism were the great American spectator sports of the nineteenth century. College football did not really come into its own until late in that century—forty thousand attended the Yale versus Princeton game in 1891—and professional football was a sideshow until radio gave way to television. A big drawback for the game is that it is not much fun to play. The participants are expected to be so highly specialized that it is perfectly possible for a boy entering the game in high school as right tackle to retire from football twenty years later without ever having played any other position and without ever having touched the ball in play except by accident. Though in theory the game has a playing time of an hour, the ball is actually in play for about fifteen minutes, and even this fifteen minutes is split between two squads: the defense and the offense. College players who fail to get signed up as professionals do not continue with the sport as amateurs in adult life. Those who have played the game at school or college are surprised when they are asked why this should be so. Wilson Morris, a congressional aide from Alabama, explained: "You spend the afternoon getting hit hard and that is hardly enjoyable unless you are a masochist." Edward Scharff, a journalist from Saint Louis, said: "Most kids only play it at school because it is the macho thing to do."

At the professional level the game is about as much fun for the participants as going a round or two with Larry Holmes. So much is obvious in the locker rooms after a Super Bowl, even one as exciting as the 1976 game in the Orange Bowl at Miami, where the Pittsburgh Steelers beat the Dallas Cowboys 21 to 17. The Pittsburgh fans were joyful, though not as joyful as they would have been if a last-minute touchdown by Dallas had not deprived their team of the seven-point spread the odds-makers had decided was the margin for an even-money bet on favored Pittsburgh. Pittsburgh players, like Jack Lambert, Joe Greene, and L. C. Greenwood, seemed overjoyed, too, as they took their turns standing on boxes to be questioned by dozens of press and television reporters, but once they were off camera, they stopped smiling. There was little sense of camaraderie or celebration. Exhausted and bruised, these were athletes who earn good money for a few short years at a hard trade that demands an aggressiveness that does not come easily to big men. Old baseball players, by contrast, tend to look back fondly on their playing days, as Roger Kahn discovered in *The Boys of Summer,* his where-are-they-now story of the Brooklyn Dodgers of the early 1950s. It is doubtful whether many ex-professional football players do the same.

College football is different, even though it long ago lost most of its amateurism. The Ivy League colleges once dominated the game. In 1888, Yale went through an entire season without conceding a point. It did it again in 1891, when, in winning all thirteen of its games, it scored 488. Today Yale, Harvard, Princeton, and the rest are also-rans. Their students do not try to pretend otherwise. Go to a Princeton game, for instance, on a Saturday afternoon and you will find the band performing with playful, and sometimes satirical, zest rather than competitive enthusiasm, team mascots dressed as tigers fraternizing with the visitors' cheerleaders, and stands uncrowded even late in the game, when students drift in to shout token support. The Ivy League colleges were shouldered aside by those that share the opinion once expressed by Knute Rockne of Notre Dame: "The only qualifications for a lineman are to be big and dumb. To be a back, you only have to be dumb." At football colleges, athletic scholarships are granted to a boy who cannot master the more difficult letters of the alphabet but who can throw a football. Such boys are students in name only. At Michigan, Oklahoma, Ohio State, USC, Alabama, Nebraska, and other big universities that take football seriously, players live cut off from the rest of the students. It is recognized, if not fully accepted, that they are there not to learn but to play football and perhaps open the way for a pro career. Bright players are rare. Talking to many of them, as a baseball manager once said of George Scott, the big Red Sox first baseman, is "like talking to concrete." The system's critics are many. They are outshouted by supporters. College football, say its defenders, unites sprawling universities as little else does. Team success brings in money, through gate receipts, to finance athletic programs and to encourage alumni to pay up when the university asks for funds. The college game, it is often said, leaves scope for personal flair and variety lacking in the more regimented, defensive professional game. The rival merits of college and professional football are the source of ceaseless debate, partisans of "amateur" football arguing that the pros cannot run, advocates of the professional game claiming that college teams cannot pass.

Foreigners are easily impressed by the violence of American sports. Pro football and ice hockey are rough, collision sports, but no more so than soccer or rugby football. What violence there is in American sports tends to take place in the game itself, not among the spectators, and this violence is, in turn, diminishing, though the newspapers may give a contrary view. Boxers no longer fight to the finish as they did in the days of John L. Sullivan, Jake Kilrain, and Peter Jackson. The last professional player to die on a football field, Chuck Hughes, collapsed from a heart attack. The public would never tolerate today a college football season like that of 1905, in which nineteen university players were killed. President Theodore Roosevelt summoned representatives of thirteen schools to the White House and told them the slaughter must stop. The President was not asking the colleges to turn out "mollycoddles," he explained in a speech to the Harvard Union, but then said: "I trust that I need not add that in defending athletics I would not for one moment be understood as excusing that perversion of athletics which would make it the end of life instead of merely a means of life."

Compared to sports crowds in other countries, where fighting, bottle throwing, and rioting have long been common, American spectators, certainly at professional games, are curiously passive. Inventive and unprintable abuse of referees or visiting teams is still not the rule. Crowds, unready to cheer spontaneously, are whipped on by electronic cheerleading on illuminated screens saying "Chaaarge . . . !" in house-sized letters to the sound of amplified organ music. Baseball and football games are family affairs and the staid, well-behaved Americans who go to them would be appalled by the rampages that follow British soccer games. In 1980, a man was murdered on the train carrying Scottish supporters to London for a game against England and 450 Scottish supporters were later arrested and charged with drunkenness, indecent exposure, and assault.

The language of American team sports is admittedly highly competitive. Vince Lombardi said: "Winning isn't everything, it's the only thing." Bear Bryant said of victory: "It beats anything that comes in second." Woody Hayes said: "I used to think winning was important. Now I think it's everything." According to Lombardi again: "To play this game you must have fire in you, and there is nothing that stokes fire like hate." The Washington Redskins' George Allen said: "Every time you win, you're reborn; when you lose, you die a little." Frank Maguire of South Carolina said: "In this country, when you finish second, no one knows your name." And Leo Durocher of the Brooklyn Dodgers put it most memorably: "Nice guys finish last." This win-at-all-costs spirit intrudes even into sports organized for small children. Consider the list of instructions given to eight-year-old boys in Santa Ana, California, by a team called the Packers. Under the heading "Rules for a Successful Packer Back to Live By," it advises these children to: "Become an all-round runner: Dig for more yards! Punish the tackler! Put fear in his eyes! Bruise his body! Break his spirit! Bust his butt! Make him pay a price for tackling you! Dig for more yards! Become a competitor! A competitor never quits. Be hostile! Be angry! Be violent! Be mean! Be aggressive! Be physical! Remember always— loosing [sic] is nothing! Winning is everything!" What is more striking than these sayings and slogans is that many Americans today would treat them as so laughably old-fashioned.

American rivalry in international sports that provoke such strong passions elsewhere is mainly confined to what used to be called the country club sports—tennis and golf. It is perhaps another sign of a popular culture growing steadily more middle class, more staid, and less boisterous that these two games should have increased so steadily in popularity. It was calculated that in 1980 there were more than 35 million tennis players in the United States, seven times as many as there were twenty years before, and some 20 million golfers. Soccer, too, mistakenly thought of as a less rough game than American football, is making gains among American youngsters, especially those from better-off families in the suburbs.

The image of violence in sports is not borne out by a glance at the attendance figures for major sporting events. In 1980, 51 million watched auto racing, 50 million horse racing, 44 million major league baseball, 36 million college football, 31 million college basketball, 27 million harness racing, 21 million greyhound racing, 13 million NFL football, 13 million minor league baseball, 11.5 million ice hockey, 11.4 million soccer, and 10.7 million professional basketball. Though neither tennis nor golf attracts anything like the size of audiences for college football or baseball, the people turning on the television to watch these former country club sports are, on the average, more affluent, and so relatively more attractive to advertising sponsors. The popularity of such sports, in which the aggression depends less on sheer brawn, is likely to grow, these being games people of all ages and of either sex can play without risking much more by way of injury than tennis elbow or a bee sting on the putting green.

Sports and society reflect each other. If American sports are becoming less raucous, more passive, and more commercialized, they have already become notably less racist. It is one sign of how racial barriers in American sports have crumbled that thoughtful blacks worry today that sports stardom offers false promise to too many black youngsters.

Formal discrimination in professional baseball dates back at least as far as 1887, when eight members of the Saint Louis Browns sent a letter to their owner, Chris von der Ahe, on the eve of an exhibition game against the Cuban Giants at West Farms near New York. "Dear Sir: We the undersigned, members of the St. Louis Baseball Club, do not agree to play against Negroes tomorrow. We will cheerfully play against white people at any time, and think, by refusing to play, we are only doing what is right, taking everything into consideration and the shape the team is in at present." Like other owners, von der Ahe capitulated to such pressure from players, and fans. Major league baseball remained lily white until after World War II. Most of the white followers of the game never saw Josh Gibson, a left-handed slugger in the Negro leagues, who was rated by Satchel Paige as the best batsman he ever faced. Paige himself was described as the greatest-ever pitcher by, among others, a great pitcher, Dizzy Dean, and a great hitter, Charlie "The Mechanical Man" Gehringer. The best estimate is that Paige in his career pitched about 2,500 games for 2,000 victories, with 250 shut-outs and 45 no-hitters. The color bar excluded him from the major leagues until the far end of his great career. This was after the Brooklyn Dodgers broke with apartheid in 1947 by signing Jackie Robinson, the first black to play in major-league baseball since the 1880s. Robinson did not have an easy time of it. When the Dodgers traveled to bigoted towns, he had to stay in a different hotel from his teammates. Opposing players, in a game against the Saint Louis Cardinals, taunted him from the dugout by shouting such things as "Hey, porter, git my bag" and "Here, boy. Here, boy. Shine."

In college football, Paul Robeson earned a great name for himself at Rutgers during World War I. Teams from integrated colleges continued to get into color-bar trouble in the South. Football teams, like college basketball teams, were confronted with the choice of dropping the black players from the team or having the game canceled. In November 1946, the University of Nevada called off a scheduled game against Mississippi State and Penn State a game against the University of Miami when their Southern opponents objected to black players in their lineups. It was not until September 1950 that the first black player appeared in a Southern Conference game. Even in boxing, superficially the most color-blind of big professional sports, American blacks for long suffered discrimination. Jack Johnson, the first black heavyweight champion of the world, was hated in much of white America and the writer Jack London was among those behind a frantic, frustrating search for a "White Hope" to defeat him. Bands played "All the Coons Look Alike to Me" when fight fans surged into Reno to see James J. Jeffries come out of retirement to challenge Johnson, unsuccessfully, for the title. When Congress in 1912 passed the Mann (White Slavery) Act to stop men from taking women across state lines for immoral purposes, Johnson was a target. In 1913 he was arrested, convicted of this offense, and after several years in exile, eventually jailed at "The Walls," the federal penitentiary at Leavenworth. When first Johnson and then a strong black heavyweight called Harry Willis challenged Jack Dempsey to a title fight, Dempsey drew a color line. He had announced, upon winning the championship, on July 4, 1919, from Jess Willard, that he would "pay no attention to Negro challengers, but will defend against any white heavyweight as the occasion demands." Florida did not permit a black man to fight a white one until 1952, when Kid Gavilan, "The Hawk" from Cuba, outpointed a local white hope, Bobby Dykes, in Miami.

It is another sign of the progress in sports made by blacks that talk of discrimination in sports today is likely to be taken to mean discrimination against women. A better term might be neglect, itself a form of discrimination. At one large state university, quite recently, the athletic budget of $3.9 million devoted $31,000 to women's sports, even though there were as many women students as men. Sports coverage tends to concentrate on games between men. Women in sports got separate but unequal status, but not because they threatened to beat men, as blacks threatened to beat whites, at their own sports. Games, serious games at least, were simply not part of women's sphere. These old patterns are going, though not as fast as they might. On television, there is plenty of women's tennis and women's golf. Boys and girls play soccer together. Women, as much as men, are targets of the sporting goods and leisure market advertising. Whatever social usefulness there was to keeping women out of the sphere of sports is passing, just as it passed thirty years ago or more for blacks.

14

IN GOD WE TRUST
Religions

IT WOULD BE SURPRISING if a narrowing of economic horizons, heavier pressures on men and women in the family, and the subtle crowding of American life had not cast their reflections in the religious sphere or had left unchanged what Americans see when they look into themselves. However much cold water is kept on hand to douse the hotter talk of a national religious revival or a new American self-absorption, it is impossible for anyone who has watched the United States recently with even half an eye not to have asked himself what was up when two candidates for President in the 1980 election were born-again Christians or when Fortune 500 companies encouraged employees to attend sensitivity training seminars. It is impossible, too, for students of trends not to ask themselves how the Me Decade of the 1970s and the Culture of Narcissism fits in with the Moral Majority and the growth of evangelical Protestantism, or how either of these apparently irreconcilable cultural forces could have usurped in such a short space of time the prevailing wind of only ten years ago, the youth movement and the counterculture. This is a cloudy matter, and in finding a way through, it is useful to keep in mind a trenchant summary made by the pollster Daniel Yankelovich of the changed circumstances that confront today's Americans as opposed to those that faced Americans of thirty years ago. In the years after World War II, he has said, Americans had a permissive economy and a restrictive morality. Today, by contrast, they have a restrictive economy and a permissive morality. That is putting it much too starkly, as Yankelovich might agree. Such change is neither so neat nor so brief, but this distinction is good to remember in considering what has been happening recently in American religion—an apparently strong conservative reaction among a large number of churchgoers—and at the opposite pole, what has been happening, among a different group of Americans, to many traditional moral conventions.

Gibbon wrote of the Romans at the time of the early Caesars that "their conduct of this life was never regulated by any serious conviction of the rewards and punishments of a future state." At first blush, much the same seems true of Americans. They strike the casual observer as one of the least other-worldly people on this earth, far more interested in the here and now than in any putative future life. The evidence seems overwhelming, however, that materialistic Americans have remained a God-fearing people despite all those "-ations" that are supposed by sociologists to cause a falling off of interest in religion: modernization, secularization, urbanization, and industrialization. More than nine out of ten Americans say they believe in God and prayer; seven out of ten that they believe in an afterlife. Over a third describe themselves as born-again Christians. Over 40 percent reply Yes when they are asked by pollsters: "Did you, yourself, happen to attend church or synagogue during the past seven days?"

These same polls indicate that the young are less likely to be religious participants than the middle-aged or the old, but this has always been so and it is possible that the decline in regular church and synagogue attendance from 1955, when 49 percent of Americans attended on a regular sabbath, to just over 40 percent in the late 1960s and in the 1970s was due mainly to demographic changes in the age profile of the population as a whole. Thus the temporary increase in the percentage of young adults in the population, as a result of the postwar and the 1950s baby booms, and the temporary decrease in the percentage of older adults probably for a while much exaggerated the apparent overall national decline in religious participation.

On this assumption, church and synagogue attendance should be expected to pick up again during the 1980s as the young adults of the 1960s and 1970s have families of their own and decide their children need a religious upbringing. The increasing mobility of Americans will also help to fill the places of worship, since the church and the synagogue perform a social as well as a religious function. In the absence of secular clubs, they are places to get to know the neighbors; places where the newcomer, the stranger, may get integrated into the community. The way the population is growing in the South at a faster rate than elsewhere, largely through internal migration, will aid the religious recruiters; at least it will if the newcomers do as Southerners do. Religious observance is higher in the states of the Old Confederacy than in other parts of the country. George Gallup, a devout Catholic, reports that 44 percent of the people in the South go to a religious service in any week, compared to only 32 percent in the West. California has more religions and a lower percentage of religious participants than other states.

Paul Sherry is among those who argue most strenuously that it is a mistake to conclude that relatively low religious participation among young Americans indicates a lack of interest in religion itself. His office is in a run-down part of the garment district in New York City, not far from Madison Square Garden. A large bookshelf in his otherwise bare workplace suggests he is a voracious reader of religious books. The titles are often catchy: *Changing of the Gods*, *The Staggering Steeple*, *Caution—God at Work*. Sherry displays a similar flair in the titles for articles in his *Journal of Current Social Issues*. "Sex Is Awe-ful" is typical.

Sherry is not a passive observer of religious trends. He makes frequent sorties out of New York to talk on college campuses and is struck by the way the questions have changed. Ten or fifteen years ago his student audiences were mainly interested in civil rights, Vietnam, and social questions. Now they are more preoccupied by questions of individual faith, and not always of the conventional kind. There is, he says, a reaction against institutions, including religious ones, as well as a lively interest in cults and in meditational literature. A visit to Boulder, Colorado, bears him out. Young Buddhists are almost easier to find there than young Episcopalians or young Presbyterians.

Firmer ground on which to say that it is wrong to treat young people as heathens or agnostics simply because they are less regular church- or synagogue-goers than their parents or grandparents can be found in the Princeton Religion Research Center of George Gallup. He has found, in a youth survey conducted in eleven nations by Gallup-affiliated organizations, that young adults in the United States are far more religious than their counterparts in many other lands. About 41 percent of young Americans say they think religion should be "very important" in life, far more than in seven of the ten other nations polled: Australia, Britain, France, Japan, Sweden, Switzerland, and West Germany. Only in the Philippines (83 percent), India (60 percent), and Brazil (52 percent) are higher proportions recorded.

The manner in which many Americans worship is changing in a way that has shaken the three mighty pillars of religious faith in the country: Protestantism, Catholicism, and Judaism. For Catholicism and Judaism the struggle is to find a working compromise between modernism and assimilation on the one hand and distinctiveness on the other: a distinctiveness married to continued integration in universal faiths that seek to embrace adherents in other continents. The mainline Protestant churches—Episcopalians, Congregationalists, and Presbyterians—are even more shaken. They are losing members and influence to those denominations that are stricter in their demands on their members, and more severe in their strictures against society.

Recent years have brought great shifts and debates among American Jews, Catholics, and Protestants, but these have provoked little comment, except in the religious journals. Growth in Jewish marriage to non-Jews, declining size of Jewish families, and concern about renewal of anti-Semitism have sharpened debates between reform and conservative traditions, and given fresh sense to the old question: "What is a Jew?" Among Catholics, liberals and traditionalists have still to find common ground definitively lost after Vatican II. Less noticed still is the increase among Catholics of charismatics, the Catholic counterpart of Protestant evangelicals. These last have not only grown among new denominations and in electronic churches associated with the New Right, which have had much attention in the press, but they have grown noticeably, as well, within the old Protestant denominations.

The huge attention given the recent engagement in politics by evangelical Protestants in newer sects may well have exaggerated both the significance and the novelty of the movement. The evangelical right, typified by well-financed organizations using the latest communications techniques, such as Jerry Falwell's Virginia-based Moral Majority, Inc., have all the strength of simplicity and conviction, especially since the targets at which they rail—secular humanists, the great universities, the Eastern press, tolerant politicians, and liberal clergymen

—are so diffuse. Particularly after the 1980 election, in which the evangelical right gave Reagan and many conservative senators strong support, it may have looked as if the evangelicals were set to lead the nation on a politico-moral crusade. The matter was far from this simple. Though this general lack of interest in religion and the very attention given the evangelical right seem extraordinary in a country where so many people of all political persuasions are active believers, those who take a professional interest in religious trends are not at all puzzled by the silence. The reasons they put forward to explain the absence of national debate on matters of religious importance are as intriguing as the changes themselves.

Among the reasons commonly cited for religion's being either ignored or sensationalized is the supposed emergence among the country's opinionmakers and intellectuals, though not necessarily among its politicians, of an attitude of secular humanism. This is an imprecise term, especially when used, as it frequently is, as a term of abuse, and a difficult term to get to grips with, since so few Americans would accept the label. It is safe to say that it suggests a general outlook on the world—tolerant according to its defenders, ungodly to the less tolerant believers—in which the part played by religious faith is either strictly private or incidental. American academics, intellectuals, and journalists in the Boston–Washington and San Francisco–Los Angeles corridors are an old and easy target. Neither acquaintance with them nor studies made of them as a group suggest they share a single outlook —on politics, religion, or any matter, although they are perhaps open to the charge of being professionally reluctant to accept much on faith.

There are many other reasons that might spring to mind for the relative absence of religious news outside of old heavily Catholic cities, like Boston or Chicago, or of religious news that is not a papal visit or a vile deed, such as the Jonestown slaughter, done in religion's name. The very existence of so many denominations and such distinct religious sensibilities is one reason that the prudent course for editors is often to keep clear of a difficult subject.

Books about Christianity, especially of the uplifting, devotional sort, have large and rising sales. Between 1972 and 1977, for instance, their sales expanded 112 percent, compared to 70 percent for books generally. Religious books, however, are rarely reviewed in the secular press and are in effect not eligible for the best-seller list. This is because most of the hundred or so religious-book publishers are private, denominational firms that sell their books by direct mail, through religious-book clubs, in discount stores and convenience markets, and in about five thousand small religious-book stores. As a result, even runaway religious best-sellers do not get into the best-seller lists of *The New York Times Book Review* and other publications, which report only the sales of trade and "general interest" books.

Partly because of this neglect and because of the apartness of the religious presses, the growth of strict churches and of strict strains within existing denominations and the decline of liberal churches were not given widespread attention until the evangelical right burst into politics. There ought to have been less consternation about this than there was, for religious activism in politics—across the political spectrum—is as old as the Republic, despite the constitutional separation of religious and secular life. In the nineteenth century, Northern Presbyterians and Evangelicals, among others, joined the crusades against slavery, city vice, and alcohol. The Catholic Church played an active part in the anti-Communist Great Fear in the late 1940s and 1950s. Black clergymen marched for civil rights. "Israel has become the Jewish Religion for American Jews," Nathan Glazer wrote recently. Many priests and nuns were active in the movement against the Vietnam War, like the sister who said in a speech to demonstrators amid the tear gas outside the Republican convention in 1972 when Nixon's war was dragging on: "Not only must we read Thomas Aquinas on peace, we must do Thomas Aquinas on peace." Famously, there was the Episcopalian clergyman who was asked in the 1950s what his religion stood for and said: "Belief in Jesus Christ and the admission of China to the United Nations."

The First Amendment to the Constitution says, in part: "Congress shall make no law respecting an establishment of religion, or prohibiting the free exercise thereof." There is no established religion, the last established churches in the states having been disestablished a century and a half ago. Even the strangest religious sects have escaped modern persecution. Indeed, religion is one of the few areas of national life—universities and psychiatry are two others—in which something close to a true free market in services prevails. Lord Bryce thought it fortunate for the Americans that lines of religious allegiance and state boundaries never neatly coincided and that no single denomination ever held complete sway over any of the nation's great regions. Utah's Mormon theocracy might seem the exception, but Utah could only enter the Union on condition that its practices in the relations between church and state—including the abolition of polygamy—conformed to those in the nation at large. The scattering of religious creeds has contributed to Americans' having managed to mute the worst religious conflicts in their political life. The very existence of so many creeds has also meant that, in modern times at least, there was not even a candidate—had there been any demand for one—for the role of established church or national religion. The growth of sizable Chinese and Japanese communities, as well as the institutionalization and acceptance of varieties of Buddhism, mean that the United States is not only no longer exclusively Christian or Judeo-Christian in religion, but not even exclusively monotheist.

Churches have tax-exempt status, but all have this equally providing they can convince the Internal Revenue Service they are truly religions, which they usually can, although some, like the Unification Church, have run into trouble. Its task of maintaining tolerance for different creeds aside, the government's dealings on religious matters are complicated. There is no wall between government and religious life. This is most obvious in symbolic ways. There are more important ones, as well.

The words "In God We Trust" still appear on the coinage. Recitation of the Pledge of Allegiance to the flag was amended to include the words "under God" during the cold war years of the 1950s. Conscientious objection on religious grounds or grounds of personal ethical conviction is an accepted reason for refusing to perform military service. In *Pierce* v. *The Society of Sisters* in 1925, the Supreme Court said it was constitutionally improper for a state to require children to attend its schools and thus sustained the right of parents to choose parochial, which means mostly Roman Catholic, schools. The Army, the Navy, and the Air Force have chaplains paid for and promoted by the armed services, not by the religious denominations they serve. The armed services claim that if the chaplains did not have a military rank, they would have no influence within the system and other officials would push them around. Each house of Congress also has a chaplain's office.

The churches play a central role in state funerals. Christmas is a national public holiday, though none of the Jewish holidays are, and each year a Christmas tree is erected behind the White House. American Presidents are expected to make at least a show of religious piety, and three of the past six of them, Presidents Eisenhower, Ford, and Carter, have been openly religious men. Carter, a born-again Christian, often drew a comparison between God-fearing Americans and atheistic Russians, notably when he invited OPEC Moslems to contemplate where the truer threat to their interests lay. This was an advance on the American delegate to the U.N. from 1947 to 1953, Warren Austin, who beseeched Arabs and Jews to settle their disputes "in a Christian manner."

On the other hand, the United States has no formal diplomatic relations with the Vatican. Public money is withheld from parochial schools though their pupils can benefit from some government programs, and religious observance is prohibited in public schools. In public education, the attention given to separation of church and state is relatively recent. It emerged from efforts to keep religion in public schools and out of a controversial Supreme Court decision in June 1962 resisting these efforts. Then, with only Justice Potter Stewart dissenting, the Court said New York State in using its schools to encourage recitation of a prayer had "adopted a practice wholly inconsistent with the establishment clause of the Constitution."

The prayer that provoked this fuss was both short and bland: "Almighty God, we acknowledge our dependence upon Thee, and we beg Thy blessing upon us, our parents, our teachers and our country." The Supreme Court ruling on this, and an earlier one on the use of classrooms for religious instruction, was bound to cause argument. For most of the Republic's history, school children have said prayers and been taught religion, commonly of an amorphous Protestant kind. But the public schools are also taken to have a duty to foster pluralism. A visitor would doubtless conclude from all this that religion is central in American life but that the country has muddled through cannily to a workable compromise between the conviction of the majority of its citizens that there is some form of divinity and profound disagreement between them on the character of this God and on the proper worship.

One consequence of the constitutional separation of church and state, minor in itself but important when it comes to describing religion in America, is that government censuses of religious affiliation are not permitted. Religious bodies count their members in different ways and since some may have an interest in exaggerating their numbers, these are not always reliable. Thus, a further reason for the neglect until quite recently of the growth in strict creeds, alluded to earlier, is the awkwardness of religious statistics. Roman Catholics and Southern Baptists report only baptized members, but then Southern Baptists are usually baptized later in life than Catholics. United Methodists, United Presbyterians, and the United Church of Christ report communicant membership. The Episcopalian Church and the three main Lutheran denominations report both baptized and communicant membership.

This makes comparisons between sizes of denominations risky. The statistics can be used as a fairly reliable guide to membership trends of the various denominations relative to one another. The broad picture that emerges is not blurred. Strict churches are waxing. Liberal churches are waning.

The growth of the strict churches and of strict strains within tolerant churches will increase ecclesiastical choice in the United States, which is already a place of astonishing religious variety when compared to Europe, and also to its immediate neighbors. In Mexico, 96 percent of the people are Catholic. In Canada, the three largest denominations —the Roman Catholic Church, the United Church of Canada, and the Anglican Church of Canada—together account for 86 percent of total membership of religious bodies. The United States can, in contrast, be fairly said to have a free market in religion. To embrace 86 percent of the membership of America's religious bodies it is necessary to add together nineteen different groups. The 72.4 million Protestants in the United States belong to 186 denominations and worship at 300,000 churches. The country's 5.8 million Orthodox, Conservative, and Reform Jews have 5,000 synagogues; its Eastern churches, with 3.8 million members, are divided into seventeen different religious bodies with 1,500 churches; and its 50 million Catholics have 25,000 churches. And each year thousands of mainly young Americans leave home, school, or job to follow one or another of the gaggle of gurus, messiahs, and pied pipers. There are about 1,500 major and minor religious cults in the United States, with a total of about 3 million members. The range of options offered to would-be worshipers within the bigger religious bodies is impressive. The options offered to Americans by the smaller religious bodies is astounding.

Wonderful names abound among the more obscure Christian denominations. Duck River (and Kindred) Associations of Baptists; the Fire Baptized Holiness Church (Wesleyan); House of God, Which is the Church of the Living God, the Pillar and Ground of the Truth, Inc.; the International Church of the Foursquare Gospel; the Pillar of Fire; Triumph the Church of God and Kingdom of God in Christ (International); the National Baptist Evangelical Life and Soul Saving Assembly of the USA. The range of religious beliefs and practices cater to diverse, and quirky, enthusiasms. The Advent Christian Church withdrew from the American Millennial Association between 1854 and 1860 as a result of controversy over the questions of immortality. According to the *Yearbook of the American and Canadian Church:* "As a corollary to their belief in conditional immortality, the group also held to the utter extinction of the wicked after the judgment." The Christian Catholic Church (Evangelical-Protestant) has as doctrines the necessity of repentance for sin and personal trust in Christ for salvation, baptism by triune immersion, and tithing as a practical method of Christian stewardship. The doctrines of the Bible Church of Christ include miracles of healing and the baptism of the Holy Ghost, with the initial evidence of speaking in tongues. The Church of the Brethren has no other creed than the New Testament and holds to the principles of nonviolence, temperance, and voluntarism, stressing religion in life. The Universal Fellowship of Metropolitan Community Churches was founded in October 1968 by the Reverend Troy Perry in Los Angeles, with particular but not exclusive outreach to homosexuals. The National Spiritual Alliance of the United States, founded in 1913, believes in supernormal personal and impersonal manifestations, and in intercommunication between denizens of different worlds.

This multitude of religious bodies fascinates foreigners and Americans alike. The country is not renowned for its tolerance of eccentrics and it is generally a compliment to be described by an American as a regular guy, which usually means an amiable conformist. In politics, an advocate of a radically different system—a Communist, a Socialist— is not just outside the pale; his or her patriotism is called into question. In religion, Americans are tolerant to an extreme. Hare Krishnas, with shaven heads and wearing saffron robes, are permitted in the name of religious freedom to behave in ways that strike some as amiable lunacy.

Amish fundamentalists claim and receive the same tolerance when they slow traffic and sometimes, it is said, cause accidents by relying on real horsepower rather than the internal combustion kind to get around Lancaster County in Pennsylvania. Religious enthusiasts are allowed to stick flowers into the buttonholes of travelers at airports and aggressively to beg money for religious causes.

A sinking feeling pervades the solider Protestant churches that provide the spiritual props for the white Anglo-Saxon Protestant tradition in the United States. Strictly speaking, of course, it is misleading to describe these as WASP churches. The Presbyterians came out of a Scottish rather than an English movement; the Wesleyans' challenge to an Anglican Church they found effete was as strong in the valleys of Wales as in the countryside of England. As the term "WASP" is understood in the United States, it certainly covers the "Big Three," the Presbyterians, the Episcopalians, and the Congregationalists, whose denomination was rechristened the United Church of Christ in 1957. More arguably, it is also extended to embrace the eighteenth- and nineteenth-century revivalist rivals to these three denominations, notably the Methodists and the Baptists.

Until a few years ago, the traditional Protestant churches appeared unconcerned with, almost unaware of, this increasing religious pluralism. Their complacency was especially marked in the colonial "Big Three." Members of other faiths, it was implied, would soon discover that in seeking status it was necessary for Americans to move up from Anabaptism, up from Methodism, up from Pentecostalism, up from Roman Catholicism. And this complacency seemed almost justified during the 1950s, when the mainline churches benefited from a national resurgence in churchgoing.

Their brief cold war revival probably resulted from several passing things, such as the example offered by President Eisenhower's uncomplicated faith, the widely propagated conviction that religion was a shield in the nation's fight for survival against atheistic communism, and a lingering dissatisfaction with a materialist culture. These denominations benefited, too, from a then current assumption that religious participation in the traditional Protestant churches was an important sign of upward mobility. In the fifties, much more than now, what it meant to be an American was to move to the suburbs, to have two or three children, and to give them a good Christian upbringing in one of the more liberal Protestant faiths. Because the motive for joining these churches was for many more social than anything else, the faith of professed believers was often very shallow, like that of Marilyn Monroe, who told a reporter: "I just believe in everything—a little bit."

Though the congregations started melting away by the end of the Eisenhower era, the collapse of the mainline churches into a mood of self-doubt did not begin until the mid-sixties. Since then they have taken constantly to feeling their pulse, and have discovered real, not imagined, symptoms that confirm they are suffering from a wasting disease. For year after year during the past two decades, they have seen their membership decline not just as a proportion of an expanding population but in terms of actual numbers as well. The Southern Baptists, perhaps the least liberal of the mainline Protestants, are the only notable exception. They have succeeded in winning more than enough members to replace those who have defected or died.

At the most mundane level, this has caused what industrial managers would call excess capacity. Churches built during the 1940s and 1950s, when the congregations of the mainline Protestant churches expanded, are ever emptier on Sundays. Would-be clergy emerging from Protestant seminaries find that there are more applicants than vacancies for people of their calling. Church collections are insufficient to meet the present payroll or to pay for the upkeep of religious buildings. To do these churches justice, these are the least of their concerns. They fret far more about their failure as preachers of the Christian gospel to retain the loyalty of so many of their old members and their inability to win new ones.

Several explanations for this state of affairs are professed by those who write about church membership trends for religious journals. Some see a natural life cycle, from growing adolescence to comfortable decline in old age, in churches as in people. They regard it as perhaps regrettable but quite normal that the Methodists and the Baptists, though not yet the more fervent Southern Baptists, have gradually become as easygoing and unevangelical as the more venerable Episcopalians, Presbyterians, and Congregationalists. Others see it as due to a lack of resonance, of religious trappings, since the church adopted a decidedly unmajestic liturgy and put aside the seventeenth-century English of the King James Bible in favor of modern translations that have the commonsensical, flat prose of *U.S. News & World Report.*

Still others believe that congregations will begin to grow again when the mainline Protestants succeed through the ecumenical movement in negotiating away most of their differences by patching together some form of church unity. The evidence for this is slight. The United Church of Christ, formed by the merger of the Congregational Christian Churches with the Evangelical and Reformed Church in 1957, has not proved any more successful in keeping and winning adherents than the other mainline congregations. The chances are that greater unity, especially if it leads to the creation of a supersized Protestant Church, will repel more people than it attracts in a country that has grown suspicious of bigness. For instance, the continuing reluctance of Presbyterians to close a regional schism that dates back to rows over slavery is certainly based in large part on a fear by Southern Presbyterians that they will lose their identity in a merger with the Yankees.

More persuasively, it is argued that the WASP denominations have lost ground and vitality by their exclusiveness and their unwillingness to make members of other ethnic groups feel at home in their churches. A sampling of sermons gives this theory some credence. Episcopalian preachers have a tendency to adopt the well-rounded vowel sounds of their Anglican counterparts; Presbyterian preachers to roll their r's, as in "crrrooked," "disrrreputable," "rrreaction," in the best Edinburgh pulpit manner. The difference in warmth between the mainline and evangelical branches of Protestant was obvious in attending, on successive Sundays, the services of two of the best preachers in the United States: the Reverend David Read of the Madison Avenue Presbyterian Church of New York, a transplanted Scot, whose sermons sell well in book form, and the Reverend Robert Schuller of the Garden Grove Community Church in Orange County, California, and of *Hour of Power* on television. At Dr. Read's church, the congregation showed a shy politeness to newcomers, a studied avoidance of any hint of intrusion, a demeanor that could be easily mistaken for standoffishness. At Dr. Schuller's church, newcomers were exuberantly greeted by lay officials as they entered the building and the minister himself began the service by chatting rather than preaching to the congregation and by posing for snapshots alongside people who had seen him on television and wanted photographs to prove to their friends that they had met the famous evangelist.

The most compelling, and polemical, explanation for the decline of mainline Protestantism comes from an improbable source in the shape of Dean Kelley, a minister of the United Methodist Church, who has a mild-mannered Pickwickian look about him with his longish gray hair, gold-rimmed spectacles, and small, stout build. As "executive for religious liberty" of the National Council of Churches, he wrote and in 1972 caused to be published a slim book called *Why Conservative Churches Are Growing*, which is perhaps the most influential, and surely the most roundly denounced, work of church scholarship to be published in the United States in the past twenty years. The reverberations from it grow each year as his arguments stand the test of time.

Like all good religious controversialists, Kelley revels in the storm he has caused, not least because the mischievous side of his character is amused by the obvious discomfort its assertions have brought to many of the well-meaning people who staff the offices of the National Council of Churches he occupies, overlooking the Hudson River on the upper West Side of New York, not far from Columbia University. A majority of them are liberal almost to a fault and, funded mainly by the Presbyterians and the Methodists, are both professionally and personally committed to work for greater Christian unity through the creation of a formal or informal coalition of the mainline Protestant churches. This greater unity necessitates for many of them a softening of dogma and a planing away of the liturgical and doctrinal differences among the denominations.

In Dean Kelley's unhumble opinion, they could hardly be more wrongheaded. His conviction is that churches can be "strong" or "weak" and that strict churches grow while permissive churches contract. Strong churches are marked by an insistence on a high commitment from their members, including loyalty and social solidarity. They expect obedience to the commands of a charismatic leadership. They have a missionary zeal, with eagerness to tell the "good news" of one's salvation to others. They are intolerant of deviance or dissent and are absolutist about beliefs ("We have the Truth and all others are in error"). In their dealings with outsiders they are "all talk, no listen." Weak churches, in contrast, are characterized by a belief that no one has a monopoly on truth, that all insights are partial. They are tolerant of internal diversity and their leadership is institutional, not charismatic. They lack any enforcement of canons or doctrine, have an attitude of dialogue with outsiders rather than proselytism, expect only a limited commitment to the church, and engage little effective sharing of convictions or spiritual insights within the group. It is obvious from all this that a more accurate title for the Kelley book, as the author himself proclaims, would be *Why Strict Churches Are Strong,* since in theory at least there is no reason why a church should not be strict in applying liberal doctrines.

In the preface, Dean Kelley quotes the following as widespread and reiterated misconceptions: It is generally assumed that religious enterprises, if they want to succeed, will be reasonable, rational, courteous, responsible; restrained and receptive to outside criticism. That is, they will want to preserve a good image in the world, as the world defines these terms. It is expected, moreover, that they will be democratic and gentle in their internal affairs, again as the outside world defines these qualities. They will be responsible to the needs of people, as currently perceived, and will want to work cooperatively with other groups to meet these needs. They will not let dogmatism, judgmental moralism, or obsessions with cultic purity stand in the way of such cooperation and service.

Though Dean Kelley is exaggerating for effect, this assumption is strongly held in many denominations. Most of the mainline Protestant churches would indeed risk a schism if they required their members to pledge total obedience for, say, an experimental period of a month to just one of the Ten Commandments. Some members would doubtless argue that killing can in certain circumstances be justified, that adultery can sometimes bring new meaning to and enrich a marriage, that coveting a neighbor's house, wife, manservant, maidservant, ox, and ass is an essential contributor to upward mobility and the American free enterprise system. And when a chart is drawn starting with the strictest churches at the top and the most permissive churches at the bottom —an exercise called "the exclusivist-ecumenical gradient" by sociologists—it almost exactly mirrors the changes in religious observance. Churches at the top, strict half of the chart, such as the Jehovah's Witnesses, the Latter-Day Saints, and the Southern Baptist Convention, have expanded their membership mightily during the past two decades. Churches at the bottom, or most broad-minded, end of the chart have experienced a steady decline in their membership and include the United Methodists, the Episcopalians, the United Church of Christ, the United Presbyterian Church (USA). Much the same pattern is seen in the Lutheran denominations. The starchiest of the three largest Lutheran denominations, the Lutheran Church–Missouri Synod, has become even starchier since its president, Dr. Jacob Preus, purged its main seminary in Saint Louis of dissenters in the early 1970s, and it now shows signs of bucking the trend that is emptying the pews in the softer Protestant denominations. A coincidence?

Even so, the growth of the stricter churches needs to be kept in perspective. Exclude 13 million Southern Baptists, who anyway veer more toward the mainline Protestants than to the more fundamentalist faiths, and the largest of the stricter churches are still only of middling size. The Latter-Day Saints, about 2.5 million members, the Assemblies of God, about 1 million, and the Jehovah's Witnesses and the Seventh-Day Adventists, both well under a million, are still heavily outnumbered by just under 10 million United Methodists, by 8 million members of the three biggest Lutheran bodies—the American Lutheran Church, the Lutheran Church in America, and the Lutheran Church–Missouri Synod—and by over 3 million Presbyterians in split Northern and Southern wings: the United Presbyterian Church in the USA and the Presbyterian Church in the U.S. Though such membership statistics are notoriously unreliable and comparisons between the membership figures of one religious body and another are fraught with pitfalls, the mainline Protestants continue to tower over the evangelical religious bodies.

Yet a puzzle remains. Why are Americans in this day and age becoming even more pluralistic in their religious observances when the current in other areas of their national life runs so robustly toward greater uniformity? Simply to pose the question is to suggest the tentative answer that comes from Professor John Wilson of the Department of Religion at Princeton University. He suspects that religion offers a safety valve for diversity in a still essentially pluralistic society that has become increasingly integrated economically since the Civil War and ever more integrated culturally since World War II, as the South has entered into the political mainstream and as the three national television networks, together with nationally syndicated columns and news services, have tended to reduce regional differences in the way Americans think, vote, live their lives, and even talk.

Churches remain, informally but effectively, far more segregated than public schools, workplaces, sports, and even buses have been since the civil rights struggles of the fifties and sixties. Nationally, only about two million blacks are members of predominantly white churches and all the signs are that most Americans, black and white, blue collar and white collar alike, prefer to become Christians without crossing either racial or class barriers. For many church professionals, this is a standing rebuke to their teachings. It particularly upsets the staff at the headquarters of the National Council of Churches, who try so hard to be blind in their working relationships to the class and color and even the sex of their colleagues. So C. Peter Wagner of the Fuller Theological Seminary in Pasadena, California, provokes the utmost irritation when he claims, as he often does, that a preference for single-class, single-color churches does not mean that the Christian ethical code permits deliberate discrimination or racism but only that the most natural way for a church to grow is among one people at a time. "Churches that realistically evaluate themselves culturally and that gear their ministry toward meeting the needs of people most like themselves are in a position to grow. On the other hand, churches which decide to try to meet the needs of a variety of people usually find that they have growth problems. It is not possible for one church to meet the needs of everyone in the community for an extended period of time. Conglomerate congregations that grow well are a rarity." Predictably, such opinions are deplored when they are not actually denounced as heretical in the more liberal Protestant denominations. Yet the continued separation of whites and blacks when it comes to worship and the success of comparatively strict religious bodies that offer something distinctly different from that available in less rigid alternatives, including the mainline Protestant churches, indicate that in religion at least, a good chunk of the American population is indeed seeking acceptable expression for minority views, and at times prejudices, that are no longer tolerated in the political culture at large.

The resistance to cultural conformity is spectacularly confirmed in the so-called electronic churches, which have made a nonsense of claims that fundamentalism is condemned to eventual extinction in a sophisticated modern materialistic society. Far from contracting, religious broadcasting has grown into a big business in the United States. More than 1,300 radio and 36 television stations devote all or most of their time to religion. Gospel programs that buy time, sometimes prime time, are also proliferating. The concrete signs of success are impressive. The Reverend Oral Roberts, a once shrieking preacher who has toned himself down and is now a veteran of evangelical broadcasting, has raised enough money from his followers to go ahead with a City of Faith at Tulsa, Oklahoma, that by some reckonings will cost as much as $400 million and will encompass a sixty-story clinic, a twenty-story research center for cancer, heart, and aging diseases, and a thirty-story hospital with 777 beds because Roberts believes in lucky seven. The Reverend Jerry Falwell of the Thomas Road Baptist Church in Lynchburg, Virginia, and of the *Old Time Gospel Hour* on television, the leading apostle of the new Religious Right, has $50 million a year rolling in and has started work on a Christian university for, eventually, 50,000 students and no nonsense: no movies, no dancing, and no mixed-sex dormitories. The Reverend Pat Robertson of the Christian Broadcasting Network, which puts out a talk show called *The 700 Club*, is busy building a similarly ambitious international headquarters at Virginia Beach, Virginia. North Carolina's Jim Bakker is also doing well with *The PTL Show*, which is loosely modeled on the Johnny Carson show. The initials PTL are supposed to stand for "Praise the Lord" but have other connotations in the Carolinas; a Charlotte radio station broadcasts a parody called *Pass the Loot*. Exact figures are hard to come by, but by all reckonings the religion of the airwaves is a financial success. The Reverend Charles Swann of the Union Theological Seminary in Richmond, Virginia, and general manager of WRFK-FM, estimated in early 1980 that Robert Schuller pulled in $12–$15 million a year; the Reverend Rex Humbard, $25–$30 million; the PTL Club, $25–$27 million; Billy Graham, $30 million; Jerry Falwell, $45–$50 million; the 700 Club, $50 million; Oral Roberts, $55–$60 million; and the Worldwide Church of God, $75 million.

The liberal Protestant churches are disconcerted by both the medium and the message. Studies they have commissioned indicate that more than eighty out of a hundred people who decide to join a church do so at the invitation of a friend or relative; fewer than one person in a hundred comes in after listening to an evangelical broadcast.

Martin Marty of the University of Chicago, an associate editor of the *Christian Century*, is not lost for an explanation.

> Late Saturday night Mr. and Mrs. Invisible Religion get their jollies from the ruffle-shirted, pink tuxedoed men and the high-coiffeured, low-neck-lined celebrity women who talk about themselves under the guise of born-again autobiographies. Sunday morning the watchers get their jollies as Holy Ghost entertainers caress microphones among spurting fountains as a highly charismatic (in two senses) leader entertains them. Are they to turn off that very set and then to make their way down the block to a congregation of real believers, sinners, off-key choirs, sweaty and homely people they do not like but are supposed to love, ordinary pastors who preach grace along with calls to discipleship, pleas for stewardship that do not come well-oiled? Never. Well, hardly ever. Since the electronic church, you remind me, at least "preaches Christ" and thus may do some good, let it be. Let its members pay for it. But let the church catch on to what is going on, and go its own way, undistracted by the offers of "cheap grace" or the language of the cross without the mutual bearing of the cross.

His gibe at cheap grace displays conviction, especially when directed at the religious programs that plagiarize the slickest techniques of the commercial television talk shows. For the electronic evangelists, or at least most of them, are not the holy rollers of old who, in fire-and-brimstone sermons to people seated on hard chairs in tents, denounced the world as a wicked place that their followers should turn their backs upon in pursuit of salvation in the next world. Instead, the pitch is that a commitment to Jesus offers a shortcut to happiness. Not earning enough money? Give your life over to Jesus and you may well become as rich as rich Guest A. Is your sex life a flop? Listen to Guest B tell you how fulfilled his Christian marriage has become since he found salvation. Your kids are disobedient brats? Then take a look at these handsome, delightfully well-mannered children who are a typical product of a Christian home.

The talk is not sophisticated. A guest on one of them explained: "You know, when you eat onions, you're going to burp a foul onion smell. But when you eat God, you'll burp a sweet odor to the world." The commonly achieved aim is to offer as an advertisement for Christianity well-washed, well-groomed, well-heeled people, although the old and afflicted are brought up on stage for the television crusade of faith healer Ernest Angley. Charity, at least when it comes in the form of welfare payments or food stamps through government, is considered un-Christian, when it is not actually labeled Communistic. The substance of the message of the electronic churches, both in the talk shows and in the more conventional sermons, has a distinctly reactionary bias. Jerry Falwell calls for the registration of all Communists: "We should stamp it on their foreheads." In a typical sermon, he denounces homosexuals, welfare cheaters, sex education, pornographic books, drug peddlers, the Equal Rights Amendment, and, in a dig at women pastors, "sermonettes by preacherettes." The Worldwide Church of God, founded in Southern California by Herbert Armstrong, believes Israelis are ersatz Jews. God's chosen people, the real Jews, left the Middle East for England and are the Anglo-Saxons. The behavior of this church's leaders has raised as many eyebrows as its views. Herbert Armstrong quarreled publicly, and scandalously with his son, Garner Ted, who then left the sect to strike out on his own. The Reverend Pat Robertson of the 700 Club supports political candidates with extreme conservative opinions and has got prominent right-wing activists, including Congressman Philip Crane of Illinois and Congressman Larry McDonald of Georgia, a member of the John Birch Society, to appear on his program.

Not all television and radio evangelists are gargoyles, and the liberal Protestant churches, confronted by pews emptied by the electronic church, are gradually realizing that they are going to have to learn new tricks. Unless they, too, can make converts and raise cash from religious broadcasting, they risk being shouldered off the airwaves by the fundamentalists.

The National Council of Churches is fighting a losing battle in attempting to insist that radio and television stations have a public responsibility to provide free time for religious programs. The television stations are increasingly unmoved by this argument. In fulfilling their duty to find time for religious broadcasts, they have a profit motive to award it to evangelists, who pay for it, rather than to the churches, which do not. By 1978, over 90 percent of religious broadcasts were paid for, compared to only 53 percent in 1959. The United Methodist Church has seen the future in deciding to invest $25 million mainly to acquire its own television station. Other big Protestant denominations are bound to follow. They are already listening hard to electronic preachers who wish them well, like the Reverend Robert Schuller of *Hour of Power.* Mr. Schuller, a believer in "bouncebackability," is a clone from the Norman Vincent Peale school of positive thinking. He has run into criticism because he invested in a star-shaped, all-glass Crystal Cathedral on his twenty-two-acre "shopping center for Jesus Christ," one exit past Disneyland on the Santa Ana Freeway, and because many of his parishioners seized the option he once gave them to listen to his sermons in their cars in the drive-in part of his church. The objections are based more on tradition than on anything else. An expensive Gothic church built of stone is treated as less extravagant and more religious than a glass cathedral, even a glass cathedral designed by Philip Johnson. And most churches continue to want families to come inside, even when this means bringing in noisy babies who disturb the service and embarrass their parents. Such grumbles over Schuller's style reveal more about the crustiness and blinkered minds of his critics than anything else. On a more serious level, he is subject, and vulnerable, to the criticism that his televised sermons, like politicians' promises, are carefully tailored to attract as many and repel as few potential converts as possible. But then, Schuller retorts, it is called broadcasting—not narrowcasting.

When Pope John Paul II came to the United States for a week in October 1979, an editor of the *New York Post,* Steve Dunleavy, beseeched his correspondent in Boston: "Find me a miracle. We've got to have a miracle." He was denied his scoop. Newspaper and magazine readers had by then been saturated in schmaltz by journalists writing about the leader of the Roman Catholic Church in the prose of Hollywood fan sheets. Americans were told he was a "husky, handsome" Pope who demonstrated a unique combination of "passionate humanism, intellectual depth and moral certitude." That he was "a man for all seasons, all situations, all faiths, a beguilingly modest superstar of the church . . . the kind of incandescent leader that the world so hungers for." The TV networks carried specials every night he was in the country. CBS even brought veteran commentator Eric Sevareid out of retirement.

Only after the Pope left did the realization sink in that his visit had not healed the ills of a Roman Catholic Church in the United States that embraces 50 million of the world's 730 million faithful. Instead, his tour, if anything, added to the difficulties of those Americans who try to obey, or feel guilty about not obeying, papal teachings. The Pope from Poland, a keep of conservative Catholic theology, insisted priests must remain celibate, that the priesthood was forever closed to women, that sex outside marriage was wrong, that homosexual acts were sinful. He condemned contraception. He quoted with approval a pastoral letter composed by American bishops in 1976 which said of abortion: "To destroy these innocent unborn children is an unspeakable crime."

Whatever the wrongs and rights of these teachings, it is apparent that many of them do not square with what a high proportion of American Catholics either do or think. This is evident in Chicago the biggest diocese and greatest stronghold of Roman Catholicism in the country. More than half the Catholics in this diocese go to church every Sunday. Only one in eight never goes to church. Four-fifths of them were married by a priest. Four-fifths of them are married to other Catholics. Yet even they have become pick-and-choose Catholics, complying with only those papal doctrines they see as sensible. The Reverend Andrew Greeley, a teacher and a prolific writer on Catholic affairs, reported in his book *Crisis in the Church* that fewer than half of the Catholics in this diocese acknowledge the right of the Church to teach what they should believe on abortion, and that the ordination of women is supported by 44 percent of the men and 34 percent of the women, in defiance of the Pope's teachings. But the great divide between the Church's leadership in Rome and the faithful in Chicago is the 1968 encyclical *Humanae Vitae*, even though in their reaction to this decision they have confounded the prophets of both the left and the right. The conservatives predicted that now the Holy Father had spoken, Catholics would throw away their birth control pills. Liberals foresaw a massive defection from the Church. Both were mistaken. Catholics have continued to practice both their faith and contraception. Even in Chicago, where church attendance remains so high, less than one Catholic in five agrees with the 1968 decision on contraception.

Conservative Catholics in the United States continue to hope Catholics will become more obedient. When Karol Wojtyla was elected in October 1978 they rejoiced. The Mother Church, they reasoned, had won applause from ecumenically minded non-Catholics and from non-believers during the reformist period begun by Pope John XXIII, but within the church itself the changes had excited more confusion than enlightenment. As they saw it, Roman Catholicism in the United States was suffering. Since the end of the reforming Second Vatican Council (1962–1965), an estimated 10,000 American priests had left the ministry. The number of seminarians had dropped from 49,000 to 11,200. There were 50,000 fewer nuns in 1979 than in the mid-sixties, when 180,000 were counted. This shortage of nuns as well as the decision of so many of them to pursue their vocation outside the traditional areas of teaching and nursing had pushed Catholic schools into a financial mire. Nuns had taught for nothing. The lay teachers needed to replace them had to be paid. The schools could not afford to foot the bill. In partial consequence, an unofficial moratorium was put on new school construction and three-quarters of all Catholic students in the United States did not attend parochial schools.

Catholic conservatives had no doubt that the Polish Pope would at least try to put a stop to "Pope John's revolution" and to move the church back to older verities. Catholicism has been anchored in Poland for ten centuries. More than 33 million of its 35 million people adhere to the faith and they have proved outstandingly earnest in their devotion. Just as Irish Catholics have seen their religion as an affirmation of their nationhood in a long struggle against British imperialism, so the Poles have regarded Catholicism as one important affirmation of national identity. Unsurprisingly, they are more resistant than other Catholics to reformist ideas that threaten to dilute the authenticity of their faith. This and everything American conservatives heard about the new Pope tended to buoy them up. They were especially delighted when Monsignor Zdizislaw Peszkowsky, of the Polish American seminary in Michigan, an old acquaintance of Wojtyla, reported that while the Pope was well aware of the advanced views of the liberals on women priests, celibacy, divorce, and so on, he intended to restore order through "priestly zeal," not compromise.

Pope John Paul II fulfilled the conservatives' expectations on his visit in 1979 to the United States when he counterattacked against the liberal demands and was unapologetic about it. "Brothers in Christ, as we proclaim the truth in love, it is not possible for us to avoid criticism, nor is it possible to please everyone." Feminists in the Catholic

Church, whose opinions are intensely felt but not universally shared, were given no quarter. The Vatican told American priests to cancel their own masses if necessary so that no laymen or women would be needed as "extraordinary ministers" at the crowded papal masses. The Pope on his tour refused to grant an audience to the Leadership Conference of Women Religious. He was unequivocal in rejecting any possibility of women priests and suggested that American nuns, most of whom have long since ceased to wear a habit, should revert to "a simple and suitable religious garb" as a "permanent" sign of their calling. Since then the Pope has continued his counterreformation, and further dismayed the liberals by, for example, approving the publication of a document proclaiming that "undue experimentation, changes and creativity bewilder the faithful." Among the "abuses" cited was "the manipulation of liturgical texts for social and political ends."

Many conservative Catholics assume the papal insistence on less permissive doctrine and modes of worship will after a lag be rewarded by a Catholic renaissance in the United States. They recall that before Vatican II, it was common for Protestants otherwise unsympathetic to Catholicism grudgingly to concede that "at least the Catholics know where they stand." They are reassured, too, by compelling evidence that doctrinal strictness has helped bring a greater sense of commitment and membership gains for the more fundamentalist Protestant denominations while the less strict Presbyterian, Episcopalian, and Methodist denominations have suffered an implosion. The assumption may be founded on a fallacy. While it certainly seems true that people will not make a substantial commitment unless the Church leadership knows what the Church is about, it does not necessarily follow that the lay members are so anxious for a lead they do not mind where it takes them. It is one thing for a Southern preacher to tell his congregation that homosexuality, welfare, and pornography are abominations in the sight of God. Most of those listening to his fire-and-brimstone sermon have these prejudices anyway and rather like to hear them given legitimacy from the pulpit, particularly as living them out demands no sacrifices. It is quite another thing for the Roman Catholic Church to attempt to persuade its members that the only system of birth control open to the faithful is the rhythm method, widely considered an unreliable defense against fecundity that can land a couple with six children when they can only afford to have two. As one Catholic woman replied, with more common sense than piety, when she was asked about the Pope's contrary opinion: "It is no good saying God will provide. The fact is he doesn't."

In the current ferment, intellectual leaders of the Church are wryly aware of the irony that for most of its history the American Catholic Church was a docile immigrant church, castigated by a small minority of dissidents for its lack of original ideas and its unswerving loyalty to Rome. Its temper was set by the Irish Catholics who gradually overwhelmed the previously dominant German-Americans when they flooded into America in the wake of the potato famines of the 1840s. They were more papal than the Pope and created what critics like Evelyn Waugh have described as the problem of "guarding them [the Irish] from the huge presumption of treating the Universal Church as a friendly association of their own." The defensive conformity of American Catholics was reinforced by the promotion of nativist anti-Catholicism by the Know-Nothing movement, so called because when its members were questioned by outsiders, they answered "I know nothing"; by the Ku Klux Klan, by the temperance crusade, and by campaigners for restrictive immigration laws. The Irish were caricatured as a brawling, boozy, illiterate threat to traditional American values. The Catholic immigrants who followed from Eastern and Southern Europe excited even more alarm. At least the Irish spoke English. The country, said the bigots, would be changed beyond recognition and for the worse unless the gates were shut on an immigrant invasion that by 1920 had brought the number of Americans of Italian parentage to 3.3 million and of Polish parentage to 3 million. Even when immigration was much reduced by quotas introduced in 1921 and subsequently strengthened, anti-Catholicism continued to flare up. It motivated only a minority. Then as now the great majority of Americans were more friendly to newcomers, even such exotic ones as the recent arrivals from Vietnam and Cambodia, than perhaps any other people on earth. Nevertheless, anti-Catholicism was a political force and at its most extreme bore a striking similarity to the red scare of the 1950s. Just as paranoid anti-Communists detected a worldwide conspiracy directed by the Kremlin to subvert and then to take over America, so anti-Catholics detected a dastardly plot, masterminded by the Vatican, cunningly to convert their country to Catholicism.

Confronted by such prejudice, American Catholics naturally

tended to be inward-looking. Pluralism was accommodated by the creation of a multiplicity of ethnic churches in the big cities: a Saint Patrick's, say, for the Irish, an Our Lady of Loreto for the Sicilians, a Saint Anthony's for the Italians, a Saint Stephen's for the Hungarians, a Saint Boniface for the Germans, a Sacre Coeur for French-Canadians, a Saint Cyril for the Croatians. Catholics, though, aimed for solidarity in their dealings with the outside world lest their enemies exploit divisions among them, and their unity was founded on almost unquestioning obedience to Rome.

American Catholics sought to win acceptance by convincing themselves and their countrymen they were superpatriots. The ranks of the revolutionaries against King George III were combed for people the Church could claim as its own, most of them soldiers with Irish surnames who, if truth could be known, would just as likely turn out to be Scots-Irish Presbyterians. In the American Civil War and again in the wars of this century, the exploits of Catholic servicemen were singled out and celebrated, as were in peacetime the contributions of Catholic authors, scientists, and engineers, especially converts. This superpatriotism may also help explain why, less innocently, Catholics were so prominent in supporting the excesses of McCarthyism.

Anti-Catholicism has since retreated to the margins and can no longer be counted a force to keep the faithful in line. There is still sting in the remark of Peter Viereck, the conservative writer, in 1959, that "Anti-Catholicism is the anti-Semitism of the intellectual," and the Church has forfeited much of the goodwill it accumulated among liberals during the civil rights struggle by its uncompromising stand against abortion. But Catholics in private life no longer encounter the virulent antipathy that confronted Al Smith when he was the Democratic candidate for the presidency in 1928, or even the suspicion that swirled around John Kennedy in 1960. Then the evangelical Dr. Norman Vincent Peale told 150 clergymen at a meeting of Citizens for Religious Freedom at the Mayflower Hotel in Washington: "Our American culture is at stake. I don't say it won't survive but it won't be the same." By 1979, the governors of twelve states were Catholics, and the states included the two most populous, Jerry Brown's California and Hugh Carey's New York, and while in the 1980 Democratic primaries Senator Edward Kennedy's moral character was an issue, mainly because of Chappaquiddick, his Catholicism was hardly mentioned.

This greater tolerance has made American Catholics less defensive; readier to feel their oats and to question orders from Rome. Their church has come of age. It is no longer overwhelmingly an immigrant church, even though Hispanics from Cuba, Mexico, and Puerto Rico are growing more numerous in its ranks. Neither is it overwhelmingly working class, as it used to be. While members of unions are disproportionately Catholic and the quiet but firm Catholicism of the late George Meany helps explain the aggressively anti-Communist traditions of the AFL-CIO, the industrialists across the bargaining table are often now also Catholics. Catholics, in short, are as varied as other Americans and like the rest of their countrymen are increasingly critical of institutions they regard as insufficiently responsive, not excluding their church.

However much goodwill is preserved on both sides, differences between the American Church and Rome seem sure to widen. Pope John Paul II, in ecclesiastical terms an archconservative, even a reactionary, has all but guaranteed this by trying to impose more uniformity at a time when American Catholics, like American Protestants, see religion as a safety valve, a way of peacefully asserting their ethnic, social, and other differences. To take the extremes, the richly traditional Catholicism of Irish and Italian Philadelphia could hardly have less in common with services at Our Lady of Charity Catholic Church in the Bedford-Stuyvesant section of Brooklyn, where a black priest, Father James Goode, routinely falls on the floor in an ecstatic transport after working his congregation up into Pentecostal ecstasy.

Even if Pope John Paul II were less assertive, differences with Rome could not be avoided. The Roman Catholic Church is a universal church that serves a worldwide community, and the relative strengths of its regional constituencies are changing. Its Western European base is weakened, it is holding its own in parts of Eastern Europe and growing fast in the third world, spectacularly so in Africa. The emerging strongholds are in areas where Catholics are most traditionalist in their outlook and least influenced by the assumption, so strong in America, of diversity and democracy in religious life. It would be difficult for Rome to accede to the demands of the liberal Catholics in the United States without compromising the church in the third world. Even radical Latin American Catholics can be ambivalent about birth control and few are ready for women priests. African Catholics tend to be conservative on both issues, and on their continent male chauvinist Islam is Catholicism's great rival for the souls of the unconverted. This leaves the Pope with little room to maneuver and suggests that a dissident Catholic Church in the United States will over time become ever more American and less Roman.

To examine the Jewish experience in the United States, or anywhere else, is not done lightly. Even the rabbis who represent the three main branches of the Jewish faith in the United States—Orthodox, Conservative, and Reform—sometimes find the Jewish experience more overwhelming than explicable. Rabbi Ronald Sobel of Temple Emanu-El in New York, the largest Reform Jewish congregation in the world, with a membership of about three thousand families, concedes: "After four thousand years it is still not altogether easy to answer two seemingly simple questions: What is Judaism and who is a Jew?" Nearly all agree that a Jew can be a member of either a faith or an ethnic group, or both. The 50 percent of America's six million or so Jews who are unaffiliated with any synagogue and beyond the reach of Jewish organizations, even those who are skeptics or unbelievers, are just as Jewish as those who do belong. Some Jews who never walk into a synagogue may be more pious than those who do attend.

For Judaism is not defined by a creed. Much more than Christianity, it is founded on custom and practice, on ceremony, tradition, a shared history, and a vast body of literature, on a sense of family and a sense of belonging to a worldwide community and, since 1948, of having a special relationship with the state of Israel. Few claim authoritatively to say that one strand in the design is more important than another. Each Jewish congregation is independent and the role of the rabbi is usually that of an interpreter rather than a leader. As Rabbi Sobel explains: " 'Rabbi' means 'my teacher.' He is to teach God's laws so that the population can know God's will and thus become a cocreator with God in the evolution of a more humane universe." And woven into the faith of all practicing Jews is the belief that an ignorant person cannot be a pious person, because only by study is it possible to understand what God requires.

Central to the Jewish experience in the United States, where 40 percent of the world's fourteen million Jews have made their home, has been a tension between particularism and universalism, between ethnicity and assimilation. In those European countries where Jews were for centuries treated not much better than lepers, they had no difficulty, perforce, in preserving their distinctiveness. In the United States, an estimated 40–50 percent of Jews now marry Christians, and Rabbi Marc Tanenbaum of the American Jewish Committee reports a general sense of "deep concern" about the consequences of this assimilation on the future continuity of the Jewish people, especially as Jewish couples in the United States tend to have smaller families than either Catholics or Protestants. "But beneath that surface reality there is another layer: the way Jews have become accepted in American society. Because you don't have such intermarriage if Jews are looked upon as outsiders, foreigners and aliens. Jews have become more American than Jewish, and this has caused a great ambivalence. They want to be part of the mainstream but they also ask themselves what price will they pay for this in their survival as a people."

The question is posed far more pressingly than it was twenty or thirty years ago. Up until the end of the Eisenhower era, American Jews accepted the then prevailing assumption that to become good Americans it was necessary for immigrants, or at least their children, to discard almost all the cultural baggage they had brought over with them: their language, their customs, their nationality, everything but their religion. Since many of the Jewish immigrants were fleeing first persecution in the Ukraine, Byelorussia, Lithuania, and Poland and then death in the Auschwitzes, Treblinkas, and Belsens of German Europe, they were more eager than most immigrants to leave behind the foreign ways of their parents and grandfathers. They felt more aversion than nostalgia for the countries they had left and took on the character of Americans so successfully that Will Herberg in his famous celebration of the success of the triple melting pot, *Protestant-Catholic-Jew*, published in 1955, excited more praise for his insight than criticism for oversimplification when he claimed that differences between Americans now boiled down mainly to the ways they chose to worship God. "By and large," he wrote expansively, "to be an American today means to be either a Protestant, a Catholic or a Jew because all other forms of self-identification and social location are either (like regional background) peripheral and obsolescent, or else (like ethnic diversity) subsumed under the broader head of religious community."

A minority of American Jews have, of course, always sternly resisted assimilation and determined instead to worship the God of Abraham, Isaac, and Jacob in a transplantation of the Eastern European shtetl on American soil. While they stand for much else besides, these communities serve to illustrate the immense cultural leap made by their coreligionists who have become Americanized. Take the Hasidic group, called the Lubavitch after a town in White Russia, who live in Crown Heights in Brooklyn and who are followers of a charismatic leader known simply as "the Rebbe." To the outsider they are both quaint and impressive. Quaint because this ghetto seems as much an anachronism as the brick-by-brick recreation of a colonial town at Williamsburg, Virginia. The men wear black hats and patriarchal beards. Sausage curls hang from their temples. Their suits are as somber as those of a Victorian undertaker. The children are dressed as diminutive versions of the adults. The clothing of the women is also old-fashioned, though more homely than severe. As Rabbi Yehuda Krinsky, one of the followers of the current Lubavitcher Rebbe and an interpreter of the group's way of life to outsiders, says, matter of factly: "Our women do not wear slacks or pants. They do not wear short skirts or bathing suits in public or low backs or short sleeves. They dress very modestly." The shops along the main commercial strip, Kingston Avenue, are a period piece, too, filled with the religious bric-a-brac of the ghetto and the shtetl: matzoh covers, seder plates, kiddush cups, tallis bags, shabbos cloths, havdallah candles, leichter trays. The synagogue, where women are unapologetically confined to the balcony, is only a short subway ride from Wall Street yet deep in eighteenth-century czarist Russia. Men, looking collectively like ravens, are perched on benches at battered wooden desks. Most of them, chain-smoking, talk or argue constantly in Yiddish. A few others, seemingly impervious to the racket, pore over their books. When asked about the Lubavitcher Rebbe, a leader for life who emerges rather than is elected from their number, they all speak with the most pious respect for a modern Moses: as much a political and cultural as a religious leader. Rabbi Krinsky, the father of six children, is not at all defensive when he is challenged on the eccentric, not to say downright reactionary, Lubavitch attitude to women. "Men and women do not sit together in the synagogue, not because the woman is inferior but because everybody has their function. . . . According to basic Judaism, women have their role to play in life and it can be as varying and rewarding as men's. But the biological differences between men and women are undeniable and a woman's primary role is to continue the species." Divorce, marital infidelity, and juvenile delinquency, the inquirer is told, with smugness but also with apparent sincerity, are not problems that occur in this community. These ideas seem foreign to other Americans, and of course they are. The Lubavitch are part of a Hasidic revival that occurred partly in reaction to the alleged aloof, arid intellectuality of many Eastern European and Russian rabbis in the eighteenth century. While the Hasidim are certainly not indifferent to the learned traditions of Judaism, they are intensely pious and believe that to have meaning, prayer must be infused with the love of God.

Quaint though they are, it is hard not to feel respect, even reluctant admiration, for these people. Crown Heights is squeezed between two of the most blighted slums in New York City. Brownsville on one side is devastated and dangerous. Bedford-Stuyvesant on the other side is not much better. In this setting Crown Heights is incongruous, with its safe, clean streets, handsome houses, and stately trees. Strong-arm methods were used to secure this gentility and they continue. Members of the Lubavitch community go out of their way to make it known that if a black man beats up a Jew he will "get paid back with interest." Give out a yell on these streets after dark and men in black suits, hats, and beards will rush out of their front doors ready to beat the assailant insensible before the police can extricate him.

Scoldings have come from what are derisively called "civil rights workers who live in Westchester," the tony suburban county north of New York, but these Jews claim that blacks living in Crown Heights have gradually come around to supporting a system of rough justice that protects their property and property values as well as those of their Yiddish-speaking neighbors.

The Hasidim are the odd men out. They remain on the fringe of American Jewish life, even though their numbers are growing fast as their rebbes urge them to have large families and as they gain as new adherents young defectors from undevout Jewish homes, once again demonstrating the truth of the law promulgated by the historian Marcus Hansen: "What the son wishes to forget, the grandson wishes to remember." The great majority of Jewish immigrants to the United States—first those mainly from Germany, who helped push the American Jewish population up from 15,000 in 1840 to 250,000 in 1880, and then the much greater wave from Eastern Europe, who helped to increase it to 4.2 million by 1927—opted instead to become Americanized as quickly as possible. Many had every reason to forget, to put behind them the persecution they had endured in Europe. Most were influenced by the special attraction the United States has had for Jews everywhere, an attraction that dates back to the eighteenth century.

The United States seemed to them then, in its Federalist Papers, in its Constitution, in its Bill of Rights, more committed than anywhere else to those ideals of the Age of Enlightenment that promised to bring Jews into the mainstream. In the United States, Jews have not been immune to discrimination: exclusion from country clubs, second-class status at Ivy League universities, the division of Wall Street into Jewish and non-Jewish banking houses. Even today reflex anti-Semitism persists in many parts of rural America, perhaps because American Jews are overwhelmingly an urban people. Well over half of them live in just six cities—2 million in Greater New York, 455,000 in Los Angeles, 295,000 in Philadelphia, 253,000 in Chicago, 225,000 in Miami, and 170,000 in Boston. But whatever the reason, in the Texas panhandle it is still common for cattlemen and oilmen to talk of "Jewboys in New York" making money out of Texan sweat and not serving in the army when America is at war. And Jews from Manhattan still confess to feeling like outsiders when they venture to places like Stuttgart, Arkansas, or Hazard, Kentucky. American prejudice against Jews is on the retreat and has in recent times nearly always stopped cold at the steps of the courthouse. Justice in the United States is meant to be blind to a person's religion and many rabbis can quote by heart a passage from a letter that President Washington addressed to the Jewish congregation of Newport when he visited that city in the summer of 1790: "It is now no more that toleration is spoken of as if it was by the indulgence of one class of people that another enjoyed the exercise of their inherent natural rights. For happily the Government of the United States, which gives to bigotry no sanction, to persecution no assistance, requires only that they who live under its protection should demean themselves as good citizens in giving it on all occasions their effectual support."

The sons and daughters of the German-Jewish immigrants of the nineteenth century responded readily to the promise and prospect of full integration into American life. They were eager to be accepted. They moved quickly to discard those precepts and practices of Judaism that made Jews seem exotic or divisive to the Christian majority in their new homeland. Also those practices that were downright inconvenient, like the dietary laws that continue to cut Orthodox Jews off socially from their neighbors. Dr. Norman Lam, president of Yeshiva University in New York, can, for example, invite anyone he wants to his Orthodox home, but if he is invited back to a Christian home or to a Jewish home where the dietary laws are not observed, he has to ask his hosts to serve him something he is permitted to eat: "a vegetable plate or a fruit plate with cottage cheese." The lead for the nineteenth-century German Jews in America came from such advanced thinkers as Rabbis Arthur Wise, David Einhorn, and Kaufmann Kohler, all of whom were in turn much influenced by the German Reform movement that sought to adapt Judaism to modern conditions. Reform Judaism was a grass-roots movement as well. The Reform Jews in America were as determined to prove themselves good Americans as the Reform Jews in Germany were to prove themselves good Germans.

In particular, members of the resolutely upwardly mobile Jewish immigrant families who had made good in America—the Lehmans, the Seligmans, the Hallgartens, the Heidelbachs, the Goldmans, the Loebs, the Sachses, and others—desired their places of worship to become more decorous and middle class. They and their rabbis borrowed freely from the services of the Protestant churches of the American WASPs. Synagogue services were made shorter and more intelligible to the unlearned. English was permitted to replace "German and Slavic dialects." Protestant-like sermons, organ music, and choirs were introduced. Family pews allowed wives to join their husbands during the service. Theological change was as startling and reached an apogee in 1885 when Reform rabbis meeting in Pittsburgh drafted what Rabbi Wise of Cincinnati, himself an immigrant from Bohemia, called the "Jewish Declaration of Independence." Parts of the Mosaic law were thrown overboard as "not adapted to the views and habits of modern civilization." Jews, the rabbis declared, were "no longer a nation but a religious community" and they expected neither a return to Palestine nor the restoration of a Jewish state. Instead, the hope of Reform Judaism was for a "kingdom of truth, justice and peace among all men."

Though pragmatism and a longing to belong undoubtedly had a large role in Reform Judaism in the United States, it is wrong to dismiss the movement as mainly an effort by Jewish chameleons to take on an American coloration—a charge frequently leveled by those Orthodox rabbis who continue to refuse to sit with their non-Orthodox counterparts. The movement has in the past led to synagogues forbidding male members of their congregations to wear hats. It has also come out of a profoundly moving reconsideration of Jewish religious traditions. Doubters should ponder the idealism of Rabbi Wise. As summarized in a Princeton study, *The Shaping of American Religion*, Wise insisted Jews were a chosen people because God had endowed them with a special mission, one that was not narrow or particular, but universal and general. That mission was to spread through the world the divine spirit and the ideals of social justice of which God had made Jews the custodians. Israel was not like other nations, limited to a particular time and place, but was rather a world people, carrying to all times and places its message of social redemption. On that basis, Wise saw a growing identification between Judaism and Americanism, for the United States supplied Jews with a social context altogether hospitable to their ideas. In this democratic society, ancient ideals could be realized in practice, and as American liberty spread through the world it prepared the ground for the universal recognition of the Fatherhood of God and the brotherhood of man, which, for Wise, constituted the messianic end of days.

For the Jewish refugees whose great exodus from the Pale of Settlement to the United States started at just about the time of the Pittsburgh Platform, such teachings were nearly incomprehensible. Isolated from progressive Western thought, they knew nothing and cared less for these newfangled ideas. As victims of czarist terror, some of them relied upon strict orthodoxy as their carapace against a dangerous world. Others, as members of a long-oppressed pauper class, thought economic equality more important than political equality and were idealistic, and often militant, socialists.

The assimilationist German Jews of America were scandalized.

Were all the gains they had made to be compromised by these huddled masses with funny clothes, strange dialects, and decidedly uncomfortable ideas? The German-Jewish press fumed over the "un-American ways" of "wild Asiatics." For the Jewish press, the *American Hebrew* posed the question: "Are we waiting for the natural process of assimilation between Orientalism and Americanism? This will perhaps never take place." The *Hebrew Standard* censoriously declared: "The thoroughly acclimated American Jew . . . has no religious, social or intellectual sympathies with them. He is closer to the Christian sentiment around him than to the Judaism of these miserable darkened Hebrews."

Yet within the past few decades, for all non-Jewish Americans and for most Jewish Americans as well, the distinction between Jews whose families originally came from Eastern Europe and the others has ceased to have much meaning. The newcomers were members of the American underclass, "Orientals," for a generation or at most two. Many of the children and grandchildren of pushcart peddlers, cobblers, tailors, on the lower East Side of Manhattan, and of socialist trade union officials, have prospered in the financial world and in the professions. In big part through their own efforts, but in big part also because after their initial shock and horror at the intrusion, members of the mainly German-Jewish establishment in the United States recognized their duty to help their coreligionists. In a gesture of extraordinary vision, several well-to-do Reform Jews even dug deep into their pockets to help finance the struggling Jewish Theological Seminary, the intellectual redoubt of Conservative Judaism in New York. They saw it as offering Eastern European Jews a halfway house between the Orthodox and Reform movements and thus giving them the opportunity of a more gentle adjustment to American life than the Reform movement offered.

This absorption of Jews from the Pale of Settlement into the American Jewish mainstream and the continuing Americanization of the generality of American Jews was until twenty years ago much remarked upon, usually with approval. Has anything much happened since to delay or reverse the assimilationist trend? Superficially the answer is no. At a time when half of American Jews are unaffiliated to any synagogue or Jewish organization, when nearly as many marry outside their religion, when the Jewish voting bloc is fragmenting, it seems that they are becoming a less distinctive, less cohesive minority.

The contrary evidence of a reaction against assimilation is more a matter of feel than of hard statistical or sociological fact. In seeking to make it tangible, those who believe such a reaction is indeed occurring tend to put exaggerated attention on small but visible signs of a reassertion of "Jewishness": on claims that seven out of ten children of mixed marriages are now brought up as Jews, versus only two or three a few years ago; on the decision of Temple Emanu-El, the modern epitome of Reform Judaism, to reintroduce in 1972 after a lapse of one hundred years the practice of conducting bar mitzvahs; on the way an increasing number of Reform Jews are now lighting candles on Friday night or returning to some form of conformity to dietary laws at home.

What makes the assertion impressive is that the return to "Jewishness" is sensed, too, by religious leaders as different as Rabbi Sobel of Temple Emanu-El, Rabbi Krinsky of the Lubavitch community, and Conservative Rabbi Wolfe Kelman, an intellectual who comes from an unbroken line of eleven rabbis and whose two brothers, son, and father-in-law are also rabbis. Jews, like others, have it seems begun to focus on the way they are different from the rest of Americans; to see their religion or ethnicity as a way of asserting and preserving their identity, their peoplehood, their sense of community, in a country where a planing away of regional and economic distinctions threatens otherwise to make them indistinguishable from the mass. "Jewishness" for them is an escape from homogeneity just as membership in the stricter, and sometimes dotty, religious denominations is an escape for so many non-Jewish Americans.

Reassertion of Jewishness is connected, too, to an "uneasiness"— the word of the Harvard sociologist Nathan Glazer—felt since the late 1960s about new questions facing American Jews. Jews had always played a large role in liberal politics and in the civil rights movement, but preferential schemes for black advancement cut against the Jewish tradition of a color-blind—or religion-blind or national-blind—approach toward rooting out discrimination. Affirmative action has meant for many Jews a break with past allies, and a division of loyalties within the liberal camp. If, before 1967, it was still just possible for the dwindling number of American Jews who had not embraced the Jewish state to separate their Judaism from the fate of Israel, the Arab-Israeli war made this unthinkable. The commitment of American Jews to Israel today is of a closeness that makes criticism of particular Israeli governments or particular Israeli government actions difficult if not impossible for them to speak aloud. American Jews are not faced by any immediate conflict of loyalty. At the same time, American Jews know they matter politically in the United States, but as Nathan Glazer has put it, they ask themselves, if it came to a test of the American commitment to Israel, would American Jews matter "decisively"?

15

ONE EYE ON THE MIRROR
Self-improvement, Health, and Psychiatry

THERE IS A FROZEN supermarket dough which divides up by itself in the oven into small buns. Capsule histories of the immediate past are rather like that. They come apart in decades. The 1950s are often fondly looked back to as a time of contentment for most Americans. The comforting memory leaves out Korea, McCarthyism, the cold war, the anti-Communist Great Fear, Little Rock, Sputnik angst, and all those disoriented suburbanites the sociologists worried about. The 1960s were a time of commitment, were they not? For many Americans they were, but rather more could not be bothered by civil rights campaigns, by marches to end the Vietnam War. Plenty of Americans loved George Wallace. Plenty thought that black Americans were asking for too much, especially after the ghettos burned. Plenty thought Nixon was right to call protesting students "bums." The 1970s, by contrast, were a time of religious revival for the more traditional Americans, and for the more forward-looking ones, a time of cultural experimentation and self-absorption.

The "Me Decade" Tom Wolfe called it, slipping between mockery and approval; Christopher Lasch called it, disapprovingly, the "culture of narcissism." The American tradition of self-improvement took on exotic forms. Pop psychiatry flourished. A successful magazine named *Self* was launched. Ordinary Americans experimented with sensuous massage, Erhard Seminars Training, Transcendental Meditation, biofeedback, zazen, through-the-wall jogging, Inner Tennis, Nirvana 24 or Arica, sensitivity training, and sensory deprivation in a Lilly Tank.

Carly Simon, of the New York publishing family, sang, "You had one eye on the mirror." She meant, it was said, Mick Jagger, but she could have meant any one of countless Americans on a restless, frequently expensive, search for themselves.

This much-noticed self-preoccupation—together with a counterpart revival among more traditional Americans of strict churches—is often contrasted with the political activism of the 1960s and early 1970s. Art Levine, an education specialist at the Carnegie Endowment, is not surprised by the change. In a study of American university students, comparing those today with those at college during the Vietnam War, Levine suggests that activism and togetherness normally rise during a war, meism and contemplation during peace. Adapting charts from the social scientist Peter Altbach, Levine says that Community Ascendancy (CA) is high during wars, Individual and Religious Ascendancy (IRA) during peace. The lines on his charts look rather like brainwaves. The CA line rises slowly, advancing, like Woodrow Wilson, toward the American declaration of war in 1917. On Armistice Day, CA goes down, the way a bootleg martini would later, and the IRA line goes up with the stock market. After 1932, the CA line begins creeping upward again, peaks in 1944, and on V-J day, drops faster than the atom bomb, while the IRA rises higher than an upwardly mobile Texan. The Korean War did not for some reason register on this socio-feedback machine, but the rhythm is the same for Vietnam. There is a heavy rise in CA between 1965 and 1973. Then, before Nguyen Duy Trinh's ink is dry on the peace treaty, the CA line drops again and the IRA line goes up before one can say, "It's my reality" or "Christian Baptist Fellowship."

Something happened, as Joseph Heller, a literary godparent for so many of today's Americans, might have said. Big cultural change was afoot, but unlike these tidy charts, it was moving at different speeds among different people at different times. The young men and women who grew up in the 1960s, give or take a few years, and who took part in the struggles of those times, did not change into self-absorbed pumpkins at midnight on December 31, 1969, any more than the Me Generation of the 1970s, which supposedly followed them, vanished when the ball fell in Times Square ten years later. Commitment did not suddenly become narcissism, communards conformists, or Maoists mortgage-holders, even if someone did remark that most of his friends in the Harvard radical class of 1966 were, within a few years, doing up the Victorian houses they had bought. For every blissed-out Rennie Davis who sought a Maharishi, for every Jerry Rubin who returned to Wall Street, this time to work there, there were Tom Haydens and Sam Browns who stuck, radical or mainstream, to politics.

Given the chance, Americans would like to bury their immediate past, mumble a few words over the grave, like John Wayne in *Red River*, and get on with business. The past stays busy, too, however. Most Americans who lived through the civil rights struggles, the Vietnam War, or the flowering and wilting of the counterculture as spectators were changed as well, even if the changes were slower and more difficult to see.

These Americans were the Silent Majority, the Middle America rediscovered by dozens of journalist Columbuses on their court-sponsored journeys out of Washington during the 1968 presidential campaign. The Silent Majority, baptized by Nixon and cosseted by Agnew, was sought out by almost every Democratic politician as well after George McGovern had shown once again the perils of ignoring the center. This Middle America was Yankee granite that the soft rain of Charles Reich's Consciousness III—as he described the outlook of the counterculture in his ephemeral best-seller, *The Greening of America* —would never penetrate, it was a hard-hat with no room for mind expansion, it was the Great Plains, which wanted to raise wheat, not consciousness.

Or so it was comfortably thought by those who mistakenly believed that conservatism in politics went inevitably with traditionalism in morals and cultural style. When the Silent Majority did speak up, however, it showed that while it may have been silent, it certainly was not deaf. Jerry Falwell and the New Right aside, it was certainly not all moral, either. Middle America, true, was bothered about "Acid, Amnesty and Abortion," the clever, nasty slogan the Republicans stuck on the Democrats in 1972. As the decade wore on, in matters of economic self-interest it became ever more openly conservative, if this is taken to mean a desire to stop conspicuous consumption by government at all levels. Yet at the same time, big changes were at work, within the family, concerning women's work and the size of families. There was a freer sexuality and greater tolerance of the milder drugs. Coupled with a new restrictiveness in the economy, all this was rewriting the familiar road map of many ordinary Americans' daily lives.

Under pressure of these changes, it was not surprising when Middle Americans began asking if God or the Rotary Club would really strike them dead if they openly questioned the stiffer traditions. Nor was it strange, with the public weakening of old standards, that so many should ask, mantra-like, "Who am I?" or that others, affronted by "permissiveness," should gravitate to strict churches or flirt with the evangelical right.

Daniel Yankelovich, in his book *New Rules: Searching for Self-Fulfillment in a World Turned Upside Down,* which came out in 1981, charts just such changing attitudes among a large group of Americans toward work, the family, and themselves. Americans today, according to Yankelovich, can be split into three broad groups: those looking for self-fulfillment in a strong form (the "strong formers"), just under a fifth of the total population; the broad mass of Americans—about three-fifths in all—who have been influenced by the cultural upheavals of recent times, but less strongly so, the "weak formers"; and the third group—accounting for the rest of the country—a conservative rump resting squarely on traditional values of self-denial and giving in order to get.

The "strong formers" are on the whole younger than other Americans, according to Yankelovich, better educated, more middle class, less married, less religious, politically more liberal, and likelier to have professional jobs. Nowadays they find themselves in a triple bind. They are burdened by freedom. They face more "life choices" than they know how to cope with. Secondly, they need a large income to support this problem, for their preoccupation with a better, more varied and satisfying life presumes a high material standard of living. Thirdly, they have been taught, ever since they were small children, to accept the authority of their wants, and encouraged by the prevailing pop psychiatry of the day, to treat them as needs which it would be sinful to let go unanswered. If all this sounds preachy, any thought of criticizing Yankelovich on this score vanishes as soon as his subjects talk. Abby —he uses pseudonyms—says she feels "all the doors are opening . . . and at the same time they're closing." Lyndon Hendries, a $100,000-a-year-plus public relations man in Houston, complains that "Our culture doesn't even come close to preparing for the concentration and pain involved with self-fulfillment." There is a strong temptation to dismiss these as the moans of spoiled heirs or overgrown children.

Yet their complaints are in the American grain. Tocqueville noticed a similar shifting dissatisfaction and wrote of Americans' "restlessness amid prosperity" in an uncharacteristically dark, biting passage:

> In the United States a man builds a house in which to spend his old age and he sells it before the roof is on; he plants a garden and lets it just as the trees are coming into bearing; he brings a field to tillage and leaves other men to gather the crops; he embraces a profession and gives it up; he settles in a place which he soon afterwards leaves to carry his changeable longings elsewhere. If his private affairs leave him any leisure, he instantly plunges into the vortex of politics; and if at the end of a year of unremitting labor he finds a few days' vacation, his eager curiosity whirls him over the vast extent of the United States and he will travel fifteen hundred miles in a few days to shake off his happiness. Death at last overtakes him, but it is before he is weary of his bootless chase of that complete felicity which forever escapes him.

What do today's restless self-fullfillers want? If Yankelovich knew, he would be in a different business. He does tell what they buy, what they eat, and what "life styles" they affect. They like new products; they try new foods and new restaurants; the word "elegant" crops up a lot in descriptions of their purchases; they read more than most and seem more eager to study foreign languages; they ski, hike, and play tennis; they eat lots of yogurt and brown bread and try to avoid eating too much of anything; they're more meditative and introspective than most and likelier to seek psychiatric help. Although Yankelovich does not say so, much of their effort at self-fulfillment is what social critics in the 1950s used to call status seeking, an eighteen-year-old's body, an unblocked mind, and a self-fulfilling life being, for them, the ultimate purchase by which to demonstrate that they have risen above the crowd. The "strong formers" as described by Yankelovich are easy to parody, if one can parody caricatures. Koren, the *New Yorker* cartoonist, does "strong formers" very well. Unlike the older, less pampered, sharper, and more frenetic Americans caught by George Price, Koren's characters are like strokable pets, knowing, aloof, world-weary, and displaying a dotty, frightening calm.

The "strong formers" are the cutting edge—bringing to mind a giant pair of Oldenburg soft scissors—of changes in "norms," according to Yankelovich, among Americans at large, or at least among everyone but the traditionalists, the stick-in-the-muds, the Main Streeters and backwoodsmen. But then, of course, these traditionalists, and most especially those marching in the vanguard of the Moral Majority, are a rather well organized, computerized, and, to many, alarming group, as it turns out, in Reagan's America.

What are the big changes wrought by the "strong formers"? An intriguing study done at Muncie, Indiana—the "Middletown" probed during several decades by the sociologists Robert and Helen Lynd—showed how in the twenties almost everyone thought that Christianity was the true religion and that all should be converted, while only two in five agreed today—a welcome change, even if against "Religious Tolerance" on Muncie's report card one would still have to put "Could do better." Back then, half of those asked—perhaps it was the men—thought being a good cook and housekeeper was the most important thing in being a good mother. Today three-quarters disagree.

In the nation at large, according to Yankelovich's poll findings, attitudes to the family and work have changed greatly in recent times. Before World War II, three-quarters thought a wife should not work if her husband could support her. Now only a quarter think so. Twenty-five years ago, four Americans in five thought a woman unmarried out of choice must be neurotic or otherwise abnormal. Only a quarter think so now. Fifteen years ago, 85 percent thought sex before marriage wrong. Today, fewer than 40 percent think so. Nowadays, more than half of all Americans, if the surveys are correct, believe both men and women should care for children. Even allowing for a wish to conform, a desire to hide reservations about modern views for fear of seeming out of fashion, these are large changes that cannot be ignored.

Yankelovich reports changes in attitudes toward work and money, although these are more difficult to interpret. How the economy is doing and how much people want to work or save in any longish period obviously affect each other and it is artificial to isolate either one. Their general drift seems to be that Americans want interesting jobs as much as high-paying ones; are less ready than before to shift cities to please their bosses; feel they should refuse promotions to jobs they do not want, and do not think they should always substitute a duller but higher-paying job for a lower-paying but more interesting one for the sake of their families. Perhaps more tellingly, Yankelovich reports that up until the end of the 1960s, a "real man" to most Americans meant a good provider. Since then, bringing home the bacon has dropped to third place or lower among the ingredients of masculinity listed by survey answerers.

Captains of industry and their morale officers in the universities, in politics, and in the press are constantly worrying that all hands are not working hard enough. This sort of report, even if many of its findings are written on water, tends to add to their fears. Social critics who have gazed too long with the naked eye at Yankelovich's "strong formers" —with all their doubts about the old Puritan "giving/getting compact" and their yen for the expressive side of life—have begun to wonder if America's middle class is not catching the British disease of cultivated idleness.

Americans have been worrying about the collapse of the Protestant ethic almost since the Pilgrims landed. They are born with a Puritan jeremiad ringing in their ears. D. H. Lawrence had fun with this in his essay on Melville:

> The *Pequod* went down. And the *Pequod* was the ship of the white American soul. She sank, taking with her Negro, and Indian and Polynesian, Asiatic, and Quaker and good, businesslike Yankees and Ishmael; she sank all the lot of them.
>
> Boom! as Vachel Lindsay would say.
>
> To use the words of Jesus, IT IS FINISHED.
>
> *Consummatum est!*
>
> But *Moby Dick* was first published in 1851. If the Great White Whale sank the ship of the Great White Soul in 1851, what's been happening ever since?

Good question. As Lawrence was implying, somehow the Great White Soul keeps surfacing again, ever ready to take another dive. Robert Lowell wrote a further obituary a century or so later in his *For the Union Dead:*

> The Aquarium is gone. Everywhere,
> giant finned cars nose forward like fish;
> a savage servility
> slides by on grease.

And that was before OPEC.

At greater length, David Riesman claimed thirty years ago in *The Lonely Crowd* to have detected among Americans a shift from the "inner-directed" personality, with its internal gyroscope that gave purpose and stability, to the "other-directed" personality, more manageable, more dependent, better suited to joining pliant, obedient troops in big offices, whether government, business, or military. C. Wright Mills differed from Riesman about social class and the concentration of economic power in the United States, but he thought a similar change had occurred in the gradual displacement of the production-oriented "old" middle class by the consumption-oriented "new" middle class, which had in it the makings of a white-collar proletariat. The portrait, in fact, of an American middle class that had lost its self-confidence and that awaited the lead of others, with little sense of its own identity, passive more than active, buyers and users more than producers or makers, has been a commonplace of much modern American social thinking.

From there to self-indulgence was but a small step in the analysis. In *The Cultural Contradictions of Capitalism*, updating the tradition for the 1970s, Daniel Bell offered an economic explanation of what was happening. Capitalism's success since the Great Depression, he argued, had depended on manipulation of economic demand and the often necessarily artificial stimulation of consumption. The better the strategy worked, the worse Americans became at saving and producing. Christopher Lasch has taken yet a further step. He draws on the work of psychoanalysts like Allen Wheelis, Otto Kernberg, and Heinz Kohut, considering the typical bourgeois of today to be suffering from a condition not far removed from that which analysts twenty-five years ago or so began diagnosing as "narcissistic disorders." In 1958, Wheelis, a San Francisco analyst, reported that patients had begun coming in with vague complaints that were hard to pin down. The common thread was that all the sufferers had an elusive sense of themselves. Older therapy sought to unblock conflicts so that patients could better get on with their day-to-day business. This new type of patient—or this patient with troubles viewed in a new way—seemed to need, before anything else, to become somebody with daily purposes to pursue. Lasch seizes this character type, generalizes it, and offers a social explanation. Public life in America—the life of work, businesses, sports, advertising, schools, and so forth—has broken down the family, Lasch believes, and is now invading the last bulwark, the individual's sense of himself, with perilous results for everyone.

The unfortunate President Carter must either not have read fully or not fully understood Lasch's book when, on July 15, 1979, a Sunday, he preached to Americans on the subject of national "malaise," saying, in effect, that Americans were unable to solve their economic problems because they were moping and groveling in an orgy of self-involvement. This neatly stood Lasch—whom Pat Caddell, the President's pollster, had encouraged the whole senior White House staff to read—on his head. For Lasch, at root, was not accusing Americans of selfishness but the big institutions—notably corporations and government—of intruding into the private sphere and robbing Americans of their sense of themselves. Right side up or down, Lasch, though a best-selling author, was too exotic fare for national television.

The President's speech was greeted with a resounding Bronx cheer. "Hold the malaise!" wrote one columnist, echoing the common view that the trouble was less in the nation than in Carter's White House. The President's odd speech had followed a season of political strange events, including a long retreat at Camp David, consultation by the busload with more than a hundred wise men and women about the condition of America, asking for the resignation of the whole of his cabinet, and then sacking three of its leading members. Beside these antics, the average American's obsession with his girth, his physical health or mental hygiene, seemed positively normal. A double standard? Not at all. Americans expect better of their Presidents than of themselves. In a Baltimore bar years before, there was a lively conversation about Spiro Agnew, a local boy, first governor and then Vice-President, undisgraced and riding high. The blue-collar workers in the bar loved his attacks on the liberals, the long-hairs, and the establishment press. But they were appalled at the thought that he might one day be President. Why, if they cheered his provocative speeches, did they think he wasn't fit for the White House? "I don't want the President of the United States," one of them said, "to sound like I do after I've had a few beers." Eleven years later, Americans, even Lasch-readers, apparently, did not want their President to sound the way they did after they had had a few kirs.

Talk of the soul is difficult to keep in proportion, especially when it is linked to the crisis in national productivity. For all the fad therapies, narcissism, and search for self-fulfillment, there is little evidence that Americans are working less hard than they used to. There is not much in permissiveness that captains of industry and their morale officers can fault on that score. Indeed, it is the brunt of much complaint from today's social critics, left and right, that permissiveness, in modern America, is intimately tied up with submissiveness. This is not a new criticism of "organizational life." To the large institutions which dominate American life and for which so many Americans work—whether these be Aetna Life Insurance, Exxon, the IRS, AT&T, the Department of Health and Human Services, or Sears, Roebuck—what employees do and think on their own time, what they wear, what styles they affect, what religion or therapy they favor, have less and less bearing on the smooth running or well-being of the organization. Not only can differences and eccentricities be tolerated at little cost. Planing them away, now that they matter so slightly, may cause more friction than it is worth.

Tell me what you eat and I will tell you what you are, promised Brillat-Savarin, the French gastronome. Faced with American eating habits, even so easy a coiner of phrases might momentarily have been stumped for words, although four would surely have quickly occurred to him: "childlike," "pretentious," "fortunate," and "ingenious." Childlike, because convenience foods and fast-food restaurants are enabling Americans to eat again as they did when they were children; pretentious, because of the antimodern countertrend which with "gourmet" cooking would bring back a largely imaginary past of elaborately cooked meals that this new food technology has just freed Americans from; and fortunate and ingenious because Americans enjoy an extraordinary system developed by Borden, Swift, Birds Eye, and others for producing food year-round, and packaging and shipping it anywhere on a continent.

Left on their own, children do not sit down to meals but eat "on demand," when their stomach tells them. This may or may not be a universal fact of human culture, but it is true in the United States, as anyone well knows who has watched small children enter a house, run into the kitchen, open the refrigerator, stand bathed in its glow for a moment, and then plunder the shelves. Meals for them are a bore to prepare and a bore to eat. Much better to eat snacks, the blander and sweeter the better. Advanced food technology has put these eating habits within reach of adult Americans, too. Just as convenience foods slowly undermined the meal, leaving it a menuless snack with no beginning, middle, or end, so the fast-food outlet, beginning with Horn & Hardart Automats in New York and reaching its triumph in McDonald's, is eradicating the kitchen. For those who cherish the family meal, this is a mixed blessing. But now that so many American couples are both working and seldom feel like buying and cooking fresh food after work, the success of convenience foods is unsurprising. From there, it is a relatively short step virtually to doing away with home-prepared food altogether. One out of every three dollars spent on food today goes for eating out and most of that is spent at fast-food restaurants, a proportion that has increased sharply in recent years. Naturally, supermarket chains and food processors are concerned with the competition. In an effort to keep up, some food processors now advertise on television products not as good as mother used to make but "as good as take-out."

But this technico-marketing triumph causes problems to Americans who are always feasting and fasting. As a result of convenience foods and fast-food outlets, according to researchers at the Center for Science in the Public Interest, Americans are eating much more fat and sugar than they did only a few years ago and almost certainly more than is good for them.

The typical fast-food diet—hamburgers, french fries, fried chicken, fish and chips—has certainly helped fatten the country. The average American, according to a federal health and nutrition examination survey, weighs six pounds more than she or he did fifteen years ago. Fifty years ago, malnutrition was the main dietary problem. Today it is "overnutrition," contributing to leading causes of death—heart disease, strokes, arteriosclerosis, and diabetes. Paradoxically, it is the poor who suffer most, for a fattening diet in America is now the most available and the least expensive.

Despite the fact that fewer candy bars per head are being eaten, sugar consumption has shot up. Some of this comes from obvious sources like soft drinks, more than four hundred bottles of which are drunk each year, on average, by each American. But food manufacturers are putting large quantities of sugar or other sweeteners into many other foods as well, such as preserved meats or bread. At the turn of the century, foods contained a quarter of all sugar consumed. The rest was added by choice. Today, three-quarters of the sugar eaten is consumed as it were involuntarily, for it is already there in the food.

Americans, on average, put away some 165 pounds of red meat each year, three times the amount of chicken consumed. White meat in chicken, besides being cheaper, is by itself much less fattening than beef. Even chicken is eaten in fattening form. Colonel Saunders' Kentucky-Fried Chicken, for example, sells the equivalent of ten pieces of chicken to each American man, woman, and child every year.

These eating habits make many Americans feel guilty. Diet foods are a subindustry in themselves. Diet books routinely lead the bestseller lists. There are several diet magazines, ingeniously puffing the simple advice to eat less. Health food shops, promising "natural" products, abound. The big food processors like Kellogg have caught on. They market "natural" cereals that are really the same as their usual products except that sugar has not been added and they have been milled to look like "homemade" cornflakes—an invention of Kellogg's advertisers, since cornflakes are not made at home, only at Kellogg's. Weight-consciousness and fear of a cholesterol-induced heart attack have affected the American diet somewhat, as the surgeon general, Dr. Julius Richmond, reported in 1980. Americans are eating fewer eggs, more fruit, and less butter than before.

Americans feel worse than they need to about their eating habits. Their fat and plentiful diet does cause medical problems, but not as many as most think. Far more Americans believe they are overweight than are thought overweight by their doctors. In the Health and Nutrition Survey of 1971–1974, about 13 percent of the men and 23 percent of the women were, by medical standards, overweight. In 1974, when a survey was taken of Americans' attitudes to their weight, almost half the women and a third of the men thought they were too fat. The average weight of Americans has risen, it is true, but so has their average height, which accounts for much of the increase.

But why all this fuss? Why this ferocious cycle of feasting and fasting? If Americans run to fat—they are, on the whole, a big-boned, large-framed people—why not live with the fact? Why strain to resemble models with a look that is confined in real life to Malibu or the upper East Side? Fashion is one obvious answer; another is that the result is a better-looking self. Both are right in their ways. But they also tell one little. For surely dieting is one of the many ways Americans express their refusal to accept their bodies the way they are. Their real or imagined blemishes must be expunged. The norm—of youth, of physical perfection, of flawlessness or grace or whatever—must be met. The body is a project, a problem, a raw material to be improved upon. And in a most highly refined cosmetic technology, the Americans have the counterpart to their ingenious but fattening food manufacturing system. With the means to straighten teeth, lift faces, change noses, and remove or implant hair, Americans can make themselves into their own works of art.

Americans agonize, too, about exercise. They are a physically active, outdoors people, many of whom happily spend Saturday morning in a pickup game of playground basketball or Sunday afternoon at softball. They get plenty of exercise, but constantly worry that they are not getting enough. Exercise is seldom allowed to be as simple as going for a stroll or knocking a ball about. Norms must be set and met. Exercisers must know how many calories per hour are expended in the different sports. Running, according to *Today's Health* magazine, tops the list at 900, while gardening is an almost sedentary 220. Dr. James Nicholas, a director of the Institute of Sports Medicine and Athletic Trauma at Lenox Hill Hospital in Manhattan, has graded more than sixty sports and games according to their mental and physical demands. Exercisers are encouraged to aim for a resting heartbeat of 51–61 beats a minute and to be able to stretch easily seven inches beyond their toes. Uniforms must be worn. Somebody calculated that $132 million was spent on exercise warm-up suits in 1976. Runners can choose from more than 175 brands and styles of footwear. Precautions must be taken against the dangers of injury or excess. "Exercise," Dr. Herman Hellerstein of Case Western Reserve University in Cleveland intones, "should be prescribed for the individual more carefully than any drug."

It is one of the presidential duties periodically to call conferences on youth fitness at the White House. After a report by two doctors at New York University about the physical feebleness of schoolchildren, President Eisenhower agreed, in 1954, to set up the President's Council on Youth Fitness. With several changes of name, this has survived. It grants medals to boys or girls who, in the space of four months, complete a course of exercise, such as fifty hours of badminton, a similar load of roller skating, or 150 games of bowling, as well as more strenuous sports. There was general disappointment when it was discovered, in the late 1970s, that the physical fitness of schoolchildren had not much changed. This is not surprising. Schools limit sports to students gifted or competitive enough to get onto the official teams. Other children get almost no physical recreation at all at school.

Americans find it very hard to shake off the competitive associations even of the most solitary of sports, such as long-distance running, the national craze of the late 1970s. When asked to distinguish "jogging" —by which the craze was known—from "running," Rory Donaldson of the National Jogging Association said: "A runner is one who competes against others. Joggers compete only against themselves."

Faith in improvability strongly colors American attitudes toward the body and so toward physical health. If others tend to think they are well so long as nothing is drastically wrong, Americans and their doctors impose more exacting standards. Like Puritans wondering if they are really among the elect, Americans do not wait for symptoms of disease to present themselves. They hunt them out in advance, with regular physical checkups as well as personality tests, at least for schoolchildren, to gauge their mental health. Feeling well is for them only part of being healthy. To qualify as well or not ill, it is necessary also to meet statistical standards of physical and mental normality. Many businesses before promoting important executives now routinely send them for medical checkups at such famous institutions as the Mayo Clinic in Rochester, Minnesota—where the waiting time for walk-in patients is ten months or more—even though studies by the National Institutes of Health suggest that such regular screening is no better at catching dangerous illnesses early than an ordinary visit to one's doctor. At such a clinic, the patient will for a full day be questioned, wired up, sampled, and analyzed. Heart rhythm, blood sedimentation, white and red corpuscles, kidney chemistry, the state of the patient's lungs or womb, all are set down and matched against the norm. "Your urine's like the gold standard," the doctor may say admiringly. "White corpuscles, absolutely normal. The usual range is 4.2 to 4.8. Yours is 4.6. Nothing to worry about there."

This industrialization of medicine is in many ways a triumph.

Americans believe theirs is the best medicine in the world. Almost nobody questioned the claim that the Shah of Iran, ill in Mexico, could be adequately treated only in New York. Billions of dollars have gone over the years to the great medical schools—Harvard, Johns Hopkins, Columbia, or Chicago. As a result, medical research, in which America does lead the world, has led to virtual elimination of diseases like polio and to unheard of virtuosity in surgical techniques.

There are doubters. The expertise was won at the benefit of the specialist, to the cost of the general practitioner, a vanishing figure. There is an old story illustrating the dangers of overspecialization. When President McKinley was shot, in Buffalo, he was taken to the city's best hospital, which was attached to the medical school. The senior surgeon naturally took charge of the case. He was a noted doctor, but had specialized in obstetrics and had never had to deal with anything from the waist up. As the medical chief, though, he would not lower himself by calling in someone better qualified to treat McKinley's wounds. After an initial operation to save the President's life, complications developed. The surgeon bungled a second operation, and after lingering a week, McKinley died, perhaps leaving an obstetrician indirectly responsible for the presidency of Teddy Roosevelt.

The professionalization of medicine was won at the expense of the average American's knowledge of what was good or bad for him. The very scale and drive for efficiency of the American hospital, impressive but impersonal, easily made patients feel incidental. And not surprisingly, there is a counterpull by patients, evident in efforts to win back some control over their health, most notably in the fashion for natural childbirth and the hospice movement.

Whether or not American medicine can take the credit, the health of Americans continues to improve. At least it does if one looks at the big indicators. Since 1900, the rise in life expectancy for the population as a whole has been almost uninterrupted. Then it was 47.3 years at birth. By 1979 it was 73.8 years at birth. Women continue to live longer than men and white Americans longer than black, although the gap between whites and blacks—14.6 years in 1900—was down to 4.5 years by 1979.

Americans for long have had a shamefully high rate of infant mortality for such a technically advanced country. This has dropped recently, and is now about fourteen per thousand live births, still high compared with Sweden, Japan, or France, but about the same as Britain and West Germany. However, the chances of a black baby dying before reaching a year in age are much higher than for a white baby. The white infant mortality rate was just about twelve per thousand in 1978, while the rate for nonwhites was more than twenty-one per thousand, with black children accounting for the overwhelming majority of deaths in this second group. In the Deep South in 1977, the mortality rates for black infants in Mississippi were 27.9, in Alabama, 26.9, and in South Carolina, 26.2.

The crude death rate has been falling, too. This moved up and down between ten and eleven per thousand in the years 1938–1947, dropped below ten in 1948 and below nine in 1975. In the ten years 1968–1978, death rates from common killing diseases, such as heart ailments, cerebrovascular diseases, diabetes, emphysema, cirrhosis, nephritis, all fell. At the same time, Americans showed a characteristic readiness to give up habits they thought bad. The numbers of smokers declined, and there were patchy efforts to improve the American diet.

Despite all this, there are dark spots. If people do not die from one thing, they must die from another. Lung cancer death rates almost trebled between 1950 and 1977. Death rates for cancer of all kinds also rose, though much less sharply, over the same period. The American Academy of Political and Social Science's report on health in the United States says tersely of this change: "Possible causal factors behind these differentials are being explored; they include cigarette smoking and carcinogenic properties of the urban-industrial environment."

Many Americans would laugh at the caution of this statement, convinced already that industrially produced chemicals are poisoning the air they breathe, the water they drink, and the food they eat. As chemical pollution is so democratic in its effects, hurting the rich as well as the poor, concern about "The Poisoning of America"—the title of a cover story on the subject by *Time* magazine—is growing into a powerful national lobby. Unlike brown lung disease, which cripples only textile workers, or black lung disease, which kills miners, chemical poisoning shows a magisterial indifference to class. How the country copes will be one of its main health issues in coming years.

There are other big clouds over the American health system. Nobody knows how to hold back its ever-rising costs, which rose steadily faster than the price level as a whole between 1950 and 1980. In that time, dentists' fees more than tripled, physicians' more than quadrupled, medical care services quintupled, and the cost of a semiprivate hospital room shot up thirteen times. A big change since 1950 is who pays the bills. Then, about seven patients in ten paid their doctor or hospital bills directly. Today things are reversed, and only three in ten pay directly. Private insurance companies today pay almost 30 percent of medical costs and federal and state governments 40 percent. Health insurance and Medicare have increased demand for services and for a higher standard of care. Yet despite polls showing that a majority of Americans favor more complete coverage, it has not politically been possible to extend the safety net further, as repeated failures to get medical insurance bills through Congress show. A few politicians, like Senator Edward Kennedy, continue to call attention to this disgrace. Despite the expansion of insurance coverage, more than 25 million Americans, or more than one in eight, have no medical coverage of any sort.

When Americans talk about their health services, many acknowledge that they would like fuller coverage for themselves. They agree that it is a disgrace that so many fellow Americans should still live in anxiety about how to meet medical bills. And yet these same Americans return from Europe with horror stories about national health services, the menacing "socialized medicine." Stories usually involve not being able to get the doctor you want when you want or not being able to get an operation of your choice at short notice.

Americans put much store by freedom of choice, and will pay a large price for this, even if the price includes consigning several million Americans to having no choice at all. Passion for choice in medicine in the United States is strange since American doctors are much more conformist and similar to one another than those in Europe. When Abraham Flexner reformed the medical schools early in this century, he raised standards and got rid of lots of bad practices. The price was an often stifling medical orthodoxy. In France and Belgium, homeopathy, for example, is considered a perfectly orthodox form of medicine and homeopathic pharmacies alternate with allopathic ones on street corners. Most Americans are shocked when they learn that the Queen of England's doctor is a homeopathist. For the President, that would never do.

Freedom of choice in medicine, it is true, means picking your own doctor as much as your favored brand of treatment. Yet the concern about this is also a puzzle. The average standard of American doctors is so high that the risks of being unable to find a good doctor under a European type of system are low. Yet well-off Americans shun group health plans, not to mention national health proposals, for fear of not being able to be treated by the doctor they want. Knowing each patient's history matters, true. But computers can now store as much information about patients as the kindliest GP used to carry about in his head. No, a more plausible explanation for the attitude of well-to-do Americans toward their doctors is that they do not want—for entirely superstitious and snobbish reasons—to share their doctors with the less well-off.

If Americans get their legendary freedom—from tradition, from authority, from each other, although not from hard work—at the price of not knowing who they are—or to use the language of psychiatry, at the price of constant anxiety about their own identity—then it is only suitable that when they seek help for real or imagined psychic troubles they should find the market governed by a totally riotous freedom of choice. Middle-class neurotics who wish to be parted from their money face as great a variety of psychotherapy as they do of universities or of brands of Christianity. In fact, these three are the only really important sectors in the land of free enterprise in which even mild competition any longer prevails. Try as it might, the psychiatric profession has never been able to impose on itself the same orthodoxy that prevails in physical medicine. A recent handbook was entitled *The A to Z Guide to More Than 250 Different Therapies Today.* And this is one of psychiatry's great troubles. For conventional psychiatrists find themselves today in a double bind. The demand for psychotherapy is as great as ever. Yet orthodox "talking cure" therapists are caught between promising advances on the one hand in psychochemical research and by a profusion, on the other, of quick-cure salesmen, some sound but most bogus.

So if American psychiatrists sound defensive today, it's because many of their enemies are real. That was a commonly heard diagnosis at the 130th annual meeting of the American Psychiatric Association when it met in Toronto in April 1977. Having survived early neglect and then excessive flattery, American psychiatry is facing something of a midlife crisis. For many of the three thousand or so psychiatrists and other APA members gathered for five days of self-analysis and job hunting, a pressing question was what product they were selling and how much it was currently worth.

As medical costs have soared, so doubts have risen about the value of expensive psychiatric treatment for poorly understood illnesses often apparently cured, if at all, by luck, not medicine. In opinion surveys of public respect for various professions, psychiatrists habitually rank lower than other doctors in public esteem. This reflects not just uninformed prejudice but an attitude of many medical graduates as well, who would rather set bones or take out tonsils than grapple with elusive emotional problems. Despite an outpouring of popular books on psychiatry, trade in the real business of psychiatric consultation is hardly brisk. At the time of the APA meeting, practitioners of psychiatric medicine with twenty years of experience were earning, on average, not much more than $40,000 a year. A few, concentrated in Manhattan and on the West Coast, can make substantially more than that, although only about 5 percent of the profession make more than $100,000. Training hospitals have been finding it more and more difficult to recruit their full quota of residents in psychiatry.

The mood in the Sheraton Hotel, where the APA held its meeting, was introspective. Dr. Robert Gibson, in his presidential address, warned psychiatrists that if they did not put their own house in order, government regulators would be tempted to do it for them. Much the same message was heard from Dr. Peter Bourne, the White House's special adviser on mental health and drug abuse, a former psychiatrist who studied combat stress among American soldiers in Vietnam. Briskly, this chubby, engaging man ran through a list of reasons for continued suspicion and misunderstanding of psychiatry. Paraprofessionals—therapists, that is, without degrees—can treat patients just as effectively as fully fledged doctors, or so many believe; and general practitioners could just as well prescribe medicines. The discipline, he said, lacks a sound basis in science, and different schools still quarrel over diagnoses and treatment. New York doctors, for example, are said to classify patients as schizophrenics with much greater readiness than doctors elsewhere. Diagnosis remains an inexact art. A few years ago, eight California psychologists, eminently sane, got themselves admitted to no fewer than a dozen mental hospitals in turn by successfully mimicking a single, mild symptom of schizophrenic delusion, claiming to hear voices. Once in, it was difficult to get out. Some stayed six weeks or more.

Dr. Bourne did not mention, though he might have done so, the unhelpful spectacle of psychiatrists offering contradictory testimony in courts, fighting with each other like Kilkenny cats, as happened in the trial of Patty Hearst. This gives psychiatry an undeservedly bad press and stirs that half-buried American yen to blow a raspberry at the expert, as the prosecutor in the second Alger Hiss trial, Thomas Murphy, did to poor Dr. Carl Binger, a psychiatrist who had testified that Whittaker Chambers, Hiss's accuser, was a pathological liar. Today the insanity defense itself is under attack from conservative lawyers.

The commonest complaint against the profession is that it serves well-to-do neurotics in the big cities and concentrates on the kind of mental problems modern life creates for the upwardly mobile. In fact, the incidence of serious mental illness is much higher in rural America than in the cities, and within cities much higher among those who exist on the fringe of urban life, bag ladies and derelicts, turned out of state mental hospitals in the 1960s in a social experiment widely believed to have misfired.

Psychiatrists would reply that the therapies offered in the consulting room are suitable only for a limited range of mental illness. At Toronto, certainly, there was a striking contrast between learned seminars on psychiatric developments in the conference rooms upstairs and the trade fair downstairs at which the drug companies touted their behavior-altering drugs, and firms like the Posey Company of Pasadena advertised straitjackets and handcuffs for use in mental hospitals.

If psychiatry had an established church it would be psychoanalysis, the Freudian practice that has an influence beyond numbers. The American Psychoanalytic Association has about 2,500 members, less than 10 percent of all psychiatrists. Common as the claim "I'm in analysis" is, there are at most 30,000 patients getting classic psychoanalysis, less than 1 percent of the more than 30 million Americans who get some kind of psychiatric help every year. Psychoanalysts still hold many of the top jobs in the psychiatric establishment, at the National Institute of Mental Health or in the American Psychiatric Association. Even so, many question the old rituals, which are becoming almost as rare as the Tridentine mass. Dr. Judd Marmor, a psychoanalyst and former president of the American Psychoanalytic Association, is one of many who believe that for most patients classical analysis simply costs too much and goes on too long to be practical.

Psychoanalysis, in its most austere form, is an ascetic discipline that promises little in return for pain and hard work. Among a few hundred doctors, concentrated in New York and influenced by, if not directly trained at, the New York Psychoanalytic Institute, a purified version of Freud's disputed legacy continues to be practiced. Patients go for five fifty-minute hours a week for as many as eight years or more. The doctor's main job, far from being to offer sympathy or support, is to record and eventually to interpret how the patient defends himself against the strains of this artificial and taxing regime. In her book, *Psychoanalysis: The Impossible Profession,* Janet Malcolm tells of several conversations with a New York analyst, a member of the Institute, whom she calls Aaron Green, although that is not his real name. Green is a purist, in the tradition of Hartmann, Kris, and Loewenstein, a follower of Charles Brenner, whose work on psychoanalytic method is considered to be the basic handbook for the American classical tradition. Analysis, according to Green, does not undertake to change the patient's life in radical, semimiraculous ways. "This is a popular myth about analysis," he is quoted as saying, "that it makes the patient a clearer thinker, that it makes him wise and good, that people who have been analyzed know more than other people do . . . the changes achieved are very small. We live our lives according to the repetition compulsion and analysis can go only so far in freeing us from it." This recalls a remark during a television interview years ago by Theodor Reik, a popular analyst, who was asked by David Susskind if Eisenhower might profit from psychoanalysis. No, replied Reik firmly: "Psychoanalysis is no substitute for intelligence."

More Americans than Europeans took Freud to their bosoms, which is odd because psychoanalysis, at root, makes the most guarded claims as a therapy and offers an extremely unboosterish outlook on life. It holds out only a slim chance that the patient may become more reconciled with his compulsions than when the arduous business of therapy began and does not undertake to adjust him to his family, his fellows, or society around him. Put like this, psychoanalysis sounds pessimistically, even subversively, un-American.

It is not difficult to think of possible factors that might explain its

American success. To begin with, when Freud introduced his new therapy to Americans in person with a course of lectures at Clark University, in 1909, there were few home-grown products to compete. And American psychoanalysis, once it took root, was constantly refreshed and reinforced, especially after the rise of the Nazis, with a flow of gifted, powerful minds from Europe.

American psychoanalysts insisted, early on, that practitioners of the new art—or science, rather—be medical doctors, even though Freud himself was more open-minded on the question and several leading American analysts themselves eventually rebelled against this stricture, opening the gates to popular therapies of all kinds. To begin with, this requirement helped entrench psychoanalysis within the medical profession, making it solid and respectable. That analysts be doctors was important to them in getting custom, since it enabled their patients to cloak an illness that an outwardly tough, masculine culture readily dismissed as softness of character.

The very sweep of psychoanalytic thought, when stretched, as it was by Freud himself, beyond the consulting room to society, politics, and art, appealed to the impatiently reductionist, "let's get down to basics," side of the American mind. By offering, in its most popularized forms, a clue to character, psychoanalysis gave Americans, a nation of strangers, unsure of who each other were, a marvelously simple-seeming way of answering the perennial question: "What makes him tick?" Drenched as it was in subtleties of language, the "talking cure" had strong appeal to literary intellectuals and deeply colored American criticism in the 1930s and 1940s.

Much of this is to say that twentieth-century Americans had an appetite for psychology and that, to begin with at least, psychoanalysts, with their import model, simply cornered the market. To be acceptable, to reach a wider public, Freud's theories had to be given a more optimistic coloring. Almost from the beginning, American neo-Freudians like Harry Stack Sullivan and Karen Horney, who championed lay analysis, and even self-analysis, began altering psychoanalysis to fit the American preoccupation with the troubles of adapting to society, with not fitting in, with problems of loneliness, anxiety about identity—in sum, with questions of adjusting more to society than to oneself. The Freud of the unconscious, of the instinctual drives, was quietly tamed in the process. Depth psychology kept its name but became ever more shallow. American neo-Freudians put a liberal, optimistic cast on psychoanalysis. They looked back to the Mind Cure practitioners of the late nineteenth and early twentieth centuries, who mixed religion with psychiatry and gave the unconscious mystical properties. They looked forward to the human potential movements of Fritz Perls and Carl Rogers, for whom "the self," once found, would prove bland and benign.

Disputes among the Freudians were as nothing to the multiplication of sects that followed. Perls, who was to become the apostle of Gestalt therapy, was among the trainees whose analysis Karen Horney supervised. A friend of Paul Goodman, he worked for several years at the Esalen Institute in Big Sur, a ravishing spot overlooking the Pacific in California, south of Monterey. An ex-analyst, Perls was a tireless critic of conventional psychiatry, which he liked to call "mind fucking." Perls wanted to make people aware of their feelings for the moment, to become "unblocked," to achieve "self-realization." The command "Do your own thing" originated with Perls and was taken up as a stock slogan of the counterculture.

From the Austrian Kurt Lewin came sensitivity training, a mild form of informal group therapy vastly popular with American management. From J. L. Moreno of Beacon, New York, a practitioner of psychodrama, came the notion of Encounter, a centerpiece of the human potential movement. Carl Rogers, who wanted to make psychotherapy "client-centered," was another psychiatrist-leader of this movement, who encouraged followers to search for a "personal growth experience."

From Wilhelm Reich, the socially minded Freudian apostate, came, by indirect way of his notion of "character armor," Alexander Lowen's bioenergetics and Ida Rolf's Rolfing. Arthur Janov in Beverly Hills and Daniel Casriel in New York, reviving old ideas of ventilationism, encouraged their patients to scream away buried emotional pains. All these had a following. Perhaps the most popular and typical of all were Eric Berne and Thomas Harris, promoters of Transactional Analysis.

Berne's book *Games People Play* was widely read, setting out, as it did, in simple diagrammatic fashion the supposed struggle within everyone between parent, child, and adult. Berne's pop psychology was a cleverly watered down and simplified Freudianism, complete with an easy jargon of its own. "Strokes" meant praise or blame. And then there was the all-important "script," an optimistic twist to the old psychiatric notion that the child is father to the man. "Each person decides in early childhood how he will live and how he will die and that plan . . . is called the script."

Americans seek, through psychiatry, to identify and then to overcome their faults—not to adjust to them. John Nicholson is an English behavioral psychologist and popular broadcaster. He wrote a short book called *Habits*, about those many important aspects of daily or nightly life—eating, sleeping, walking, talking, scratching, washing—over which most of us exert little conscious control. The book did enormously well in Britain and the secret of its appeal was not hard to see. Noticing, treasuring, and mocking each other's behavioral tics is a British national pastime, and here was a book full of them, written up with the authority of science. In the United States the book did badly. The title alone smacked of a subversive fatalism. Its neutrality was offensive to the positive-minded American. The book might have had more pull if it had taken a stand about habits and offered some hope of change. Calling it *How to Cure Your Habits* or *A Guide to Better Habits* might have given it more pull. Even *Learning to Live with Your Habits* might have tweaked the would-be buyer's conscience with the thought that his or her self-criticisms were too strong or self-esteem lacking. But no, Americans did not want to read about any aspect of themselves that would be with them for the rest of their lives.

The rest of one's life was what Gail Sheehy's best-selling *Passages* was really about. It did very well in the United States, even after its guiding thread—the idea of psychological life stages—was properly accredited to Daniel Levinson and Erik Erikson. In Britain, where a passage is something between two rooms, the book did badly. Sheehy's book brilliantly combined psychological determinism with American optimism, in the old tradition of American popular psychiatric thought. At any stage of life, the book said, in effect, the tasks and problems are pretty well fixed and predictable for everyone. This message, far from making people feel trapped by circumstance, was triply reassuring. For it said bury your regrets and anxieties, so you can concentrate on the stage you are in; however bored, however desperate you may be, there's another stage and a new set of problems coming which you may do better at; and it arranged the seven ages with the best last—old age, a time of psychological maturity and fulfillment.

This optimism is not all self-deception. Americans do try to change their habits. They are great renouncers. This is the country, after all, of Prohibition. If a fad catches on, Americans will show great powers of self-denial. Look at the change in smoking habits. According to the surgeon general, in 1980, the number of men aged twenty or over who smoked had dropped by nearly 30 percent in the preceding decade. The number of teenage boys who smoked dropped in the same period by a fifth. The bad news—for antismokers—was that smoking among teenage girls was up by a half, although from a lower starting point, and this rapid increase was quickly leveling off. Airplanes were obliged by law to provide nonsmoking seats for those who wanted them. The question "Do you mind if I smoke?" ceased to be a polite form of words and it became acceptable to reply "Yes, I do." Restaurants opened nonsmoking sections.

Laws and regulations helped nudge smokers to quit. Many lawyer-hours have been spent quarreling over the precise wording of the warning that appears on each package of cigarettes: "The Surgeon General Has Determined That Cigarette Smoking Is Dangerous to Your Health." To say that it had been "discovered," the tobacco industry lawyers argued, would leave no room for doubt about the scientific findings, and there was doubt. To say the surgeon general had "decided" made it sound too capricious, as if he'd thought it up in the bath. "Determined" was the compromise.

Cigarette advertising was banned from television. Later President Carter came under strong pressure from Joseph Califano, a zealous ex-smoker, to step up the antismoking campaign. Carter, a Southerner, knew better. In North Carolina, the heart of tobacco country, he gave a famous, weaseling speech in which he assured the tobacco industry that his administration's aim in the matter was to "make smoking even safer." The Reagan administration lobbied hard to reduce the size of school lunches but not of the safety net for tobacco growers.

The national appetite for quick-cure books that promise to break a smoking habit or to take inches off a waistline is another symptom of that mildly severe hypochondria affecfing Americans' attitudes to their bodies and to physical health. That it is supplied so copiously has to do with the collapse of the doctor-expert within psychiatry and with the profusion of sects in the absence of any orthodoxy. The form that it takes—the self-help manual—is an old American genre. There has never been any lack of advice books for Little Engines That Could. Benjamin Franklin drew up checklists for earthly happiness. "Lose no time, be always employed in something useful." "Rarely use venery but for health and offspring." Franklin prompted D. H. Lawrence to write:

> The Perfectibility of Man! Ah heaven, what a dreary theme. The perfectibility of the Ford car! The perfectibility of which man? I am many men. Which of them are you going to perfect? I am not a mechanical contrivance.

The latest crop of self-help mental hygiene books has old roots. The following advice from Frank Haddock's *Power of the Will* (1907) will be quite familiar to any reader of today's psychiatric advice books. The voice is sterner, the manner stiffer, yes. But the message—"You are weak now, but you will feel strong if you do these simple tasks"—is the same. Haddock's tenth exercise, quoted by Donald Meyer in *The Positive Thinkers,* is as follows:

> Stand erect. Summon a sense of resolution.
> Throw Will into the act of standing.
> Absorbed in self, think calmly but with power these words: "I am standing erect. All is well! I am conscious of nothing but good."
> Attaining the Mood indicated, walk slowly and deliberately about the room.
> Do not strut. Be natural, yet encourage a sense of forcefulness. Rest in a chair.
> Repeat, with rests, fifteen minutes. . . .
> Repeat every day indefinitely.

Spiritual automation, Meyer calls this. The same description applies today.

In *Imagining America,* the English critic Peter Conrad suggests that it is preoccupation with the stresses of personal identity and the "collective unease of national identity" that makes Americans such unusually critical spectators of themselves, such private eyes for their

hidden faults, such consumers of self-help manuals. He could have gone
two steps further. Unease about who they are underlies not only the
Americans' passion for self-improvement, but the methods they use.
For the improved self, sought in dieting, running, or reading Orestes
Swett Marden's *Success* magazine, or half a century later, Fay and
Lazarus's little paperback *I Can if I Want To,* is above all a self that
fits in, a self defined by the average, by what's normal. The sense of
self must be supplied from outside. Self-improvement, characteristically, becomes meeting norms. The passion for being normal underlies the Perlsian Gestalt prayer: "You do your thing. I do my thing."
Implicit in this slogan is reassurance to those terrified of breaking rules,
and it could sound radical only in a conformist culture. Self-improvement, secondly—and this has been tirelessly pointed out—involves
personal repairs that need almost no cooperation from others, often in
disregard of the old Yankee maxim "If it ain't broke, don't fix it!" Like
jogging as defined by the National Jogging Association, self-improvement is a competition against oneself.

But this is only half the puzzle. For while Americans happily embrace the improvability of individual men and women, they treat the
improvability of man as a dangerously socialist doctrine. Suspicion of
government and fear of the mass—even Whitman's hopeful "I *en
masse*"—runs out of the Constitution as a red thread through the
American political tradition. That Americans' view of individual men
and women is so sunny, but of man, so dark, colored the American
greetings given Freud and Darwin. Americans welcomed Freud but
they tamed him, banished or bowdlerized the unconscious, unable to
accept the mind as the place of instinctual struggle. They welcomed
Darwin, too, yet readily adopted the blind struggle of species, of combat for survival of the fittest, as a model of social life. In American pop
psychology, the unconscious has become a smiling neighbor saying
"Have a nice day." In American pop anthropology, society is blandly
represented as the most savage and bestial spectacle. It is as if the
Americans are all too ready to believe that taken together, men and
women can be beasts, but never taken one by one.

This tension between confidence in the perfectibility of individual
men and women and deep skepticism about improving people together
in society is the American riddle. So long as the economic machine gave
Americans rising prosperity and so long as two oceans gave them free

security, the tension between political pessimism and individual optimism gave more life and energy to the country than it drained away. But those two historic gifts have become luxuries that today's Americans have to work for. Their individual optimism seems unshakable. It is political pessimism Americans cannot any longer afford.

ACKNOWLEDGMENTS

Countless people gave us their time and advice. It was tempting to mention everybody. Even a long list, however, would not have been complete. Rather than overlook a few we decided to extend a general thanks to all.

That said, some of the credit must be shared by name. We have plundered conversations, ideas, and articles from many colleagues on *The Economist,* including, in particular, John Grimond, Dudley Fishburn, Margaret Cruikshank, Ann Wroe, Peter Martin, Andrew Neil, and Rupert Pennant-Rea.

To John Midgley, contributing editor in Washington and for many years American editor, we owe a quite special debt. A surer guide and better colleague would be difficult to imagine.

We thank the editor, Andrew Knight, who spared us as his correspondents in the United States with leave to finish this book. Gordon Lee, the literary editor, read the book in typescript and made several helpful suggestions. The opinions are ours, not *The Economist*'s.

The constant help of Doro George in Washington and Muriel Davis in New York was invaluable. Unasked, they were always ready to lend their skill and efficiency to our extra work. So were Ann Norman, Amanda Raymer and Cheryl Younson, to whom special thanks as well.

Without the unguarded readiness of *Economist* correspondents in many cities across the country to share their fund of local knowledge we could not have begun. For their help and hospitality, our gratitude.

Ivis Steele produced finished copy at short notice, amazing us with her command of the word-processor. Gail Lynch kindly agreed to take our photographs.

Daniel Davidson in Washington scrutinized the book in draft, saved us from several errors of logic or fact and pointed us toward many improvements.

To speak of "research" for a book of this sort would be rather pretentious. A bibliography was out of place, we felt, in a book without scholarly ambitions.

Besides conducting many, many interviews and talking over some topics at length with friends, we have devoured books, magazines, and newspapers. Obviously, at many points we have relied heavily on others' work. To those whose books and articles we have borrowed from, though not, we trust, their exact words, we give thanks.

Americans have a great appetite for facts and, on the whole, an allergy to secrets. This openness lightened our job at almost every turn. We were told that America was famous for hospitality but learned this for ourselves.

Among the many we have visited or taken ideas from over the years, we would like particularly to thank Michael Barone, Tom Bethell, Peter and Vicky Bocock, Peter Brewton, Paul Burka, Robert Chambers, Edward Cowan, Katy Costello, Frank and Sheila Dear, Jack Davis, Sarah and Alvin Duskin, Dr. James Gordon, Tom and Roses Graham, Maxine Hitchcock, Ted and Lenore Jacobs, Michael and Penny Janeway, Hella Junz, Dean Kelley, Rabbi Wolfe Kelman, Paul Kemezis, Rabbi Yehuda Krinsky, Morton Kondracke, Saul Landau, Mary Ellen Leary, Bob Lenzner, Anthony Lewis, Brian Loar, Charles and Eileen Lowe, Christopher Lydon, Thomas Mansbach, William Mares, Jurek Martin, Peter McGrath, Marty Merzer, Sarah Miller, Bill Montalbano, Catherine and Carol Moremitsu, Daniel Morgan, Bailey and Wilson Morris, Howard and Margarita Naish, Kathy Neumeyer, Kathleen Newland, Antonia Phillips, Jim Ridgeway, Ned Scharff and Louise Lague, Georgiana Stevens, Chuck Storer, Bob Stovall, Jan Stucker, Sanford and Beth Ungar, Austin Wehrwein, John Wilson, Diana and James Zurer.

For thoughts on America, we would like to thank, in New York, Brock Baker, Alexander Cockburn and Andrew and Lesley Cockburn, Murray and Diane Rossant, Emma Rothschild, Nicholas Wahl; in England, Perry Anderson, Richard Blackburn, Guy de Jonquieres, Fred Emery, the late Gareth Evans, Fred Halliday, Louis Heren, the late Fred

Hirsch, Charles Hope, Mary Kaldor, Andrey Kidel, Michael Leapman, Herbert Nicholas, Peter and Laura Wollen.

Toby Eady, our agent and friend, had the idea for this book, presented it with flair, and gave, when needed, just the right prodding. We thank him, in the words of a famous Yankee catcher, for making this book necessary.

Times Books gave early encouragement. We are grateful to Ned Chase for setting us on the proper path. At Harper & Row, Edward L. Burlingame provided keen interest and support. For his unfailing help and sound advice, we thank our editor, Aaron Asher.

Tony Thomas owes a great debt to Sarah, who made everything worthwhile in the end.

A final word from Edmund Fawcett. The patience of my wife, Natalia Jimenez, was tried many times but never her gaiety. Unconsulted, Marlowe and Elias put up with an unfather. Natalia already knows how much difference they all made, but it bears repeating.

INDEX